# THE GUN DIGEST
# BOOK OF KNIVES

## 3rd Edition

**By Jack Lewis
and Roger Combs**

## DBI BOOKS, INC.

## ABOUT THE COVER

Three state-of-the-art factory knives grace the cover of this third edition of *The Gun Digest Book Of Knives.* From left to right are: Remington's "Big Game" locking folder, Buck's "Kalinga" fixed blade hunter, and Browning's Damascus "Classic Fighter." **Photo by John Hanusin.**

**Publisher**
Sheldon Factor

**Editorial Director**
Jack Lewis

**Production Director**
Sonya Kaiser

**Art Director**
Denise Comiskey

**Associate Artists**
Gary Duck
Paul Graff

**Copy Editor**
Shelby Harbison

**Production Coordinator**
Pepper Federici

**Photo Services**
Kelley Grant

**Contributing Editors**
Dean A. Grennell
Chuck Karwan
Bob Learn
Jack Mitchell
Russell Thurman

**Lithographic Services**
Gallant Graphics

# CONTENTS

# INTRODUCTION

OBODY knows when knives were invented by Early Man, but it's certain this was one of the first tools to evolve among cave dwellers. Whatever the origins, the basic tool has remained the same for millions of years: A sharp cutting edge and a handle to hold it.

The materials and techniques for making knives, however, have changed drastically over the past few years. Steel, wood and plastic are still the basics, but new designs incorporating the most modern Space Age materials are introduced with almost bewildering regularity. New and old-line knife companies are competing for the attention of consumers all over the world. The importance of the potential market in the United States is obvious from the number and variety of knife importers found on our shores.

Knives have been the traditional product of certain areas of the United States, England, Germany, Switzerland and Japan for years. Many of these factories continue in production today, some in the same locations they have occupied for hundreds of years. Other upstarts began making knives only "yesterday." Some have become successful with a design or material innovation new or radical enough to catch our fancy.

The *Second Edition* of *The Gun Digest Book Of Knives* was published six years ago. Since then, the world economy has seen numerous changes, with another invasion of foreign-made goods seeking our approval. Knives have been among them. Those companies that have studied the market have found success; others have fallen by the wayside.

This all-new *Third Edition* is an in-depth study of major knifemakers all over the world; some old and some new. We are also taking a look at the basics of knifemaking: the steel and the handle materials, as well as some of the newest sheaths. We shall see a number of specialty knives and their makers and we will learn how to sharpen, maintain and repair our favorite blades. Knife collectors, too, will have a chance to see what is hot and what is not in this always changing aspect of knives.

We hope you will have as much fun reading about knives as we did writing about them. Chances are, you will run across some knives you never heard of before. We did — and found every one fascinating!

*Jack Lewis,*
*Roger Combs,*
*Capistrano Beach, California*

The Bowie knife probably received its greatest exposure in the movie, "The Iron Mistress," with actor Alan Ladd as Jim Bowie. People assumed the knife he carried was a true copy of the original knife, but it was a Hollywood design.

# Chapter 1

# THE BOWIE MYSTERY

### Either — Or Both — Of These Knives May Well Have Been With Jim Bowie, When He Died At The Alamo!

THERE IS such a thing as a Bowie knife. In fact, there are literally thousands of Bowie knives around the world. At least, the manufacturers refer to them by that term. Most are based upon a concept rather than the actual design of the knife with which Jim Bowie was reputed to have defended himself through much of his life, the final chapter coming at the fall of the Alamo on March 6, 1836, when a tiny band of frontiersmen sacrificed their lives against a horde of Mexican soldiers.

Over more than a century and a half since the first Bowie knife was allegedly made by blacksmith James Black, there have been detractors; those who claim there never was such a knife as the one supposedly carried by Bowie; that the knife was created long after his death as a marketing idea; something that would sell.

Most of these doubters have been discredited over the years, but to the average citizen, the Bowie knife is the huge blade that Alan Ladd carried in the film "The Iron Mistress." More than one person is convinced that this particular knife was the one Jim Bowie actually carried at the Alamo. Actually, it was designed by art director John

Beckman, who was assigned to the film, and was made by a property man, Arthur Rhoades, at Warner Brother studios.

Today, there are two known knives, both of which may have been made by James Black over his forge in Washington, Arkansas, for Jim Bowie.

But before we get into that, one probably should know something of the man from whom Bowie is supposed to have ordered these knives.

James Black was known to have been born in New Jersey in 1800. When only 8 years old, he ran away to Philadelphia, where he was seized by local authorities. Since he refused to tell where he came from, he was apprenticed out to a manufacturer, in keeping with the customs of that era. Because of his size, he was considered to be about 11 and was indentured to a manufacturer of silver plate.

Black served this trade until he was supposedly 21 years of age, although he actually was three years younger, 18. Freed of his apprenticeship, he decided to move west, taking a stagecoach to Cincinnati, then a steamer down the Ohio and Mississippi rivers, until he reached New Orleans.

He worked on a ferryboat for a time, then got a job as a deck hand on a steamer that would take him up the Red

River to the edge of what was considered the wilderness.

Joining forces with another adventurer named Elijah Stuart, Black left the boat and the two of them moved about fourteen miles inland from the Red River. There, in early 1824, they staked out a settlement that came to be known as Washington. It is located in Hempstead County, Arkansas.

Black was close to penniless, but went to work with a blacksmith named Shaw. The shop catered to the freight-hauling wagon trains headed southward to Texas or to Santa Fe. The agreement was that Shaw and his sons would handle the work of shoeing horses or installing iron tires on wagon wheels, while Black would devote full time to making knives and handling gunsmithing chores. Ultimately, Black became a full partner in the enterprise.

In time, Black sold his share back to Shaw and moved on westward. However, he found more problems there and ultimately returned to Washington, marrying Shaw's daughter, Ann, in June 1828. He also set up a blacksmith shop in competition with that of his father-in-law.

According to legend, James Black developed his own means of tempering and hardening steel, refusing to pass his secrets on to anyone. His test of excellence was called the "hickory test." When a blade was finished, it was used to whittle a block of hickory for an hour. At the end of that time, the blade still was expected to shave the hair from his arm. As a result of his earlier training in silver plate, Black also worked in precious metals, incorporating them in his knife designs.

Jim Bowie came riding up from Texas in 1830 and, according to legend, stopped at Washington to see James Black and order a knife from him. Seemingly, he had whittled the model from wood. Black looked over the model and agreed to transfer the design to steel.

That's the way the legend goes, but Arkansas Territorial papers held in our National Archives indicate that Jim Bowie was in the area of Washington, Arkansas, selling land off and on from 1826 until 1831. Black, of course, could have made the knives — or any number of them — at any time during this period.

According to legend, Bowie returned sometime later to claim his knife and found that Black had made two versions. He accepted Black's variation, which featured a double edge along the length of the blade's front curve.

The fame of the Black-made blade came long before the Alamo. On his way back to Texas, Bowie reputedly was attacked by three men who had been hired to kill him. Jim Bowie reportedly killed all three with the knife in close combat.

Ann Black died in 1835, according to the Arkansas *Gazette*. Her father, still angry at Black after so many

*This is the Bowie knife bought by Joe Musso with some gun parts. When he started to clean the knife, he discovered evidence that led him to believe it might well be one of the knives made for Bowie by James Black, a blacksmith.*

At the re-created James Black blacksmith shop in Washington, Arkansas, the Bowie owned by Joe Musso is inspected by trio of experts. From left are, Bill Hicks, Don Montgomery and Gene Godfrey. Musso made trip to Arkansas for research.

years, found him ill in bed and attacked the blacksmith with a club. When the beating was over, part of James Black's eyesight was gone.

Journeying to New Orleans to see a specialist, he was told that here was no chance of recovering. In fact, by that time, he was totally blind. Unable to care for his five children, James Black failed to protest when they were indentured to his father-in-law who had caused his blindness.

Black went to live with the family of Daniel Webster Jones, who was later to become governor of Arkansas. The blind blacksmith lived with the Jones family for some thirty years, finally dying at the age 72 in June 1872.

After Black had made the so-called Bowie knife for Jim Bowie, he reportedly made hundreds more of the same general design. Thus, somewhere perhaps, is the "original" made for Jim Bowie. After that, came the Black knives that were close in design and using similar steel. Later came the copies, many of them manufactured in the cutlery centers of Sheffield and Birmingham, England, finding their way to these shores to be purchased by those headed for the Western frontier.

Perhaps the saddest note of all lies in the fact that near his seventieth birthday, James Black tried to write down the formula for the knife steel that he had developed. Daniel Webster Jones recalled that Black was near despair, when he found that of the ten or twelve processes used to harden and temper the steel, he could remember none of them!

James Black is buried in a cemetery on the north side of Washington, Arkansas. However, since the original markers were of wood and long since have rotted away, no one is exactly sure of his grave site.

Today, a re-creation of the James Black smithy stands in Arkansas' Old Washington State Park. Some of the tools of the era are in evidence and several elderly blacksmiths show how knife blades and other steel items were made in James Black's era.

As for Jim Bowie, the legend has been recounted so many times that any school boy should be able to recite it by rote. Let it only be said that Bowie and his fabled knife captured the imagination of the frontier and led to thousands upon thousands of styles called "Bowie knives" being sold. Some of them, incidentally, look as much like

Joe Musso (left) shows his Bowie knife to the late John Wayne on the set during the filming of a Wayne starrer. The actor was interested as a result of the film he had made earlier, "The Alamo." Several so-called experts have said that there was no actual Bowie knife and that the design did not appear until the 1870s. However, an editorial in the *Arkansas Gazette*, published in Washington, Arkansas, in 1841, made mention of James Black and the fact that he had made knives for Jim Bowie. Paralleling today's anti-firearms hysteria, the editorial criticized such knives and their makers, suggesting that manufacture of such blood-letting weaponry be banned. That was published 150 years ago!

*This concept, drawn by artist Paul Graff, illustrates what probably was the forerunner of the Bowie knife. Based on the Mediterranean dirk or so-called Spanish dagger, this knife was made for Jim Bowie's brother from his own design.*

the accepted concept as we look like Greta Garbo — if anyone knows what she looks like these days!

In spite of the fact that Bowie allegedly brought a wooden model to James Black for reproduction in steel, there is one school of history that contends that Jim Bowie did not design the knife at all. Instead, they insist, the credit should go to Rezin P. Bowie, his brother.

It is known that Rezin Bowie did design a knife of Mediterranean influences. It became known as the Spanish dagger in the southwest and resembled nothing more nor less than an over-sized butcher knife. It is known that Rezin Bowie had such a knife made for his own use by Henry Schively of Philadelphia, Pennsylvania, a respected cutler of the day. Some years later, Schively began to sell what was termed an "improved Bowie." It had a steel guard and the scales often were of checkered ivory.

Whether Rezin Bowie was truly responsible for the design with which his brother died in defense of the Alamo is a fact that probably never will be determined, but it is a recognized fact that he did design a number of fighting knives and was recognized as something of an authority on such cutlery.

But let's move forward to the early 1980s. A Hollywood studio conceptual artist and historical illustrator, Joseph Musso had purchased an old Bowie knife from a dealer in gun arts. In addition to being a gun and history buff, Musso also spends considerable time in meeting the requirements as president of the Motion Picture Illustrators and Matte Artists.

"I was cleaning some old guns and decided out of curiosity to see whether the solvent I was using would dissolve some of the crud on the cross-guard of the old Bowie knife," Musso recalls. The date, he reports, was April 1, 1981.

The solvent did remove the accumulated dirt and tarnish and, as Musso puts it, "I saw something I never had spotted before. The guard had the initials, *JB,* on it beside one of the six-pointed star designs."

Musso had long been a student of the Bowie legend and pondered whether the initials and star really meant anything. Could they stand for James Black as the maker or even Jim Bowie as the owner? Or was it just another phony copy of a Bowie knife?

Musso pondered this for some time and finally contacted Peter Hurkos, believed by many to be the world's greatest psychic.

For those who may not be familiar with Hurkos and his seeming powers, he is supposed to have acquired his psychic powers after he fell from a ladder in his native Holland in 1941. He lay unconscious in a hospital for four days. When he regained consciousness, it is reported, he had developed a talent for piercing the past, present and even the future. The hospital staff, according to reports of the time, was stunned; there was no medical explanation, no logical reason for Hurkos' seeming powers.

The Hollander has gained a degree of fame in his country and in Europe as what might best be described as a "psychic detective," working on cases involving missing persons and murder victims. He has worked on a number of cases with various police departments, helping to solve the mysteries including the murders committed by the Charles Manson followers in which actress Sharon Tate died. Incidentally, Queen Julianna of Holland decorated Hurkos for his work with the Dutch underground during World War II and there is a statue commemorating his work in Rotterdam.

Hurkos — born Pieter Van der Hurk — was brought to the United States in 1956 to be tested at the Round Table Foundation Research Laboratory in Glen Cove, Maine. He spent more than two years taking part in experiments under scientifically controlled conditions. The doctors and experts apparently were convinced that Hurkos' psychic faculties were the greatest they ever had tested. His feats of seeing past, present and future have been reported on in *Time, Newsweek, Life, Look, Reader's Digest* and countless other publications. The International Police Associations made Hurkos a member and His Holiness, Pope Pius XII, decorated him, stating at the time, "I hope you will use your God-given gift for the betterment of mankind...use it as an instrument to touch people, to help them."

Whether the reader chooses to believe in Peter Hurkos' powers is up to the individual. Joseph Musso, however, is a believer. Since Hurkos resides now in Studio City, not far from Hollywood, the owner of the Bowie decided to contact him, not telling him the reason.

"Hurkos agreed to see me," Musso recalls. "I took the knife to him in a brown paper bag. I still had told him nothing about what I was bringing to him or my reasons for wanting to see him.

"I simply laid the bag in front of him and asked what he

could tell me about it. Peter Hurkos told me that my knife was the largest and the favorite of at least fourteen knives owned by Colonel James Bowie. He allowed me to tape record the entire event.

"Hurkos said that this knife was made for Bowie by James Black and Bob Lovel Snowden and was the only knife Bowie had with a brass strip along the back of the blade."

The knife was still inside the brown paper bag, on a table in front of Hurkos. It had not been opened...and the knife did have the brass strip described!

James Black, the Arkansas blacksmith mentioned at some length earlier, "had a process for hardening steel," according to Hurkos and used the process on this knife. Snowden then finished the knife, including installation of the brass strip. According to Hurkos' vision, if one chooses to call it that, Black and Snowden — the latter in Black's employment — made other knives, including a knife now owned by Bart Moore II, which the psychic said was carried by a lieutenant at the Alamo. (This could possibly be Lieutenant James Butler Bonham, who rode with Bowie when the latter took command of the San Antonio-Alamo post.)

"Hurkos, also showed me what several of Bowie's other knives looked like," Musso reports. "One of these was made by Henry Schively, the cutler in Philadelphia. This latter knife had an eleven-inch blade with a sharp false edge and an S-shaped hand guard."

Hurkos also contended that another blacksmith, Noah Smithwick of San Felipe, Texas, made and sold copies of the knife in Musso's possession.

Hurkos added that all of the knives Jim Bowie had made featured sharp false edges and clipped points, the latter his trademark, and that he didn't like the dirk-style knives favored by his borther, Rezin. If true, this would tend to negate the claim that Jim Bowie's knife actually was designed by his brother.

The psychic also stated that Bowie carried three knives and a sword during the Texas Revolution. He wore the knife owned by Musso on the left side at his waist and another knife on his right. A third knife, smaller in size and made by John Sowell of Gonzales, Texas, was carried in a special sheath sewn into his boot.

"Hurkos said that the six-pointed star design on the hand guard of my knife was the mark of an officer and that Bowie had the knife made after he became a captain in 1832," Musso reports. "I have since documented the fact that American officers wore such star devices on their forage caps from 1825 to 1850."

But instead of wearing the stars on his hat, Hurkos said Bowie wore the stars on this knife and on the band around the tops of his black boots. During the Texas Revolution, he wore no uniform, but was clad in a buckskin shirt.

Hurkos told Musso that Bowie didn't like guns, but was "crazy about knives" and that he fought with them like "the Roman gladiators," charging into battle carrying the big knife owned by Musso in his right hand to block and parry, using another smaller knife to thrust and kill.

Carrying the experiment further, Musso laid out several photos — all of them facedown on a table. The psychic selected the picture of Jim Bowie without seeing it. He also mapped out Mexican troop positions during the battle of the Alamo, correctly stated that Bowie spoke three languages — English, Spanish and French — and identified two copies of Bowie's handwriting. These were Xerox copies of documents written by the frontiersman, one of which had come from the Mexican archives. Musso stated that one was written while Bowie was in good health, the other while he was sick. The one from the archives was written in Spanish and was written after he was wounded at the Alamo. Both copies were facedown on the table, when Hurkos made these pronouncements.

"Even though Bowie was a colonel, Hurkos kept referring to him as the commander," Musso recalls. "That puzzled me, but sometime later, while doing research in Texas, I saw letters in which Bowie referred to himself as Commander of Volunteers during the Texas Revolution."

During the recorded interview, Hurkos also went into elaborate details of Bowie's final days and his fall from the Alamo church.

According to the psychic, Bowie was suffering from a lung disease during the thirteen-day Mexican siege on the Alamo. (Historians contend that Bowie had typhoid-pneumonia or tuberculosis at the time of his death.) However, when the final attack came, Hurkos claims, Bowie was able to rally enough strength to fight on the walls with his men. When the Mexicans started to breech the north wall, Bowie, directing the defenses from atop the Alamo church, was ordering his men to reinforce the troubled position when he struck his head against a beam and fell about twenty-five feet in front of the Alamo facade.

"I see him lying there, still alive, but bleeding from the mouth," Hurkos said and added that the Texans then carried the now dying Bowie inside the Alamo church. When the Alamo finally fell to the Mexicans, they found that Bowie was already dead (or close to it) and was unable to offer any further resistance.

In a book, *The Bowies And Their Kindred,* published in 1899, Walter Worthington Bowie stated that Jim Bowie died an hour before the final battle in such a manner. One might question how the author had such knowledge. While the popular concept is that all occupants of the Alamo died in the onslaught, this is not true. After the battle, women and children in the fort were released by the Mexicans, thus the information could have come from one of them.

"Hurkos said that my knife was found after Bowie's death in the Alamo by a Mexican soldier, Alphonso Roberto and that it was acquired later from Roberto by a man of German descent named Hans Fisher. I subsequently read in the Time-Life book series on the Old West that a Ger-

*In this painting of Jim Bowie, still owned by descendants, he appears older and more resolute than some expect him to be after having seen him portrayed by a host of actors. In his hand, he appears to be clutching a sword. When a soldier, he did carry a saber that is still in the family.*

Now supported by the State of Arkansas as a tourist draw, the re-created James Black forge and blacksmith shop in Washington is as authentic as researchers can make it. A staff of blacksmiths produce products of 1830s period.

man named Henry Fisher attempted to start a German colony in Texas in 1844. I later showed this article to Hurkos, who said this Fisher was the same man who acquired my knife," Musso reports.

Hurkos also told Joe Musso that the wooden handle on the knife he possesses was replaced in the 1890s, as the original had rotted and was cracked. He said also that the original butt cap had been replaced. Originally it had been a brass cap with the six-pointed star in the center. The psychic contended that all other parts of the knife, including the brass strip on the top of the blade, are original as made by Black and Snowden.

Still not satisfied, Joe Musso took the knife to the Truesdail Laboratories in Los Angeles. Founded in 1931 by Dr. Roger W. Truesdail, the laboratories are staffed by nationally recognized scientific engineering experts in many fields that include chemistry, engineering, food technology, forensic science, pharmacology, physics, metallurgy and microbiology.

Technicians at the laboratories subjected the knife to a number of tests, including emission spectrographic chemical analysis, X-ray diffraction compound analysis and macroscopic analysis. The result was a report of more than fifty pages signed by Charles H. Avery, a registered professional engineer. The report is dated Novemeber 23, 1981 and is listed as laboratory report No. 812263.

In this report, the engineers opined that the knife was made about 1830 and that there was absolutely no phony aging on the blade. The lab report concludes that the blade was forged by hand in a charcoal furnace using ores low in sulphur and phosphorus by a cementation process. (Variations of this process include the making of ancient Damascus and Wootz steels.)

The lab report states that the brass strip along the back of the knife's blade was installed at the time the knife was made; it was not a later addition. The initials, *JB,* were placed in the mould before the hand guard was cast. They also concurred with Hurkos that the original butt cap had been replaced with one of later manufacture. Hardness of the blade, three-quarters of an inch above the blade cutting edge, tested at 46C on the Rockwell scale. Knives of modern manufacture usually have a hardness of 55 to 60 on the Rockwell scale, incidentally.

The report from Truesdail Laboratories also recommended additional research and comparison tests for further verification of the source of the iron used in making the knife. To date, according to Musso, this has not been done.

What does all this mean? In his heart, Joe Musso is certain he possesses the knife that was Jim Bowie's favorite; the one with which he battled at the Alamo. However, when he talks of it, the collector tends to be cautious.

"Scientifically, I have a 150-year-old Bowie knife with a brass strip that belonged to an American officer with the initals, JB," he says. "Peter Hurkos is quite insistent that the initials on my knife stand for Jim Bowie."

But there is more. Some pages back, mention was made of a knife owned by Bart Moore. This particular knife popped up as early as 1975, when Moore contracted B.R. Hughes to tell him about it.

"Surely every person who has studied James Bowie has wondered what happened to this knife after his death," Hughes says. "A number of knives reputing to be this knife have shown up in recent years, but each has proven to be a fake."

But in reading a letter from Moore, Hughes found himself becoming interested — perhaps excited. "For one thing," he recalls, "Moore is not a knife collector nor is he a Jim Bowie fan. In fact, he has no interest in this particular knife, except for the fact that it has been in his family since 1890."

According to the Moore family records, Bart Moore's grandfather obtained the knife in 1890 from a Mexican who purported to have been a soldier in Santa Anna's army at the battle of the Alamo. The Mexican gave the knife to Moore's grandfather in payment of a $5 debt. The Mexican, incidentally, was thought to have been in his mid-seventies at the time of the transaction. Assuming he was seventy-five, that would have meant he was about fifteen years old when — and if — he served with Santa Anna at the battle of the Alamo; not an impossibility.

The Mexican, according to accounts handed down in the Moore family, claimed to have found the knife the day following the slaying of the Alamo garrison. It was found near the spot where the bodies of the defenders were burned. He took the knife with him and used it during the years he worked as a ranch hand near Wichita Falls, Texas.

According to Bart Moore, the knife has been in the family since that time, being passed from one generation to another. However, not much attention had been attached to it until recent years.

The knife measures 13¼ inches in overall length; the

*This knife was made by a cutler in New York State named Todd. It is alleged that Jim Bowie commissioned him to make the knife as an improvement on the original design. The blade on this particular knife is nine inches long.*

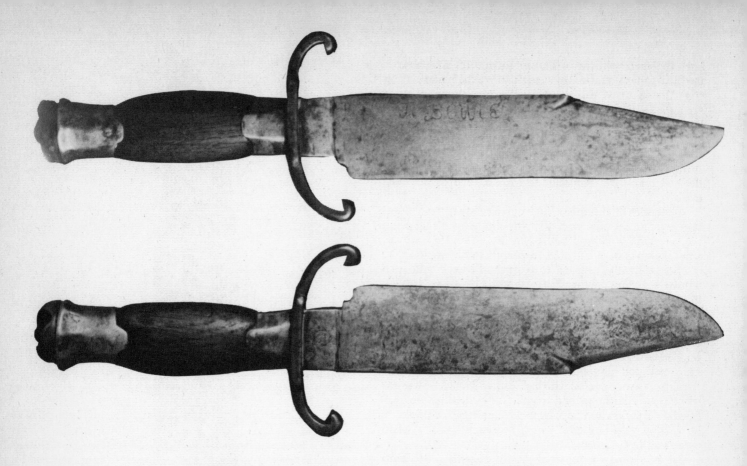

*This Bowie knife owned by Bart Moore II, a California resident,
bears markings which appear to lend credence to its authenticity.
The knife has been in the family since the 1890s and allegedly
was given to a Moore ancestor by a Mexican who was at the Alamo.*

length of the blade is 8¼ inches and measures 1⅝ inches in width. The knife appears to have been made from quarter-inch stock and was hand forged. The clipped section on the back of the blade is about three inches in length and is almost straight. Behind the clipped section are a number of tiny saw-type teeth that measure fourteen to the inch. Purpose of these, experts contend, would be much more efficiency in catching and helping to misdirect an opponent's knife during a fight than for sawing. The brass strip on the knife owned by Joe Musso, incidentally, probably was installed for the same purpose.

The scales of the knife have been fashioned from oak, while the rather ornate butt cap is of some base metal that has been plated, although both show the effects of much wear.

The guard on the Moore family's knife is long and curved with a hook at each end, again designed to deflect an opponent's blade, it would appear. On one side of the blade, etched in crude letters is J. BOWIE in capitals. On the opposite side are the initials, JB, which are enclosed in a crudely shaped acorn.

The initials, of course, lead to some conjecture. They are found on the knives held by both Moore and Musso. Do they stand for "Jim Bowie" or is it "James Black," the maker?

The dubious may be quick to discount both of the knives. However, it must be considered that the Moore knife has been in the family's continuing possession for nearly a cen-

tury. In 1890, there certainly was not the interest in collecting that is shown today. Therefore, is it logical that someone would attempt to create a fake a hundred years ago or more? It's doubtful. In those days, it was just another old knife just as the knife that Musso found among his old gun parts was considered in the same light.

In 1982, Jay Casell, who operates the Alamo Theater and Museum at 315 Alamo Plaza in San Antonio, Texas — only a stone's throw from the rebuilt Alamo — contacted Moore and asked that he be allowed to put the knife on display among the other artifacts relative to the Alamo battle.

Casell's two on-site historians, Kevin Young and William Beach, conducted research at the state archives in Austin to gain further documentation concerning the Moore knife. Don Montgomery, park historian for Old Washington Historic State Park, the site of the rebuilt James Black blacksmith shop, also investigated the background of the knife.

Montgomery went on record as stating he was "'eighty percent'' convinced that the Moore knife is one of Jim Bowie's originals and that it was forged by James Black.

"I know of three knives in existence today that have a claim to being original Black creations,'' Montgomery said at the time. "One of them, I have no faith in, but two of them, I am convinced, were made by Black, most probably for Bowie himself. He was a collector of knives and more than likely carried a number of his creations with him into

The continuing mystique surrounding Jim Bowie and his big battle blade has been the subject of countless movies, both in the silent film era and since. Actor McDonald Carey was one of those who portrayed the frontiersman in the film, "Comanche Territory," made in 1950. The knife may be the same one that Alan Ladd carried in "The Iron Mistress."

the Alamo. I am eighty percent convinced that the Moore specimen is one of these."

Again, early in 1982, a descendant of Rezin Bowie said to Bart Moore that "I am of the firm conviction that you have in your possession James' original knife, which he had made."

Mrs. Gwendolyn Moore Burk, then 87, was a resident of Picayune, Mississippi, who related the tale of the creation of Jim Bowie's knife. The legend was told to her by her own grandmother, Nathilda Bowie Moore, who was said to be present "when Bob Snowden and Grandfather (Rezin Bowie) attempted to kill a heifer. Grandfather held the knife, which struck a bone in the calf's neck and the blade was driven back through his hand. He remarked to Bob later that, if the blade had a guard, that never would have happened.

"So to the shop they went and Bob fashioned a knife from an old file. When Jim (Bowie) saw the knife, he exclaimed that it would make a fine hunting knife and he would go to Arkansas and have one made for himself and some to give friends."

Until the knife was put on display at the San Antonio museum, Moore had kept it in a safe deposit box, planning on passing it on to his son as a family heirloom. At one point, however, it was taken from the box and sent to Japan with an eye to having it reproduced there for sale in this country.

Oddly, about the time the insurance ran out on the knife, it disappeared! After trying frantically to locate the knife or to learn what had happened to it, Moore contacted the Federal Bureau of Investigation and told an agent what had happened. It was the opinion of the FBI that the knife fell under the category of a national treasure. Based upon that premise, the bureau agreed to handle the problem.

Two weeks later the knife reappeared and an FBI agent turned it over to Moore once again. The knife now is registered with the FBI, but Moore never did learn how or where the agents found it.

Today, the knife is shown occasionally at knife or gun shows, but always is well guarded. It is displayed without a fee from the promoters of such shows, as Bart Moore feels that the knife is a part of Americana and that citizens should be allowed to view it. This, of course, is a far cry from the days of more than thirty years ago, when the present owner's father carried the knife in combat in Korea!

William P. Bagwell, a resident of Arkansas and a widely respected authority on such edged weapons, examined the blade some years ago and reported in the Arkansas *Gazette,* "I think this knife is the finest example of an old fighting knife, the most intelligently contrived pure fighting knife I've ever seen. The guard, the shape of the blade, the length, the weight, the balance — all these factors point out that the man who made this gave a great deal of thought and consideration to the ultimate use to which the knife would be put.

"The guard on Moore's knife is somewhat strangely shaped by our standards today, but at the same time, is eminently practical. The Bowie knife of the 1830s did not have a guard. It looked more like a butcher knife. Most of the Bowie knives that had guards were straight, not curved like the guard on this knife. This particular specimen is curved on both ends. The quillions are curved toward the point of the knife. But the most interesting feature is the knobs on each end which would really lock onto a blade and catch it.

"It really intrigues me," Bagwell added, "that the guard is made of iron. Iron was a common material that blacksmiths had to work with. Steel was scarce and so was brass. If a frontier blacksmith made a knife, the most common material available was iron — and the guard on this knife is made of iron!

"The way this knife is put together, the way it is pinned...all the techniques used to make this knife are consistent with what a blacksmith would have available to him and his forge, using primitive tools in a primitive area.

"In my estimation — judging from all the other old knives I've seen — this knife has the strongest claim to being James Bowie's knife of any other knife I have ever seen. I would say, from what I know about knives, knifemaking and James Black and James Bowie that I'm ninety to ninety-five percent sure that, yes, this knife is James Bowie's!"

During his examination, incidentally, Bagwell put the Moore knife to the acid test, literally. He rubbed the blade with citric acid and wavy, watery lines appeared, convincing him that it is of Damascus steel, a process for which James Black held the secret.

Don Montgomery, the park historian at Old Washington Historic State Park, made his own investigation of the Moore-owned knife in early 1982.

"As the historian at Old Washington Historic State Park, I have had many opportunities to examine several old Bowie knives, as well as the written records concerning James Black, the Washington blacksmith often credited with making the first Bowie knife," he reports.

"From my studies, I have concluded in my own mind that James Black definitely made a Bowie knife for James Bowie, although I cannot say it was the first Bowie knife. The major argument used against James Black's inventing the Bowie knife has been the non-existence of a Black-made knife and that there is no written documentation supporting the James Black story which dates before 1890,

*An ancestor of Bart Moore II accepted this knife from the Mexican who claimed to have been a soldier at the Alamo, picking up the knife after the battle. It was in payment of a $5 debt. Etched on the blade is "J. Bowie" name. Several experts feel that the knife is truly authentic.*

when the first written accounts of James Black were published based upon the remembrances of Governor Daniel Webster Jones of Arkansas.

"My research has found many documents from the life of James Black which, in most cases, support the James Black story told by Daniel W. Jones. Even more exciting was the discovery of an editorial attacking the Bowie knife published in the December 8, 1841, issue of the Washington *Telegraph* in which the publisher said, 'This far-famed deadly instrument had its origin, we believe, in Hempstead county (Arkansas). The first knife of the kind was made in this place (Washington), by Mr. James H. Black, for a man named James Bowie, who was killed at the Alamo in Texas, and hence it is sometimes called the Black knife, sometimes the Bowie knife....'"

Montgomery contends that this editorial completely destroys the argument that the James Black story was merely the fanciful stories "of a bitter old man who had never been much of anything," meaning James Black. Also, the argument that all documentation has come from Daniel Webster Jones, who was too young to have ever seen Black make a knife is refuted, since D.W. Jones was only a couple of years old when the editorial appeared in the newspaper.

Montgomery goes on record by stating, "There is only one knife that I know of which I would consider to possibly be the original knife made for James Bowie by James Black. It is the knife owned by Bart Moore which has been in the family since about 1890.

"The knife itself is rather unique for a Bowie knife and was made by a skilled blacksmith, since several of its features were not the easiest to make. The fluting on the butt cap, the pommel collar and the ferrule was a difficult and time-consuming task which would require a skilled craftsman. The etching on the blade, which has 'J. Bowie' on one side and an acorn with the initials 'J.B.' on the other side tends to confirm for me that this knife was owned by James Bowie and made by James Black, since it would seem unlikely that Bowie would have his name on one side and his initials on the other.

"Finally," says Montgomery, "if one studied the typical patterns of silver-plate ware in the early Nineteenth Century, one would see a resemblance between this Bowie knife and a table knife, which would not be surprising in a James Black knife, since Black was an apprentice to a manufacturer of silver plate in Philidelphia.

"I have come to the conclusion that James Bowie was a collector of knives, perhaps having as many as twenty at one time," Montgomery adds. "It will probably never be known what happened to most of them, but in looking at the Bart Moore knife, I believe that it is very possibly one of the collection."

The case rests.

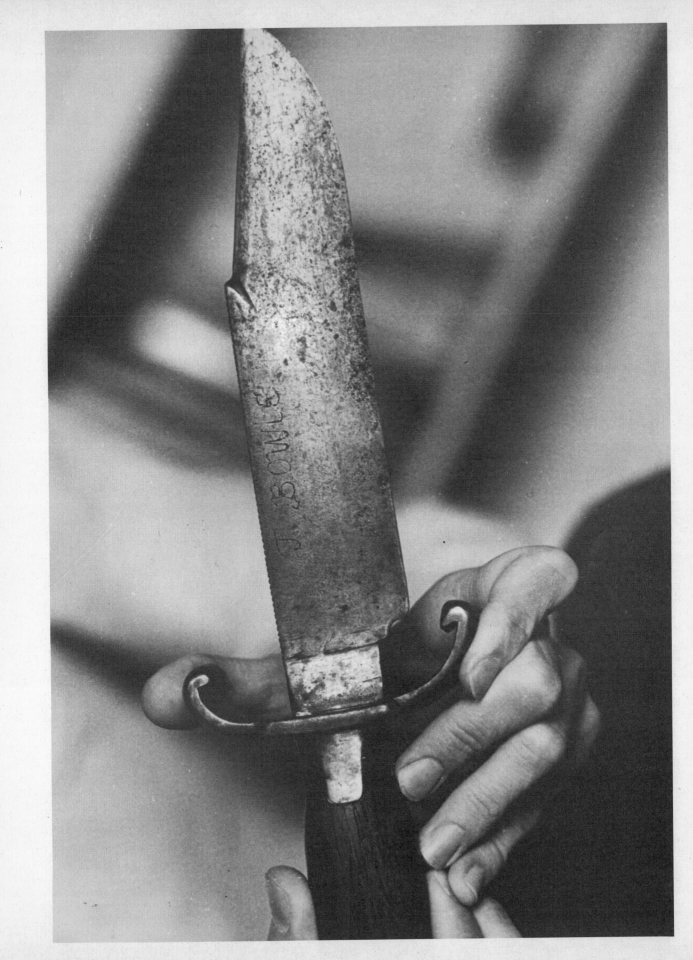

Molten steel is tapped from induction furnace at Allegheny Ludlum plant. All steel must start somewhere and this is an early step in the process.

# Chapter 2

# A FEEL FOR STEEL

## There Are Steels That Are Fit For Knives — And There Are Those That Aren't. Knowing The Difference Is The Mark Of The True Cutler!

OVER THE centuries, the materials favored for knives seem to have gone full circle. There was the era known generally as the Middle Ages when the Damascus blade was considered the ultimate in cutlery. Now, in the Eighties, many custom knifemakers have gone back to the ancient rituals and are boasting of the fact that they are making knives by hand of Damascus-forged steel!

But there have been a lot of knives — and many different alloys of steel — in between. In fact, so many types have led to a great deal of confusion among those who are less than expert when it comes to knowing what constitutes good cutlery and what does not.

The modern-made Damascus, incidentally, is being used primarily by custom knifemakers, while the factory blades still are fashioned from alloys that allow knives to be turned out *en masse* for the cutlery trade.

A century and a half back, when a blacksmith or a cutler decided to make a knife, he was not able to order up a roll of 440C stainless as is the case with today's manufacturers. He had to rely on the steel that he made and tempered himself to come up with a knife blade that would perform all of the chores demanded in a frontier society.

Today, there are any number of types of steel that will make good knife blades and there are several stainless — more realistically, stain-*resistant* — steels that are favored by knifemakers. It should be pointed out, perhaps, that the older types of steel that were ever in danger of rusting are rapidly becoming things of the past in the knife industry. More and more custom makers and manufacturers as well are relying upon the so-called "stainless" alloys for their blades.

Among custom knifemakers, for example, the favored stainless is 154-CM, which is made by Crucible Steel. A close copy of this particular alloy is ATS-34, which is produced in Japan. Many custom makers are switching to the latter, because it is priced at roughly half the cost of 154-CM and the Japanese manufacturers are willing to pro-

This is an argon oxygen decarburization furnace at the Allegheny Ludlum Steel plant at Brackenridge, Pennsylvania. This is another step in perfecting the types of steel that are favored by both manufacturers and custom cutlers.

duce the shapes and widths a maker wants instead of his having to accept what comes out the door of the steel mill.

We discussed this with Bob Loveless, who is famous for his handmade drop-point hunting knives. Most of the knives he makes today are gobbled up by knife collectors who pay as much as $2000 for a rather plain, undecorated knife. However, it does carry the Loveless name and that has become important in itself among collectors.

"I started out using 154-CM when a customer ordered a stainless steel blade," Loveless states, "but I have switched to ATS-34 because of price and availability. Stain-resistant alloys have caught on among knife users and even collectors who probably never will use a knife in the field. As a result, most of the custom knifemakers I know seem to be concentrating on stainless knives or they have turned to making Damascus, because those are the things their clients want."

In his own experience, Loveless has found that a number of custom knifemakers still are using 440C or D-2 steels. These have the stain-resistant properties being sought, but are somewhat cheaper in price than either 154-CM or ATS-34.

There are some other things to consider. A number of the alloys being used today cannot be forged with any great ease. That means that the knifemaker is limited to the stock-removal method of forming a blade, if he uses one of these alloys. For those who do not understand the difference, in forging, a bar of steel is heated and pounded into proper shape on an anvil, being tempered while still in the cherry-red state. That is putting it rather simply, but the explanation covers the basics.

With the stock-removal method, the steel usually is bought in billets — steel bars of proper length, width and thickness — or in long rolls that can be unwound, then stripped out into acceptable lengths. The rolls are available in various widths, of course, which means that a man tends to order the width that suits his needs; or else designs his blades to fall within the width of the roll of steel. Flat stock also is available.

These strips of steel are flattened out, then the shape of the blade and the tang are inscribed on the metal as a pat-

Steelworkers watch gauges closely as rolls of steel come from a three-strand tandem cold rolling mill's machinery.

tern. Then powered stones and grinders are used to remove excess metal, bringing the billet of steel down to the dimensions sought. With the knife thus roughly formed, the custom bladesmith, making one knife at a time, must indulge in a good deal of handwork to complete the knife.

In the case of manufacturers, the roll of steel may be fed onto a reel and simply unwound through a series of dies and cutters, where the shape of the knife or the blade is stamped out, pinholes drilled and grinding done automatically. Fitting of handguards, bolsters, pins, et al., is accomplished pretty much by hand.

For centuries, cutlers were content to fashion quality carbon steel into knife blades. While the primary ingredient of steel is iron, the element that has most to do with its hardness is the amount of carbon that is introduced into the alloy. The addition of carbon to molten iron causes hardness, but too much carbon can make the resultant steel brittle as well.

At the other extreme, if insufficient carbon is added, we will have a blade that does not snap easily, but it also will not hold an edge when put to serious use. The problem, of

course, is to find a happy medium for cutlery; we want a steel that is hard enough to hold an edge, yet tough enough that the blade will not snap under tough or extended use.

The carbon content in steel is rated on a percentage basis, if one wants to look at it in those terms. However, those who work with steel use what they call a "point" system of measurement. With this measurement, each one-hundredth of a percentage is a "point." Or it can be defined as .01 percent being a point. Thus, if we are working with 0-1, a cold-rolled die steel, we find that it has .90 percent carbon in its composition — or 90 points.

The point system of measuring carbon added to the iron is used with other mineral additives as well. Working with the same 0-1 steel, we find that it also contains 50 points of chrome, 100 of manganese and 50 points of tungsten. This combination creates a steel that has been used for many years in knifemaking. It is versatile in that it can be forged or the blade can be shaped by the stock-removal method. When tempered properly, this particular steel has a hardness factor of 57 to 62 on the Rockwell C scale.

Carbon is introduced into most steels as they are made,

At Camillus Cutlery factory, basic knife materials are stored, distributed to work stations along assembly line. Note that most of the metal is in varying width rolls.

Workmen at Camillus factory use stamping units to cut blades, brass linings and center scales fast. Automatic equipment turns out thousands per hour.

but the points may differ from as low as 5 to as high as 100. The problem here is that steel must have at least 40 points of carbon before it will harden. The craftsmen who make custom knives by hand seem to favor steel with 50 to 60 points of carbon, if they are seeking to build a flexible blade. If the blade is meant to carry an edge for a long time, they may want a steel carrying 70 to 100 points of carbon. Again, the edge will last, but the blade tends to be brittle.

In today's manufacture of steel, in addition to iron and carbon, any number of other elements may be added to give the resultant steel special characteristics.

Listed alphabetically rather than by order of importance in the manufacture of steel are: chromium, lead, manganese, molybdenum, nickel, phosphorus, silicon, sulphur and tungsten.

In stainless steel, as much as twenty percent chromium may be added. This makes the material difficult to forge, as it tends to crack when being worked at the forge. Addition of this element, however, causes the hardening process to penetrate more deeply into the knife blade and the steel is easier to heat-treat properly.

Knowing the properties of lead, it may seem strange that

this element would be added to a formula for steel. Actually, it is used seldom and then only on special order by the customer. The proportion usually runs no more than .03 percent and usually less. Addition of lead allows the steel to be machined more easily, but such stock is not likely to be used for knife blades.

Manganese is present in almost all steels, but usually in no greater amount than two percent. It acts as a deoxidizer and brings a degree of strength to the steel. It also is an aid in proper heat-treatment.

Molybdenum has received a great amount of publicity in the past couple of decades, usually in connection with steels made for the firearms industry. It tends to increase the toughness of the alloy in which it is introduced and aids in the penetration of the hardness quality. If the molybdenum content is high, the steel is poor forging material.

Nickel is used largely in the various formulae for stainless steel. As much as thirty-six percent of stainless may be nickel. It also is said to increase toughness and strength of the steel, but hardness may suffer in proportion to the amount of nickel introduced.

Considered an impurity in most alloys, phosphorus is

At Buck Knives, big rolls of steel in varying widths and thicknesses are delivered to the factory for cutting. In this photo, steel looks flimsy, but it surely isn't.

Heavy reels of steel are moved into position on a chain hoist to be mounted on a spindle. Once mounted, steel is fed into a straightening machine that will flatten it.

present in all types of steel. It is alleged to reduced the possibility of atmospheric corrosion, among other things.

Silicon is introduced as a means of improving tensile strength of an alloy and also aids in the hardening process. When used in combination with other elements, it produces a tougher type of steel.

Sulphur is an impurity and every effort is made to remove it from the steel mixture in the molten state. Any steel with a more than a minute inclusion of sulphur cannot be considered a good steel for cutlery.

Tungsten is introduced in small amounts to steels that are meant to be used for tool making. This particular element causes a dense-grained structure in the steel, which allows for a hard cutting edge. However, it also results in the steel retaining its hardness even at extreme temperatures. This makes it difficult to forge and thus goes largely ignored by those knifemakers who fashion knives with hammer and anvil rather than by the stock-removal method.

For the custom knifemaker who is going to forge his blades, either oil-hardening or water-hardening steels are preferred. Tests have shown that air-hardened steel usually is tougher than either of the other two, but it presents problems in forging. When the metal begins to air cool, if the knifemaker is working it to shape, it may crack, which means the end of that particular project.

D-2 is one of the air-hardened steels that makes a superior knife, but it is used primarily by knifemakers who use the stock-removal method. However, if it is forged properly, it provides an edge that will last a great deal longer than some of the competitive alloys. The carbon content is high — 1.50 percent or 150 points. It also contains twelve percent chromium, one percent molybdenum, one percent vanadium and suffers little distortion when being heat-treated. The resultant hardness, as measured by the Rockwell method, ranges from 54 to 61 C.

There are several series of steels that are used by custom knifemakers, each with differing carbon and other elemental content. Some are chosen for specific properties sought in a knife, others simply because they are easy to work. All of them, however, feature Rockwell hardness in the range of 50 to 65 C, which makes them good working knives. Among these are the 10-Series steels that include 1050, 1060, 1070, 1080 and 1095. Each differs primarily in its

Steel bands move through straightener, then a stamping hammer cuts out the various components. Scrap is dumped into barrels and will be sent to salvage later.

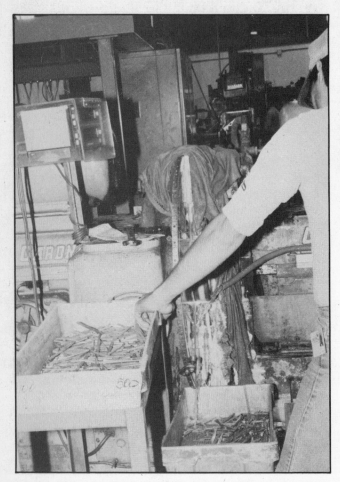

Buck Knives has become highly automated over the years. Locking components for maker's line of folding knives are stamped out automatically, go into a tray to sort.

content of carbon and manganese. Hardness, when tempered, ranges from 55 to 62, depending upon the carbon content.

As mentioned earlier, favorites among custom knifemakers differ from one to another, but many use 440C, which is a high-carbon chromium stainless alloy. While it can be forged with no great difficulty, most custom knives made from it are produced by the stock-removal method. It contains .95 to 1.20 percent carbon, plus copper, chromium, manganese, molybdenum, nickel, phosphorus, silicon and sulphur in its composition. It is known as a steel with high wear resistance, which is one of the greater reasons for its popularity.

Among the factory knifemakers, 440B is favored. It has much the same properties as 440C, but contains less carbon. The reason for favoring 440B lies in the fact that commercial knifemakers use high-speed grinding equipment and the higher carbon content of 440C tends to load grinding wheels too rapidly. Thus 440B, while a slightly less tough steel, is more workable on a mass production basis.

Another steel that is used today by at least one mass pro-ducer is M-2. This is a high-speed tool steel that makes up into an excellent cutting blade. The carbon content is .85 percent, so it can be ground on high-speed equipment in the stock-removal method.

Those who forge blades on an individual basis tend to steer clear of M-2, however, because it is prone to crack during the forging process. This particular steel has a reputation for being both tough and wear resistant. In addition to carbon, the formula contains varying amounts of chromium, manganese, molybdenum, silicon, tungsten and vanadium. When properly heat-treated, hardness registers at Rcokwell 58 to 62 C.

Roughly two decades ago, Vanadium Alloys, a Pennsylvania firm, introduced Vasco Wear, an alloyed steel that was said to be exceedingly tough and highly wear resistant. Custom knifemakers thought, at first, they had discovered the ultimate steel.

"But it turned out to be a disappointment for us," says Bob Loveless, who is continually seeking steels with improved properties for a cutting edge. "The first thing we discovered was that the moment this material was introduced

*Stainless steel blades are arranged in trays according to production order. Largest factories can turn out several thousand knives daily. Grinding is next step.*

*Buck blades are tested by random selection for hardness after sub-zero quench. Machine records Rockwell reading.*

to blood, the metal stained and discolored. That didn't make it very popular among hunters who would be cleaning game in the field.

"The other problem most custom knifemakers experienced was that Vasco Wear had an unpredictable way of going dull. Most steels are linear in that there is a direct proportion as to how much cutting one can do with it before it goes dull. Then you resharpen the blade and go back to cutting. With Vasco Wear, there was no linear dimension. It might be cutting perfectly well, then go dull all at once."

There are cutlers, however, who say Vasco Wear can be made into highly serviceable knives through forging. The greatest problem with this is that the material is extremely hard, tough and difficult for the cutler to work after it has been hardened. The finished Vasco Wear blade generally has a Rockwell hardness of 58 to 62 C when forged. Some commercial knife manufacturers are turning out kitchen cutlery from this particular material, but custom knifemakers have turned away from it.

As mentioned earlier, Loveless and a number of other custom cutlers have come to favor 154-CM and its Japanese-made look-alike, ATS-34. Both have virtually the same makeup, which includes 1.05 percent carbon, fourteen percent chromium, .50 manganese, four percent molybdenum and .30 percent silicon.

Both of these steels are used to make knives by means of the stock-removal method, however, as they have been found difficult to work in forging. Both have high wear resistance and are described as medium in toughness. When heat-treated, hardness rates at 56 to 62 C Rockwell.

As indicated earlier, Damascus — or a modern version of this ancient steel — has become suddenly popular among knife collectors, users and, resultantly, custom knifemakers.

When one thinks of Damascus steel, it tends to bring on thoughts of Middle Eastern potentates, the Crusades and many other memory pictures that may be more legend than truth.

Back in the Thirties, the late Cecil B. DeMille made a film concerning the Crusades. The film since has been shown on television, but even fifty years ago, one par-

Rockwell testing is done by all knifemakers, whether big or small, to ensure that the hardness of blade is such that it will take an edge and maintain it.

Considered by many to be the nation's leading maker of custom knives, Bob Loveless turns his blades out one at a time with minimum equipment but a lot of skill in his California shop.

ticular scene did much to impress young minds — and some not so young — with the cutting qualities of Damascus steel.

In the scene, Richard the Lion-Hearted has come face-to-face for a meeting with the Middle Eastern potentate, Saladin, who is really the villain. The actor portraying the English knight put a thick bar of iron between two chairs. Then, swinging his broadsword, cut the bar of iron in two.

The Turkish villain appeared amused and announced this was a show of strength, not of blade sharpness. He took his own blade — a scimitar of some sort, as we recall it — turned the cutting edge upward, then tossed a light silk scarf in the air. As the scarf floated gently down across the blade, which was held steady in the hand of the Turk, the fabric was cut nearly in two.

Admittedly, the scene was accomplished with what the film studios tend to call "movie magic," but it did leave an audience impression as to the qualities of Damascus steel.

The individual who probably has done more than any other to return Damascus to its current state of popularity has been Bill Moran, who operates his forge in the Maryland backcountry.

Moran was one of the pioneers, with Loveless and a few others, in bringing the custom-made knife to its present level of popularity among both users and collectors.

Originally, Damascus steel was used in making battle swords and the craft is thought to have originated in Damascus in what now is Syria; hence the name. However, there are numerous examples of ancient Damascus-type blades that have come from India and Persia — what now is Iran — and even from Scandanavia, where the Vikings apparently perfected the steel-makers art. The Japanese, too, used a Damascus-design steel in many of their early samurai swords.

As with many innovations and even sciences, it is not impossible that the technique was developed in all of these geographic areas at about the same time or that tradesmen and such travelers as Marco Polo may have carried the art from one area to another.

The mark of a Damascus blade, of course, is the wavy pattern that is seen throughout its length. The pattern is created by as many as a thousand layers of iron and steel

*While a large-scale manufacturer can turn out many thousands of knives in a day, Loveless and fellow custom knifemakers do a lot of handwork that cuts their production. He makes about 20 knives a month.*

being welded together, then etched with acid to bring out the pattern.

The reasons Damascus virtually became a lost art are not determined easily. The most obvious is that cutlers and bladesmiths found a less time-consuming way of making good steels and the economic factor led to Damascus losing favor.

The reason that a Damascus blade requires too long to make lies in the fact that the layers of alternating steel and iron must be welded at the forge with the blacksmith's hammer. This means a great deal of hammering out, folding over the molten metal and hammering it into a single mass again. This is repeated time after time, until the layers are virtually welded together into a single strip of metal. It is from this that the blade is formed.

Moran, for example, feels that 512 layers make an ideal knife, the patterns being properly eye-catching, while the blade offers excellent cutting quality. Incidentally, at the prices that Bill Moran gets for his custom knives, it is not likely many are going to be used for field-dressing deer! They are highly prized collector items, since he is able to

make no more than a dozen a year and his Damascus knives sell for several thousand dollars each.

Following Bill Moran's lead and learning from his efforts, a handful of other custom knifemakers today are turning out Damascus steel knives at their own forges.

The technique is simple to start with, at least. All you need is a bar of steel and a bar of iron. However, the knowing maker has his own preferences as to the type of steel he will use. The pieces are forged together — welded, actually, — with heat and hammer in the same manner that no doubt was used centuries ago.

Bill Moran has worked at the blacksmith's forge most of his life and even before he began making Damascus blades, his earlier custom knives were forged. He has found that, in welding the two bars together — one of iron, the other steel — he must have exactly the right temperature. If it is too hot, the steel will be ruined. If not hot enough, of course, the two bars will not fuse together in a weld.

When the two pieces of metal adhere properly, the combined bar is folded and hammered out with an iron blacksmith's hammer. This creates another weld and results in a

In spite of the automation and computerization used in mass manufacturing of knives, a great deal of handwork still is used in the assembly phase of the operations.

At Camillus Cutlery, blades on all knives are sharpened on wheels by hand to achieve a specified cutting edge.

block of material that is roughly three inches square with four layers of alternating steel and iron. This block is hammered out on an anvil to a length of about six inches and is folded again; a slow, time-consuming process. When one stops to consider that, in his experiments, Moran has tried up to 2048 layers, there is no way of judging the worth of a knife when compared to the time involved.

The first knife he made had a hundred layers of alternating steel and iron, but Moran felt the grain was too coarse. The next knife had 2000 layers, but the grain was so fine that, even after being acid etched, one could not differentiate between the layers. Tie to this the fact that the knifesmith does not really know how successful he has been in creating the pattern he seeks until the forging has been completed, the blade has been ground, then hardened and polished. He finally settled on six hundred layers as his ideal.

There are other dangers, too, according to Moran's ex-

perience. He says that the more welds, the greater the possibility of a mistake. Discoloration may appear in the metal or one of the welds may turn out to be bad. If the latter is the case, a crack usually will appear, running lengthwise up the blade. Moran has found no way of repairing such a crack and simply discards that particular piece of work, starting once again with a bit of iron, another of steel.

In his initial experiments, Moran used W-2, a tool steel that contains up to 1.40 percent carbon and .25 percent vanadium. He had difficulty in welding this steel to iron and went to 0-1, described in detail earlier in this chapter.

Based upon Moran's findings, there are a great many more facets to making Damascus, ranging from the type of coal that is used to make coke, to the temperature — 3000 degrees Fahrenheit — that must be attained for welding the two metals into a single bar, then folding, hammering, folding, *ad infinitum*.

These knives have been ground to shape by the familiar stock-removal method, which is favored by a majority of today's custom knifemakers. The final edge comes later.

Bill Moran (left) and Bob Loveless were founding members of the American Knifemakers Guild, which was founded to improve quality of custom knives.

Once the blade is forged, it is annealed by soaking it in a hot bed of coals overnight. Moran says this will bring the steel down to what he calls "its maximum softness."

Then the blade is ground, the knifesmith taking care to remove the small hammer marks that may appear on the metal. Actually, the blade has been shaped pretty much to its final dimensions in the forge, so grinding is held to a minimum.

The blade now is ready for heat-treating. A fire of coke is prepared and a bar of hot iron is dropped into a bucket of oil to heat it to 125 degrees. Moran warns against trying to quench a Damascus blade in cold oil.

While everyone talks about quenching when the steel is heated to a "cherry red" tone, Moran is a bit more scien-

tific. He uses a magnet and keeps touching the blade with it. At the point that the steel becomes magnetic and adheres to the magnet, he lowers the blade point-first into the special heat-treating oil.

Damascus blades can be drawn for extra toughness, but Moran does not do this. Instead, he allows the blade to remain in the oil until the latter cools. This may take up to two hours. Once the blade has cooled, Moran checks it for imperfections or determines whether it is likely to break. He uses a pretty basic approach, placing the blade on his anvil and hitting it hard with an iron hammer!

If the knife passes that test, he uses an 80-grit belt to grind on an edge. After that, comes treatment with 240 grit, then 500, before going to the buffer for a final polish.

When the buffing is completed, there should be some semblance of a pattern in the steel. This is created when the buffing wheel removes a little of the iron, which is softer than the steel on each side.

To etch the blade, muriatic acid is used. This is poured into a large glass container that is deep enough to cover the blade. The blade is lowered into the acid and allowed to stay for about half an hour. At the end of that time, the Damascus is removed and washed in clear water to halt the action of the acid. Baking soda may be sprinkled on the blade, too, thus halting the acid action. The blade then is soaked in water before it is buffed once more to remove the acid stains. Moran Damascus blades test Rockewell 62C to 67C.

After that, comes installation of the handle, pommel and guard. The latter two, Moran also fashions from Damascus and uses exotic woods for his handles.

Other makers of Damascus knives have their own techniques, but by necessity, they must parallel those used by Bill Moran. After all, he led the way!

Damascus-type patterns also are obtained by forging knife blades from steel cable. In fact, a number of knifemakers are using this material for their Damascus blades these days.

"With the average Damascus blade, you're never really sure of the composition," opines Bob Loveless. "Some are exceptionally well made and will hold an edge. Others don't hold an edge for any great length of time."

He does feel, though, that the patterned blades created from steel cable — or wire rope, as it is called by some knifemakers — holds a good deal of promise.

"To start with, we know what's in that cable," he explains, "and we know how to handle it to get a decent cutting edge."

Welding such cable into a blade is not a new technique. It's been done for at least a century, but in recent years, the system for making a knife blade has been all but lost.

"The blade made from wire rope," Loveless contends, "is rugged, durable and carries an interesting pattern that we call watered steel." Such cable also can be used in creating a number of what are called twist patterns.

The material used here is cable made of all-carbon steel, but one must be certain it has no properties meant to make it stainless and has not been galvanized. Most commonly used are lengths of cable from the oil-hardened 10-Series steels. These include 1065, 1075 and 1095, all of them

*With the increased interest in Damascus knives in recent years, forged-to-shape blades have begun to appear on the market. These are from Damascus USA. Many blades and blanks are being forged in Pakistan, India for export.*

described as plowshare steel in the industry. Sizes may range from as small as a quarter-inch up to a full inch-and-a-half in diameter.

Some of the wire ropes have cores of fiber or plastic. These will not serve for knifemaking, since the steel surrounding them will not weld properly. The number of strands in such cables can range from as few as seven to as many as three hundred, depending upon the thickness of the cable. Most of the cable also has a coating that combines petroleum, some type of asphalt-based lubricant and a rust-preventative. This material needs to be removed — or as much of it as one is able — before proceding. The best material found to date for stripping this coating is gasoline. It is suggested,

however, that stripping this material be done outside of the shop in an area where there is no likelihood of fire or an explosion.

The first step is to cut a piece of cable about a foot in length. Most makers prefer to use cable that is three-quarters to an inch in diameter. The ends should be welded immediately so that the individual wires will not unravel. This should be done at the forge. The length of cable is brought to weld temperature slowly.

When the cable reaches an orange shade, not the usual cherry-red that blacksmiths consider the ultimate, it should be taken to the anvil and pounded with a hammer, turning it all the time so that the round cable comes to resemble a

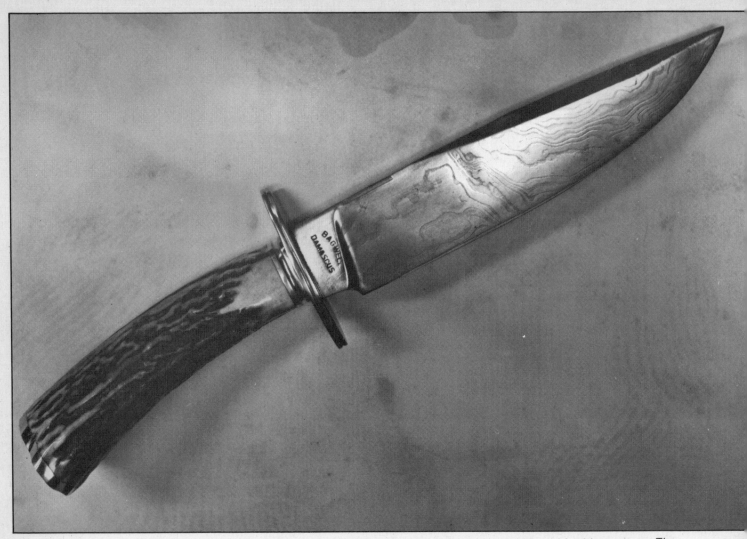

*This Bowie style by custom knifemaker Bill Bagwell has a Damascus blade that he fashioned for his own use. The craftsman described edge-holding qualities as incredible, but this is less true of some Damascus being imported.*

four-sided billet. In doing this, the diameter will be reduced as much as fifty percent, because the air spaces between the strands of wire are being closed up. Slag and scale will be hammered out of the knife material, too, as the welds are closed. The weld areas must be overlapped and fluxed with borax. One must take his time in all of this, since rushing the welding or trying to work the steel when it is too hot can ruin the potential knife blade.

Some knifesmiths tighten the strands even more by heating the cable length to a cherry red shade, then using a wrench and a vise to tighten the twist. Ultimately, this will result in an almost solid length of metal. Twisting, inciden-

tally, also will have a positive effect on the cutting qualities of the knife when completed.

Once the twisting is satisfactory to the knifesmith's eye, the bar is forged down and folded, then welded in much the same manner that one would handle regular Damascus. At times, several pieces of wire rope are welded together, thus increasing the amount of pattern in the finished product.

Once the billet is prepared and properly welded, it can be forged, then heat-treated as though it was ordinary 10-Series steel. In order to etch the blade, it is polished first with 400-grit, then with a crocus buffing wheel until it is clean. Either ferric chloride or a mild solution of nitric acid

These hand-forged Damascus-bladed knives are the work of Bill Moran, the one to reintroduce this type of steel-making in 1973 at the Knifemakers Guild show.

can be used to etch the blade and bring out the Damascus pattern. A substance called aqua regis also can be used and some say it produces the best patterns. Up to half an hour of etching is normal.

The advantage of the steel cable approach is that it can save countless hours of welding and folding. Much of this combining already has been accomplished simply by the twist in cable. Making a Damascus-type knife in this fashion is much faster than the method used by Bill Moran and others and the product can be equally as good. And as Bob Loveless puts it, "You know what the steel is and what's in it, so you know what to expect performance-wise of the finished blade."

Not all Damascus knifemakers make their own steel. Today, Charlton, Ltd., is furnishing ready-made forged-to-shape blades of Damascus which are made by the firm. There also are firms in England which are producing steels with Damascus patterns for use by custom knifemakers.

Using gas furnaces and huge power hammers that drive as much as fifty tons of pressure, it is possible to produce Damascus billets in as little as twenty minutes in such a mass production operation. A number of production knives are now produced with Damascus steel blades.

A wide choice of natural materials has been used in this array of the knives favored by some custom makers as the best of what they produce.

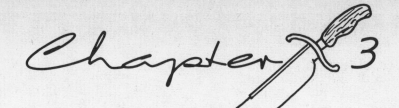

# Chapter 3

# GETTING A HANDLE ON IT

*Natural Materials May Present Problems, But
They Make Up For That In Beauty And Function*

KNIVES HAVE been with us nearly as long as mankind has roamed the face of the earth, if the evidence from archeologists is believable. There is plenty of evidence dating back millions of years that the earth's early human inhabitants used knives that were nothing more than sharp pieces of flint perhaps chipped off a large boulder by effects of weather and temperature change rather than by planned effort. These sharp flakes of flint were picked up and ultimately were found useful as cutting instruments.

There is no confirmed information relative to the origin of knife handles. It can only be assumed that early man found that he could wound himself by grasping the sharp edges of the piece of flint and ultimately decided to wrap grass or a length of vine around the stone knife as protection of the hand, finding that such wrapping also improved his grip and the feel of the implement in his fingers.

Whatever the early history, materials for knife handles have come down through the ages as being limited to a great degree, until the so-called Space Age materials began to be developed in this and other countries.

In the days of the Roman Empire, the ancient Greeks and even the Middle Ages, when knighthood was allegedly in flower, handles were being developed for cutting instruments, but many of them were more ornamental than practical.

One has only to inspect the knife and sword handles of the Crusades — on both sides — to realize that more thought was given to artistry than to practical use. All too often the handles on daggers and stilettos were far too small to fill all but the tiniest hand. This, of course, made them difficult to use.

In Italy, the artisans of Florence and other art center cities turned out beautiful work, often the handles were of gold and silver and inlaid with precious gems, but again, these were works of art, not meant for use in the field for hunting or in battle.

The type of knife that has been discussed thus far, of course, was that owned or worn by the nobility or the wealthy. Among the peasants and farmers, blades were fashioned as working tools and the usual handle material was wood, which was riveted to the steel. In most cases, little attention was given to shaping the handle or attempting to make it more practical than the simple slabs of wood

Jim Sornberger, San Jose, California, used nickel silver in the handles of these knives inlaid with gold nuggets.

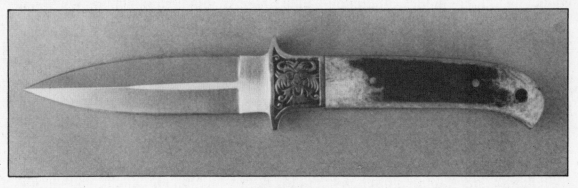

This Taylor-made boot knife is rather plain in design, but features an engraved ram's head with Sambar stag.

allowed. There were those, of course, who would whittle and cut down these cumbersome handles until they better fit the individual hand, but most seemed content to use whatever they obtained without much in the way of change, beyond maintaining a keen edge.

As might be expected, over the centuries, a variety of so-called natural materials came to be used for knife handles. This list includes various types of wood, ivory, horn, stag, bone, stone, shell, leather and other materials. Such were the standard until this century, when the man-made materials began to make their appearance. These include Micarta, Zytel, pakkawood, various types of rubber and a host of other compounds concocted in chemical laboratories with the aim of improving man's lifestyle — or his military capability. All of these materials have been touted as being far superior to natural handle materials, and they are in many respects, if one wants to discount beauty.

Even today, most of the natural materials are relatively easy to obtain. Note that we say *most;* some, such as ivory, have become premium items, as has Sambar stag.

Walnut was a favorite handle material for many decades simply because it was plentiful in this country. At the other extreme, I have yet to see a knife made in Finland with a wooden handle that was of something other than birch.

Today, the most popular materials seem to be the exotics such as cocobolo, rosewood and others such as Goncalo alves, ebony and purpleheart.

A premium price now is being asked if one wants ivory scales for his custom knife. This is based upon the fact that most of the ivory currently available cannot be imported into this country legally. Botswana still exports legal ivory and there have been recent finds in Alaska of mastodon tusks that probably are thousands upon thousands of years old. These fossilized tusks are being washed out of the frozen tundra during hydraulic gold mining operations and are being purchased by knife manufacturers and ivory dealers. Buck Knives, for example, bought a number of these mastodon tusks a few years ago and has been using them in the firm's custom knife shop.

What is termed *fresh* ivory is illegal in this country and to have it in your possession is asking for a heavy fine and probably a stiff prison sentence. Under this federal restriction, ivory from the Indian elephant, the teeth of the sperm whale, walrus tusks and horns from the narwhal all are considered contraband.

Horn of various types has been used for centuries for knife handles. India seems to control the major supply of horn from both the water buffalo and the Sambar stag. For

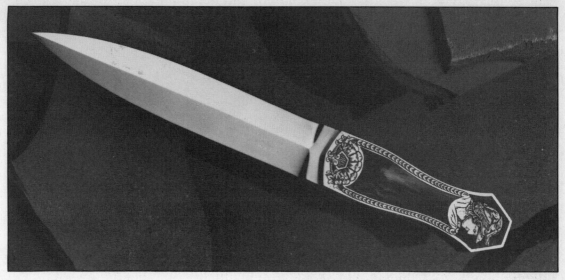

*For his War Dagger, actually a collector piece, Jim Sornberger utilized sheep's horn for handle inlays.*

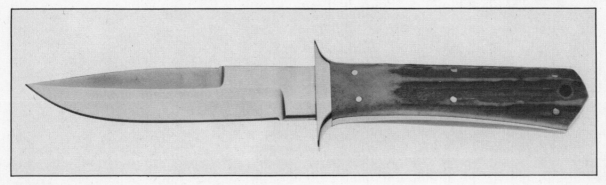

*Blackjack Knives is one of the manufacturers who try to maintain a supply of stag to dress up factory knives.*

the most part, Sambar stag exportation is controlled by the Indian government which has made a point of seeing there is not a glut on the world market, although importation into this country has increased in recent years. For a period of about a decade, a customer paid dearly if he wanted stag scales on his knife. Water buffalo horn is increasing in supply, coming in some amounts from the Philippines now to alleviate shortages from India.

Another material — once popular, but now used primarily on presentation knives — is mother-of-pearl. Most of this also comes from the Philippines. Perhaps the top importer of ivory, mother-of-pearl and buffalo horn into this country is Art Jewel Enterprises, Limited, 421 Irmen Drive, Addison, IL 60101. While this firm deals primarily in custom handgun grips, they also supply raw handle materials to knifemakers.

Divers in the Philippines bring up ton after ton of mother-of-pearl-bearing shell, but it is only the large shells that can be cut into pieces of sufficient size to make a knife handle or pistol grip. As the supply becomes more scarce, divers are having to dive deeper and the ultimate risk of life is reflected in the increasing price.

Most of the handle materials listed thus far are available in various forms. Hardwoods — including the jungle-grown

exotics — usually are available in seasoned blocks that can be used for a one-piece handle or it can be split into scales; this all depends upon the style of the knife being made, of course.

The major manufacturers usually attempt to purchase handle materials as board lumber, saving considerable cost. Gerber, for example, uses great quantities of walnut and purchases this material in large amounts that can be cut up in their own facility for knife handles and for use in presentation boxes. The latter also are made within the factory by Gerber's own staff of skilled woodworkers. If you're interested in making your own handles for custom knives or perhaps replacing those on knives in your collection, you can riffle through the Yellow Pages and probably find a dealer in exotic hardwoods who can supply you with whatever you need.

In the case of ivory, one undoubtedly could get a lot of knife handles out of a large African elephant tusk, but buying in such lots is pretty unlikely for the average individual. Ivory today is selling at $35 — and up — per pound, with emphasis on the "up." Thus, a number of dealers, including the aforementioned Art Jewel Enterprises, import tusks directly from Africa, going through customs where it is ascertained that the material is legal. Once in the shop,

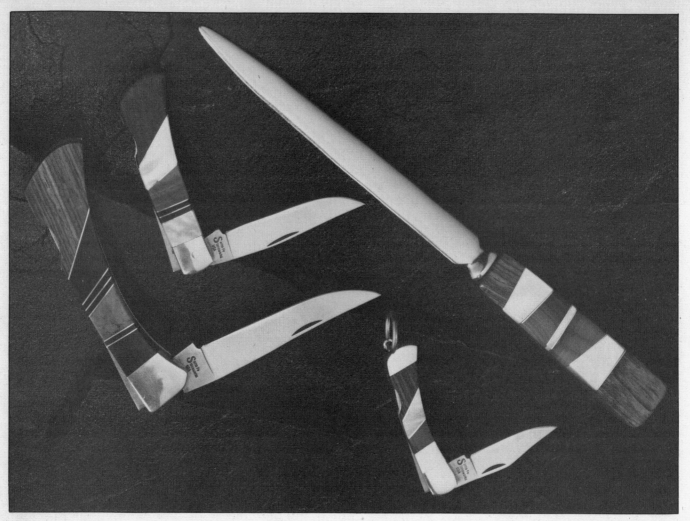

Santa Fe Stoneworks features several natural materials in these knives. Included are mother-of-pearl, turquoise, jet, cocobolo, azurite, malachite, rhodochrosite, Mexican rosewood, tiger eye and lapis lazuli; all quite fragile.

these tusks are cut up on band saws to whatever dimensions are required. With careful cutting, a pound of ivory may yield up to six pairs of knife scales, depending, of course, upon the size of the handle.

As with most natural materials, there can be problems with ivory. To start with, it is heat-sensitive and can be burned if being ground or drilled without proper care. It does carve well and is no great problem to shape. When polished to a luster, it has a beauty all its own.

That's when it's newly carved, of course. But ivory is a dentin material and a sudden loss of moisture ultimately means cracking. Most of those who handle ivory will take a secton of tusk and coat both ends with glue as a sealant. Thus, the ivory tends to dry more slowly and is less likely to crack. It should be allowed to dry for at least six months — and a year is even better. During this curing process, the section of tusk should be kept in a cool, dry place and never exposed to direct sunlight.

New or "green" ivory can be stabilized by a complicated process that requires a vacuum chamber. This is a lengthy and complicated process not available to the average knifemaker.

In working ivory, it is imperative that the craftsman wear a protective mask. It has been determined that ivory dust

that gets into the respiratory system can cause great damage to lung tissue.

Ivory also tends to yellow with age. There isn't much that can be done about this, so just learn to live with it.

Jasper is another natural material that is finding uses among knifemakers. Kershaw Knives, for example, is using it to inlay handles in some of their more ornate styles. This material, however, is a mineral — a rock, if you will — that is classified as a semi-precious gem. Mined primarily in the northwestern United States, it makes up beautifully when polished, but like mother-of-pearl, is fragile. If you should ever drop a knife bearing a handle of either of these materials, be considering, while the knife is on its way to the ground, what your replacement handle is going to be made of. Both jasper and mother-of-pearl tend to shatter easily under such treatment.

Bone has been used for knife handles for centuries, but has been largely replaced in recent decades by various plastic compounds that can be cast to look like bone. The Delrin scales used on Remington's line of replica Bullet Knives is a good example. Handles on the original were of bone.

At least one craftsman still is producing folders with handles of real bone. He is Clyde Fischer of Nixon, Texas,

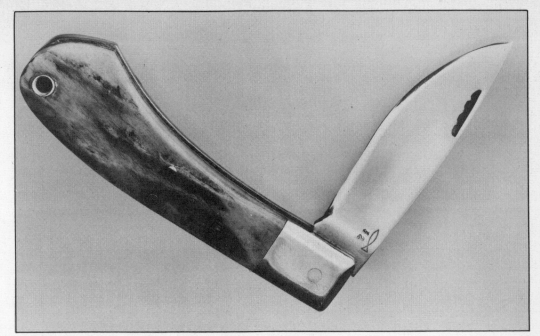

For handle scales, Clyde Fischer, a Texas custom maker, gets the fibia from over-age bulls and cows from a local slaughter house. He cuts and dyes them red, green, tan.

The beauty of natural materials is reflected in this style created by Jim Sornberger. It utilizes African amber for the handle; is inlaid with fine gold wire.

who is considered one of the great custom knifemakers.

Not just any bone will do for the scales Fischer installs on his folders. "It is the fibia from either a very old cow or an extremely old bull," he explains. "A young steer that has been slaughtered does not have the growth in the fibia that I need for the texture that appears in my knife handles."

For this need, Fischer contacted a slaughterhouse that dealt in nothing but the old bovines he sought. This outfit furnishes beef for bologna and other ground meat products, since the flesh is less than prime when taken from aged animals.

The first thing Fischer does is to boil the bones until all of the flesh and tallow have been removed. He allows them to dry, then goes at them with his power saw, cutting the slabs to the size he needs for handles. These slabs then are dyed red, green or a brownish shade he calls "antique." They later are cut to the proper shape and fitted into the recesses on his custom handmade folders.

As mentioned earlier, horn is popular with some knifemakers, because it is easy to work. By boiling it in water, it can be worked into virtually any needed shape. However, it is difficult to glue and this can present problems. It is used primarily by custom cutlers.

One type of horn makes a beautiful handle, but you aren't going to see many. This is rhinoceros horn. The rhino is becoming extinct in its native African haunts, because poachers have virtually wiped out the species. Reason is that the horn is highly sought in the Orient as an aphrodisiac. Chinese traders don't ask the origin of the horn, which is ground into a powder and sold at great cost to hopefully improve male sexual prowess.

A rhino horn of twelve or fourteen inches will bring as much as $5000. The price has gone up even more recently, because of the demand for knife handles. Rhino horn handles are being installed on daggers carried by Arab princes in Kuwait; even with the lowering price of raw petroleum, there's still enough gold available to pay for custom-made knives with rhino horn handles!

The various types of woods used for knife handles deserve a closer look. We probably should list them in order of importance or use, but everyone seems to have his own favorites — for either artistic or economic reasons — so we'll look at them in alphabetical order, instead.

**Ash** is a familiar wood, since it has seen wide use in the furniture industry in this country. It can be found from time to time with a curly grain, but usually is rather straight. It is light in color, grained with brown streaks. It is tough and

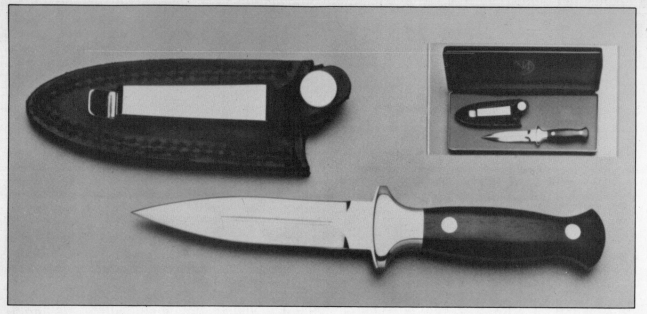

*Lending a touch of class to this Beretta USA boot knife is the ebony handle. The wood is imported from Africa.*

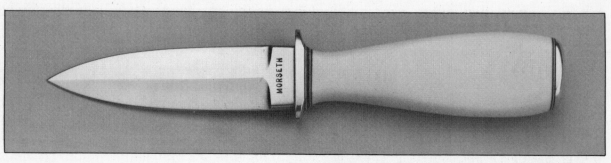

*The simple lines of this Morseth boot knife are made more attractive by addition of an equally simple ivory handle.*

stable, thus makes good knife handles, although it's not all that popular. Handles made of this material usually have an oil finish meant to bring out the grain.

**Blackwood** comes from Africa and we don't see all that much of it. It is hard, dense and stable, with a gray color that features a black grain running through it. Its density tends to make it heavy, which may be one of the reasons few knifemakers use it. It does take a nice finish and the custom is to leave it unsealed.

**Cocobolo** is imported from South America, an oily wood that is both hard and dense in texture. Those who make custom grips for handguns use a lot of this wood, since it is stable and relatively easy to work. However, it has been discovered that the oily dust can be toxic; if you decide to use it for a knife, be sure to wear a protective mask to guard your lungs. It is reddish with black and orange grain running through it, when freshly cut. As it ages, the wood tends to darken, adding to its beauty.

**Ebony** comes primarily from Africa, a black, heavy wood that can produce so smooth a surface when finished properly that it resembles a man-made product. The problem with this material, however, lies in the fact that it tends

to crack if not cared for in the proper manner. It must be seasoned well before it is cut up, then should be sealed in much the same manner as ivory.

**Goncalo alves** is another wood of South American origin that is popular for custom pistol grips. Both hard and extremely dense, it can be difficult to work. Featuring a dark brown figure, it ranges in color from a golden tan shade to brownish red.

**Hickory** is one of those woods that proably is thought of more in context with other products than knife handles; baseball bats, for example. However, this light-colored wood has a toughness and a flexibility that makes it excellent for knife handles. It has an exceedingly straight grain that can be emphasized by passing a blow torch over its surface, then sanding it down. This one should be given an oil finish, then a coat of paste wax.

**Ironwood** has been used for everything from fence posts to knife handles. In fence construction, it usually is used as a corner post so the wire can be wrapped around it and tied; it is so hard that it is difficult to drive a wire-holding staple into it!

There are various types of ironwood, some growing in

*Beretta has entered the knife business with a vengeance. These knives are made in Japan, feature rosewood scales.*

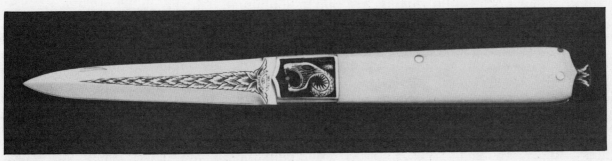

*This art piece made by Jim Sornberger features an ivory handle. Bolster is carved, set with emerald and ruby.*

the Midwest, other types in the North American deserts. The latter tends to be the most colorful, offering an array of colors that can range from dark brown to a light yellow shade. The figure running through this background can range from near black to light brown. The wood is difficult to work and, because it is so dense, is heavy. However, a knife handle will last through many generations and it doesn't require a sealer.

**Lignum vitae** is even harder — and more difficult to work — than ironwood, but it offers a range of grains, some of them straight, others beautifully figured. Because the grain is so tight, it adds to an almost polished finish. If not cared for, however, it tends to check, so an oil finish is recommended. Freshly cut wood tends to be yellow with a darker gold-colored grain. As it ages, however, darker yellow and shades of green may appear in its grain.

**Maple** is a wood that can be exotic in appearance, if not in origin. It is light brown in color and offers a variety of grains that once were highly sought for rifle stocks. The makers of early Kentucky muzzleloaders sought curly and fiddleback maple for their better rifles. This native material responds well to moisture, heat and changes in weather

and can be used for beautiful knife handles, if the right grain is chosen, then given a proper oil finish to enhance the pattern.

**Oak** isn't given any great consideration for custom knives or those designed for sporting purposes, but there are kitchens over the nation that have knives handled with this type of wood. There are many varieties of oak, depending upon geographic location where it grows, but virtually all of them have a straight grain that doesn't leave much to the imagination. It is, however, sturdy wood that makes a good handle for heavy knives of the type used in butcher shops and for other major cutting projects.

**Purpleheart** is light in color when first cut, but turns darker within a few hours. This is caused by oxidation. It also is a close-grained, dense wood that tends to have some toxic qualities and should not be ground or otherwise worked without a breathing mask. It takes an oil finish well, the treatment tending to enhance the grain.

**Rosewood** comes in several varieties and from numerous climes. For example, the rosewood that is imported from the Amazon jungles of Brazil is easily worked, but requires sealing to avoid warping. It is heavy and dense

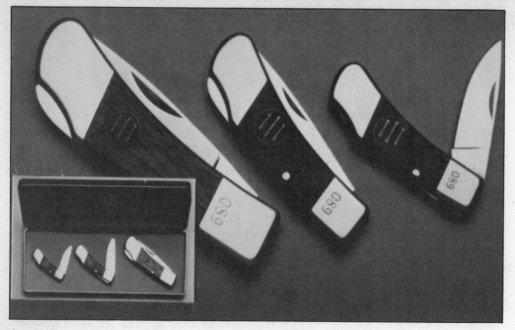

In an effort to grab a piece of the U.S. knife market, Beretta USA is using many materials, walnut included.

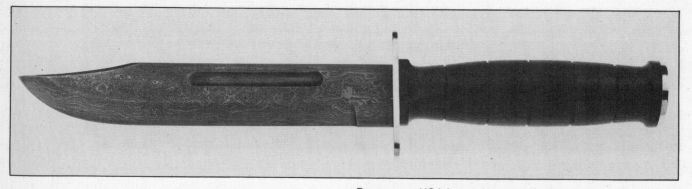

Damascus USA is turning out this Damascus reproduction of the Marine Corps Ka-Bar of World War II fame. The original had a handle of leather washers. This version, however, features a handle made from a hardwood.

and colors, ranging from light brown to reddish shade, usually feature a good figure. Mexican rosewood — also known as *bocote* or *cordia* — tends to be light in color, almost a golden shade, with a black figure throughout. Hard and heavy by comparison with the Amazon variety, a sealer helps to bring out the grain figure. Most custom knifesmiths use an oil finish.

East Indian rosewood contains a great amount of resin and this can make it difficult to work. Some users soak the blocks of wood in acetone for a week or so, changing the chemical daily. This causes the resin to leech out of the wood, although the color of the purplish wood will be lighter when the treatment is completed. No sealer is required, but an oil finish is recommended.

**Walnut** is a wood with which most of us should be familiar. It has been the favored wood for rifle stocks, military and civilian, for centuries. It grows through most of the United States in one species or another. Classified as a hardwood, it tends to be somewhat softer than the other

woods discussed. Properly figured by nature, it is beautiful when finished with oil, then given a coat of paste wax. The wood is stable and easy to work, but requires a sealer for best effect.

With virtually all of the woods mentioned, a good paste wax that carries carnauba in its formula will help to bring out the grain and protect the surface at the same time.

Leather is another natural material that has seen continuing use for knife handles over the centuries, but moisture and heat have a definite effect.

The most used method of making a leather handle is to punch out a series of discs or oblongs, then drill a hole through the center of each and thread them onto the tang. A butt cap is threaded onto the end of the stick-type tang and tightened down to hold the leather washers firmly in place.

We recall an era in the Thirties, when the Buster Brown Shoe Company was giving away a hunting knife with each pair of youngster's shoes. Everyone in the neighborhood had to have one, it seemed — whether they liked the shoes

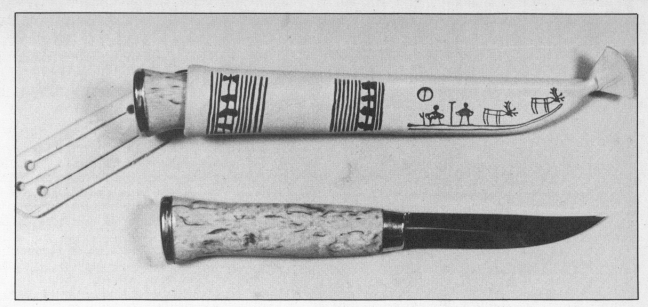

*Because it is in great supply in that country, Finnish knifemakers tend to install birch handles on knives. The burled pattern comes from a diseased tree, though.*

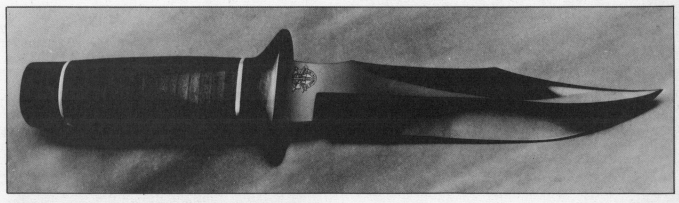

*The leather washers of old are featured in the handle of this Special Forces Vietnam Commemorative made by SOG Specialties, but leather has been impregnated with resin. This treatment makes the handle material more stable.*

or not. As we recall, this premium was made by Marble Arms and boasted surprisingly good steel in the blade.

However, the handle was another matter. In time, the series of leather washers broke the bond of varnish that was supposed to hold them together and they would turn, get out of alignment and the result looked like a real mess rather than a serious using knife.

The Marine Corps Ka-Bar of World War II was made in similar fashion. However, rather than a round tang, it was simply ground down from the same flat bar stock in the blade. The washers were punched in the center with a rectangular cut that fit over this tang. Thus, while the washers might become loose in time, they did not tend to turn around the tang.

One of the authors has such a knife that he carried in World War II, Korea and again in Vietnam. The handle is badly dented in spots, where it has been used as a hammer, but the leather is still tight and firm. Some of the early World War II Ka-Bars were not tempered properly and the blades tended to snap long before their handles showed the effects of rough use.

Such leather washer handles still are being made. Al Mar uses this type of handle on one of his combat knives. SOG Specialties, producing what they call a Special Forces Vietnam Commemorative model, is using a leather washer handle that has finger grooves cut into the leather. As with the knives being marketed by Al Mar and others, the leather has been impregnated with a hardening resin that leaves a smooth, polished finish and tends to negate the effects of water and sun.

There no doubt have been other natural materials used in knife handles over the ages, but those mentioned have been the most popular and — for the most part — still are being used.

With the advent of man-made materials, some manufacturers have begun to shy away from the natural approach ...but the true knife fancier still likes the feel and beauty inherent in the natural materials.

## "IN COUNTRY"
Limited Edition Vietnam Commemorative
Handmade Knife by,

### Jim Sornberger

**O**nly 365 knives will be made, one for each day of a tour in "the Nam"

**E**ach knife individually serial numbered 01 thru 365.

- All stainless steel construction
- 6½" blade of ATS-34 steel
- "Camo" color textured handle
- Full Tang design for maximum strength
- Leather scabbard.

Handle inlaid with miniature replica of Republic of Vietnam Service Medal

**Price $395⁰⁰**
(without medal $365⁰⁰)
CA residents add appropriate sales tax.

**DELIVERY:** Beginning April 1987, as these knives are handmade, delivery may spread over a two year or longer period.

**DEPOSIT:** $95⁰⁰ deposit required to reserve each knife, upon receipt of deposit you will receive acknowledgement of your deposit with the serial number of your reserved knife and approximate delivery date.

**SEND ORDER TO:** JIM SORNBERGER
5675 Meridian Ave.
San Jose, CA 95118

Custom knifemaker Jim Sornberger chose a camouflage Micarta to handle this limited edition to commemorate vets of Vietnam. Micarta usually is in solid colors.

Some of the Space Age plastics used for knife handles are cast in a camouflage pattern, as is the case with survival model produced by Coleman/Western Cutlery.

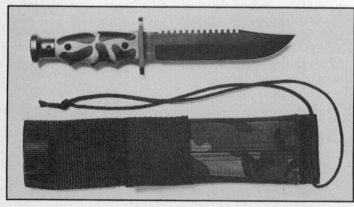

**W**HILE THERE is no doubting the beauty of most of the natural materials, the fact is that most of them tend to provide problems for the owner sooner or later. Wood will dry out, splinter or ultimately rot. Stone and shell are fragile and shatter easily. Ivory tends to crack or check in time, as it dries. In short, time tells on these materials.

For the most part, the man-made materials that are enjoying their present heyday have about as much personality as a Sherman tank, but whether you like the appearance or not, they're here — and it looks as though they're here to stay.

Perhaps the earliest of these materials to see any major use by both commerical knife manufacturers and custom bladesmiths was micarta — or if you follow the dictates of the patent holder, Micarta.

The advantage of Micarta over some of the other man-made materials is that it can be manufactured in a range of colors and can be polished to a high luster. The product comes from Westinghouse, which originally used it as an insulating material in transformers, since it does not conduct electricity. At that time, Micarta was formed in a rather lifeless brown tone and didn't offer much in the way of beauty. Some knifemakers began to use it, however. Ultimately, the manufacturer turned out a deep green shade and the venerable Bob Loveless finally convinced them that they should try a maroon shade as well. All have been used on knife handles, along with black and white — or ivory, as it is often called for sales effectiveness.

Micarta is technically described as a "fabric-reinforced phenolic laminate." It is created by pouring a resin into a flat pan, then laying down a strip of cotton cloth that is soon impregnated with the resin. Comes another layer of resin, then another layer of cloth. The cotton ranges from extremely light in weight to that which has the texture of canvas — because it is canvas!

In this fashion, the material can be cast, if that's the correct word, in whatever thickness is desired. There are those who refer to "linen Micarta," but it's not. It is just another grade of cotton that is being used in the mixture. The bonding between the cotton and resin is achieved by a combina-

Blackjack Knives' folding Mamba is equipped with handle material which has been formed from rubber polymer.

*Above: Custom knifemaker Gene Harrison used nylon cord used for parachute shroud lines to wrap this handle.*

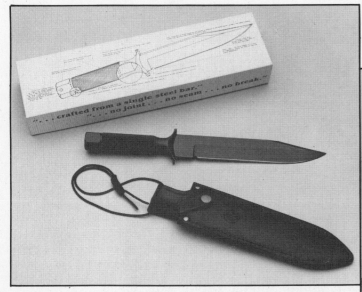

*This Chris Reeve-designed combat knife features small checker pattern filed into the handle for good gripping.*

*For Remington-marketed line of Bullet knife replicas, a nylon-based material called Delrin is being utilized.*

tion of pressure and heat. The resin is described as a thermo-setting plastic resin. One of its advantages is that it won't return to its original shape if heated after it has set.

Another material that is seeing use among knifemakers is called pakkawood. This is created in the same fashion as Micarta, except that sheets of wood measuring only one-hundredth of an inch in thickness are substituted for the cotton content of true Micarta. Once this material has been cured properly, when its edges are ground down, there is a beautiful pattern that appears to be laminated wood. Of course, that's what it is to a degree.

Ivory Micarta actually does not contain cotton. Instead, paper and the syrupy resin are combined to come up with the cream-colored material that resembles ivory, but isn't likely to suffer the same time-inspired blemishes.

"However, ivory Micarta is not nearly as strong as the true Micartas made with cotton," Loveless insists. "It is more easily damaged and, if a customer demands paper Micarta as the handle on a custom knife, I tell him of all the drawbacks before I go ahead with the product. But he's the buyer and I give him what he wants."

Loveless does point out that, in its favor, the so-called ivory Micarta does work well for scrimshaw work. "It is soft enough to take the fine needles and some excellent art work has been accomplished with it."

Loveless still favors cotton Micarta for the handle on a working knife in spite of the fact "that it now costs five times what it did when we first started working with it."

General Electric, incidentally, has a similar product, but as yet, it has not seen wide use among the custom makers.

A host of other materials are being used today, too, most of them by factory knifemakers. Many of them are using the same materials, but for the sake of advertising, tend to personalize it by giving it what would appear to be an exclusive name.

A material that is being used by Gerber Legendary Cutlery for a number of its combat and survival knives is a type of rubber polymer. It comes in thick tubes, with a hole in the middle for the tang to be inserted. The material then is put under several hundred pounds of pressure to force it down upon the guard before the butt cap is installed.

Once this material is in place, it goes to the grinding

Ka-Bar is utilizing a knife material called Stratawood. This material is fashioned by utilizing alternating layers of thin wood and resin.

wheels, where material is removed and the handle section shaped as desired. When completed, this material has a rather tacky-feeling resiliency that feels good in the hand. For what it may be worth, the same material is being used in modern auto bumpers.

Ka-Bar is using a material they call Stratawood, which they say is "natural wood laminated by phenolic resin in stratified layers." This is another name for pakkawood.

A number of other materials are being used, too, most of them born of the Plastics Age. We went to Tom Hawkinson of BASF Engineering Plastics in Orange County, California, to get some insight into the composition of the various materials.

One of Dupont's products being used on the series of Remington Bullet folders is Delrin. According to Hawkinson, this is a homopolymer polyacetal — known in the trade simply as "acetal." He describes it as a special plastic used for load-bearings in small machinery for the most part. It is used extensively in faucets and in the irrigation and plumbing industries. The material has a slippery surface which reduces wear, when used in gears. When used

in the Remington knife handles, it is cast to look like shinbone stag, which was used on the original Remington knives of half a century and more ago.

Zytel is another Remington product that is created by mixing fiberglass with nylon. The two are combined, then heated to about 600 degrees Fahrenheit before being injected moulded.

It is possible to color Zytel by introducing the desired color concentrate, blending it before the pellets of nylon and fiberglass are heated to a liquid state. The new Armed Forces bayonet is being made with a handle of Zytel and has undergone extensive tests to ensure that the material will not become too brittle when cold and will not snap off in extreme heat.

A number of manufacturers are using materials called Velox and Kraton. The latter is an imitation rubber, actually a plastic compound, that is created by Shell Petroleum. Velox has a polyester base that is used for such items as the distributor cap in your automobile's electrical system. It is used for a number of other electrical applications as well, according to Hawkinson. It can be either moulded in its

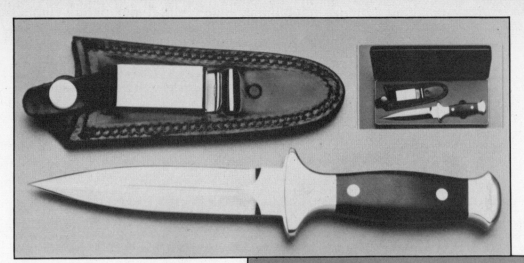

Beretta's double-edged stainless steel knife from Collector's Series features scales fashioned of ebony.

Beretta's new Hunter's Series utilizes black Micarta as handle material. Model also is made with clip blade.

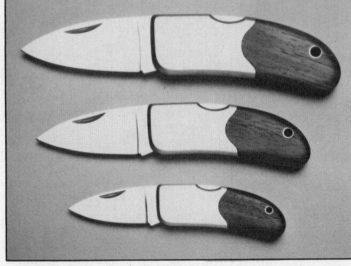

Stainless steel is another man-made material that can be used in knife handles; it's combined with rosewood.

original form or can be mixed with heavy additions of fiberglass for additional strength. This particular material is manufactured by General Electric.

Another knife handle material in current use is Butyrate, which is material that combines plastic with rubber. The result is a clear substance — unless dyed — that feels and acts like rubber. In industry, it often is used for small fasteners.

Resin-impregnated hardwoods also are finding favor with some knifemakers. This is exactly what it says it is:

Hardwood that is impregnated with resins under pressure.

And an obvious use of a man-made material is the same material from which the knife blade is made: steel. A number of one-piece knives are being made, primarily by custom knifemakers, wherein the handle is simply an extension of the blade, but usually is skeletonized in order to reduce the overall weight.

Other makers are using steel for handles that are hollow, as with many of the survival models. These may either be wrapped with nylon cord or some other type of material that could substitute as fishing line or whatever is needed. Still others feature the metal, itself, which often is checkered for a better grip.

Aluminum also is being used for knife scales, since it is light but durable and can be engraved or stamped for decorative purposes.

As time goes on, there no doubt will be other new materials — or variations of the old — that knifemakers will want to try. If the knives so equipped sell, these knives undoubtedly will remain in the line. If the fickle choice of the buyer rejects it, they'll shrug and try something else. Needless to say, cost of the handle material for mass-produced knives always is a factor.

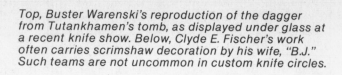

*Top, Buster Warenski's reproduction of the dagger from Tutankhamen's tomb, as displayed under glass at a recent knife show. Below, Clyde E. Fischer's work often carries scrimshaw decoration by his wife, "B.J." Such teams are not uncommon in custom knife circles.*

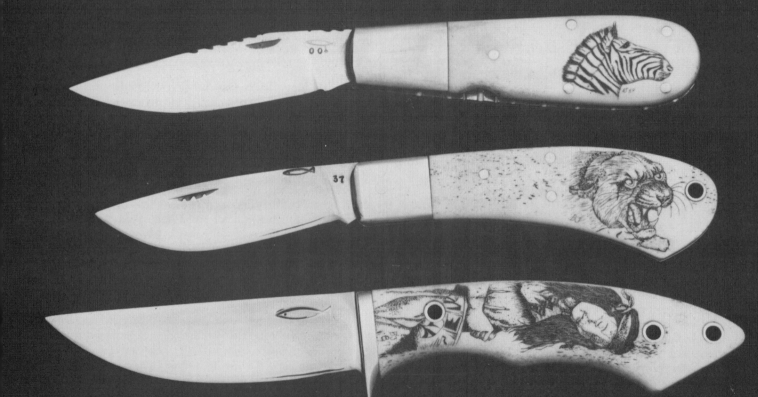

# Chapter 4

# DECORATING KNIVES

*Fancy Finishes Do Not Make A Knife Cut Better,
But Make Them More Pleasant To Look At!*

IT SEEMS possible that some prehistoric cave dweller may have gotten a bit of bright pigment, such as ochre, daubed on his shaped piece of flint, admired the effect and left it in place until it rubbed off in routine use. The knife, as many have noted, is mankind's oldest tool and a vast amount of time and attention has been expended in dressing up innumerable specimens," opines Dean Grennell, who researched this chapter for us.

In the Fourteenth Century, B.C., King Tutankhamen — of the Eighteenth Egyptian Dynasty — admired ornate cutlery to the extent that two of his favorite knives were entombed with him. In recent times, custom knifemaker Buster Warenski went to great efforts to create an exact replica of one of the knives found beneath the mummified remains when the tomb was opened. Warenski's creation uses thirty-two ounces of pure 24-karat gold for the basic framework and an incredible amount of patiently applied decorative touches. It is said to be valued at up to $100,000, currently.

Most decorated knives are less elaborate, but more practical. You would not, for example, be overly inclined to use a knife such as Warenski's masterpiece for opening the morning mail!

A more contemporary art form, having most of its inception in the Nineteenth Century, is scrimshaw. It is said to have originated aboard the Yankee whaling ships, whose crew members tended to pass the time on long voyages by engraving artistic images on the teeth of the sperm whale. The shallow lines were pointed up with inks or pigments and the really gifted artisans produced work of true artistic merit.

With the passing of the sailing whalers from the scene, the scrimshander — that being the accepted term for the art's practitioners — went into decline and scrimshaw faded to a nearly lost art. It continued to be done at a more hasty and casual level to produce gewgaws for the gift and tourist markets and, in time, was taken up again as a serious medium. Many of the present generation of scrimshanders are turning out really exceptional work.

Scrimshaw offers more than ample subject matter to fill an entire book and Bob Engnath has produced two such volumes, titled *The Scrimshaw Connection* and, logically enough, *The Second Scrimshaw Connection*. These are expertly produced and superbly illustrated. They are published by The House of Muzzle Loading, Box 6217, Glendale, California 91205.

"My son, Bill, owns a dropped hunter made by H.J. Schneider in 1976, the year he moved from Cub Scouts up into the ranks of Boy Scouts. The Schneider knife has handle scales of ivory, bearing expert scrimshaw work by William Metcalf of Taos, New Mexico. Schneider tells me

Bob Loveless usually employs a more prosaic etched trademark on his knives, but uses this for select customers on request. Photo-etching is the process.

As discussed, Loveless recently made up a dropped hunter for himself and went on to have a modified version of the trademark made up for the reverse.

Metcalf has drifted away from scrimshanding, continuing to work as a painter," Grennell reports.

Schneider's output of knives includes a goodly percentage of high-art examples, often ornately engraved. Two examples are illustrated here with photos by Weyer of Toledo, Ohio. One is a double-edged dagger, designed and engraved by Gary Blanchard of Burney, California, with metal sculpture on the blade that shows an aroused African bull elephant in the foreground, other members of his herd in the background. The handle is — naturally enough — of ivory, worked in a spiral pattern with gold wire inlay and the hilt is in the shape of two elephant tusks. The beehive-shaped butt cap represents a thatched African hut.

"The other Schneider knife also has a handle of ivory, with a woman's face carved in intaglio and engraving by

Ron Skaggs of Princeton, Illinois, in a classical Greek motif."

Bob Loveless confines the bulk of his output to utilitarian "using knives," of exceptionally high quality, only rarely producing an engraved specimen. An exception was one of his dropped hunters, made up for inclusion in a set to be auctioned at the 1987 meeting of the Safari Club International. It has a gold inlay bas-relief of a lion's head set in the hilt, with engraving by Terry Wallace and Bob Swartley of Napa, California.

"Loveless' usual trademark reads *R.W. Loveless/maker/ Riverside, Calif.,* set as three lines in a lens-shaped pattern. Customarily, this is applied to the left side of the blade by a photo-etching process. He has a special trademark he uses occasionally for friends who appreciate that sort of thing, incorporating a reclining nude and my own Loveless knife carries both trademarks, one on each side of the blade."

Loveless finally lucked out in drawings for a deer permit

Two ornately decorated daggers by H.J. Schneider, with carved ivory handles and engraving by Gary Blanchard and Ron Skaggs, as discussed in text here.

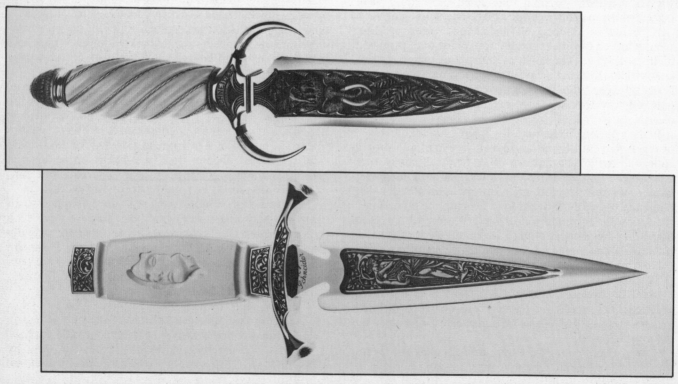

*Mel Wood's engraving features a fine blend of delicate artistry and a subtle sense of just-rightness to go with the basic image of the given knife decorated.*

*Bill Grennell's H.J. Schneider knife dates from 1976, with scrimshaw by William Metcalf. Although an Eagle Scout since 1985, Bill never took it on a camp-out!*

near the Riverside area for the 1987 season and, in high glee, celebrated by producing a dropped hunter for his own use. Naturally enough, eternal urchin that he is, it carries the figure trademark on the left side, partially occulting the last half of *California*. On the right side of the blade, he had a new stencil made up, with the model shown from the back and the missing *-fornia* superimposed over the figure. It is just the sort of pawky, tongue-in-cheek touch you might expect from the irrepressible gent. Loveless' personal knife also carries a small compass set in the butt of the handle; a feature included no more than rarely in his routine production.

Pete Kershaw, president of Kershaw Knives, Wilsonville, Oregon, worked up a unique production for presentation to the fastest qualifier for the 1987 Budweiser/G.I. Joe two hundred-mile race in Portland, Oregon. Twelve inches in overall length, it has a hand-carved ivory handle that is an exact replica of Billy Vukovich's 1953 Indianapolis Five Hundred winner. The knife was carved by internationally renowned Erhard Gross of Oregon City, Oregon. Working with an ivory elephant tusk from the Republic of Congo — taken in 1964, before the exportation of ivory tusks was outlawed to deter poaching — Gross worked hundreds of hours to duplicate the Howard Keck Fuel Injection Special that Vukovich drove to victory. Kershaw estimates the knife's value at $4000.

Clyde E. Fischer and his wife, "B.J.," constitute a knifemaking team reasonably common in the trade. Mrs. Fischer not only does scrimshaw work of truly exceptional quality on Fischer's knives, but does custom work on knives or gun grips for others. The Fischer duo can be reached at Fischer Custom Knives & Supplies, Box 310, Nixon, Texas 78140.

*Michelle "Mike" Ochonicky is a full-time scrimshander whose work is entirely done by hand, without the aid of patterns or stencils or use of power tools.*

Mel Wood gets his mail out of Box 1255, Sierra Vista, Arizona 85636 and his address for UPS shipments is Bushy Canyon Road, Elgin, Arizona 85611. Wood is a former engineer in missle and space systems who made the transition to engraving knives and guns. He spent several years in perfecting his engraving techniques before accepting his first professional commission. His shift to engraving on a full-time basis dates from 1978.

Wood's current backlog of work is reported to be on the order of five years, but his method of operation avoids taking the client's hardware out of action for such extended interludes. He accepts reservations, by mail or over the phone, entering them in his logbook. As the client's name works its way down the ladder, Wood notifies that it's time to ship and, as of that time, he reaches an agreement as to the amount of coverage, design and price. It is rare for such a client to cancel, but when it happens, it shortens the time for the next in line.

Wood does custom engraving for several knifemakers and many of those have him work upon their knives prior to the larger knife shows of the given year. His work embodies a graceful and intricate scroll pattern that is entirely, distinctively his own. In addition to such engraving, Wood has developed a technique for silver amalgam inlay work for ivory or Micarta knife handles that is unique. He also does carving or applique work, upon request.

Schrade Cutlery, 26-30 Canal Street, Ellenville, New York 12428, now has a growing line of sheath and folding knives they call Schrade Scrimshaw, as photo-etched upon the blades, with attractive scrimshaw in additional designs on the handle scales.

Larry R. Cole operates as American Craftsman, HC 84, Box 10303, Broadbent, Oregon 97414. Primarily an engraver, he is the factory engraver for Kershaw Knives, doing limited edition work for them. He also does engraving for several knifemakers and can produce presentation cases or knife display stands in a variety of styles and exotic hardwoods.

Michelle "Mike" Ochonicky, 4059 Toenges Avenue,

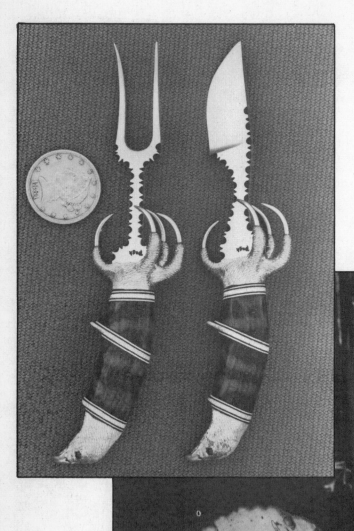

*Jim Pugh's fanciful knife and fork set, left, have eagle head butts and claw hilts, may not be dishwasher safe. Lower photo shows three examples of Tom High's work as a scrimshander, with accent on wildlife motif.*

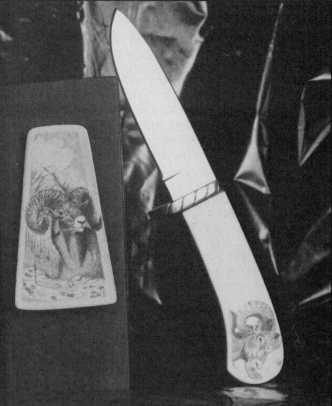

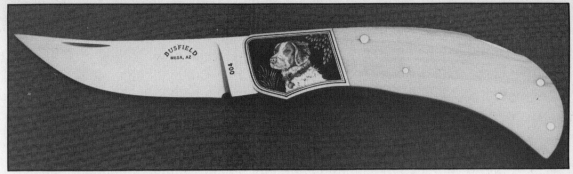

Top, this graceful lock-blade folder was made by Jack Busfield and engraved by Steven Lindsay of Nebraska.

Racing enthusiast Pete Kershaw had this knife made up with an ivory handle duplicating Vukovich's car. Below, a sample of the work of Dennis B. Brooker.

St. Louis, Missouri 63116, styles herself a full-time scrimshander and goes on to note all of her work is hand-done, without patterns or stencils. "She uses only hand scribes — no power tools — in her work. She prefers traditional black ink in both line and stippling techniques, with the stippled version bringing higher prices," Grennell reports.

"Ochonicky has a degree in art — specifically sculpture — with extensive graduate studies in various mediums. She enjoys doing one-of-a-kind pieces and working with the customers to develop unique designs.

"Although Ochonicky does a lot of scrimshaw work on custom knives, she stocks a full line of factory knives she scrimshaws. The knives are all bone-handled, from makers such as Parker, Frost, Kershaw, as well as knives with synthetic handles by Buck, Gerber or A. G. Russell. Illustrated here are a pair of Russell's Sting knives with her scrimshaw. She notes that the Micarta Russell uses scrimshaws nicely and makes handsome display pieces."

Tom High operates as Rocky Mountain Painting & Arts, 5474 South 112.8 Road, Alamosa, Colorado 81101, specializing in handmade color scrimshaw, with the work engraved, not just painted on. His brochure illustrates a broad variety of original designs on knives as well as belt buckles, bolos, and the like.

Steve Lindsay operates as Custom Hand Engraving, Rural Route 2, Cedar Hills, Kearney, Nebraska 68847, specializing in engraving the work of custom knifemakers such as Ron Lake, Jack Busfield or Steve Hoel. The quality of his work speaks for itself.

Jim Pugh takes his mail at Box 711, Azle, Texas 76020. A custom knifemaker with an excellect and well-deserved reputation, one of Pugh's specialties is the ornate decoration of the butt cap, often in the representation of the head of a bird or game animal. His usual material for handle scales is exotic, highly figured hardwood, set off with intricately contrived spacers. Another distinctive touch is what might be termed the talon hilt.

*Franz Letschnig is an engraver of jewelry, operating in Quebec. He enjoys doing engraving of wildlife, as illustrated by these examples, but finds little demand for such work locally. His address is given on the facing page.*

"Pugh is prepared to furnish virtually anything his customers desire, such as precious metalwork or high-grade jewels, ivory and so on. His wife, Raymonde, works as the engraver of the family enterprise. The basic leaflet of information on their products and services is free on request. A Pugh specialty is the collector-grade miniature — not trinkets, but genuine knives, five inches in overall length, with Swedish steel blades heat treated to 59C Rockwell, some with 2mm AA-grade ruby eyes. The set of the four basic designs goes for $7500, price subject to change."

Pugh requires no deposit at the time of ordering, unless gold is involved and then only sufficient to cover his investment in it.

"Minting is a process that produces a bas-relief image in moderately malleable metal by use of a hard die and great impact pressure that causes the metal to flow into the configuration of the die. This is the process used in producing coins and it has seen limited use in decoration of knives: particularly in the handle scales of knives. Production of the dies is extremely expensive, thus limiting the process to

*Top, Wayne Clay acknowledges Bob Loveless and W.C. Davis as having gotten him started, but he now incorporates features uniquely his own. Above, a Ron Post hunter, with a wistful leopard scrimshawed by Charles Hargraves.*

*An elegant folder by Jimmy Lile, skillfully engraved by Billy Bates.*

knives produced in a fairly high volume of output," Grennell's research tells us.

Kershaw/Kai Cutlery USA Ltd., 25300 S.W. Parkway Avenue, Wilsonville, Oregon 97070, produces a lockblade folder with minted, die-struck scales in nickel silver, depicting three geese in flight formation, at a current suggested retail price of $37.95 and they may offer additional designs at a later date.

Billy R. Bates, 2905 Lynnwood Circle S.W., Decatur, Alabama 35603, does custom engraving on knives and guns and offers custom knifemakers the option of trading his services for knives. Dennis B. Brooker is an engraver/designer/artist residing at 502 Highway 92, Prole, Iowa 50229.

Wayne Clay, Box 474B, Pelham, Tennessee 37366, freely acknowledges his thanks to Bob Loveless and W.C. Davis for their help in getting him started in the right direction and their influence is clearly apparent in some of his work, while many another example is uniquely a feat of Clay. He makes an impressive variety of cutlery for every use and application. Some are starkly utilitarian, others carry tasteful cosmetic touches, including engraving, scrimshaw and handle scales of ivory, fossil ivory, sambar stag, sheep horn, desert iron wood, cocobolo, African blackwood, mother of pearl, ivory Micarta and numerous other options.

Charles Hargraves, 1839 Kingston Road, Scarborough, Ontario, Canada M1N 1T3, has been doing scrimshaw for about fifteen years, having started on powder horns and branching into knives and guns. He displays a

fine knack for fitting the subject comfortably within the available space.

Franz Letschnig, 210 Chemin Marieville, Richelieu, Province of Quebec, Canada, J3L 3V8, is an engraver of jewelry who also enjoys engraving wildlife art on the handle scales of knives and similar articles.

George Marek, Box 213, Westfield, Massachusetts 01086, does both engraving and scrimshanding. A considerable portion of his work is done on knives by Jim Siska, who works out of the same city.

Byron Burgess, 710 Bella Vista Drive, Morro Bay, California 93442, is a custom engraver specializing in knives and firearms.

Larry H. Peck, 14 Patricia Lane, Hannibal, Missouri 63401, has a commercial illustration background, with twenty-four years in the field. A 1962 graduate of the Kansas City Art Institute, he began scrimshadning in 1976 as a hobby and went into it on a full-time basis in 1987. Most of his work is on wearable items, because that represents the bulk of his ongoing trade. Knives, mostly of the custom variety, are done on a single-order basis, as are grips for handguns. While he welcomes industrial contracts, most of his work is one at a time. He favors the point scribe, used in a linear pattern, or stippling, depending upon the material and subject matter.

"Occasionally, Peck uses the knife on hard line illustrations. Inking is done with India ink, artists oils, etchers ink or engravers enamel, depending upon the base material and the envisioned use of the work. Most of his orders are for black ink, but he also does color work."

Paul "Hoagy" Holguin, 13718 Alma Avenue, Gardena, California 90249, is a custom knifemaker of several years experience, with a pronounced fondness for tiger-striped Oregon myrtle wood as a material for handles.

Dale Fisk, Box 252, Council, Idaho 83612, has been scrimshanding for over ten years and for several of those has served as the scrimshander for the custom department at Buck Knives. He also works on private orders. Fisk offers some cogent comments on contemporary scrimshanding that, we think, warrant inclusion here.

"The basic technique of scrimshaw is a simple process. The surface of the ivory must be sanded and polished to the point that ink placed upon it will wipe off easily, with no trace left behind.

"The basic image of the picture to be scrimshawed is drawn onto this surface with an all-surface pencil. The polished surface is then disturbed by means of a sharp point that is pressed into it to make holes or scratched across it to make grooves, or by a blade which is used to make slices into the surface. Ink is then rubbed across the surface, where it is caught in these depressions, being wiped off of any undisturbed areas.

"To achieve a result worthy of being termed fine art, these holes, scratches or slices must be placed at depths and locations measured in the smallest of increments. For one example, on an etching of a human eye, one-eighth-inch in width, a difference of a few hundredths of an inch — or even a few thousandths — can make the difference between depicting an expression of amusement or anger.

*If Mother Nature and Jack Frost were to pool their considerable talents, they'd still be hard-put to rival Steve Lindsay's engraving!*

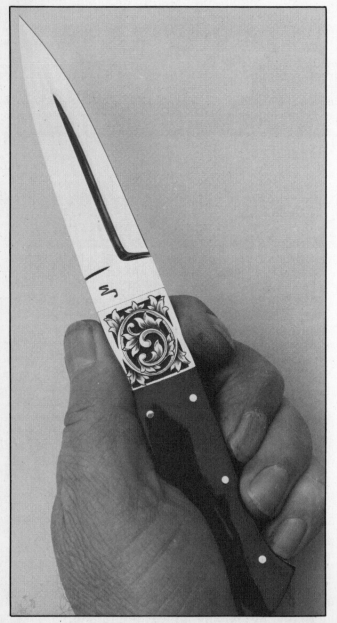

*The work of scrimshander/engraver George Marek is a sheer symphony of restrained elegance, as epitomized by this dagger.*

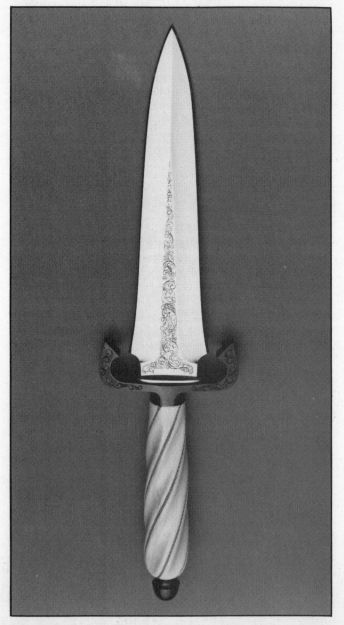

Paul Holguin made this dagger, engraved in classic Greek motif by Morris Carson.

Scrimshawed Indian head by Larry Peck graces this custom knife by Atkinson.

"The #11 Exacto knife blade is the number one tool among most modern scrimshaw artists. It can be used for all three types of surface disturbance. Other standard tools of the trade include scribes, or a pin vise holding a sharpened sewing needle.

"Not long ago, I told Bob Engnath about a motor-powered scrimshaw tool of my own invention and it turned out that he had already started using a similar machine and even had one for sale in his Glendale, California, shop. Basically, the tools have a sharp point that reciprocates up and down, powered by a small electric motor. They can make a lot of holes in a short time. It would appear that the use of such time-saving devices is becoming more common and, if used properly, can accomplish textures previously impractical, if not impossible. It should be emphasized that these tools are hand-guided, and they should not be confused with some of the automated techniques in current use, such as lasers.

"Of the 'scrimable' materials available for knife handles, there is a great difference in the quality of the results obtainable from each. The best material is elephant, mastodon or mammoth ivory. Walrus tusk also works well.

Some artists achieve great results with sperm whale tooth. Personally, I find the surface of this ivory to be a bit hard. Stag is a little fibrous, but it can result in scrimshaw of moderate quality, if fine detail is not essential. Antler is one more rung down the ladder toward less detail, with bone being at the bottom. Both are more suitable for heavy, line-type etching and tend to absorb some of the ink, giving the surface a dingy gray color.

"There are several plastics that are used for scrimshaw, the most common of which is paper Micarta. Linen Micarta will not work. Some nice work has been done on this synthetic, but I don't like it for two reasons: First, the scrimshaw tends to have a slightly fuzzy effect, making detail difficult. Second, Micarta yellows quite quickly. I have had no experience with Corian, a countertop synthetic, but have seen some work done on it that equals or exceeds that done on Micarta," Fisk concludes.

Bladesmith Sean McWilliams, 4334, C.R. 509, Bayfield, Colorado 81122, specializes in making forged stainless steel blades and has been one of the pioneers in forging stainless. He works with such alloys as 440-C, ATS-34, 154-CM and the ultra-tough T-440-V.

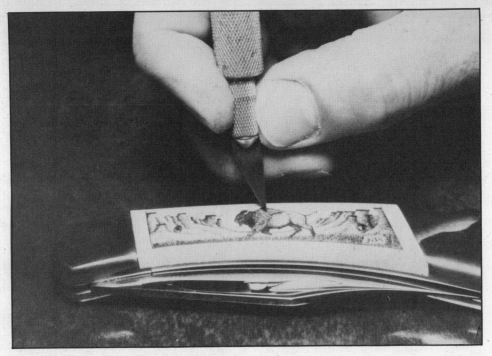

*Dale Fisk rates the #11 Xacto knife as the number one tool of the scrimshander. He's using one here on woolly mammoth scales of a Buck #110 folder.*

The results, he reports, have been spectacular: "Forging improves the stainless steels much more than it improves the tool steels," going on to explain that forging compacts the molecular structure, making the stainless alloys much more sharpenable than the usual expectation. Stainless steels not only take a sharper edge, but they hold it better when forged, he says.

McWilliams does a differential heat treating so the blade is hardest along the edge, but not too hard to sharpen well; softened in the tip, spring-tempered in the backbone and fully annealed in the handle. The usual approach employed by many makers is to heat treat the entire blade and tang to a uniform hardness. McWilliams started out as a blacksmith in the early Seventies, making decorative utensils and hardware, as well as edged tools such as chisels for woodcarving. That is when he learned the art of heat treating and also when he forged his first stainless steel before he had contact with the conventional wisdom

*Kershaw uses a process similar to that of minting coins to produce graceful scales of geese in flight.*

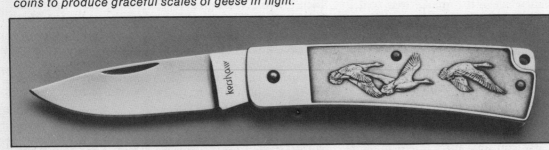

*Dan Honeycutt imports and distributes these knives with Damascus-type blades, going on to engrave them.*

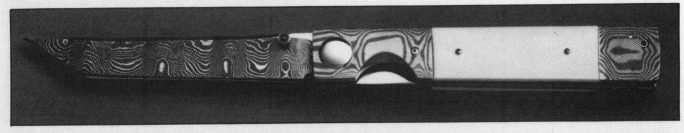

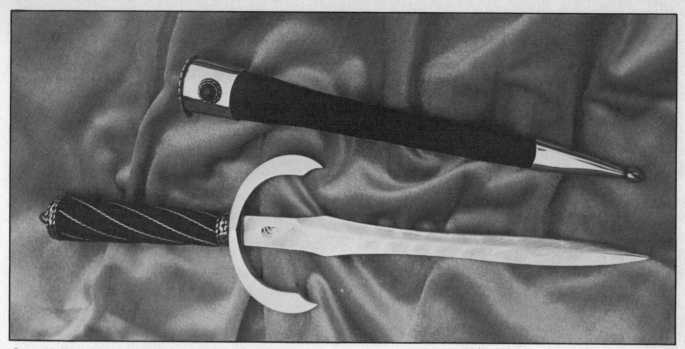

Sean McWilliams made and decorated this forged twist Damascus dagger with an eight-inch blade. It has a forged nickel-silver guard and fittings, with ebony handle and silver wire inlay. A black star diopside stone is set in the guard at the top of the sheath.

A fine example of the intricate detail in the work of scrimshander Stan Hawkins, Arcadia, California.

that says you can't forge stainless. He makes all types of blades: folders, hunters, Bowie/fighters, classical and fantasy daggers, Damascus blades, swords and Japanese styles.

Scrimshaw artist Carole McWilliams, 4334 C.R. 509, Bayfield, Colorado 81122, specializes in subjects related to her southwestern Colorado locale: Rocky Mountain scenes and desert sandstone canyons, usually done up with small figures of Indians or mountain men: the human dealing on a one-to-one basis with nature.

"Scrimshaw should make a piece more complete and should make it a personal thing for its owner," she says. "Part of the art is in finding out what the customer really wants. Sometimes, they don't know what they want and my job is to help them select something that will really please them. I want them to be happy when they get it and still delighted with it for a long, long time."

Stan Hawkins, 2230 El Capitan, Arcadia, California 91006, supplies the Lahaina Scrimshaw factory in Hawaii with several pieces a year and has about a four-month waiting list for custom scrimshanding.

Dan Honeycutt operates Ozark Knife, 3165 South Campbell #A-2, Springfield, Missouri 65807. Ten years in operation, it is the oldest and largest cutlery specialist in Missouri, he says. They stock the work of at least fifteen different makers, along with many other edged items.

Rob and Mary Davidson operate Rocket Made Knives, 2419 25th Street, Lubbock, Texas 79411. He has made knives for five years and she has done scrimshaw for four. They will be happy to discuss their work with interested parties.

Knife sheaths may come in all sizes, shapes and of any material. A variety of leather hand-crafted styles is shown at the top of the page, with latest nylon versions from Buck, right.

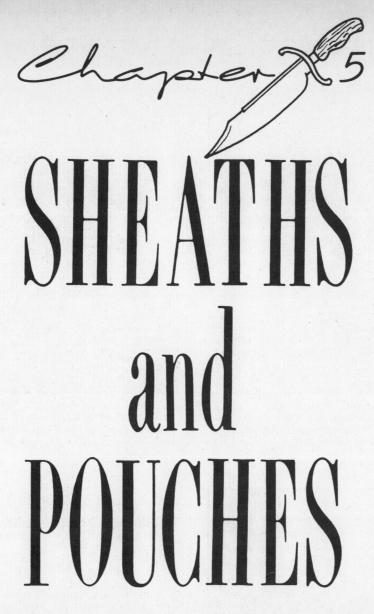

# Chapter 5
# SHEATHS and POUCHES

*No Matter How It's Carried, A Knife Needs To Be Safe, Secure And Ready For Action!*

A KNIFE is of no value unless it is at hand when needed. At home in the drawer, the knife does no service if the need is in the field, at the office, aboard the fishing boat or merely out in the backyard.

There are any number of places and methods for carrying a knife. Most men and women of our acquaintance seem to carry a pocket or purse knife all the time. A pocketknife at the factory or the office often will see hundreds of different jobs in a typical week of work. When fishing, hunting or camping, a knife will earn its original price many times over, even if the cutting tasks are simply opening a charcoal bag or slicing the plastic bag on a pack of hot dogs. We are advocates of the habit of always carrying a sharp pocket or purse knife; it is sure to be used.

But when it comes to bigger knives such as hunting, skinning, slicing, carving or fillet models, the pocket or purse is hardly the place for them. Only a fool would consider carrying a naked blade slipped through the belt, no matter what one might see in the movies. A sheath or pouch is required for any knife larger than a pocket folder with a two-inch blade.

A knife may be carried on the hip with the belt threaded through a loop on the back of the sheath; in fact, that is the most common location. But it is not the only position. Many are carried elsewhere, depending upon the type of knife, the purpose of the knife and the activity in which one may be engaged. There are dozens of variations.

Most knife sheaths are worn on the right or left side, depending upon which is the user's dominant hand in the traditional vertical mode. Such a position is probably the most useful for most tasks. When hunting, it is not likely that events will happen so rapidly that the hunter will have to drop his firearm in order to draw his knife. Things usually move at a more leisurely pace, so a fast-draw knife is not required.

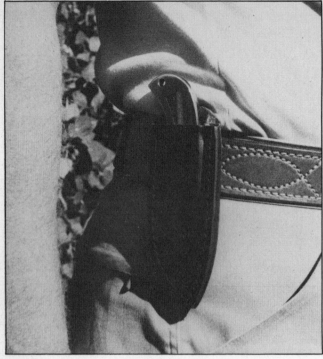

*The little two-inch blade skinner from Guttman is carried in a spring-clip sheath, at home on the belt as shown, or tucked down in your boot. The knife is narrow enough for either place.*

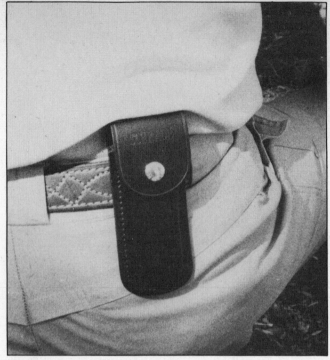

*A larger Schrade locking folder is carried in a belt pouch. Pouch is made of leather and has a positive-locking snap closure on the top flap.*

*Left: Bianchi's big Knighthawk survival knife requires a heavy leather sheath, complete with its own small sharpening stone. Grommets in sheath are lash points for arm or leg carry.*

Some hunters and backpackers prefer to carry a small axe on the trail, as well as a hunting knife. This usually is no problem, unless a canteen of water is also hanging from the belt; something should be moved over to the opposite side of the body. Too much gear on one side can become uncomfortable. Proper balance of your load is simple common sense.

When wearing a heavy backpack, a knife on the belt can get in the way. Most modern packs are equipped with a hip belt that is specifically designed to carry most of the weight. The shoulder straps merely balance the load, while it is the packer's hips that actually carry the poundage. A belt sheath under the hip strap not only would be uncomfortable, but would tend to position the knife out of reach, until the pack is taken off. The answer, providing the sheath has a large enough belt loop, is to slip the hip strap through the sheath's belt loop. The knife can be restrung on the belt in camp, if desired.

Another handy location for the knife sheath — and the knife — is on the shoulder straps of the backpack. Most sheaths are not sewn to accommodate this placement, so the sheath may have to be taped to the shoulder strap. Depending upon the design of the sheath, it may be worn right-side up or upside down. The handle-down position has a fast draw going for it, but the sheath design must

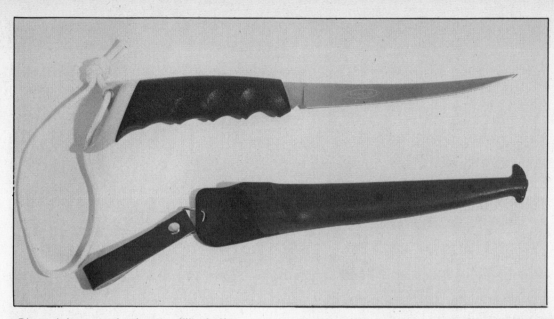

*Big stainless steel saltwater fillet knife, above, features soft handle and narrow sheath of non-slip synthetic material to resist corrosive elements. Coleman/Western Big Game System pair, at right, are carried in an unusual double-knife leather sheath.*

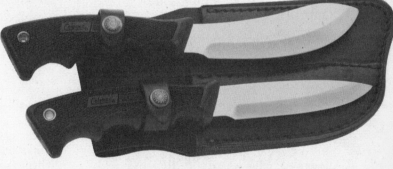

absolutely preclude the possibility of the knife ever slipping out during strenuous activity by the wearer. Positioning the sheath on the pack strap is favored by many veteran backpackers as offering the easiest access to the knife. For a right-hander, the right shoulder strap is the most practical location, with the water canteen hooked on the left side. The arrangement puts everything within easy reach.

There are a couple of custom knifemakers and at least one factory knife company that offer a fixed blade sheath which is worn in a horizontal, rather than a vertical, position on the belt. This places the knife in front, off-center to the right or left side. The position offers a couple of advantages when hunting in some parts of the country. This is especially true in the wide open spaces of the West, where hunters may spend as much time in four-wheel drive vehicles, bouncing along the foothills, as they do on the ground stalking an animal. The horizontal knife carry makes crawling in and out of a pick-up truck cab a lot easier, with less chance of the sheath getting caught in the upholstery or the edge of the door frame. Too, the sheath is less likely to hang up on brush or vines when it is snugged up against the belly, rather than belted to the hip in traditional fashion.

A knife also may be carried strapped or lashed to either forearm or along the lower leg. This is a typical carry mode for skin and scuba divers. The knife does not interfere with the diving tank or the weight belt about the waist, yet is ready for instant use should the need arise.

Some fighting or survival knives are designed to be worn in the boot. Instead of a belt loop sewn to the inner side of the sheath, a strong clip of spring steel is attached to the

*Gerber offers several different sheath designs and camouflage patterns for its boot knives. Nylon sheaths may be worn on belt using the sewn-on loop, or slipped into boot top using spring clip.*

*CAM III's latest fighting knife with non-glare, skeletonized handle is equipped with a leather sheath. Sheath may be clipped to either belt or boot, or lashed through grommets to arm, leg.*

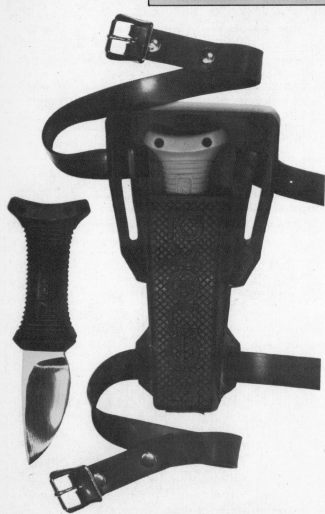

*Wenoka diving knife sheath is made of a hard, non-porous plastic material which is impervious to saltwater damage. Sheath has provisions for belt wear, or to be strapped on the lower part of leg.*

sheath to clamp both sheath and knife securely to the inside of a boot. Some law enforcement officers use this innovation for carrying a back-up knife. The arrangement is less than satisfactory when wearing tight-fitting Western jeans, because there is barely enough room for boots and none through which to reach down and draw out a knife. A spring-clip sheath also may be worn on the belt in a more conventional manner. It is a rather versatile design.

Sheaths intended for concealed wear also may include provisions for strapping or lashing the sheath to an arm, leg or shoulder strap. Three, four or more eyelets in the sheath constitute a simple addition to the design.

Another leg sheath uses elastic straps with hooks or Velcro closures to position the sheath and knife out of normal view. The knife used in this type of carry is usually a long, slender design that will not be too bulky when worn along the leg. Undercover or plainclothes police officers might favor a knife on one leg, carrying a back-up pistol in an ankle holster on the other. In hot weather, though, the arrangement can become rather uncomfortable.

A good sheath does more than simply carry a knife. If designed correctly, it also protects the blade and the blade's edge from damage. This is particularly evident with knives for fishermen. The slender, curving fillet knife takes a lot of abuse, yet needs to be ready for use at all times. Not every angler will wear his fishing knife on his belt, but will always have it along. Tackle boxes carry plenty of knives, but tossing a bare-bladed knife in a box is a sure way to quickly dull the edge, as well as present a definite hazard to one's hands when the box is opened. A fillet knife sheath is the obvious answer.

Some special knife designs require special sheaths. Several knife makers produce knives that feature a single handle and interchangeable blades. As many as four different blade shapes may be included in such a tool, requir-

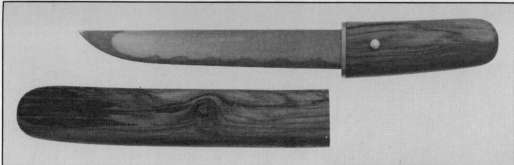

Bob Engnath, of House of Muzzleloading, is offering a series of Oriental-style knives which feature wood handles and sheaths. Closed, wood grain matches.

The military-style sheath for the Phrobus III/Buck M9 bayonet does more than simply carry the big knife. Green nylon design has provisions for a small honing stone, wire cutter, screwdriver, plus a Velcro-held accessory pouch for extra gear.

ing a larger, compartmented sheath to transport it. Another sheath design accommodates not one, but two separate knives; a hunter and a skinner in combination. Another sheath carries a knife and an axe in a neat package on the hip. This type of sheath needs to be large enough for both implements, as well as strong enough to support the considerable weight of the two. Those who carry the design are pleased with the increased readiness they enjoy.

Even the largest knife blades — Bowies, machetes and swords — need sheaths to protect and carry them. A sword or machete blade may be two or three feet long and producing a sheath for same is a formidable task, but it is a necessary item. The long blades can be heavy when carried only in the hands.

Thus far, our discussion has alluded primarily to fixed-blade knives, but larger folding knives also are carried on the belt. Rather than a sheath, a pouch is the most common carrier for a folder. Usually, the pouch is simpler in design, consisting primarily of a pocket to hold the knife, a flap over the top to retain the knife and a belt loop or spring clip. The pouch need not be formed to fit the knife blade as is the typical sheath design.

At least one knife design, the Clipit by Spyderco, uses no sheath or pouch for carrying. In the Clipit's case, a steel spring clip, is fastened directly to the outside of the handle slab. The knife is carried either inside the pocket with the clip outside, or on the belt or boot top, the same as any boot knife.

Leather and nylon are the most commonly found sheath and pouch materials. But hard plastic, metal, canvas, wood, shell, rubber and fiberglass are also used. Leather is the traditional modern material for sheaths and pouches; buckskin, shell and horn were used in much earlier times. In even more ancient periods, the Japanese warriors carried their swords in wooden sheaths that had been wrapped with silk cord or decorative fabric. The Crusaders of the Middle Ages seemed mostly to have used metal sword sheaths.

The outdoorsman will appreciate the handy leather belt sheath accommodating the small hand axe and skinning knife. Top flap and safety strap are both closed by metal snaps, unaffected by snow and cold.

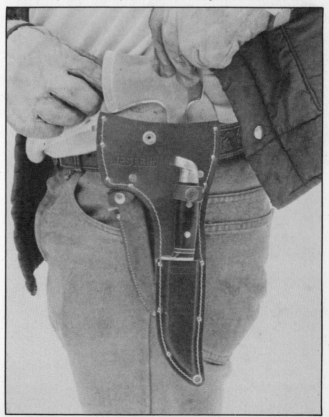

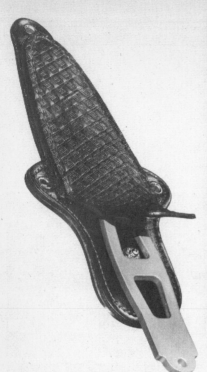

The LifeKnife survival knife is carried in a camo nylon sheath with provision for a honing stone. The belt loop is large enough to fit around pack belt.

The CAM III sheath holds the knife in place by a snap through the tang cut-out, above. When the knife is worn point-up, it remains secure until drawn. Handle is grasped, a quick outward motion unlocks the snap and the knife is drawn downward.

Buck Knives produces a paired knife and axe set, but each is carried in separate sheath. Design and leather material are matching, heavy enough for the most rugged use without restricting movement.

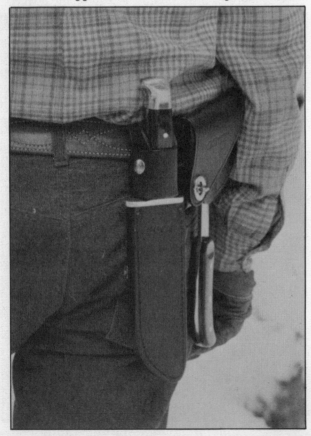

Leather is still the most popular material used for fashioning knife sheaths, although nylon, especially padded nylon fabric, has gained a large share of the market. Nylon has a much lower price going for it and producers are finding it easier to work with on a production line. Nylon can be produced in any color, including camouflage patterns. Black is the most common, but shades of gray, blue, brown, forest green and even bright reds and yellows find special uses.

For the military market, the sheath Buck includes with its M9 bayonet finds olive green as the color usually specified in the contract. For most police work, including uniformed officers who are equipped with a complete Sam Browne belt and holster of nylon, black usually is specified. Most police SWAT teams are furnished with all-black nylon web gear, including their knife sheaths. Most survival knife sheaths are black, too, although olive green runs a close second. Brown nylon is used for the Boy Scout knife that Buck makes and blue is prescribed for the Cub Scout knife. Coleman Western furnish a gray-blue nylon pouch for their Rough Cut folders.

Most leather knife pouches utilize a snap closure while the nylon top-flaps use Velcro; some use both. A larger sheath may have a tie-down to keep the bottom from flapping around or snagging on brush while hunting. Some tie-downs are leather thong or nylon cord, while others will use a buckled strap of leather or nylon webbing.

Some sheaths, especially those for large survival knives, have a provision for carrying a small sharpening stone. Many of these stones, however, are quite small and sharpening a blade with one presents a real challenge. The hard plastic sheath for the M9 bayonet has its stone affixed to the outside, protruding about a quarter of an inch above the surface. Thus, the bayonet sheath itself acts as a con-

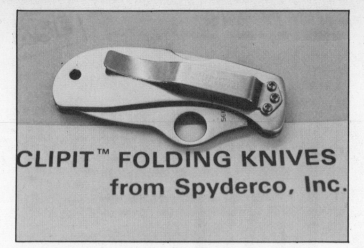

# CLIPIT™ FOLDING KNIVES
## from Spyderco, Inc.

*Neither sheath nor pouch is the answer for Spyderco Clipit folding knives. The spring steel clip is attached directly to the handle slab and designed to be carried on the belt, trouser top or in pocket.*

venient handle while the blade is being sharpened on the stone.

Some do-it-yourself knife-making kits also include material for making one's own sheath. These usually are simple designs, consisting of a pre-cut sheet of leather and a length of thong. The leather is folded over to form a pocket sheath and the two resulting edges are laced together with the thong. Two belt slots may be cut in the leather, rather than make an attempt to sew on a belt loop. It may not be pretty, but it will serve a purpose.

Should the need arise for a new sheath for an old knife, most gun and knife shows seem to feature tables displaying sheaths and pouches of various sizes and designs. Some are available with fancy tooling on the leather to enhance the value of the combo. No knife need go bare-bladed.

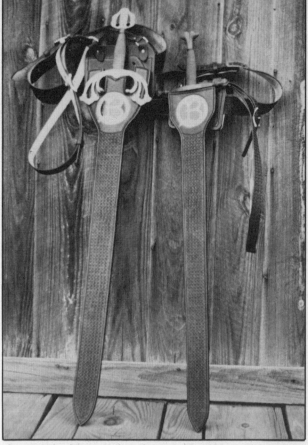

*Among the largest sheaths to be found are those for ceremonial and display swords, above. These two, from Cow Catcher Leatherworks, surround 36-inch blades. Plenty of leather goes into hand-tooled sheath.*

*Not for looks, but extremely practical is the Chuck Stapel ankle sheath knife, right. Handle is thin for concealed wear; sheath is held by Velcro strips.*

*Below: A gift set from Boker Tree Brand knives includes a two-blade folding knife, a sharpening steel and a thick, full-grain leather belt pouch.*

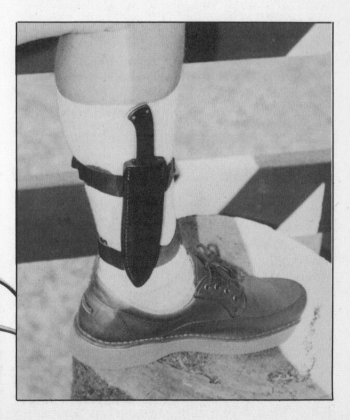

# Chapter 6

# COLLECTING KNIVES

Knife collectors may specialize in production sets, right, or in more exotic and expensive models such as the James Rodgers Sheffield, above. The Rodgers knife was made in 1848-1849 and features a stamping of "Old Zack" Taylor, twelfth President of the United States.

THAT OLD jackknife your grandfather gave you — the one with the scuffed bone handle and the badly worn blade — may be worth a lot of loot. Knife collecting has been a recognized hobby for many decades, but in recent years, it has grown in mammoth bounds. The National Knife Collectors Association, as one example, started in 1972 with six hundred members. Today, they number more than 10,000 and the association is said to be growing by more than 250 members a week.

A.G. Russell, who has been around the knife business for less than a century, but a lot longer than most of us, has some views on the subject.

"Until not many years ago," he contends, "knife collecting was a hobby that generally was enjoyed mostly by the wealthy. They seemed to concentrate on collecting exotic, custom-made knives and a lot of them went for thousands of dollars each."

Russell knows whereof he speaks. He was a founding member of the Custom Knifemakers Guild and has watched such craftsmen as Bob Loveless develop their talents and their names to the point that one has to wait several years for a Loveless knife and you may pay $1000 and even a lot more for one of these.

Or there are such collectors as Joe Musso, a worker in

## Those Who Like To Collect Things Will Find
### Plenty Of Help If Their Thing Is Knives

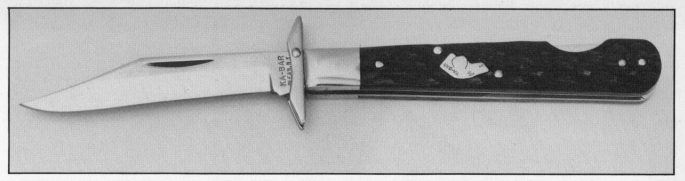

One of several Ka-Bar collector series is the Dog's Head. The Swing Guard locking folder, above, was the second model of four in 1985.

the Hollywood film factories, who is mentioned elsewhere in this book at some length. He tends to specialize in Bowie knives made in the last century as well as those that have been used in films. Not only does he have a great deal of money invested in his collection of Bowies, but he also has devoted countless hours of research and week upon week of travel to authenticate some of the knives he has collected and to track down the whereabouts of others.

But the collector who is appearing today tends to collect a different type of knife. As one expert put it, "More often than not, he's an average citizen who has accumulated a drawerful of pocketknives over the years and, until recently, had not realized they had increased in value." Most of those are pocketknives or folders of one type or another. While we've seen some of them go at gun and knife shows for as little as $3 each, there are others — the rare antique specimens — that may be worth thousands.

This is not intended to be a treatise on knife values. That

is handled in excellent fashion by a companion DBI Book, *Levine's Guide To Knives and Their Values*. That volume identifies and values almost every knife of every type known. It runs some 480 pages and has over 2000 illustrations. We recommend it to anyone wanting to know the value of knives.

Instead, we are taking a broad-brush look at the how and why of the new trend of collecting.

Some gun collectors, discouraged by anti-gun legislation, have found knife collecting a less restricting activity. The value of the U.S. dollar has had an effect, too. Collecting almost anything of value has become a good investment — although the knowing collector recognizes the fact that the items in his collection tend to go up and down the scale of value with the state of the economy.

To learn the rudiments of collecting, it might be a good idea to join a collector club. If you've never heard of one, ask around. Your local cutlery dealer probably can give you a lead. In fact, he probably belongs to one — or several.

Members of such groups hold swap meets and shows,

Above: California knife was made in Sheffield, England, by John Walters about 1848-50. Horsehead Bowie, right, is circa 1850, by Fenton & Shore, of Sheffield; a highly collectible knife.

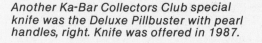

Another Ka-Bar Collectors Club special knife was the Deluxe Pillbuster with pearl handles, right. Knife was offered in 1987.

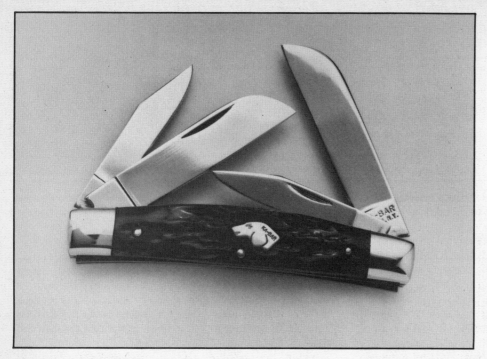

The 1984 Ka-Bar limited production collector knife was the Dog's Head four-blade Congress pattern, left. The knife has jigged bone handles. measures four inches long when closed. The Ka-Bar axe-knife combo, below, is a replica of the Union Cutlery model first produced in 1912. The 1987 collector version was made in Standard and Limited Edition models for knife club members.

meet to exchange information, to trade knives among themselves and to keep up on new trends.

If you're interested in the investment aspects of knife collecting, learn as much as you can before you start plunking down your money for some rusty old dagger that strikes your fancy. As one expert put it, "It's more profitable to collect what's popular than unpopular knives that just happened to catch your fancy. Beginners probably should specialize in knives from a certain period or knives made by one manufacturer."

And that's really the gist of this chapter: knives made by one manufacturer and what they're doing to make them collectible.

W.R. Case & Sons Cutlery has long been of interest to collectors and comprises what amounts to a whole separate branch of collecting on its own. The powers that be at the company knew the collectors were out there and decided to organize them into the Case Collectors Club. That was in 1981. Since they also had a profit motive, Case also issued at that time what they called the "1st Edition — Case Collectors Club — 1981." This was a knife that had been their Model 6151 and had not been made since 1940, when most of their production started going toward the efforts of winning World War II. The original had been made with a regular bone stag handle and chrome vanadium blades and springs. The 1981 version had a jigged bone handle, a stainless steel backspring, brass liners, nickel silver bolsters and a saber-ground clip blade of what the maker called Tru-Sharp surgical steel. Included with this knife was a cherrywood plaque and a brass plate suitable for engraving.

Members of the Case club received a newsletter, which was full of handy hints on knife care, folksy talk about knife shows and it also gave the manufacturer a chance to talk about the new knives they would be introducing. Before that time, there were hundreds of Case Knife Collectors around the country, ardently seeking rare Case production knives.

Ka-Bar Cutlery wasn't far behind with this idea and

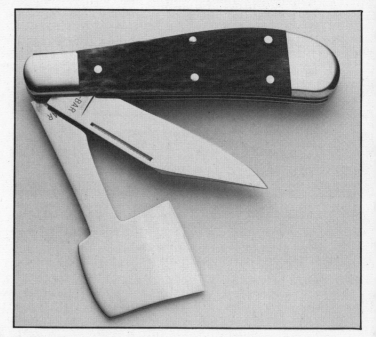

created the Ka-Bar Collector Club. There had earlier been such a club, a rather loosely organized entity, but in the late Seventies, the cutlery company got behind it and began issuing an annual member's knife, each of them suitably etched on the blade to indicate the year of issue and the fact that it was a club exclusive.

"Membership is available at nominal dues of $5 per year," according to Bob Reinschreiber, a long-time Ka-Bar executive who oversees club activities. "On becoming a member, the knife collector receives quarterly bulletins as well as the opportunity to buy special Ka-Bar Collector Knives, which are produced for club members only.

"Our members are encouraged to participate in the activities of the club and are always kept informed about progress, new plans, as well as being asked to contribute

*Ka-Bar is always coming up with interesting club collector knives, including the 1987 Grizzly folder, above, and the "Bomb" pattern, below. The handle shape is supposed to represent a World War I bomb dropped by hand from a bi-plane.*

their ideas on what the club should be doing in the way of knife production and researching company history.

"Also, in the course of the year, each member has available to him a toll-free number he can use in requesting information about Ka-Bar Knives or its history. We have a large group of over 10,000 enthusiastic members."

Of course, Ka-Bar wasn't always Ka-Bar. It started as the Union Razor Company in Tidioute, Pennsylvania, and later became the Union Cutlery Company in Olean, New York. Ka-Bar became the successor to Union.

Many of the knives being made only for club members are nearly forgotten patterns. For example, during late 1986, they introduced three different knives — or the same knife with three different markings. One had *Union Razor Co.,* stamped in the blade, the second had *Union Cut. Co.,* and the third, naturally enough, was stamped simply *KA-BAR.* This was known originally as the Sunfish model and was made by all three of the succeeding companies. The Union Razor version was introduced about 1900 with stag bone handles. The Union Cutlery style had the same appearance except for jigged bone handles. It was intro-

*Schrade's first entry into the limited edition world is a cowboy commemorative, complete with a full-color scrimshaw. Ten thousand of the five-inch lockblade folders were to be made.*

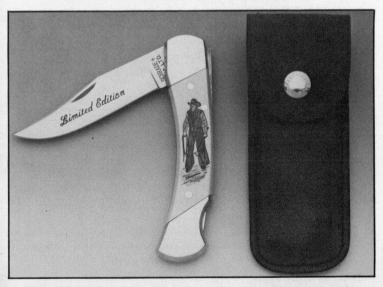

duced about 1915. The third, the Ka-Bar version, had black celluloid handles. The three were offered as a set with matching serial numbers. The serial numbers, incidentally, are meant to discourage the unscrupulous from attempting to sell these re-creations as originals.

A fourth edition of the Sunfish was issued in 1986 as a Club Special with jigged chestnut bone handles.

Much was made of the fact that, several years ago, literally thousands of Ka-Bar parts for long-forgotten models were found in an ancient water well, under the parking lot and under the driveway and the sidewalks of the factory. No one could figure out the reason for such seeming waste. Now they knew!

"Recently, we have seen some counterfeit Ka-Bar knives which, after examination, left us shaking our heads as to the source of the component parts which looked genuine," Reinschreiber reports. "We also have found occurrences of Ka-Bar knives of sub-standard quality appearing in thieves' markets; not many, but enough to make us wonder where they were coming from.

"Although it isn't hard to distinguish these knives from the genuine production, we felt it was necessary to check out how this was being accomplished. The result of our investigation was that, contrary to factory rules, some defective parts, small quantities of overruns and broken parts were being discarded in the trash bin. A well directed or enterprising junkman was picking them up and finding a market to help feed some counterfeit and sub-standard production in small shops, wherever they may be."

Reinschreiber states that this leak has been plugged by returning to the procedure of destroying discarded parts.

As time goes on, more of the long-forgotten patterns will be reinstituted for limited runs to members, company offi-

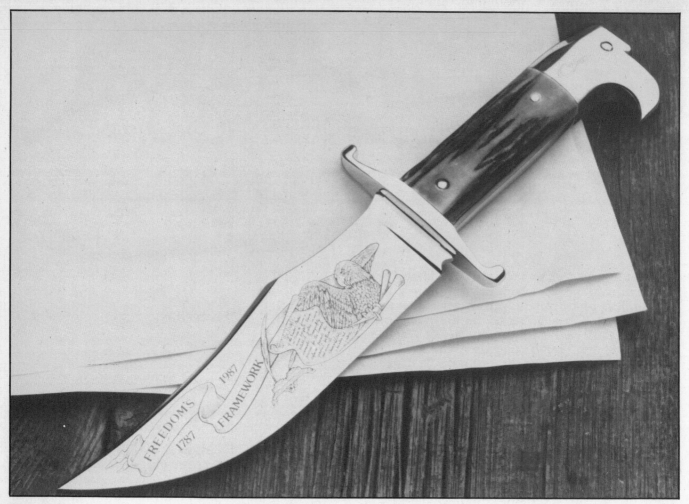

The 1987 bicentennial of the U.S. Constitution prompted Case to commemorate the year with this collector model. The pattern was used in 1976 to honor the American Bicentennial. The knife features a seven-inch blade, stag handle, gold-plate artwork denoting "Freedom's Framework," eagle head butt cap.

cials say. But one of them has been around since the early days of World War II and it's not a limited run.

"The Ka-Bar/U.S. Marine Corps fighting knife is growing in popularity, not only throughout this country but worldwide," Reinschreiber reports. "It's amazing how many of these knives are being sold to collectors, knife enthusiasts and sportsmen in Europe, Asia and the Far East. It continues to be our number one seller, being featured in prestige catalogs in the direct marketing field."

Schrade Cutlery and its marketing folks also have learned a good deal about the collecting cult. During the bicentennial in 1976, the company issued a series of commemorative knives. They found it a good source of income and have been doing it since.

Each of these knives is issued in advertised limited numbers and, because of that limitation, a built-in collector market is created.

In 1986, they finished up a series that had run for several years honoring the American Indian. The last three to appear were called the Turtle, the Bear and the Sundance. Each of these was a large folder marketed in a pouch that featured beadwork in Indian designs. The handles carried scrimshaw following the theme. In the case of the first models, 10,000 knives were issued for each. With the sixth

and final knife in the series, the Sundance, only 8000 were made.

But the firm came right back in 1987 with a new series that's expected to cover a couple of years. It's based upon the pioneers of the American West.

In 1986, Schrade also introduced a series of limited edition knives featuring Currier and Ives prints reproduced on the blades with an acid etching process. That year, two of the knives were produced in numbers of 2000 each. We suspect this may not have been a continuing series, however, as little has been said of it since.

Casting about for other commemorations, the firm decided to issue one marking the fiftieth anniversary of the Duck Stamp — officially known as the Migratory Bird Hunting and Conservation stamp. This knife was marketed with a special wall plaque describing the foundation of the stamp. There also was a bronze medallion of the Golden Anniversary Duck Stamp installed on the plaque. Only 1500 of these were made and the package sold originally for $80 per copy.

The centennial anniversary of the Statue of Liberty, of course, was a natural and Schrade dealt with the Museum of New York to produce 15,000 Statue of Liberty knives, each featuring an etching of the statue on the blade. In

*The Remington 1982 replica bullet knife was this two-blade Trapper.*

addition, there were five hundred Gold Edition knives that went for $150 each. The etching work was inlaid with gold for these.

Buck Knives, too, was able to come up with a collector knife commemorating the Statue of Liberty. They found a supply of wood from the original railings and stairs before the statue and surroundings were refurbished and used the wood for handle slabs for the knife. The knife also was furnished with a photograph of the statue and a printed legend noting the significance of the wood and the knife. Apparently, the special knife was a sell-out for Buck.

Maybe there wasn't much more to commemorate in

*1983's limited edition replica was the Baby Bullet.*

*For 1984, the Remington replica bullet knives were, for the first time, two single-blade lock-backs.*

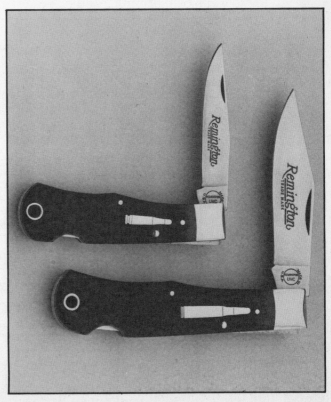

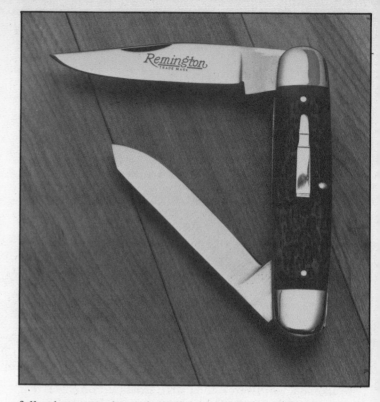

1985, but the marketing arm of the company discovered Damascus steel and issued a limited run of 2000 knives with Damascus blades. It was a standard design lock-back with Mexican rosewood scales and, for the first time, featured an etching of the new corporate figure, the Schrade Forter. Each was issued with a tooled leather sheath. The blades, incidentally, comprised 512 layers of steel.

At a recent collector show, we saw a fixed-blade Remington knife that sold for $3 in 1933. Today, it is priced at $90!

When World War I ended, Remington no longer was making great masses of military arms, so they looked about for other products. Since the gun company had a number of cutlers on the staff, who had been making guns for the war effort, knives sounded like a natural.

The first knife to come off the Remington production line in February, 1920, was called the R-103. In June of that year, they boasted that more than five hundred knives had been shipped that month.

By 1931, Remington was able to announce that more than 10,000 knives were being made each day. Considering the 5½-day work week, that added up to 2,860,000 knives per year! At one point, the company was producing more than 1000 different patterns and issuing a catalog that was thicker than the Chicago telephone directory.

But with the onset of the Great Depression, hardware stores and wholesalers were failing. This had been Remington's chief cutlery outlet and by 1936, output had been downgraded to 307 patterns. In 1939, the company introduced its first knives with stainless steel blades. But the

following year, the cutlery division suffered a $2 million loss and the division was sold.

Remington introduced what they called the Bullet knife in 1922 with bone stag or cocobolo handles. By 1930, there were twelve different styles...but they died as designs when the company was sold.

Forty years later, in 1982, Remington reintroduced the Bullet knife. The design proved so successful that there has been a new variation each year since — all based upon the

*This two-blade pen knife was the choice for Remington in 1986, called the Hunter.*

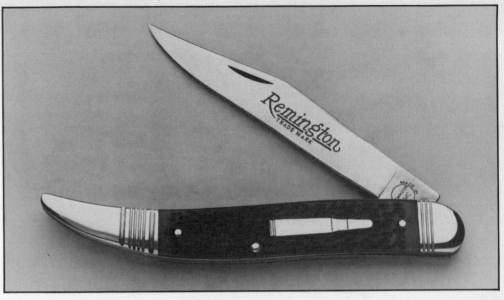

*1987 saw another change in the Remington Bullet knife pattern, with the Fisherman folding knife.*

original design. That first replica, if you will, was produced in what was called "a special collector edition that salutes Remington's new Model Four and Model Six rifles."

Instead of natural materials, these replicas have scales of Delrin, a nylon product, but it was cast to match the appearance of shinbone stag.

The next year, 1983, brought one called the Baby Bullet, a re-creation of the original R-1173. To anyone who bought a new shotgun or centerfire rifle that year, the knife was offered at half price. In 1984, two lock-backs were introduced: the R-1303 and the R-1173L. The following year, the Woodsman model (R-4353) was introduced, looking much as had the original in the Twenties and Thirties. In 1986 came the R-1263 Hunter, which carried stainless steel Turkish clip and pen blades. Like all of its predecessors, it had nickel silver bolsters.

There was a departure of sorts in 1987. The company issued one called The Fisherman, but it still was developed from the original Remington pattern, the R-1613. In spite of the fact that it was aimed at anglers, it still carried the familiar bullet outline inset in the handle.

Remington reintroduced the seventh of its limited edition replicas of its famous Bullet knife series in 1988. As this book went to press, the latest addition to this series was the R-4466 Muskrat, a double-end, trapper-style dating back to the early 1920s.

Blades are double-honed of 440 stainless steel and handles are of Delrin. One side of the handle contains the distinctive nickel silver cartridge shield. Construction also includes nickel silver bolsters and liners of rustproof brass.

The double-end style incorporates two opposed three-inch blades, of clip and spey design. Etched on one side of the clip blade is the Remington logo of the 1930s, while the shank end of each blade is etched with the original Remington UMC circle. Stamped on the reverse blade shanks is the R-4466 designation on the clip blade and 1988, signifying the year of the edition, on the spey blade.

Apparently the blade business has prospered, for Remington introduced a new and permanent Sportsman's Series of four specialized knives in 1988. These knives were in adition to the annual limited edition replica Bullet knife series.

Each of the new series will include blades honed from 440 stainless steel, handles of Delrin, nickel silver bolster, rustproof brass linings and stainless steel pins.

The Remington Upland model is of double-end serpentine design with an identifying nickel shield of a rising pheasant on one side and three specialized blades. It has a 2⅝-inch skinning-type clip blade with the Remington logo etched on one side, plus a patented choke tool for inserting and removing 12- and 20-gauge Remington, Browning and Beretta choke tubes as well as most other popular Invector-type flush-mounted chokes. There also is a strong

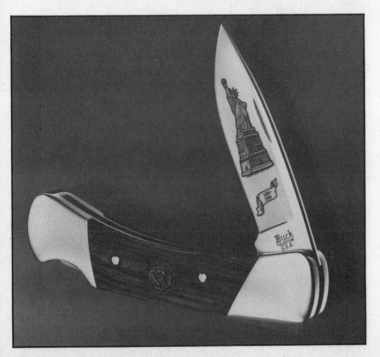

*Buck Knives got into the commemorative collector knife game with a Statue of Liberty model, left. Handle slabs are made of scraps from Ellis Island stairs, railings and other wood furnishings.*

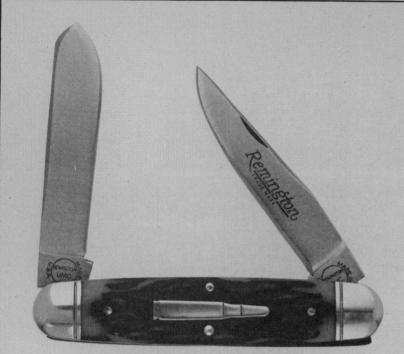

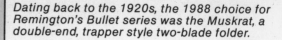

*Dating back to the 1920s, the 1988 choice for Remington's Bullet series was the Muskrat, a double-end, trapper style two-blade folder.*

*Added to the Bullet replicas in 1988 was the Remington Big Game knife, with an elk-head medallion on the side. A skinning clip blade and a self-cleaning bone saw pivot on one end.*

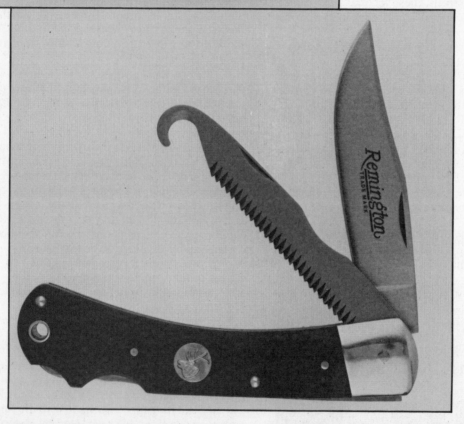

screwdriver tip for removing shotgun magazine retainer caps and other applications, plus an upland bird gut hook. The overall closed length is 3⅞ inches.

The 1988 Remington Waterfowl knife is 4¼ inches in closed length and is embossed on one side with an identifying nickel silver shield of a goose in flight. The four specialized blades include a three-inch breasting and skinning clip blade; a serrated, sheepsfoot-design cartilage and bone blade; the choke tool that fits 12- and 20-gauge flush-mounted choke inserts. The end of the tool is a sturdy screwdriver for removing shotgun magazine cap retainers. A pin punch removes shotgun fire control mechanisms.

Remington's Big Game knife is five inches in length with double lock-back design. It comes with an oil-tanned leather sheath containing a diamond sharpening tool and one end of the knife has a convenient lanyard hole. One side of the handle is embossed with an identifying nickel silver shield of an elk head.

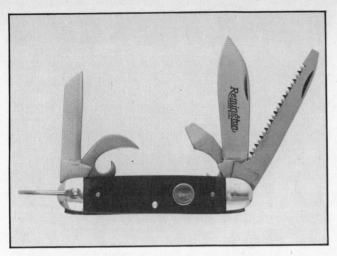

The five-blade Remington Utility knife is another limited production model introduced in 1988.

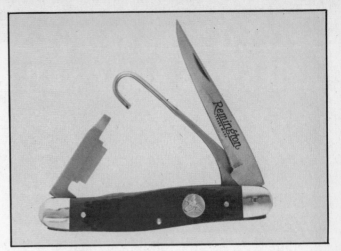

The Remington Upland knife has a clip blade, bird gut hook and a clever interchangeable choke tube with screwdriver to fit most popular shotguns.

It has a 3⅝-inch skinning clip blade with the Remington logo etched on one side, plus a self-cleaning boning saw with a skinning hook at the end. A grip notch on the back of this blade functions as a control notch for the clip blade when it is open and the saw blade is closed.

The utility model is a straight, double-end, trapper design with a circular Remington UMC logo shield on one side. One end contains a lanyard ring. Overall closed length is 3¾ inches. It is designed as a tool for hunters, fishermen, campers and other types of outdoorsmen. Five blades include a 2⅜-inch spear blade bearing the Remington logo; a standard saw blade; a safety-type, hooked can opener; a bottle cap lifter with end screwdriver and a cut-off pen blade.

Forty years hence, these may all be meat for a new breed of collector!

On a less corporate note, there are other commercially inspired collector organizations. The earlier-mentioned A.G. Russell probably started the whole thing about twenty years ago, when he organized the Knife Collectors Club from his headquarters in Springville, Arkansas.

He does frequent mailings to a list of more than 7000 knife enthusiasts, offering them special prices on knives that he has made to his own specifications in the U.S. or styles that he has discovered in Germany or Japan. Each year, he also issues a club knife, as do the knife-making firms that sponsor such clubs. Some years ago, he issued a small dagger as the year's club knife, the FH-1, which is described as a "much improved version of the old Texas Toothpick."

Using this same design, he had this knife reproduced later in a high-impact plastic and called it the CIA Letter Opener. He sold some 50,000 at up to $6.95 each, then began giving it away as a premium to those who joined his club. As he tells his customer members, "I am not interested in selling you just one knife. I want to sell you knives for the rest of your lives." It's an approach that has worked.

In fact, the Russell marketing approach has worked well enough that several others have adopted similar programs. Both the National Knife Collectors Association and the American Blade Collectors Association are headquartered in Chattanooga, Tennessee. The former was taken over in its infancy by Jim Parker as an aid to selling knives which he produced in his own factory. The American Blade Collectors Association was formed with the idea of membership aiding the circulation of an associated magazine. Both, however, offer annual "member knives."

No one maker is involved in producing the member knives for these two organizations. Instead, various commercial knifemakers submit prototypes for inspection and evaluation. A choice is made from these submissions. It is an interesting market, since selection to make the "official" club knife for the year can result in an order of up to 10,000 knives!

The Remington Waterfowl knife features a choke wrench tool that fits many shotgun choke tubes.

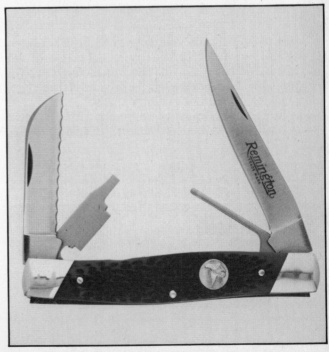

# SPECIALIZING IN BOY SCOUT AND SWISS ARMY KNIVES

Buck Knife's official Boy Scouts of America folder is a single-blade knife using a typical Buck blade shape and lightweight handle materials. The nylon belt sheath has the Scout emblem.

BOY SCOUT knife. Swiss Army Knife. These special knives have a certain romance of their own and have their share of avid collectors. Both types have had dozens of variations through the decades of their existence, making them prime collector knives.

The Boy Scouts of America was founded in 1910 and a Boy Scout knife was produced almost immediately. After

The Camillus Eagle Scout Knife is a special, good looking model for the lad who reaches that high rank.

all, what's a Boy Scout without a knife? Until about 1922, the New York Knife Company had a monopoly on the "official" knife production and was not shy about letting the world know it. Not long after the end of World War I, however, the exclusivity was ended and any number of makers joined the ranks of Boy Scout knife makers. Many of the pocket models of those early days carried the inscription, *Official Boy Scout Knife,* while others were marked with such designations as *Scout Knife; Camp Knife; Be Prepared.* Then and today, many carry the official Boy Scout shield emblem on the handle.

Most Boy Scout knives, no matter who is producing them, have folding blades; many of them, two or more. The traditional knife shows a large spear-point blade, a screwdriver blade that doubles as a bottle cap opener, a can opener and the typical leather punch blade. A good many had a lanyard bale on one end of the handle. In the days before World War II, most of the handles were of stag or bone. Today, plastic, Delrin, Kraton or other durable Space Age materials are used.

In 1985, the seventy-fifth anniversary of the founding

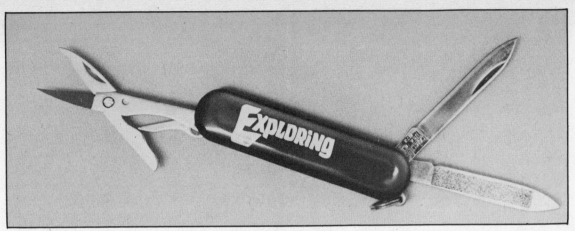

*This three-blade Exploring knife is intended for Explorers, has a green plastic handle and a pen blade, a fingernail file and a folding pair of scissors as shown.*

of the Boy Scouts of America was celebrated; Schrade issued two commemoratives. One was the familiar knife carried by virtually everyone who has ever been a Scout. This was a reproduction of the original four-blade knife produced by the long-gone New York Knife Company. The blades were in enough forms to set up houekeeping. The second knife was a lock-back with custom-etched brass-inlaid handles and etching showing the fathers of Scouting: Daniel Beard and Ernest Thomas Seton. The first knife sold for $24.95, the second for $49.95. The New

York reproduction was not a limited run. The higher priced knife was limited to 12,000 copies.

Buck makes a knife that carries the official Boy Scouts of America symbol. Called ScoutLite (Model 412), this folding lock-blade is a special model of the BuckLite series. This lightweight knife has handles of a rich red color and comes in a nylon sheath of Boy Scout khaki color. Scout-Lite is 4½ inches when closed and has a three-inch blade.

An even newer addition to the Buck line is the CubLight, a lock-back folder for Cub Scouts, somewhat smaller and

*The latest Swiss Army knife model by Wenger, imported by Precise International, features at least sixteen individual tools and blades, all inside the typical red handle imbedded with the Swiss cross on one side.*

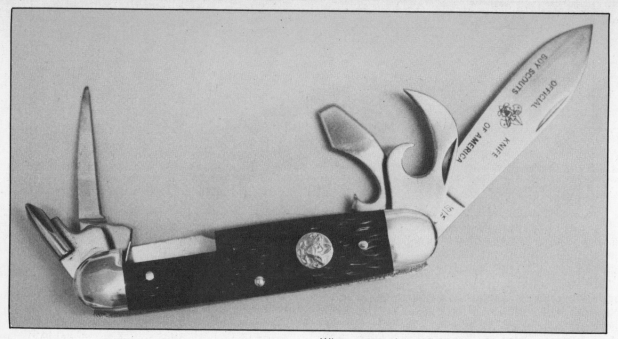

*When most of us think about Boy Scout knives, we think about something like this. A big folder, the Camillus includes a number of multi-purpose tools.*

lighter than the ScoutLite. Featuring a drop-point blade of 2¾ inches, the knife is just under four inches long when closed. The Model 414 CubLite has a blue Valox handle and a blue and yellow belt pouch. Chuck Buck has told us that the company has been criticized for producing a knife intended for boys of Cub Scout age. But Buck, who has been involved in youth work for years, believes that, with the proper adult supervision, boys 9 to 12 can handle these knives safely.

Camillus makes a half-dozen different Boy Scout knife designs. The traditional-looking five-blade folder has a Delrin handle, a main spear-point blade, a Phillips screwdriver, a combination blade screwdriver and bottle opener, a can opener and a combination punch and scraper blade. Camillus' smaller whittler's knife carries the Boy Scout shield on the handle slabs, enclosing three special whittling blades. They also produce two special models; one for Eagle scouts, another for Explorers. The Explorer model is bright green and black while the Eagle Scout is red, white and blue on one side and red on the back. Each has a pen blade, a nail file and a tiny pair of scissors.

Camillus, Buck and Victorinox Scout knives are listed in the current Boy Scouts of America equipment catalogs. Victorinox is one of two companies designated as official suppliers and producers of the famous Swiss Army knife. The second supplier of Swiss Army knives is Wenger, imported by Precise International, which also makes a Boy Scout version of its Swiss Army. Each lists three folding knives made to the typical Swiss Army pattern, also carrying the Boy Scout emblem.

The two Swiss competitors and their American importing companies each make claims about who was first and which is the "official" supplier to the Swiss Army. In fact, both supply knives to the Swiss and other armies. Victorinox traces its origins to 1891 and Wenger to 1893. In 1908, the Swiss government ordered only Swiss-made knives would be issued to citizen-soldiers; half from Wenger, the balance from Victorinox.

The original Wenger issue knife had wood handle slabs

*Another "official" Boy Scout knife from Camillus is the Whittler, carried in the Scout supply catalog. The BSA emblem appears on the Delrin handle enclosing three special whittling blades.*

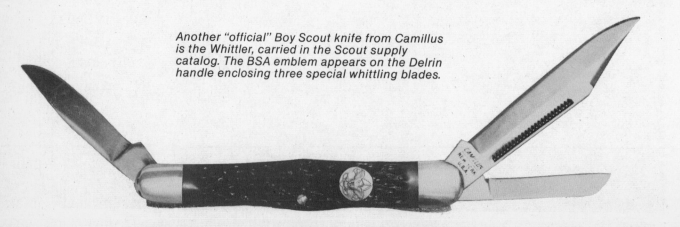

painted bright red so the knife might be easy to spot when dropped in the snow. Today's four-blade knife is made with an aluminum handle. Switzerland is one of the world's leading producers of aluminum due to the abundance of hydroelectric power used in making the metal. To distinguish the original Swiss Army knife from its many competitors, the Swiss cross has been inlaid in the red handle since 1909. The basic look of the knife continues today with the red handle and Swiss cross identifying it, although even Victorinox and its imitators are making copies in different colors.

Many companies make knives similar to those produced by Wenger and Victorinox, but those two remain the only "official" makers for the Swiss Army. Their popularity grew world-wide after World War II, when many American servicemen came home with them. Since then, millions of Swiss Army knives have been carried into combat in many parts of the world.

The number of variations is almost mind-boggling. Victorinox has more than forty different models of the knife and Precise International imports more than fifty from them and other makers. Tools available in several different models include large and small blades, corkscrews, can and bottle openers, several sizes and types of screwdrivers, reamers, scissors, files, saws, fish scalers, rulers, orange peelers, magnifying glasses, compasses, tweezers and toothpicks. The newest Wenger model from Precise features a small wrench and a locking main blade.

Boy Scout and Swiss Army knives comprise a fascinating and educational branch of knife collecting. There are dozens, even hundreds, of variations of official and unofficial knives. Many, especially the Scout knives, have been discontinued and may be found only at gun shows, swap meets and among other collectors.

One might wish to collect all versions of the Swiss Army knife by each producer or each model made during a particular year. One of each Boy Scout knife might be easier to find, but some are quite rare. Buying one of each of forty or fifty current models of Swiss Army knives could be expensive, but it can be a good place to start a collection.

*A few years ago, an unknown Oriental knife company attempted to copy the quality of the European Swiss Army knife. Close examination reveals how badly it failed. An attempt to open any of the blades was guaranteed to break one or several fingernails. Genuine Swiss Army knives are only made in Switzerland.*

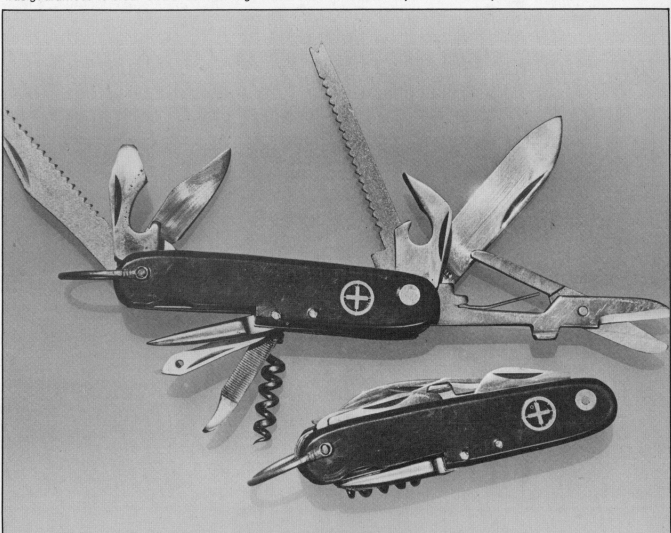

Among the best-known locking folders are the Buck Hunter and Ranger, at right. Buck recently remodeled these knives with more rounded edges on the handles, but the basic design remains the same. Typical non-locking folders from Imperial, below, include some with two or three blades, specialized shapes.

# Chapter 7

# FOLDING KNIVES

## Often Called The Pocketknife Or The Jackknife, The Folder Is The One We All Carry

THE KNIFE most of us carry a majority of the time is a folding knife. No matter what one's occupation, age or sex, there are more people in the world carrying a folding knife than any other kind of knife. The folder is the knife of choice for most of us.

A folding knife may take on any one of hundreds of forms. It may be no larger than a coin in the pocket, or it may be a giant with a blade of five inches or more and a handle to match. The little folder may fit snugly in your pocket or be encased in a pouch in your traveling kit or its big brother may be too large to be carried in any logical manner except in a belt pouch. The folder may have but one blade, or as many as four, six, even a dozen on some Swiss Army knives.

The main blade may have a mechanical locking mechanism to prevent accidental closure of the blade while it's in use. The best locking systems will not collapse under even the most severe pressure. A blade folding unexpectedly can cause a severe cut at the least, even the loss of fingers at the worst.

All sorts of locking systems have been used on knife blades. The lock release has been placed on the top and the bottom of the knife, as well as in the front, middle and rear. Ka-Bar, for one, invented a clever locking release hidden in the rear bolster of the knife. It was difficult to find for anyone who did not know the secret. But the design afforded a nice, clean appearance for the knife and facilitated an extremely thin knife for unobtrusive pocket wear. The best locking mechanisms are those which tend to become more tightly locked as pressure increases. While anything mechanical can break, given the right circumstances, most modern locking blades are as safe and reliable as design, workmanship and materials can make them.

Lock release placement is a matter of personal taste and production possibilities. There are those who prefer the front lock saying that such placement is strong and convenient. Others prefer the rear lock arguing that the location is less likely to be released accidently while working with the blade. Still others insist the central location is best, because it is protected by the palm under normal operation. Some locks have been placed as a sliding or pressure button on the side of the knife handle. The Gerber Paul knife design, as an example, requires only finger pressure on both sides on the the locking button to allow the blade to fold. The design became quite popular for several years and is only now being phased out of the Gerber line.

Not every folding knife blade is held open by a mechanical locking mechanism. Some are held in place by spring friction alone. These are the typical pocket- or jackknives, the type most familiar to all of us. There have been more of these knives sold and used over the past several decades than any other design. For routine chores — cutting string, opening letters, sharpening pencils, snipping thread, scraping paint, opening produce or snack packages, a dozen other everyday tasks — the friction-lock folding knife is perfectly adequate. For routine tasks like those, a locking blade is not necessary. Some airline security personnel will not allow a locking folder aboard an airplane.

The small friction folder will have a blade or blades of about an inch and a half to perhaps three inches long. There are some non-lockers with longer blades, but they are less common these days. You may remember the old fishing knife of several years ago which had a long, slender fillet blade and a scaler with hook disgorger on it. These did not have locking blades in those days, although they probably should have.

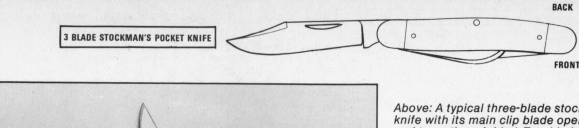

**3 BLADE STOCKMAN'S POCKET KNIFE**

BACK

FRONT

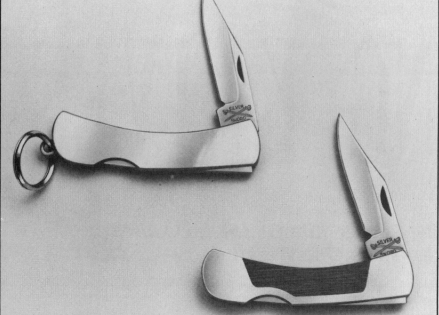

*Above: A typical three-blade stock knife with its main clip blade open and two others folded. Two blades pivot out of the main blade side, with the third by itself, opposite.*

*Two folders from Camillus illustrate how the same basic design can produce two different knives. The top folder has all-metal handle slabs, with no other material, while lower has well-fitted wood inserts.*

**BLADE AND SPRING ACTION**

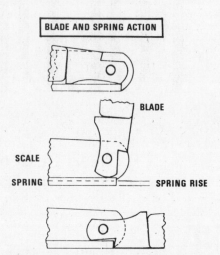

BLADE

SCALE

SPRING — SPRING RISE

*Most non-locking folding knives operate in the general manner drawn above. The shape of the knife tang is carefully made to fit precisely into the action spring when the blade is fully open. The spring must retract completely into the scales when the blade is open or closed.*

While there is no restriction to the number of blades a pocketknife might have, most have no more than three. There are larger folders with six, eight or ten blades, but one to three blades make up the typical pocket or purse knife. The two-blade design may have both blades pivoting out of the same hinge pin; this would be the typical jack-knife. The two blades may be placed on opposite ends of the knife, closing into the handle facing one another. Most three-bladers are designed with two blades on one end and one on the other.

The choice of blade shape for a small folder is unlimited, but there are several blades that are found more frequently. Probably the most common is the clip blade in several variations. The clip blade shape is used for most folding hunting knives, jackknives, stock knives, the so-called Barlow knife and in many others. The clip blade seems to lend itself to the folder, the natural peak to the back of blade offering plenty of room for the nail mark.

Another common pocketknife design is the pen knife, using, not surprisingly, a pen blade as its main blade. Many multi-blade folders include a pen blade. The spey and sheepsfoot blade shapes also have had long popularity with a lot of old-timers using the sheepsfoot for whittling away in the town square. The shapes have a utility use, though, other than whittling and still are in common usage.

Other more specialized blade shapes incorporated in the

**CLIP MASTER BLADE**

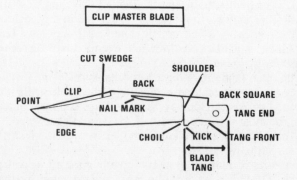

CUT SWEDGE — SHOULDER
CLIP — BACK — BACK SQUARE
POINT — TANG END
NAIL MARK — TANG FRONT
EDGE — CHOIL — KICK
BLADE TANG

*A typical folding knife blade and its nomenclature are shown above. Blade shapes may vary, but the general shapes will maintain. The closing and opening action of the folding blade leads to the expression that the knife "walks and talks." The action of the tang end moving along the spring is the walk, while the snap of the knife at the end of the cycle is the talk.*

design of small- or medium-size pocketknives are such tools as a punch blade, a saw blade or a nail file. A small camper knife might add such things as a bottle and a can opener, along with a screwdriver blade. The latter blades may be included in, but are not restricted to, the Swiss Army knife or a Boy Scout knife. Some multi-blade knives also may include such items as a magnifying glass, a pair of scissors, a Phillips screwdriver and awl, a marlin spike; even a toothpick and pair of tweezers.

For the bowhunter, particularly one who hunts from a tree stand, a folding saw blade is an essential tool. The

*Two Browning folders, both made in Japan, right, show the action of the blades and springs. The upper knife has a locking mechanism at the rear while the two-blade model uses only friction to hold the blades in place. Note how the springs extend out of the handle as the blade tang slides along them, opening or closing.*

*All kinds of tools may be enclosed in the folder's handle other than knife blades. Kershaw rigger's knife features a sheepsfoot blade, a shackle tool and a marlin spike. The shackle tool doubles as a screwdriver at the end. Handle is polymer rubber.*

*Each of the folders below incorporates a saw blade within its handle. Some also include a sewing awl, bird hook, gutting blade along with main locking blade. European saw teeth cut on the draw stroke, U.S. on the push stroke.*

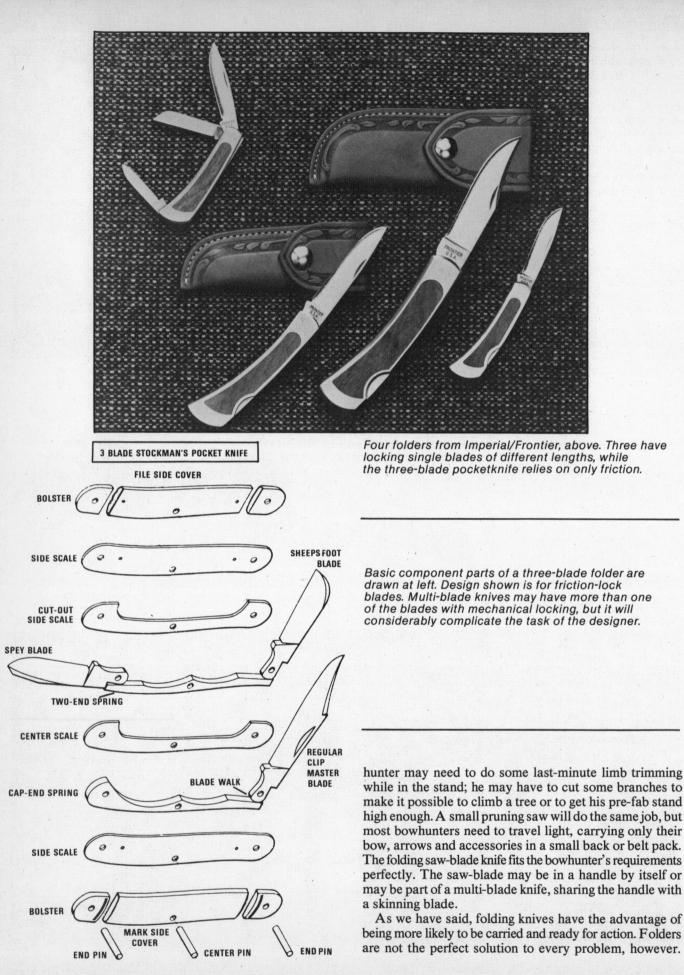

*Four folders from Imperial/Frontier, above. Three have locking single blades of different lengths, while the three-blade pocketknife relies on only friction.*

**3 BLADE STOCKMAN'S POCKET KNIFE**

FILE SIDE COVER

BOLSTER

SIDE SCALE

SHEEPS FOOT BLADE

CUT-OUT SIDE SCALE

SPEY BLADE

TWO-END SPRING

CENTER SCALE

REGULAR CLIP MASTER BLADE

CAP-END SPRING

BLADE WALK

SIDE SCALE

BOLSTER

MARK SIDE COVER

END PIN    CENTER PIN    END PIN

*Basic component parts of a three-blade folder are drawn at left. Design shown is for friction-lock blades. Multi-blade knives may have more than one of the blades with mechanical locking, but it will considerably complicate the task of the designer.*

hunter may need to do some last-minute limb trimming while in the stand; he may have to cut some branches to make it possible to climb a tree or to get his pre-fab stand high enough. A small pruning saw will do the same job, but most bowhunters need to travel light, carrying only their bow, arrows and accessories in a small back or belt pack. The folding saw-blade knife fits the bowhunter's requirements perfectly. The saw-blade may be in a handle by itself or may be part of a multi-blade knife, sharing the handle with a skinning blade.

As we have said, folding knives have the advantage of being more likely to be carried and ready for action. Folders are not the perfect solution to every problem, however.

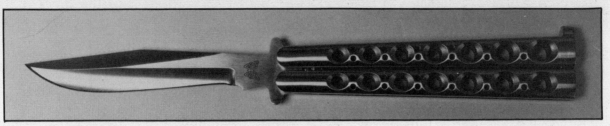

*An altogether different folder a balisong, made by Pacific Cutlery, is based on a design originating in the Far East, mostly the Philippines. The two drilled-out handle sections unlock and pivot around in opposite directions at the tang to enclose the blade. Skilled practitioners can open and close the balisong with speed.*

They have their weaknesses and we must be aware of them to be able to put them to their best use without damage.

Primarily, the folder's greatest weakness is that it has a mechanical moving part; it may have several. Anything is subject to breakage and wear, especially a moving part. The blade itself, the hinge pin, the locking mechanism; these parts move and are subject to wear and breakage. Dirt and grit, or the lack of proper lubrication tend to mar the bearing surfaces of these parts. Some wear is inevitable, but neglect or corrosion on these precision surfaces will hasten their demise.

Dirt is the enemy of any moving part and the folding knife is no exception. The simple pocket knife, carried every day to the office or factory, tends to pick up lint, sand or other foreign matter which will find its way down into the blade space. Folding knives require more cleaning and lube attention than the average fixed-blade sheath knife. This is covered more completely in the chapter on knife cleaning and refurbishing, but any folder should be inspected more frequently than other knives for dirt and rust, especially down in the blade nest. This area is ideal for cor-

*One of the lightest weight folders on the market is the Bucklite, below. It has a locking blade and a handle of skeletonized man-made material for less weight.*

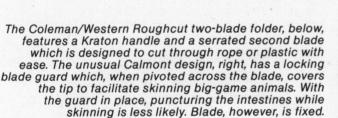

*The Coleman/Western Roughcut two-blade folder, below, features a Kraton handle and a serrated second blade which is designed to cut through rope or plastic with ease. The unusual Calmont design, right, has a locking blade guard which, when pivoted across the blade, covers the tip to facilitate skinning big-game animals. With the guard in place, puncturing the intestines while skinning is less likely. Blade, however, is fixed.*

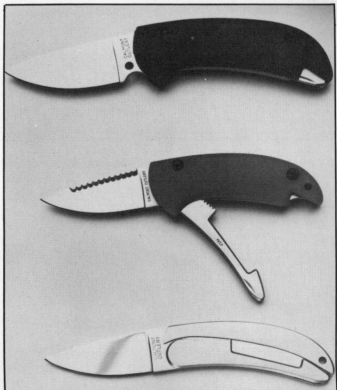

Three folders from Gerber are, from top, Folding Sportsman with locking blade, the finger-grooved Magnum Folding Hunter, also with a lock, and the two-blade Handyman with squared screwdriver tip.

rosion to start: warm, moist and dark. Once underway, such damage can be stopped and even reversed, but it is a lot more work than simply preventing it in the first place.

Other areas of potential trouble are the handle slabs. As we know, folding knife handle slabs may be made of man-made synthetic materials that are impervious to most substances. Or they may be natural materials which can deteriorate with time and neglect. Wood, bone, stag and shell are traditional folding knife handle materials, but all can be damaged and will break down in time. Because the

amount of handle material is so small, handles for folding knives lack the protective mass found on most sheath knife handles. The handle slabs are attached to the knife with pins, rivets or epoxy cement — perhaps a combination of two — but rough use may loosen them.

The folding knife blade usually is not as long as the typical sheath knife blade and presents its own problems when sharpening. Small blades are not called upon to perform many of the heavy-duty jobs of larger blades and should be sharpened with a longer edge. The traditional twenty or

The Case Pro-Lock I is a larger folder which puts the locking/unlocking lever to the front for one-hand operation. The knife measures a full nine inches long when open and has a laminated hardwood handle.

The Case prototype knife design below permits the handle to pivot up out of the way for cleaning inside, sometimes necessary with a fillet knife. Open, it illustrates how the locking spring holds the blade.

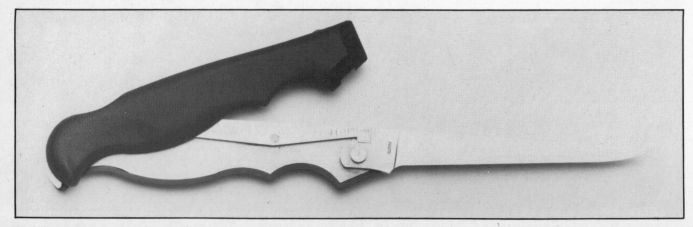

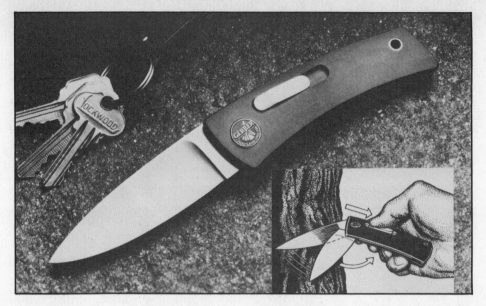

*Gerber's Bolt-Action folder is actually a slide-lock mechanism which operates as shown in inset drawing.*

twenty-two degrees of angle between the blade and the stone for big knives ought to be lowered to about sixteen or seventeen degrees for the pocketknife blade. Because the blade is only a couple of inches long, most knife sharpeners tend to hold the blade at a more shallow angle anyway.

The techniques for sharpening all sorts of knives are covered thoroughly in Chapter 12 and won't be repeated here. But when sharpening folding blades, one must remember to clean out the blade opening carefully when finished. It will do no good to leave residue honing oil, stone and

metal dust grindings collecting down in the slots. The oil will attract more lint and dirt, eventually clogging the blade and locking mechanism. Furthermore, the oil may easily stain through pockets and trousers or items in the purse. A small cotton-tipped toothpick or cotton swab will get down into the recess and clean everything out after sharpening. And don't forget the smallest drop of lubricating oil on the blade pivot pin and the locking mechanism. This treatment will keep your folding knife in good condition for years. You'll be able to pass it along to your grandchildren.

*Al Mar's big SERE folder has the lock placed almost in the middle. A folding knife this large must have a locking blade when engaged in heavy cutting tasks.*

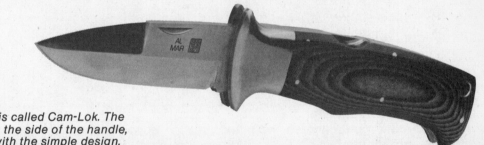

*Camillus' locking mechanism is called Cam-Lok. The operating button is located on the side of the handle, permitting one-hand release with the simple design.*

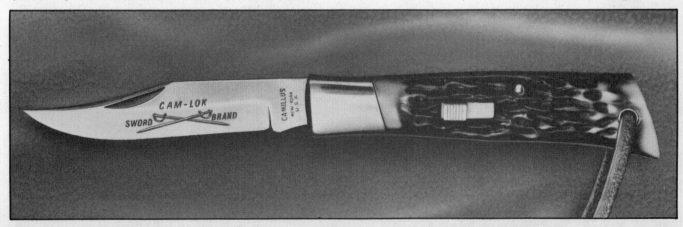

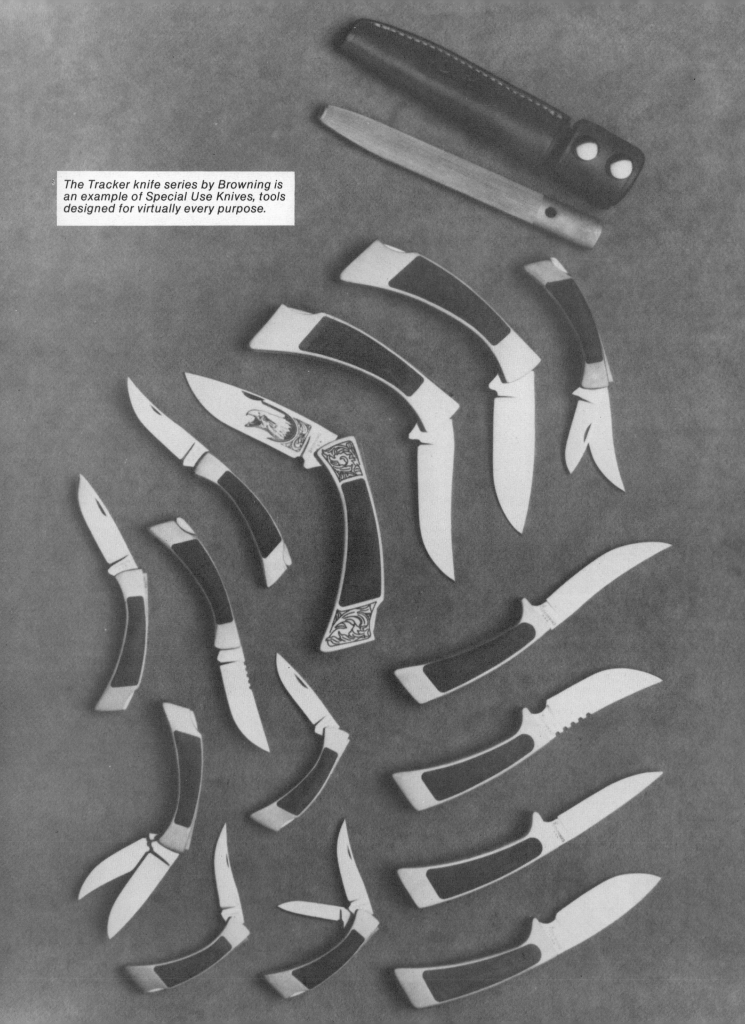

*The Tracker knife series by Browning is an example of Special Use Knives, tools designed for virtually every purpose.*

# Chapter 8

# SPECIAL USE KNIVES

## Some Knife Designs Just Don't Fit Into Any Category Other Than Their Own

THROUGHOUT OUR research for this book, we kept coming across knives that just don't seem to fit into a category with which we are dealing. They were knives designed for specific purposes and, while many of them aren't pretty, they have a practical quality about them we couldn't ignore. We asked Russ Thurman, a self-proclaimed outdoorsman, to scout around for what we call Special Use Knives.

We weren't surprised when the first knife he wanted us to talk about was a knife for horsemen, inspired by an 1865 U.S. Cavalry knife. Thurman spent twenty-one years in the U.S. Marine Corps and some time on horses, although not at the same time.

The Collins Horseman 1865 knife is a real emergency tool. It has a pick for cleaning horses' hooves, a corner bastard file for cutting wire, a flat file and three blades, one for cutting wood or trimming hooves, one locking main blade and one pin blade. It has a regular and a Phillips screwdriver, plus a leather punch, tweezers and needle pick.

Smith & Wesson's ultra-thin shooter's knife is no longer made, but if you can pick one up, you'll have a handy knife and tool. They are still found at swap meets and gun shows. In addition to a stainless steel main blade, the knife has a screwdriver blade sized to fit screws on rifles and pistols.

The Kershaw Model 1075 Twelve-Meter Rigger's knife is designed for those headed to sea under sail. It's a folding knife with a main stainless steel blade of 2¾ inches, a shackle tool, marlin spike and screw turner. For yachtsmen looking for a larger fixed blade, the Working Edition of the Myerchin Offshore System has a 3¾-inch blade with a 6⅝-inch marlin spike, nicely accommodated in a leather sheath.

Once at sea, those who skin dive will need a good knife. While there are many on the market, Thurman found one at a knife show that grabbed his attention. Made of stainless steel, the blade was engraved with inch markings and the handle, of hard plastic, was decorated with *Sea Hawk* in raised letters. The plastic sheath had drainage holes and slots for tying the sheath to the diver's leg.

According to Thurman, he's "slept on a lot of rocks" in his day and that's why he took a quick liking to the camp knife from the Wyoming Knife Corporation. Made in America, its double-curve, hollow-ground stainless steel

The craftsman of this skin diving knife built durability into his tool. The handle and sheath are of tough plastic and the blade is engraved as a ruler.

*At last, a knife for the horseman. The knife is designed after one issued the U.S. Cavalry in 1865. Small enough for the pocket, it's a real emergency tool.*

*The camp knife from The Wyoming Knife Corporation is a handy trout and game bird knife, or its double-curved blade is ideal as a steak and paring knife.*

blade reflects versatility. With an open leather scabbard, it's handy as a trout and game bird knife or as a steak and paring knife.

Hunters looking for big game have quite a selection of Coleman/Western knives to consider. The Model R16 Hunter has a 4⅝-inch stainless steel, hollow-ground drop-point blade and a rubber-like Kraton handle. The finger grooves and checkering provide extra grip when field dressing big game. Coleman/Western's RD1214 Big Game System puts two knives at the hunter's side, held con-

veniently in one sheath. The deep-bellied skinning knife has a 4⅝-inch blade; the drop-point blade is 4¼ inches long. Both have checkered Kraton handles. The Guide Series by Coleman/Western offers blades that are thicker and sturdier than their other knives. The Model C101 Whitetail has a 5½-inch skinner blade with a resin-impregnated hardwood handle which fits snugly in a brown leather pouch sheath. Famed deer expert and wildlife photographer Leonard Lee Rue III helped design the Whitetail. Legendary mountain man Billy Stockton guided

*The ultra-thin shooter's knife by Smith & Wesson isn't made anymore, but it can be found at gun shows and swap meets. The special screwdriver is designed for firearms.*

Coleman/Western through the making of the Elk, Model C103. It has a 4¼-inch drop-point, bevel-ground, stainless steel blade. The double-wide leather sheath also holds a medium-grit India field sharpening stone.

Browning's Tracker knives come in more than a dozen blade sizes, including lock-blade and non-folding models. They have mirror-polished, high-carbon stainless steel blades. Browning's hunting series also features folding and non-folding models. Included are two lightweight fillet knives and the Model 503 Big Game, a three-blade folding knife with dressing, skinning and saw blades.

Calmont's unique Retractable Point Protector gives the outdoorsman more than a knife for dressing game. A part of the handle when the blade is in normal use, the Protector swings out to protect the point while exposing the blade.

It's great for dressing game, but it can also be used for cleaning fish, cutting sails or cutting away clothing in an emergency. There are six models, four have 2¼-inch blades, two have 2½-inch blades. All are made of 440-A stainless steel. Three of the models have back serrated edges for tough cutting jobs. All come with a sheath.

The quality of Buck Knives is reflected in their outdoor series featuring Kraton handles. There are five knives in the series: The WoodsMate, FieldMate, CampMate, PathMate and TrailMate. Blade lengths range from four to 7½ inches. Each comes with a nylon sheath.

The Puma All Sport folding knife by Gutmann has a blade that locks in place for skinning, gutting and other cutting chores. There's a fish scaler on top of the blade, plus a fine bone saw.

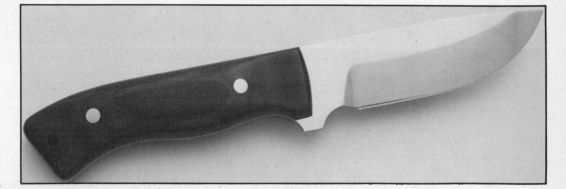

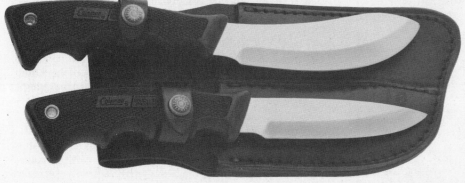

*Coleman/Western offers a full line of quality knives for the big game hunter. The Elk, Model C103 (top) has a 4¼-inch drop-point, bevel-ground blade of stainless steel. The RD1214 Big Game System (left) features a deep-bellied 4⅝-inch skinning blade, and a drop-point blade measuring 4¼ inches. The Whitetail C101 (below) has a 5½-inch blade and a resin-impregnated handle.*

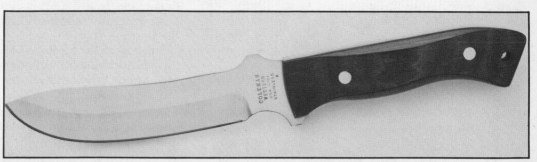

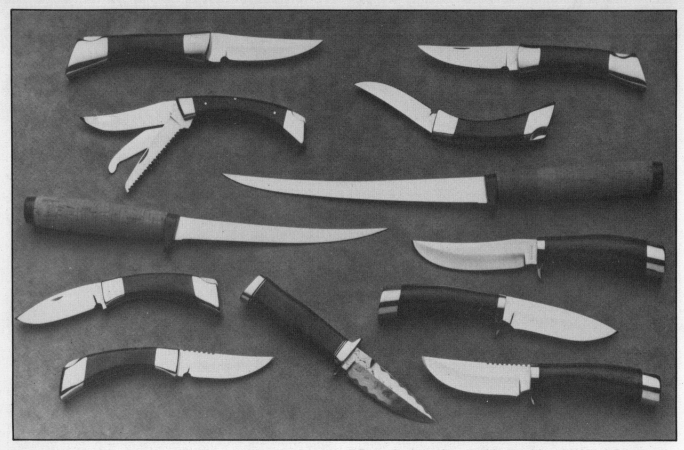

*Browning's craftsmanship is evident in their folding and fixed-blade hunting series. The lightweight fillets have cork handles and sturdy, flexible blades. The Model 503 Big Game Knife has dressing, skinning and sawing blades.*

The famous Colorado Trout Knife is perfect for cleaning fish. The Beaver Teeth Knife Company brought the knife back after it had been discontinued for fifty years. It is rust resistant and fits nicely in a tackle box. There are plenty of other uses for this simple, but extremely useful tool.

The CAM III Guthook Fisherman makes cleaning fish less messy by opening the fish up in fillet position, without damaging the intestines. The 2⅞-inch blade is of vanadium-molybdenum stainless steel and the stainless steel handle is inlaid with ebony wood and brass liners. It's also useful for dressing small game.

We weren't surprised when Thurman came up with a stack of fish fillet knives, since he also claims to be a fisherman. He was particularly impressed with Fiskars' PowerGrip fillet knife. The Fin-Grip handle is a real safety feature and the six-inch high-carbon stainless steel blade is sharpened easily with the pull-through sharpener built into the sheath.

The Fisherman's Solution is billed by Alcas Cutlery as "a total fillet knife system" and we agree. The blade of 440 high-carbon stainless steel can be adjusted between six

*Custom knifemaker Jim Barbee of Texas skins a javelina during hunt. Note Barbee's hold on the skinning knife to give maximum control. The skinning knife continues to be improved with a wide number of models available.*

The Kraton handles on these Buck knives provide a sure grip and they've proven extremely popular. The models, with blade lengths from four to 7½ inches, include the CampMate, PathMate, TrailMate, WoodMate and FieldMate.

and nine inches or removed for cleaning by use of a Cam-Lock on the side of the handle. The sheath also has some unique features. It opens to become a gripper for dressing fish or removing hooks and it has a sharpening stone for honing blades and fish hooks, plus a line cutter.

Case Cutlery has eighty years of quality behind their three Case basic fillet knives. Of surgical steel with blades of four, six and nine inches, the knives have synthetic handles. Leather sheaths are lined with plastic to protect both knife and sheath.

Buck Knives' fillet series includes three knives: the OceanMate with a nine-inch blade, the LakeMate with 6½-inch blade and the StreamMate with a 4½-inch blade. The textured Kraton hand-fitted handles have a tacky feel to them, adding greatly to safe gripping.

A comfortable, sure-grip design also is built into Brunton/Lakota's KingFisher fillet knives. You have your choice of blade lengths of four, seven and eleven inches.

Case Cutlery's folding fillet, in addition to being easy to carry in a tackle box, has a handle that snaps open for thorough cleaning. To prevent rust and corrosion, the inside of the knife is stainless steel.

The Clearwater fillet knives by Kershaw include the Folding Angler with a 5½-inch blade, and five fixed-blade models with blades from 6½ to nine inches. Kershaw also has a dandy fishing tool with scissors for line cutting and

Cleaning fish is a lot less messy with the CAM III Guthook Fisherman (above). It has a 2⅞-inch blade and stainless steel handle with inlaid ebony wood and brass. The Puma All Sport knife (below) has a fish scaler and a fine bone saw.

The Colorado Trout Knife (below) is a useful tool that isn't burdened with a lot of gadgets. It's perfect for cleaning fish, and fits easily in a tackle box. We have the Beaver Teeth Knife Company to thank for again making the knife.

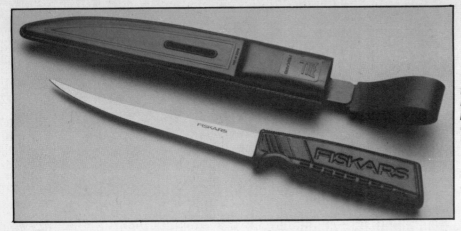

When it's time to put an extra edge on the PowerGrip fillet knife, you only have to look as far as the sheath. The pull-through sharpener is a handy idea. Fiskars also provides extra control of the six-inch blade with Fin-Grip handle.

W.R. Case & Sons Cutlery Company has created three basic fillet knives. The blades of four, six and nine inches are of surgical steel. Synthetic handles are designed for added comfort and a sure grip. Each has a leather sheath.

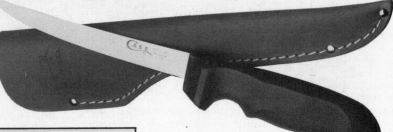

Alcas Cutlery has a unique filleting tool in The Fisherman's Solution. The stainless steel blade adjusts from six to nine inches, and the sheath opens to become a gripper for cleaning fish. The sheath also has a sharpening stone.

The folding fillet by Case Cutlery ends the problem of how to thoroughly clean a fillet knife after dressing fish for an hour. The knife easily snaps open for cleaning. The inside is made of stainless steel to prevent corrosion.

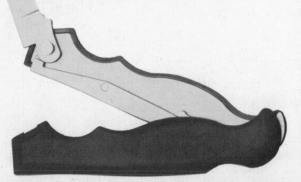

crimping split shot, plus a hook disgorger. Their Skeeter scissors are designed especially for the fisherman who makes his own flies.

If you need a really long fillet blade, the Model 9612 by Coleman/Western will meet your needs. It has a twelve-inch 440-A stainless steel blade with a Kraton handle for a sure, cushioned grip. Coleman/Western's six fillets include the Model 561, a folding fillet with a 5⅜-inch blade and reinforced Valox checkered handle.

For those "tough situations" Thurman tells us he's always getting into, he selected some outdoor tools with cutting power. The Roughcuts from Coleman/Western come in three folding-blade models. The 952 and 954 have two blades, one spear point and the other serrated for tough cutting jobs. For heavy-duty cutting, it would be hard to beat the 955 RoughCut. One "blade" is a real five-inch saw for cutting small branches or the heaviest big game during dressing. The second blade has a 2½-inch straight cutting edge, backed by a two-inch serrated tooth edge. The grooved handles of Valox have a slight palm swell for a sure grip.

An all-around camp tool that's often overlooked is the

Coleman/Western offers six fillet knives. The Model W769 has a durable resin-impregnated hardwood handle. The nine-inch blade is stainless steel, protected by leather sleeve.

Kershaw has five fixed-blade and one folding-blade in its Clearwater edition. The folding fillet has a 5½-inch blade and the fixed blades range from 6½ to nine inches.

The LakeMate with its 6½-inch blade is one of the three Kraton handle fillets offered by Buck Knives. OceanMate has a nine-inch blade and the StreamMate has a 4½-inch blade.

The folding fillet by Coleman/Western measures seven inches when closed. Its stainless steel blade is 5⅝ inches long. The handle of reinforced Valox is checkered for a firm grip.

There are three fixed blade fillet knives in the KingFisher series offered by Brunton/Lakota. The blade lengths are four, seven and eleven inches, all with sure-grip handles.

The 955 Roughcut by Coleman/Western is an ideal outdoor tool. It has a five-inch saw and cutting/serrated edge.

axe. Coleman/Western's R10 belt axe is eleven inches long with a 2¾-inch cutting edge and a finger-grooved Kraton handle. The W6610 axe-knife combination by Coleman/Western fills many outdoor needs. This axe also has a 2¾-inch cutting edge with an overall length of eleven inches. The fixed-blade knife has a 4½-inch blade. Both have resin-impregnated matched hardwood handles and are carried in a combination leather sheath.

Gutmann's Woods Man camping and hunting axe also is designed for camp chores and dressing game. The stainless steel one-piece head and shaft are riveted to the handle which features a finger-grip design. The multi-purpose folding saw by Gutmann is carried easily and ready for serious cutting.

Buck Knives' tradition of versatility is reflected in their hunter's axe, Model 106, which has a 2½-inch cutting head with an impregnated birch handle. Buck's Model 15400 SawBuck is a true multi-purpose field saw. Two-sided, one edge is for fine-tooth cutting, the other for jobs needing coarse teeth. The 10¼-inch blade is controlled easily by an ideally shaped Kraton handle. It's well protected in a saddle leather sheath.

For a pocket-size saw, the lightweight version by Buck Spin carries a lot of cutting power. Its blade is seven inches long, carried in a nylon sheath or optional nylon holster.

Including combination knives in this chapter delighted Thurman. He went about digging up several he felt worth mentioning only to be disappointed that the famed Swiss Army Knife was being featured in another chapter. However, he spoke highly of Ka-Bar's Hobo knife. While other

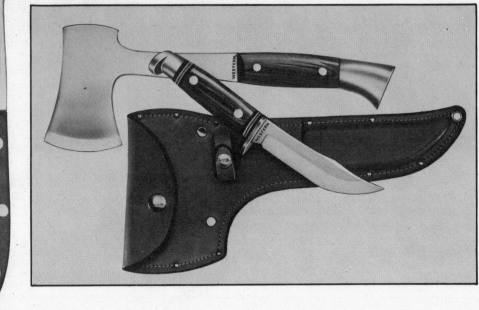

The combination axe and knife (below) by Coleman/Western is a superb idea and a nice addition to an outdoorsman's gear.

Gutmann's Explorer axe (left) is useful for many camp chores, plus the heavy-duty cutting in dressing game.

A finger-grooved Kraton handle ensures firm grip for the Coleman/Western R10 axe (right). It has a 2¾-inch edge.

knives have knife, fork and spoon combinations, the Hobo conveniently snaps apart so you don't poke yourself in the eye with the spoon while using the fork. It snaps back together easily and is carried in a nylon pouch.

For a multi-purpose outdoor/kitchen knife set it would be hard to beat Kershaw's Deluxe Blade Trader. Six blades are interchangeable on a rosewood handle. All the blades measure 7¾ inches and include a frozen food blade, bread slicing blade, carving blade, cook's blade, saw blade and boning blade. The handle and blades are stored in a zippered vinyl case. Other Kershaw multi-purpose tools include the Do It All Blade Trader which includes a fillet slicing blade, crosscut saw and clip-point boning/hunting blade.

Kershaw also makes a handy ambidextrous sportsman's shears which measures 8½ inches overall. Fiskar's Sportsmen's Scissors Collection includes the game and fish shears, seven inches long; the tackle box snip, five inches and the sports scissors, four inches.

The Leatherman Tool and Mini Tool pack a pocketful of ingenuity. The big brother has twelve tools, including two pliers and four screwdrivers. The Mini has nine tools and measures only 2⅝ inches. Both are made of stainless steel.

Never wanting to be without a knife, Russ Thurman gathered a number of what he calls Gentleman's Knives, which can even be carried into the boardroom. Gutmann's Explorer LTD Gentleman's pocketknives include five

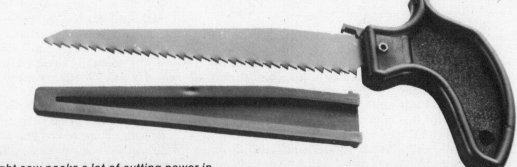

Buck Spin's lightweight saw packs a lot of cutting power in a pocket-size tool. The sturdy blade is seven inches long.

*Kershaw's Deluxe Blade Trader is an all-in-one outdoor and kitchen knife outfit.*

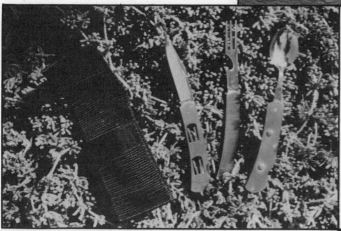

*Ka-Bar's Hobo knife conveniently snaps apart for a fine feast. Snapped together, it's carried in a nylon pouch.*

*There are twelve tools in the Leatherman Tool and nine in the Mini Tool. Folded, the Mini measures only 2⅝ inches.*

models, one a combination money clip, pen blade, nail file and scissors. Gerber and Al Mar also have money clip knives. In addition to the Escort money clip knife, Gerber's excellent Escort smoker's knife features a round tip blade for scraping a pipe bowl, and their Escort Gentleman's knife has scissors, stainless blade and nail file.

Al Mar and Tekna have added an edge to key rings with their miniature blades that are tucked safely away in sheaths attached to key rings.

Al Mar, Gerber and CAM III have given belt buckles an edge, too. Gerber's Touche and Al Mar's buckle knife are removed easily from the rest of the buckle which acts as a carrier. Both are single-blade knives. CAM III's utility belt buckle has a single knife blade, can opener and bottle opener folded inside.

Rigid Knives puts an edge in your boot. Their Classic boot knives, the Amigo and Vaquero, are crafted in the tradition of survival knives. They both have Micarta handles, 440 stainless surgical steel and leather boot sheaths. Their overall lengths are eight inches with a 3¾-inch blade.

And for true elegance, it would be hard to beat Jim Sornberger's custom-made miniature knives. Measuring two to 4½ inches, each reflects the work of a skilled craftsman. That same quality is the trademark of Iisakki Jarven-

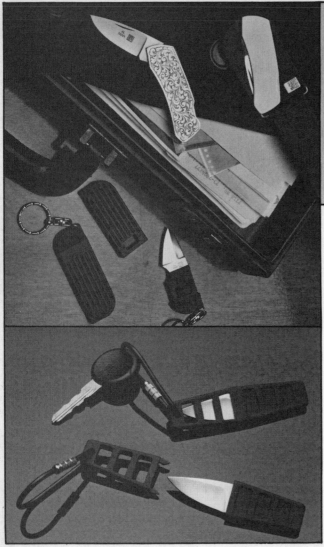

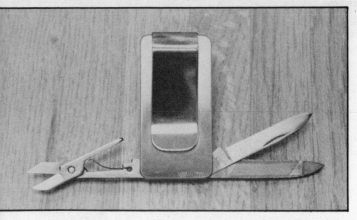

*Al Mar has added an edge (left) to its belt buckle and key ring, plus given an elegant knife to gentlemen. The Al Mar money clip (above) has a nail file and scissors.*

*Tekna has neatly placed a knife blade in a key-ring holder.*

paa, Ltd., the oldest and most famous of the Kauhva knife producers. Their Puukko, the all-purpose tool and weapon of the Finnish people, is brought to America by Ken's Finn Knives of Michigan.

Harry K. McEvoy has been making professional throwing knives since 1949. His Tru-Balance knives are famous for balance and workmanship. These are more than sport throwing knives. Several of his models are excellent all-purpose knives that can be used for throwing, hunting, camping, chopping and survival situations.

In a category Thurman calls, "Make my day, punk," is the All Weather Protection sword umbrella by Atlanta Cutlery. The high-quality nylon umbrella has a quick-draw ten-inch stainless steel blade hidden in its telescoping shaft. The precision ground, tapered point is sharp enough, Atlanta Cutlery says, to drive through a steel helmet. There's a double-lock system to prevent accidental openings.

*Gerber's Escort Gentleman's knives include a multi-purpose knife, two-blade money clip and smoker's knife.*

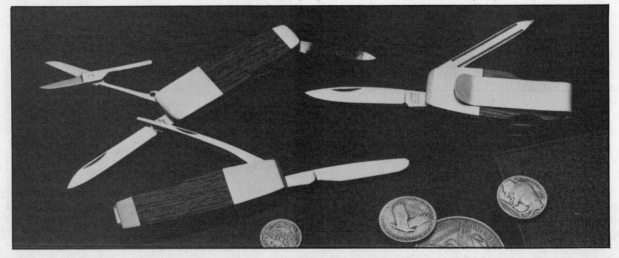

*Harry K. McEvoy's Tru-Balance knives, in addition to being used for throwing, are useful as all-purpose outdoor tools.*

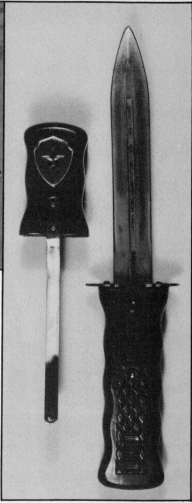

*The Chinese Armed Police Knife measures only 6½ inches with sheath, but it sports a 5½-inch double-edged blade.*

*The Amigo and Vaquero by Rigid are classic boot knives.*

It would seem the police in China also have special knives to deal with, let's say, certain undesirables. The Chinese Armed Police Knife, discovered by Bill Adams of Atlanta Cutlery during a visit to China, has a unique retractable blade. The sheath is more of a point protector with a swiveling, metal belt loop. To draw the knife, the handle, which hangs down, is grasped in such a way as to depress the sheath lock catch. In one movement, the blade is drawn out, revealing a 5½-inch blade that automatically locks in place. With practice, the action can be quite fast. To retract, the blade is lined up with the blade extension spring, the blade release catch is depressed and the blade is pushed back into the sheath. Once together, the entire knife measures only 6½ inches long. Thurman admits it's more of a novelty knife, but he seemed delighted we included it in this chapter on special use knives.

*The Fiskars' Sportsmen's Scissors Collection features the game and fish shears, tackle box snip and sports scissors.*

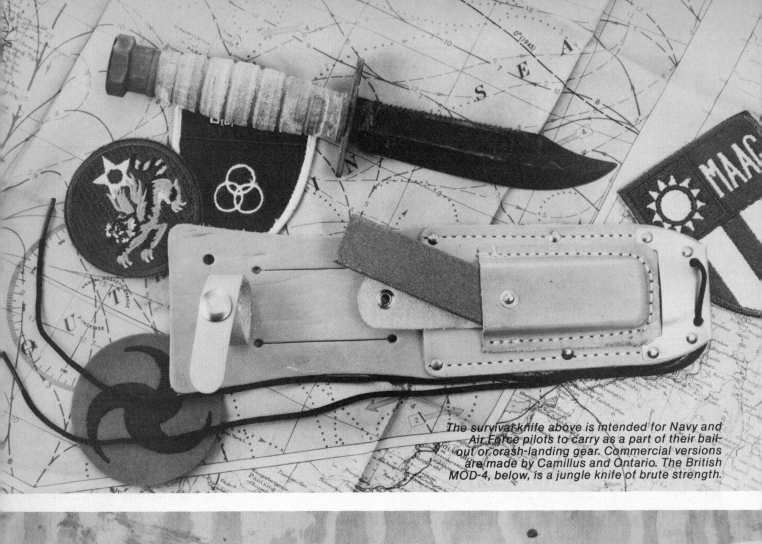

The survival knife above is intended for Navy and Air Force pilots to carry as a part of their bail-out or crash-landing gear. Commercial versions are made by Camillus and Ontario. The British MOD-4, below, is a jungle knife of brute strength.

# Chapter 9

# MADE FOR MAYHEM

## An Endless Supply Of Military And Combat Knives Has Come On The Modern Scene

THIS CHAPTER will try to throw a pretty big loop. It is going to address military knives of the surplus type in all their myriad varieties including combat, survival, parachute and utility types. In addition, it will cover military combat knives that are of actual issue patterns but are from new commercial sources rather than military surplus. Finally, this chapter will address combat type knives that are not issued by any military service, but are commercially available for private purchase by soldiers and civilians alike.

With a deadline upon us and recognizing the required breadth of this chapter, we enlisted the help of Chuck Karwan to research much of the information that follows.

Karwan is a respected authority in his own right. A combat officer in Vietnam as a member of Special Forces, he had more than his share of experience with knives designed for warfare. As a collector of edged weapons, we are lucky to be able to draw upon his expertise for this segment.

"While I spent a large part of my life in the military, my personal interest in military and particularly military combat knives goes back to my childhood in the post-WWII era," Karwan recalls. "In those days, every town had one or more Army & Navy Surplus Store. They had *real* military surplus and the prices were in keeping with a lad's paper route income.

"Some of the military knife bargains I recall include, Navy Mk1 knives for $3, Navy Mk2 knives for $5 (Ka-

Bars to you Marines), Navybolos for $4, M1917 Army bolos for $5, utility pocketknives for $2 and original British-issue Fairbairn-Sykes Commando knives for $6. Please note that these prices were for excellent to new specimens complete with original scabbards!

"Sadly, those days are long gone, but I still remember taking to the woods with one or more surplus store treasure and pretending I was in combat in the South Pacific. My childhood interest in the military blade was nurtured by attending West Point, airborne and Ranger training, service in Vietnam and, finally, training and service in U.S. Army Special Forces. Military knives became tools of my trade and my interest in them and their use never slackened."

There is, for many of us, a certain primeval romantic appeal to edged weapons in general, but more so for the knife because of its personal nature. Combat veterans in particular are prone to covet blades that were close companions during memorable service, but interest in the military blade is hardly restricted to veterans; it seems almost universal in men. Military knives, as compared to other varieties, have the additional appeal of historical association and the fact that, with rare exception, they are well-made practical tools and weapons.

Current interest in knives — particularly U.S. military knives — appears stronger than ever, but the once-abundant surplus sources have largely dried up. Once in a great

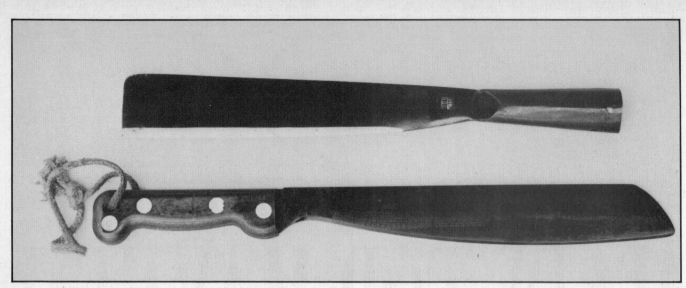

*Military machetes, above, make interesting souvenirs of war. At top is a Vietnam-era Chinese machete, captured in number by Karwan's battalion. The lower is a British pattern used by Aussie troops in Vietnam. The Cattaraugus 225 Q, left, in right photo and Case 337 Q commando knives saw WWII action in the Pacific.*

while, some dealer will come up with a case or two of something interesting, but the hunt is largely for single specimens at gun shops, military collector shows, gun shows, knife shows, flea markets and even yard sales. All can be excellent sources. As the World War II veterans are growing elderly, or at least near retirement age, more and more WWII military items, including knives, are starting to come out of the woodwork.

Prices on original military knives vary from the ridiculous to the sublime. "A couple weeks ago, I picked up a WWII Cattaraugus 225 Q 'Commando' knife in nice shape with scabbard at a gun show for a measly $5. Undoubtedly it was a bargain, but comparable specimens rarely bring over $25 or so. The Cattaraugus 225 Q is a good example of an all too commonly underappreciated and overlooked military knife," Karwan reports. "Hundreds of thousands were produced during WWII and issued to our combat forces, particularly the Marines. They were even issued to the elite Raider Battalions and saw considerable use when the fighting was the hardest.

"In my opinion, it was the most practical and sturdy of the WWII-issue combat knives, yet they receive little attention. This is probably because the Navy and Marines subsequently standardized on the Mk2 (Ka-Bar) model and the fact that the 225 Q has no military markings and is consequently often overlooked.

"The other extreme is a knife I sold to a friend last year for $1200. It was a near-mint Case V-42 stiletto of the design issued in WWII to the elite First Special Service Force (FSSF) nicknamed the Devil's Brigade. The V-42 was a high-quality knife and was reportedly well liked by troops in the FSSF. It was later adopted as the centerpiece in the Special Forces crest.

"Of all the WWII U.S. military knives, the V-42 seems to bring the most money. My friend was elated with the $1200 price I gave him, because it was well under the market value. Some have changed hands for as high as $2000!"

Other expensive military knives are the WWII Marine Corps stiletto, the Carlson's Raiders Gung Ho knife, OSS Smatchets and escape knives, Special Forces SOG knives of the Vietnam era and any of the Nineteenth Century U.S. military knives like the Hicks and the M1849 Ames. You can get good military knives for as low as $5 or you can spend thousands of dollars. It is up to you and your pocketbook.

There are so many categories and sub-categories of military knives one can take any number of interesting approaches to acquisition. One way is affiliation to a service. For instance, the U.S. Navy has issued a surprising number of knives over the years. In WWII, many thousands of Mark 1 knives were issued. There were at least ten different makers and a myriad variations and sub-variations. All had blades of about 5⅛ inches and were little more than hunting knives of the era. Other than blade length no two seem to be the same. Of those that survived the war, most were used up as utility and hunting knives in the post war "surplus" era.

The Navy's next knife, the Mark 2, is the more significant. This larger, seven-inch-bladed knife, saw wide issue throughout the Navy until recently, when it began to be replaced by the Mark 3.

Shortly after its adoption by the Navy, the Mark 2 was also adopted by the Marines as the Fighting Utility Knife. It has been produced by Pal, Conetta, Robeson, Utica and still is being produced by the Camillus, Ka-Bar and Ontario knife companies.

"It is a superb combination field and combat knife that has served its country's military forces well. It was probably the most common personally purchased knife in the hands of troops in Vietnam. This is the knife called 'the Ka-Bar' by former and current Marines as a generic term for the breed, regardless of who manufactured it," Karwan explains. "Variations in markings and manufacturer are numerous. The knife that is supposed to replace it, the Mark 3, is a sorry substitute. Its one redeeming feature is its stainless steel and moisture resistant construction. The blade is a direct copy of the Soviet AKM bayonet blade, of all things. They would have been a lot better off copying the Mk2! Such is progress."

The U.S. Army issued a number of interesting knives over the years. One of the most striking is the WWI Mark 1 trench knife that features a dagger-style blade combined with brass knuckles. It made for a vicious weapon in a close encounter of the worst kind. When WWII broke out, the only combat knife on the Army books was the Mark 1. Many were dragged out and issued for the second go-around. Airborne units, in particular, seem to have received many.

"While it was an awesome weapon, it wasn't particularly practical and its construction used up a lot of brass that could have been better used making cartridges," Karwan opines.

Thus a new Army combat knife was developed and called the M3. It was a good weapon and a pretty fair field knife that was popular with the troops. It was also to be the last standard combat knife of the Army. Though over 2.5 million were made, they are far from common for some reason. When the Army adopted a series of bayonets, M4 through M7, each had the same blade as the M3, so the Army never again thought it necessary to issue its troops combat knives.

"Soldiers needed and wanted combat knives, regardless of what the Army said or supplied. Probably no other factor than the U.S. Army's failure to issue combat and field knives from late WWII to the present has had such a strong effect on the custom and commercial combat knife business," Karwan feels.

While the Army stopped issuing combat knives on a routine basis in late WWII, certain elite units still got knives from time to time. The previously mentioned Case V-42 issued to the First Special Service Force is a good example. During the Vietnam War, there was a special procurement of knives for Special Forces. It is commonly called the SOG knife after the headquarters that conducted special operations in Vietnam under the pseudonym of

*Two of the three military combat knives are well known and collected. The Cattaraugus 225 Q saw service in the Pacific, but is not as sought after as the Navy Mark 2, center, or the Army M3, right.*

*Right: Not all the military knives found are the real thing. What appears to be a WWI French trench knife is a fake! Below: Pilot bail-out kits in 1942 included folding and non-folding machetes by Case, Imperial, Camillus and Cattaraugus.*

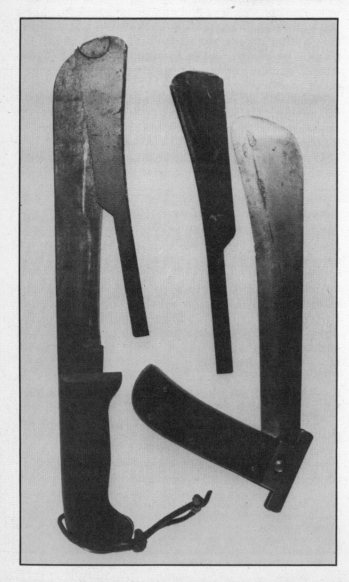

Studies and Observations Group (SOG). There was a requirement for sterile equipment for certain sensitive cross-border operations — sterile meaning unidentifiable as to country of origin.

"Unmarked knives along the lines of a six-inch Randall number 1 modified Bowie fighting knife were purchased in Japan," Karwan recalls. "There are a lot of misconceptions about these knives. Some will be found with the Special Forces crest; engraved on the blade with the inscription *5th SPECIAL FORCES GROUP (Abn) VIETNAM.* Collectors often pay a large premium for such knives.

"Ironically, those were *not* issue combat knives. They were purchased from Japan by the Special Force mess associations and given away as mementoes to SF NCOs when they rotated home. The same holds true for the similarly marked chrome-plated Fairburn-type stiletto that is occasionally encountered.

"Real SOG knives are unmarked or only serial numbered, though some had inscriptions engraved on later. SOG knives vary considerably from batch to batch as to blade shape. Crossguards are of iron, brass or aluminum in several different shapes. Spacers in the handle are both black and white and blades are finished in several different shades of blue as well as brown. Quality borders on crude for most batches. It is an area ripe for fakery, so be careful.

"Another special unit issue knife was supplied to U.S. airborne troops, beginning in 1940, and continued into the Sixties. While it was hardly a combat knife, the M2 Paratrooper knife was specifically intended for the airborne mission. A number of minor variations were manufactured by Schrade Cutlery Co., George Schade and Colonial.

"The knife was a switch blade (push button) design with a blade slightly over three inches, black plastic handle scales and a lanyard ring. It was intended that a parachutist who was entangled, particularly in a water or tree landing, could cut his way out. The idea behind using a push-button knife was that it could be opened with one hand should the other be injured or occupied at the time.

"The German army also issued and still issues to its parachutists a knife that can be opened with one hand. Rather than a push-button spring-bladed knife, theirs is a gravity knife. These operate by pointing down and throwing a lever. The blade drops out and locks into place. To put it back in, one only needs to point it up and repeat the process."

Original Nazi airborne examples of WWII vintage are highly coveted collector items, many of which still probably lie in footlockers across the country as war souvenirs.

The current West German army-issue version — which has a stainless steel blade and metal parts and an olive drab green plastic handle — is imported currently by Hansen & Hansen. It is considered a far better knife than the WWII version.

Even the U.S. Air Force got into the parachute knife act by issuing to pilots, beginning about 1958, a switch blade quite similar to the Army M2. Called the MC-1 Survival and Parachute knife, it differs from the M2 by having bright orange handle scales, the lanyard loop on the blade

Military kukries come in all sizes. Clockwise from left: Assam Rifles kukri, British Gurkha Regiment kukri, Border Patrol Scouts kukri, huge ceremonial kukri, standard military issue in Indian regiments, smaller officer's kukri; all from Atlanta Cutlery.

hinge end and a folding shroud line cutting hook on the end opposite the blade. These were made by Schrade and Camillus. Contrary to popular belief, federal laws do not prohibit the possession of switch blade and gravity knives, except on federal property. However, local laws may have such prohibitions.

"Besides the MC-1, the Air Force and Naval air arm have issued a number of other interesting knives over the years to their pilots and air crews," Karwan's research shows. One of the more useful was a large folding knife put in Navy and later Air Force survival kits. "It has a 4⅝-inch blade that locks open and a five-inch saw blade that really works. Some have lanyard loops and some do not. They were made by Colonial and United Machine Tool."

Another pilot's survival knife is the fixed-blade one designed by the Navy Weapons Bureau with the help of the Marble Arms Corporation in 1957. Its original configuration sported a six-inch blade with a clipped point and a saw back. The leather scabbard has a pocket for a sharpening stone. The six-inch version was made by Marble and by Camillus. In 1962, the blade was shortened to five inches and this is the type that is standard in the Air Force and Navy to this day. They have been made by Milpar and Utica and are still being made by Camillus and Ontario. Another "survival" knife that was military issue to pilots in some bail-out kits was a small, three-bladed stockman's knife. They were identical to the commercial variety, though some are marked *PROPERTY OF U.S. GOVT* on the blades. Manufacturers were Ulster, Imperial, Kutmaster and Camillus.

"Many of the other military knives available are folders also. All U.S. services have at one time or another issued a pocket utility knife like the typical Boy Scout knife, with a spear point blade, a can opener, a combination bottle opener and screwdriver, plus a punch or small knife blade. Depending on vintage, they have carbon steel or stainless steel blades and handle scales of bone, plastic or stainless steel. Practically every maker made one at one time or another and Camillus still makes the all stainless variety. They have a wide variety of markings with a plain *U.S.* being the most common. They are still an issue item in the Army and probably other services as well.

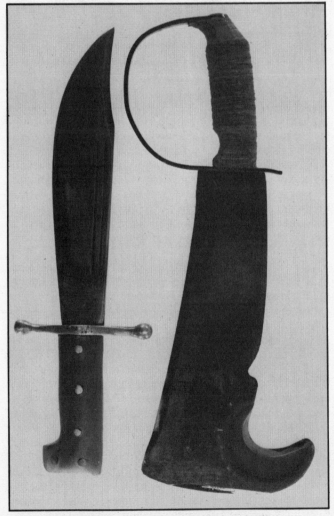

At left is a V-44 survival knife used in tropical areas from 1934 to 1942. The survival axe Type IV is slightly shortened version of WWII Woodsman's Pal. This one was carried on aircraft in Vietnam.

The West Germany Army Kampfmesser (combat knife),
below, is a sturdy, useful stainless steel tool.
At right, the German Army model compares with
the British issue MOD4 jungle survival knife.

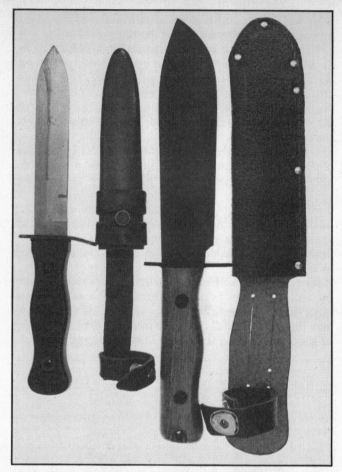

"The other most commonly encountered military folder is the TL-29 which is a lineman, signalman or electrician's knife with a locking screwdriver blade and a spear point main blade. Issued by all services — but particularly the Army — variations in markings, manufacturers and handle material run into the dozens. There are myriad other military folding knives, including square-pointed sailor's knives, some with marlin spikes and some without; two-blade utility knives; Medical Corps folders and even a folding fishing knife. Folding military knives, both U.S. and foreign, are a huge area with good condition specimens often tough to find because most got used up."

Large machetes, bolos and the like are issued by the United States and many foreign militaries. Most commonly seen are U.S. and British Commonwealth varieties. While most were intended to be just tools, some, like the U.S. M1917 bolo, also were superb weapons.

"One machete in my collecton is of Chinese manufacture and was one of a large group captured by my battalion of the 1st Cavalry Division during an incursion into Cambodia," Karwan reports.

"They proved so popular with the troops that our battalion supply people kept several cases. Their shorter and heavier hand-forged blades made them far handier and efficient than the U.S. issue. For nearly a year after that, a request for a machete in my battalion would get you issued a *Chinese* machete. This is the only instance to my knowledge where regular U.S. troops were issued Communist Chinese manufactured equipment!"

Far more interesting than machetes are the Gurkha kukries. The Gurkhas are people from the Himalayan mountain country of Nepal whose major export is mercenary troops for the British and Indian armies. Their fighting prowess is legendary. After trying to fight them, the British decided to hire them instead! The traditional combat knife of the Gurkha is a knife with a nine to twelve-inch blade that is distinctively wider and curved downward in the front. It is a formidable chopping, slashing and even stabbing weapon.

An example of Gurkha fighting prowess and ability with the kukri is the WWII incident involving Lal Bahader Thapa, an officer in the 2nd Gurkhas. When faced with a German patrol, he killed five with his Webley revolver in his right hand and three with his kukri in his left hand. "I suspect he was kidded by his comrades for wasting ammunition!"

It is a little known fact that troops in the elite American Provisional Unit 5307, better known as Merrill's Marauders, often carried and used kukris during their distinguished action in Burma in WWII.

The miliary kukries came in many varieties, depending on the particular Gurkha unit that carried it and the period of manufacture.

"For a long time, about all that was ever encountered in the way of kukries was tourist souvenir junk. The real thing can now be purchased from Atlanta Cutlery. They have four different real military kukri variations, as well as an officer kukri and a ceremonial monster-sized version.

"I can personally attest that Atlanta Cutlery is offering the real thing, because a former Special Forces buddy, who had been working with troops from the British Gurkha regiment, sent me one of their issue kukries. It is virtually identical to the one Atlanta Cutlery sells as a British Gurkha Regiment kukri right down to the markings."

Of other interesting foreign military knives, one of the most distinctive is the Chilean corvo. There are two versions: the standard military type, which is the most practi-

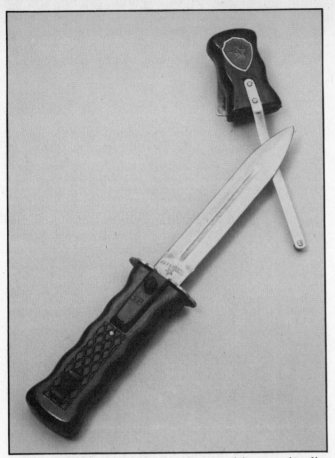

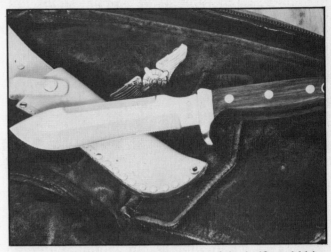

From opposite ends of the world: two knives, two philosophies. The Chinese retracting-blade police dagger, left, and the German Air Force utility knife approach combat issue with different views.

cal by our standards, and another used by certain elite units which features a more curved and upswept blade tip. Both are double edged and of excellent robust construction. "The Chilean military has developed a unique fighting style with these which entails using them almost like a sharpened hook. The exaggerated curve comes from a Chilean mining tool that was converted to weapon use in the Nineteenth Century. Unfortunately, I can not report a commercial source for these knives."

Even more unique are the People's Republic of China police daggers that have become available recently through Keng's and Atlanta Cutlery. These compact knives have their blades telescoped partially into the handle when they are sheathed. In the carrying mode it is only 6½ inches long. To extend it, one only has to grasp the handle, push a button and pull. The 5⅜-inch blade is extended automatically and locked in the outward position, giving an overall length of 9½ inches. "It is an ingenious design that allows the carrying of a relatively large knife in a small package while still being lightning quick to put into action."

Probably the most commonly encountered foreign combat knife is the British Fairbairn-Sykes (F-S) Commando knife. Besides being issued to British forces, many were purchased by U.S. and other allied troops in WWII. There are dozens of manufacturers and variations, but particuarly the early models can get rather pricey.

"It is just a guess, but I suspect that more Axis soldiers died on the points of F-S Commando knives than all other combat knives combined. It is a poor utility tool at best, but an outstanding killing weapon.

"Colonel Rex Applegate, of WWII OSS fame, told me

that Captain Skyes, the co-designer of the knife, told him he and Fairbairn had taken the design from the medieval daggers they had examined in the Tower of London museum. The F-S is still in production for the British Army. Fortunately, contact overruns, complete with military markings, are sold here by a number of importers and dealers. The first F-S Commando knives were made by the Wilkinson Sword Company and the basic design owes much to the efforts of that company," according to Karwan.

Wilkinson also collaborated on the development of another British military knife, the Ministry of Defense (MOD) jungle survival knife. Like the F-S knife, the MOD survival knife has been produced by a number of contractors with overruns occasionally making it to the U.S. market.

"It is a big brute of a knife with a seven-inch blade, 7/32-inch thick, having a rather blunt drop point. It has a full tang handle with simple wood slab scales. The scabbard is often flimsy-thin leather. These are issued to all the British services. Army units assigned to tropical areas use them as a jungle knife."

One last English military knife on the market is another survival knife of sorts. It is a four-inch-bladed knife designed to be carried on the pilot's or aircrew's person with its sheath attached to the uniform. The knife is locked into its scabbard by levers in the handle that must be squeezed to withdraw it. The British air crew emergency knife is designed to serve the purpose of the previously mentioned USAF MC-1 pilot's knife as an aid to crewmen in cutting themselves free from their parachutes.

Another foreign country that has a wide selection of military knives that can be procured commercially is West Germany. Already mentioned is the West German parachute knife imported by Hansen & Hansen. Another is the *Bundeswehr* (Army) *Kampfmesser* (combat knife). These have been standard in the West German army for many years and are historically significant, because they probably were the first stainless steel combat knives ever adopted by any army. The knife has a 5⅝-inch single-edged blade with a spear point and an OD green plastic handle. The scabbard is one piece aluminum with a friction re-

Two knives which have similiar appearances and uses are the highly collectible V-42 stiletto used by First Special Forces, on top, and the British Fairbairn-Sykes commando knife, below. At right is the Australian Navy diver's German-made knife.

point main blade, a combination saw, can opener, bottle opener and screwdriver blade (believe it or not, they all work), a punch, and the ever necessary cork screw. I have seen these made by Victorinox of Switzerland, of German manufacture, and by an Italian manufacturer on contract for Germany. The scales are OD green plastic and genuine contract overruns have the Bundeswehr marking. This is an excellent folding utility knife.

There are a few other notable military knives around on the market from still other foreign countries. One of the most wicked looking is the standard combat knife of the Spanish army. These are made by Aitor, one of Spain's largest and best cutlery manufacturers. It has a 7⅛-inch blade of 440B stainless steel that is wider in the front than the rear. "The back of the blade has three inches of double-cut saw teeth that really work. The handle is well shaped and made from black polyamide plastic with a checkered

tainer. A retaining strap on the leather belt frog attaches to the scabbard. They have been made by a large number of German cutlery firms and at least one Italian contractor. Contract overruns often make it to the U.S. market.

"These are excellent field knives. Back in my days in the 10th Special Forces, several of us were fond of the German Kampfmesser for parachute jumps, because there was no danger of the knife poking through the solid aluminum scabbard as can happen with leather scabbards on a bad impact. The blade on mine takes and holds an excellent edge, too."

The other two German military knives on the market are quite similar to each other. The first, the German Air Force knife, is a dead ringer for the Puma Whitehunter. It is a practical and sturdy knife with full-tang construction, wood handle scales and a six-inch high-carbon stainless steel blade. The blade has a dropped point with a good amount of belly and features a sharpened section on the blade's spine for hacking.

The other is allegedly standard with the German Border Police, a quasi-military unit. It has the same blade except the spine of the blade has double-cut saw teeth instead of being sharpened and the handle is a moulded rubber substance. "You couldn't ask for a better or more practical military field knife."

"Another available military knife is not from the German military, though it is made in Germany. It's the Australian navy diver's knife. It has a 6¼-inch heavy stainless steel blade with a cast alloy handle. The back of the blade has double-cut saw teeth and the edge on the front 2¼ inches is finely serrated to aid in cutting lines. The only retail source I know of for the last three knives mentioned is Atlanta Cutlery," Karwan tells us.

One last German army knife you may encounter for sale occasionally is a folding utility knife. It is basically the same as the Victorinox Safari or Trooper. "It has a spear-

surface. The scabbard is also of plastic with a nylon web belt loop and keeper. True issue types sport the Spanish eagle crest on both blade and scabbard.

"The Austrian army combat and field knife is a particular favorite of mine. It has a 6⅜-inch blade that is 3/16-inch thick and fairly narrow. The handle is of a comfortable thermo plastic as is the knife scabbard.

"The standard is a masterpiece of design, because it is made in one piece with a positive spring latch retainer and a quick-detachable belt fastener.

"The standard Austrian issue variety is all black. Two varieties can be found on the market. One is made in Germany and is sold here by Springfield Armory. The other is made by Glock of Austria, the same company that makes the superb Glock 17 9mm service pistol. Both are excellent, but I prefer the Glock variation.

"Glock also offers a similar knife with OD green scabbard and handle with double-cut saw teeth on the blade's back. Like most of the European double-cut type teeth, these work. These are light, tough and practical knives that I highly recommend. Glock calls their all-black version the Model 78 and the OD version with saw the Model 81.

"A gun dealer who handles the Glock handgun can get you the knives. If he does not stock them, contact Atlanta Cutlery for the Model 81."

*The Chilean Army combat knives, called corvos, are unusual with an exaggerated curve descended from a Nineteenth Century mining tool. Regular army units get the model on left, elite units get sharper curve.*

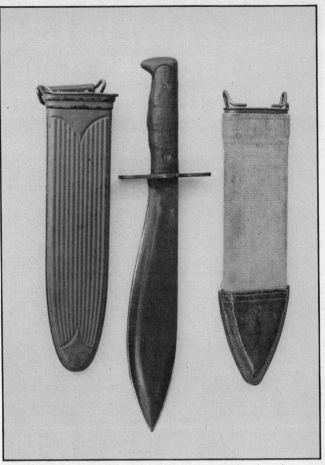

*The U.S. Army Model 1917 Bolo is a good tool and sought-after by collectors. The issue canvas scabbard is at right; sheet steel was experimental.*

Military knives from Finland, Australia, New Zealand and other countries are equally interesting, but less frequently encountered. It is only natural that we emphasize U.S. and, to a lesser extent, English military knives, as these are encountered most commonly and, in most cases, hold the most historical association for us.

In the beginning of this chapter, it was mentioned that the U.S. Army has not issued a combat or field knife since the WWII M3. The Army brass evidently felt the series of knife bayonets that evolved from the M3 would fill the bill and no knife was needed. The average soldier, particularly one actually operating in a field environment or in combat, did not agree. The net result is that soldiers have had to purchase their own combat and field knives. Probably nothing has been more of a boost to both the commercial and custom production of combat-type knives than that single fact. There also has been a renaissance of interest in the knife as a weapon. The reason for this could be the experiences of hundreds of thousands of young men who served in Vietnam. It could be due to the rise of interest in Oriental martial arts. Possibly the seemingly ever-increasing restrictions on firearms has fed the interest in alternative weapons. Emphasis on the blade as a weapon in a number of recent movies has not hurt. Regardless of the reason, the American public and the American soldier never have had such a broad selection of truly excellent military type commercial knives.

# A HOST OF COMBAT-STYLE KNIVES ARE BEING MADE HERE AND ABROAD. THERE'S ONE FOR EVERY NEED AND EVERY TASTE!

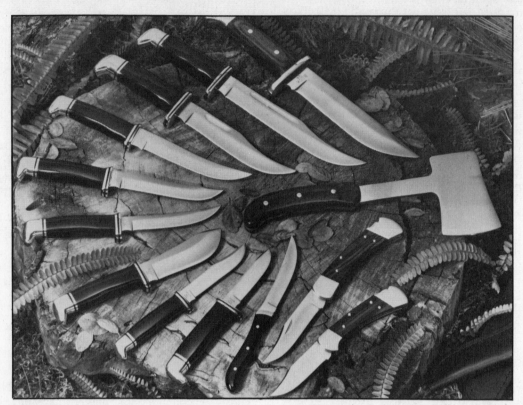

Several Buck knives saw actual combat service in Vietnam, among them the models Special, General and Frontiersman, the top three in photo above.

T HE "I CAN skin and butcher an elk with my two-inch pocketknife" crowd will ask "What are they good for?" Many are good for a lot of things.

It was mentioned earlier that, if a U.S. Army soldier wants a combat or field knife, he has to buy his own. It remains to be seen whether the new M9 bayonet designed to be all-purpose, will slacken the troop's interest in having that personal field knife. Not all troops will be issued the M9 bayonet, anyway.

There are also all those Marines, Seabees, sailors, Coast Guardsmen and airmen who may want a sturdy combat utility knife, or they may want one that is better than they are issued. There also has developed a strong market among the police, particularly those in the SWAT, counter terrorist, and hostage rescue business. For example, Al Mar told us that most of the FBI hostage rescue team (HRT) now carry the smaller of his SERE fixed-blade series with a serrated back. It would not take much imagination to think of many uses for a good blade in that line of work. Even regular state and local police often carry large combat-type knives in the West when they operate against the illegal marijuana growers. They are used to cut down the plants that are found and for other utilitarian uses. Civilians also have found that many of the large combat knives are just as useful for them in the great outdoors as they are for the soldier operating in the field.

Buck's newer Kraton-handled sheath knives are particularly suited to military field duty.

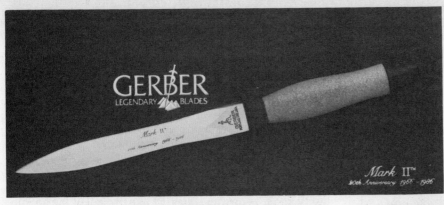

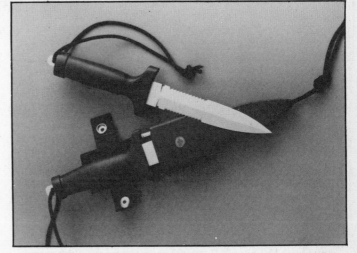

Presentation version of the Gerber Mark II with unique five-degree blade cant was re-introduced in 1986, left. Gerber TAC II double-edge knife is one of three such designs in Gerber's line. Hard plastic sheath holds knife firmly until button-released.

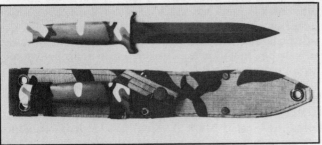

A fine combat weapon by any standard is the older Gerber Guardian II double-edge knife, camo-handled.

For a long time, there was a trend to see who could get by with a smaller knife and anyone with a blade of over four inches was labeled an obvious tenderfoot. Currently, the trend is in the opposite direction.

"Many of the best and most experienced woodsmen I know now carry large field knives, usually in conjunction with a smaller fixed-blade or utility folding knife," Chuck Karwan has found. These large knives often are given the less aggressive name of "camp knife," but are about the same as a military field knife. Within reason, a large knife can do anything a small knife can do, but the opposite is not true. Everything else being equal, a large knife holds its edge longer, because there is more edge to stretch the cutting over. Finally, the large knife makes a far better weapon should one be needed against predators of the four- or two-legged variety.

"Probably the most dangerous animal in the United States, from the standpoint of frequency of attacks, is the domestic dog gone wild. I have encountered several instances of people who have come out of such encounters much better off because they had a large knife for a weapon.

"The large knife also substitutes when a weapon such as

The Gerber BMF, left, is available with saw teeth, as shown, or without. Blade is stainless steel, handle is of Hypalon. Gerber LMF model, below, is also to be found with or without saw teeth.

*The nylon belt sheath is designed to convert to either fixed blade or folded mode for Gerber Parabellum.*

has the same Kraton handle in OD green. This one features chisel-tooth saw teeth on its back as well as a serrated clipped edge for cutting rope; a practical and useful field knife.

Buck offers two other knives that could be considered for military service, though they perhaps better fit the category of survival knife. These are the Buckmaster with its heavy 7½-inch blade and tubular handle and the all-steel Buckmaster LT with a similar blade and skeleton handle. The Navy repeatedly has placed a small order for Buckmasters, presumably for use as diving knives by Navy SEALS.

"Of the two, I prefer the Buckmaster LT as a combat utility knife," Karwan states. "I like the feel of the handle better and I don't see much need for the cross-guard, anchor pins or tubular handle for normal use."

Buck is also the manufacturer of the new M9 multi-purpose bayonet system. These are also being sold commercially under the Buck name.

In Portland, Oregon, is a manufacturer that has made combat-type knives a cornerstone in an extensive line. It all started in 1966, when they offered a 6½-inch dagger called the Gerber Mark II. That first Mark II has gone through numerous minor changes, but it is still prominent in the Gerber line. It made its reputation in Vietnam, primarily in the hands of elite troops like Special Forces, Marine recon and Navy SEALS. It was not as popular with regular troops, because it was not a good utility tool. What it was and is good for is as a weapon for silent killing or emergen-

a firearm isn't available. Typical circumstances would be in national parks where firearms are prohibited or when traveling overseas. A large knife has been quite comforting for me in several instances when traveling in South America and other places — and that was before Crocodile Dundee showed why he carries his!"

Even if a person really has no need for a large weapon-type knife, there is no denying the fascination some of us have with the breed. It would not surprise us if the reason was some genetic memory of our ancestors who, not so long ago, held personal edged weapons in high esteem, because they all too often meant the difference between life and death.

In the previous section, we covered military patterns that are still in production by such manufacturers as Camillus, Colonial, Ka-Bar, Queen and Ontario. In some cases, civilianized versions are also offered. When one looks at the locations of the major manufacturers and importers of combat-type knives, it becomes obvious they are centered in the West, particularly Oregon and California.

"Buck knives were the most commonly seen in Vietnam of all the civilian combat-style knives," Chuck Karwan recalls. "In my unit, the preferred model was the Buck Special, with its six-inch rust-resistant Bowie-type blade. Light in weight, it was a nearly ideal field knife that could make a good weapon as well. The Buck General is the same knife with a 7½-inch blade. It would make an even better jungle knife than the Special.

"The other knife Buck offered back then that was well thought of by the troops was the Model 124 Frontiersman. It is a heavier-duty knife with a 6⅞-inch blade and is probably the best of the three for military purposes. It would have been more expensive than the others, costing about double, as I recall."

All three knives are still in the line, but Buck has variations on the Special and General that are even better for heavy service: the WoodsMate and the CampMate. With basically the same blades as the Special and General, these boast extremely comfortable and practical black, rubber-like Kraton handles. There also is a 5½-inch FieldMate that

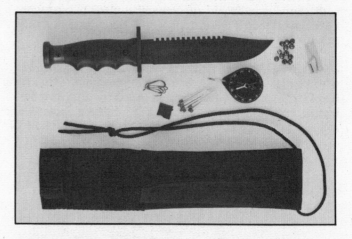

*Coleman/Western's survival knife system is available in either black, above, or camo. Either will serve as an excellent combat knife. Large zippered pocket in sheath is designed to carry chosen emergency items.*

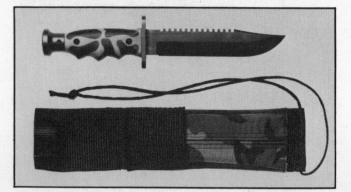

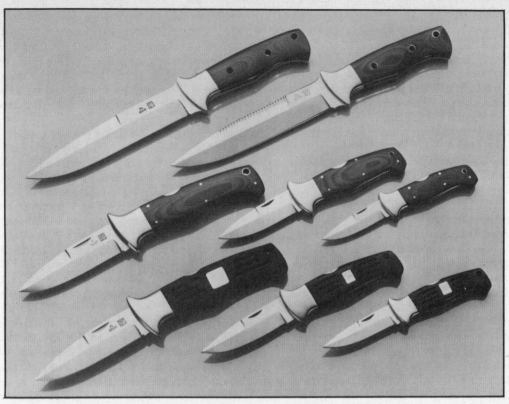

*Top to bottom, left to right: Al Mar SERE series knives, VI, V, III, II and I are all designed with combat in mind. The top five designs have layered Micarta handles while the lower three use black neoprene. Six are folders.*

cies. Its doubled-edged blade, a full quarter-inch thick, and solid one-piece aluminum handle make it extremely rugged. The handle has a textured epoxy finish to ensure a solid grip, even if wet.

The Mark II has a brother, the Guardian II. It has a 6¾-inch double-edged blade shaped with straighter sides and without the serrations found on the Mark II. The aluminum handle also is shaped somewhat differently and, if anything, is even better. Currently it is available only with a blued blade and a camouflage colored handle.

When Gerber bought the Bench Mark line, the firm got still another double-edged dagger-type knife called the TAC II. It is a lighter, thinner knife than the other two, but shares the double-edged dagger configuration. The six-inch blade has serrations on the side. The TAC II's handle and scabbard are made from DuPont Zytel. The knife is

retained in the scabbard by a unique patented locking mechanism that combines a positive lock with an instant thumb release.

While we call the Mark II, Guardian II and TAC II "double-edged daggers," they also could be called stilettos or fighting knives. Gerber calls them "survival knives," presumably because they are designed to aid one in surviving encounters of the lethal kind. All three are superbly designed and manufactured to accomplish that mission, but are not terribly useful for more utilitarian work. For this reason, Gerber has added a number of other knives that better serve the dual role of weapon or tool.

The biggest of these additions, the BMF has proved to be tremendously popular with both military personel and civilians alike. The name BMF ostensibly stands for Big Multi Function, but we suspect it really stands for some-

*Left: New Al Mar SERE IVB features a serrated top edge designed to cut easily through rope, nylon straps, used by members of the FBI's Hostage Rescue Team. Below is the newest version of the SERE/Attack III. At right are Al Mar's Shogun I and II, martial arts-oriented fighting knives, based on ancient Oriental-type blade configurations.*

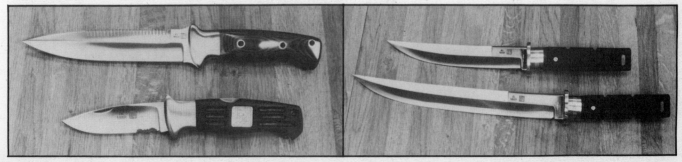

thing less innocuous. It has an eight-inch blade a full quarter-inch thick and is made from high-carbon stainless steel tempered to a Rockwell hardness of C54-55. The blade is basically of the clipped-point Bowie design and comes with or without chisel-tooth saw teeth on its back. The saw teeth are designed for aggressive cutting of wood and other materials and they do work.

"One of my old Special Forces team sergeants stabbed an NVA in Vietnam with a custom combat knife that had large saw teeth angled to the rear. He did it from the rear in a bony part of the NVA's anatomy. The result was a dead NVA, but he could not get his knife out," Karwan recalls. "Frankly, I do not know if the teeth on the BMF would hang up in a lethal encounter or not." If it is a worry, just buy the BMF without the teeth.

The handle of the BMF is superb state-of-the-art DuPont Hypalon fitted under compression. Hypalon is a dense, closed-cell foam rubbery substance that affords a positive grip and cushions the hand from shock during heavy use. It cannot absorb water or moisture, because the air cells in the foam are closed, meaning not connecting. Since the outside layer is sanded to shape, it leaves a finely textured roughness due to the outer layer of air cells being opened up.

"There is no doubt in my mind that such rubbery substances as Hypalon are the best way to go on a knife intended for rugged use. The handle construction of the BMF has a major advantage over other rubbery substances that are molded to shape as knife handles. With this material, the owner can customize the handle to shape to suit his own hand simply with the use of sandpaper," Karwan observes.

The BMF sheath is as impressive as the knife. Made from heavy DuPont Cordura, it has a Bianchi belt clip fastener for ease of attachment to a pistol belt or equivalent. On the back, covered by a nylon web strap with a snap, is a sizable diamond-impregnated stainless steel hone. After extensive testing, I consider the diamond hone supplied on the BMF scabbard as the best field sharpening system available," Karwan contends. "It does not require the use of oil or water, will not break and will sharpen the hardest blade quickly and easily.

"The sheath also has a pocket at the top that holds a quality liquid-filled, jewel-bearing compass. An accessory strap on the front of the sheath allows the piggy-back attachment of an accessory pouch. This pouch can hold a folding knife, survival kit items, medical supplies — or anything that will fit. Gerber's approach with this sheath was to offer a superior solution to the concept of using a hollow knife handle as a survival kit reservoir."

Besides the saw-tooth and plain-bladed BMF, still another variation is available exclusively through the Cutlery Shoppe. It differs in that there is no top guard, there are thumb grooves on the back rear of the blade and the blade is a still longer nine inches.

"It could have been called the EBMF for Extremely Big MF, but Cutlery Shoppe calls it the Predator. I have yet to handle one, but I suspect it will make a dandy camp knife, jungle knife, bush knife and weapon," Karwan opines. The Cutlery Shoppe is a retail mail order source for the entire Gerber line as well as those of other makers and importers. They also offer an exclusive Gerber re-creation of the original Mark II with a unique five-degree cant to its blade.

For people who feel the BMF is too big and heavy, Gerber has a superb answer in the form of the LMF, standing for, what else, Little MF. It features a dropped-point six-inch blade and all the same basic features of construction

*This is Al Mar's version of the famous Applegate-Fairbairn fighting knife, so well-known from WWII.*

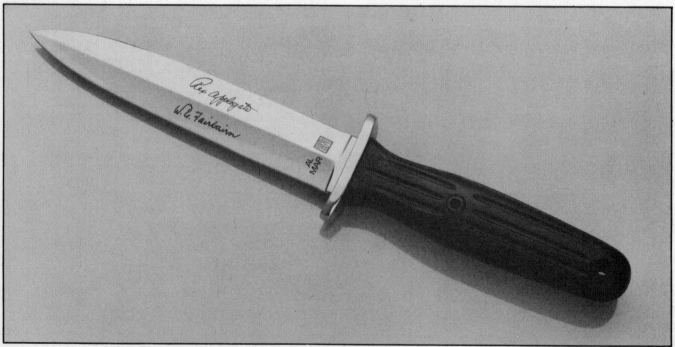

Two rubber practice knives from Al Mar, above, at right. Chalk is used on "edges" to note cuts and thrusts on partner. An original handmade A-F knife is shown below.

At top, the Al Mar Pathfinder is an unusual design, essentially a double-edge machete which will serve as a combat knife, also. Special Forces SOG knife, above, is newest version of design from Al Mar.

as the BMF. It even comes with or without saw teeth and with an appropriately sized Cordura scabbard like the BMF's.

Gerber makes a sort of folding combat knife called the Parabellum that should be mentioned. Large for a folder, it has a 4½-inch blade and an open length of 9½ inches. The handle is made from injection-moulded DuPont Zytel, an extremely tough plastic, and uses the same lock system as the famous Gerber Bolt Action series. "The Parabellum is unique among folders of my acquaintance in that it is designed to be carried either as a folder or a fixed-blade. The scabbard even converts from folded to fixed-blade carry. When the knife is stored in the open position, the storage pouch can be used for a compass or other survival items.

"This knife should have particular appeal for uniformed police, as it could be carried on the equipment belt innocuously in the folder mode, but readily switched to open-blade carry before going in on raids or other high-risk missions."

Western Cutlery makes a couple of military-type knives that may remind one of heavy-duty versions of the old Ka-Bar fighting utility knife. Like Gerber, Western chooses to call these survival knives. These are heavy knives with 6½-inch blued chrome-vanadium steel blades of the clipped-point Bowie-type, with saw teeth on the back. They come in two versions. One has a plain black Valox plastic handle and nylon scabbard and another features a camouflaged handle and scabbard. The fabric scabbard is designed to hold survival items in a large zippered pocket on its face. Like all Western knives, they come with a one-hundred-year warranty.

Western's Bowie strongly resembles the V-44 survival knife of WWII. While a bit ostentatious, Western Bowies saw more than a little service in Vietnam. Reportedly they made one hundred on special order for the Special Forces, complete with SF crest etched on the blade. I suspect these were used for presentation pieces, but would make an excellent heavy field knife and no one should question its ability as a weapon.

The other military-type knife is the Western Seabee, a re-creation of Western's version of the Navy Mark 1 knife. This comes with a leather scabbard marked *USN*.

*Original version of the Al Mar SOG knife, which was replaced by newer design on previous page.*

It seems appropriate that a firm with the motto "The Warrior's Edge" should lead off mention of the importers. This firm is Al Mar knives.

"Al Mar is an impressive person. Former SF, avid martial artist, accomplished shooter, a deputy sheriff, an instructor on officer survival, and a knife designer and importer all rolled into one causes his knives to be an extension of his own personality. I like both him and his knives," Karwan declares.

"The main offerings in the Al Mar line that I considered excellent combat tools are the SERE fixed-blade series. They come in two sizes, one with a 5¾-inch blade, the other with a 7-inch blade. Both also come in optional versions with the back of the blade serrated for cutting rope, straps and the like. The blades are hollow-ground from AM-6 high-carbon stainless steel with a versatile dropped point and false edge. The handle scales are of attractive and durable Micarta. Either size would make a superb

combat utility knife. It is the new SERE IV B that is popular with the FBI hostage rescue team members."

Al Mar also offers two sizes of martial-arts-oriented fighting knives. These come with either a seven-inch or a 10¼-inch blade. The single-edged models are called the Shugoto I and II. The double-edged models — new addition to the line — are called the Shogun I and II. In many ways, they are modern versions of the true Japanese tanto, which had a rather long blade by knife standards. Handles are of DuPont Zytel. These, with a couple others, are in Mar's Tanken line. Tanken translates as "short sword" and the Tanken line offers a unique blend of Oriental sword styling with Western function. "While these look a bit foreign, they will perform the fighting knife function extremely well."

Another Tanken knife is a double-edged dagger called the Phantom. It has a 5¾-inch blade and a handle similar to those of the knives just mentioned. It is one of the handiest of its breed and is an extremely efficient weapon. Unlike most double-edged fighting knives, the Phantom is hollow ground high up the blade. This allows the Phantom to slice efficiently and to be a far more useful knife than most double-edged stabbing blades.

The Phantom is not Mar's only double-edged fighter. He also offers a production version of the superb Applegate-Fairbairn knife.

"Effective as it was, the Fairbairn had a number of drawbacks in both blade and handle design," Karwan feels. "Rex Applegate, then with the OSS, collaborated with Fairbairn on an improved design, but the war ended before it could be produced.

"Many years later, Colonel Applegate dug out his prototypes and drawings, refined the design further and had it produced by a custom knifemaker. It has since gone through a

*Southern California's SOG Specialties has a stainless steel version of their SOG design. Micarta handle and black nylon sheath make it extremely useful.*

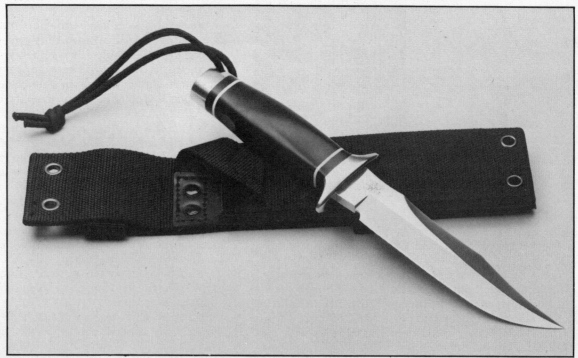

Left: Chris Reeve-designed Blackjack Knives Jereboam I, Jereboam II, Sable I and Shadow I, all made of single pieces of steel, hollow handles and Kalgard finish. The big Jereboam II, below, has an 8¾-inch blade of Bowie styling; an ideal combat fighting knife.

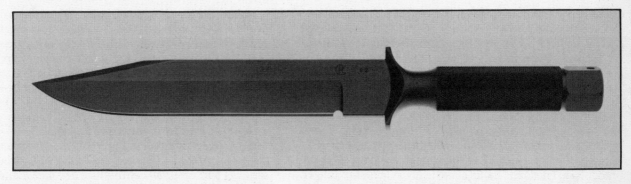

further evolution and Applegate offers hand-made versions built by Oregon knifemaker Bill Harsey. Unfortunately, they are a bit expensive for the average knife user."

Consequently, Applegate and Al Mar collaborated in a production version of the Applegate-Fairbairn. It has a 6¼-inch double-edged blade hollow ground on both edges from AM-6 stainless steel, a simple brass cross-guard, and a black Lexan handle made in the same moulds that form the handles for the hand-made version.

Like many simple masterpieces there is a lot of subtle design development in the Applegate-Fairbairn that make it stand out in the field. Mar also offers a rubber training version designed to use chalked edges to show where cuts would have been on one's training partner.

The new Al Mar Pathfinder machete is unique in a number of ways. First, it is double edged; second, it is stainless steel and third, it has a cross-guard. Basically, it is designed to be a machete that is useful as a tool but also devastatingly effective as a weapon. A trained person equipped with a Pathfinder could inflict tremendous damage. The blade has a slight drop in the front, a la kukri, and shares the kukri's tremendous chopping power. At the same time, it can perform the functions of a similar sized machete.

"Mar also has a re-creation of the Vietnam War Special Forces SOG knife mentioned in the military knife section. Al called his the One-Zero for the numerical call sign of the Special Forces recon team leader.

"The knife has the same shape and general construction of the SOG knife, but is made from far better materials and with much better workmanship," Karwan feels. "Most of these will be bought, I am sure, as memorabilia-type collector's items, but there is no reason it could not be used. Incidentally, Al is making a few changes in the the One-Zero, so the first version is likely to be a collector's item."

Al Mar is not the only company selling a newly made version of the old SOG knife. SOG Specialties has an entire line based on the SOG knife. Recently, they an-

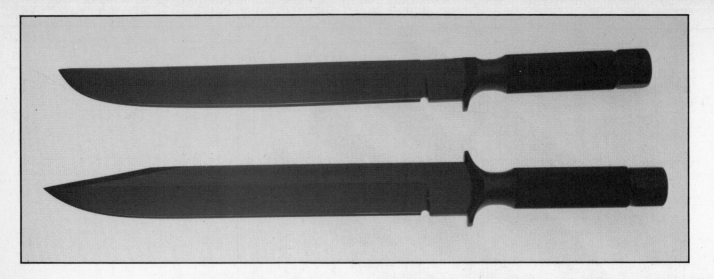

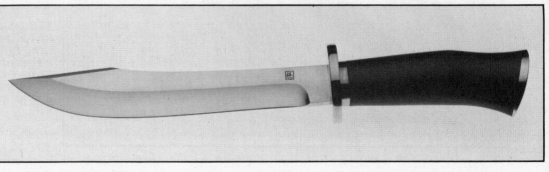

*Longest Blackjack knives, above, could serve as machetes when required. Chinese Fighting Knife, right, was designed by Bob Lum and is produced by Blackjack Knives.*

nounced a stainless steel version with a stacked Micarta washer handle and a Cordura scabbard. It promises to be the most field-useful rendition of the SOG knife to date.

Down California way, Blackjack Knives handles a line of knives made by Chris Reeve of South Africa. Though they are billed as a custom series they actually are semi-production knives. The entire line is oriented toward the hollow-handled survival design, but these knives gain their hollow handle in a unique way. The entire knife, cross-guard and hollow handle are machined from *one piece* of high-carbon tool steel. The line comprises many different models, at least nine having blades seven inches or longer. Every one would make a good combat utility knife.

"I particularly like the looks of the 8¾-inch Jereboam II and the seven-inch Mark V. In spite of the one-piece con-

struction, the knives are well balanced and not excessively heavy," Karwan finds. All have a rust-resistant gray-black Kalgard finish. Not surprisingly, they are expensive.

Blackjack Knives also is about to bring out a production version of a knife designed by nationally known custom knifemaker Bob Lum. Called a Chinese fighting knife, it is based on a classic Chinese sword design. It is a large knife that could serve quite well as a field knife as well as a weapon. It is to be produced in Japan.

Cold Steel is another importer of knives with an Oriental design inspiration. The leader of their line is their Tanto series. Their original Tanto has a 5¾-inch stainless steel single-edged blade with a reinforced point like a Japanese sword. The handle is moulded checkered Kraton, a rubbery substance similar to that used on Pachmayr pistol grips. It affords an extremely secure grip, at the same time being shock absorbing and virtually unbreakable. "These are extremely rugged and serviceable knives, popular in both civilian and military circles," Karwan has learned. A similar knife with a dull finish is called the recon Tanto and still another, the Master Tanto, has a three-layer laminated stainless blade; a hard layer is sandwiched between two softer layers.

"I've seen the results of torture tests done on the Master Tanto and it is the closest thing there is to an unbreakable knife. The reinforced point allows these knives to penetrate bullet-proof vests and even car doors."

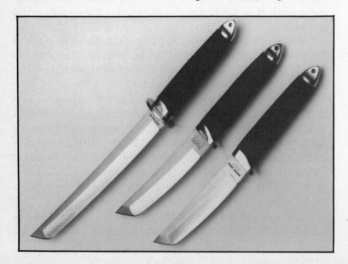

*Three models from Cold Steel are definite combat knives: The 8¾-inch Magnum Tanto, 5¾-inch regular Tanto and the laminated-blade Master Tanto.*

There is no doubt about Cold Steel's Trail Master knife combat heritage, with its 9½-inch blade and Kraton rubber handle for shock absorption. With its Carbon V Bowie-type blade, the knife weighs slightly more than a pound.

"Cold Steel has yet another knife of the same size blade and handle called the Outdoorsman. It has a more conventional upswept point and a sharpened section on the blade's back for chopping. Ironically, the blade is shaped more like that of a typical Japanese tanto than is their Tanto, but regardless of what you call it, this is a fine utility field knife that is large enough to do excellent service as a weapon."

If a 5¾-inch blade is not big enough for you, Cold Steel offers a Magnum Tanto with an 8¾-inch blade with same sword tip as the original tanto and basically the same handle with the addition of an oval guard. Though its oriental styling might appear strange to Western eyes, it is still a practical tool and weapon.

Not all of Cold Steel's large combat-types knives are Oriental or imported. Just added to the line is an American-made Bowie knife, called the Trail Master, that promises

Springfield Armory imports a number of German-made combat knives, including, from left: a copy of the Marine Ka-Bar, Austrian Army issue combat knife, short, long wire-cutting bayonet types, boot knife.

to be an outstanding performer. It has a 9½-inch blade, simple brass cross-guard, and a checkered Kraton handle.

Lynn Thompson, the president of Cold Steel, set out to design a production Bowie that would equal or surpass the performance capabilities of the best hand-forged custom-made Bowies. The Trail Master blade is 5/16-inch at its thickest, lending tremendous strength and stiffness to the blade. At the same time, the high, flat grind leaves the edge area narrow enough that the knife can slice efficiently. It is made from a proprietary high-carbon steel called Carbon V.

In the Midwest, combat knives are being imported from West Germany by Springfield Armory. The line includes a copy of the Marine Ka-Bar, a version of the Austrian combat knife and two unique wire-cutter knives. The latter two are variations of the commercial bayonets Springfield Armory imports from the same source. There are long and short versions, both with blades modeled after the Soviet AKM bayonet. Each has a clipped point, serrated back and a hole in the blade to accept a stud on the knife sheath that converts the knife to a sort of wire-cutter.

There also are several large military knives being imported from Spain by Catoctin Cutlery. These are made by Aitor and Muela and we have good reports on their products.

"Less than twenty years ago, when I went to Vietnam, there were few choices of suitable commercial combat-type knives. Today, it would take several footlockers just to hold one of each," is Karwan's comment.

It should be pointed out that, with several hundred custom knifemakers in the country today, almost all of them make one or more combat knives. Some are totally practical and are based, perhaps, on the makers' own combat experience. Others tend to be more artistic than practical.

An entire volume could be filled with knives by these makers and comments about them. That, though, will have to wait for a future edition of this book.

*Bayonets are manufactured in many countries and are available for every military rifle, past and present. Springfield Armory sells the German-made bayonets for rifles, left to right: M1 Carbine, M1 Garand, the FAL, M14 (Civilian M1A), H&K Model 91 G3, M16 (civilian AR15), Beretta BM59. Right three have wire-cutting capabilities.*

IRONICALLY, IT was the restrictions imposed on the importation of military surplus rifles in 1968 that fired the interest of many collectors in bayonets. Even though the rifles could not be imported, the bayonets could. And, unlike firearms, they could be purchased readily and easily through the mail. As a result, many former military surplus gun importers brought in thousands of bayonets from all over the world and interest in bayonets reached a new high.

"Recent changes in importation laws now allow most pre-1946 military surplus rifles to be imported again. If anything, this factor has given interest in bayonets an even stronger boost, as military gun collectors seek the proper bayonets for their newly acquired military rifles," Chuck Karwan has found. Consequently, never before has the bayonet collector had so many good options so readily available on the market.

"There is one thing to beware of, though. Original foreign military bayonets are an area of tremendous potential price volatility. What might be a rare and valuable bayonet today could well be a common and cheap bayonet tomorrow, if some foreign government unloads its stocks on the world market all at once. Since this is happening to some extent with military surplus guns, it should not be surprising that the same thing would be true of bayonets.

"My best advice is to avoid paying high prices for bayonets that were produced in large quantities, but are uncommon or rare on the U.S. market. For example, the British Enfield jungle carbine bayonet is a fairly uncommon and moderately expensive bayonet. The reason it is uncommon is that when Britain released her No. 5 Enfield

jungle carbines as surplus, she kept the bayonets. This was for the simple reason that they also fit the standard British Sterling submachine gun still in service. Should the large quantities of such bayonets on hand in England be released as surplus, the value of jungle carbine bayonets would drop like a stone. Similar situations hold true for many other models of bayonets. An expensive bayonet could become a cheap bayonet overnight. Be careful what you buy and for how much!"

Fortunately, most of the bayonets on the market are quite reasonably priced. This too has helped spur the interest in collecting bayonets of one kind or another. Currently there is a large selection of British and British Commonwealth bayonets available. These range from socket bayonets for the old Martini single-shots up through those for the various long and short Enfield rifles of the Boer War, WWI and WWII fame. They even include bayonets for the British L1A1 self-loading rifle (SLR) that saw recent service in the Falklands.

"Some, like the funny little No. 9 bayonet with its Bowie blade and no handle, have previously been difficult to find," Karwan reports. "The British No. 9, No. 7 and No. 4 bayonets all fit the No. 4 Enfield rifle. Enough such variations are currently available to make it a collecting field in itself. Prices for common No. 4 bayonets are as low as $2 in some circles and rarely exceed double that amount. Other interesting Commonwealth bayonets on the market include large quantities of U.S.-made P14 bayonets, several interesting Indian short-bladed variations of the P1907 SMLE bayonet and a previously unknown Indian long SLR bayonet."

At the Buck Knives factory in California, cases of M9 bayonets await shipment to Phrobus III where final inspection is carried out under supervision prior to final acceptance, delivery to Army.

From left: Type M4 bayonet is mounted on M1 Carbine, Type M5 on M1 Garand, Type M6 on a military M14 and Type M7 on M16A2. Each of the German-made bayonets is of the wire-cutter type, fitting M16 or AR15.

Century Arms recently brought in large quantities of most of the major French military rifles from the M1886 Lebel up through the post-WWII Mas 44. Along with them came many previously hard to find bayonet variations. Some of the more interesting include WWI period Lebel bayonets with cruciform blades over twenty inches long; some even have solid brass hilts. Century also has imported large quantities of Swedish Mauser bayonets with tubular steel handles and double-edged blades. "Previously these were uncommon and hard to find. Currently, they are cheap and one could hardly find a higher quality piece of cutlery at a better price."

Quite a broad selection of bayonets recently has come into the country from South America. These are from Brazil, Argentina, Chile, Venezuela, and other countries. Virtually all are for one variation or another of the Mauser rifles so commonly used in South America.

"Most of the bayonets were made in Europe. While some are identical to European army bayonets, many are distinctively different or have distinctive crests or markings. This whole area of South American bayonets is largely unexploited with little written about it. An added bonus is that mint condition specimens are not uncommon, even at moderate prices," Karwan has found.

"There is a little bit of everything available right now including Swiss, Italian, Russian, German, Austrian, Portuguese, Chinese, Japanese, American and others to whet the appetites of bayonet aficionados no matter what their tastes."

Understandably, one of the most popular field of bayonet interest is that of U.S. bayonets. The most common available U.S. bayonets on the market today are the series beginning with the M4 for the M1 carbine, proceeding to the M5 for the M1 Garand, the M6 for the M14 and M7 for the M16. The entire M4 through M7 series actually represents a family of bayonets, as they all have exactly the same blade and differ only in the latching mechanisms and attachment fixtures. Appropriately, the entire series is derived from the U.S. Army M3 combat knife of WWII. All, except the M3, are readily available and moderately priced, though some M4s can get pricey. All were manufactured by a large enough number of manufacturers to become a lifetime project for anyone trying to obtain one of each.

"Importers have been finding large quantities of U.S. bayonets of the WWI and WWII periods overseas," Karwan tells us. "The M1905 bayonets for the M1903 Springfield tend to be a bit expensive, but the M1917 bayonets and the later Model 1942 and M1 bayonets are not so bad. The M1905 bayonets were made only by Springfield Armory and Rock Island Arsenal and are all dated. Some collectors try to assemble a complete set of dates, which is quite a challenge.

"The other WWII vintage bayonets are usually collected by maker. Many M1 bayonets are nothing more than Model 1942 or M1905 bayonets that have had their sixteen-inch blades shortened to ten inches by grinding. Should you encounter such cut-down bayonets and the blade has been reparkarized, chances are you have a valid arsenal modified bayonet and not a ruined one."

Recently the U.S. Army added a new bayonet to its arsenal of weapons. It is the much heralded and impressive looking M9 bayonet for the M16 series of rifles. It is being issued to all close-combat troops such as infantry, combat engineers, Rangers, Special Forces and the like. The rest of the Army will continue to use the M7 bayonet. Interestingly, the Army recently has adopted an improved scabbard for the M7 and is still letting contracts for M7 manufacture.

The M9 was designed by Phrobus III of Oceanside, California, and is manufactured by Buck Knives for Phrobis. Phrobis designed the M9 to meet U.S. Army specifications for a more versatile, sturdy and useful bayonet than the M7. Indeed, its full name — M9 Multi-Purpose Bayonet System (MPBS) — indicates the intention for it to be much more than just a bayonet.

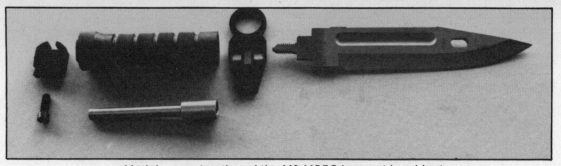

*Modular construction of the M9 MPBS bayonet is evident in photo above. Complete disassembly and assembly may be accomplished with only a screwdriver and wrench.*

*A Buck employee puts the government-prescribed edge on an M9 bayonet. The abrasive grit is quite coarse, reflecting the peculiar sharpness test from Army specifications. Twine-cutting tests date from 1917.*

"The Phrobis entry competed in rigorous trials against five other entries. The two other U.S. entries were from Imperial and S-Tron. Foreign entries were from Eichorn of West Germany, Royal Ordnance of England and Marto of Spain. The competitive trials were conducted by a diverse group of soldiers that included elite Ranger and airborne troops, combat veterans and inexperienced young troops.

"Tests included performance as a bayonet, field knife, and wire cutter. One of the original specifications called for the bayonet, when combined with the scabbard, to be capable of cutting double-twisted barbed wire, ribbon-type barbed wire and standard metal bands.

"In addition it was required to cut through light sheet aluminum such as the skin of a military aircraft, using the saw teeth on the bayonet's blade back. Presumably, this is so a soldier who survives a plane crash, where the aircraft does not burn up or explode, can cut his way out if none of the escape doors work.

"Somehow, I don't think that such situations occur very often, maybe once every war or two," Karwan opines.

"The bayonets in the trials were inflicted with a great deal of abuse including bending, dropping, sub-zero temperatures, impacts on the point, torque — and much more.

"After the dust settled, the clear winner of the trials was the Phrobis entry. It was the only bayonet tested that had not one single performance failure. All entries also were rated for personal preference by each tester for the individual functions of bayonet, field knife, combat knife and wire-cutter as well as for overall preference. The Phrobis entry came out number one in all categories," Karwan's research shows. "This bayonet also was the second most expensive in the trials. To the Army's credit and many people's surpise, the contract was awarded to Phrobis for their entry and not to the lowest bidder."

The M9 MPBS is a truly handsome piece that has a number of unique features. First, the blade is shaped like a Bowie knife with its clipped point rather than the typical spear point of most bayonets. It is hollow ground which greatly aids the cutting and slicing ability of such a thick blade. The blade is also made from a modern stainless cutlery steel called 425 and is zone hardened, whereby the edge has a Rockwell C hardness of about 54 with the tang in the 40s and the threaded tang extension in the high 30s.

"This system of zone hardening allows good edge-holding, providing at the same time, extreme resistance to breaking. Zone hardening is difficult to do on a production stainless steel blade and is, to my knowledge, unique to the M9, certainly among bayonets. The M9 also has a unique modular construction that allows the bayonet to be disassembled in a matter of minutes with simple tools or by using an integral screwdriver on the scabbard. This allows damaged components, including even the blade, to be replaced readily at low unit level rather than having to be returned to a depot for repair," Karwan states.

The handle is made of olive drab Du Pont Zytel 8018. This extremely tough material lends considerably to the substantial strength of the M9 MPBS. The scabbard is made from the same material and is nearly as impressive as the bayonet. It features an integral screwdriver on its tip, a built-in sharpening stone covered by a snap-down web strap, a Fastex quick-release buckle that allows quick removal from the soldier's belt, plus a stud and plate that convert the combined bayonet and scabbard into a sort of wire-cutter. The excellent Bianchi belt fastener — used by the Army on the M12 holster for the M9 9mm pistol — is used to attach the scabbard to the soldier's belt. The bayonet is retained by a friction retainer as well as two straps with snaps.

"I trust that soldiers will have very little luck trying to explain to their supply sergeant how they lost their bayonet out of its scabbard," Karwan observes.

"All in all, the M9 MPBS is an extremely impressive piece, though it is far too heavy for my tastes. Troop reaction has been enthusiastic for the bayonets that have been delivered to date. The Army is buying 315,600 M9 MPBSs over a three-year period at a cost of $49.56 per copy.

"Buck also is producing a version for commercial sale. It varies from the military version in a couple ways. First it is marked *BUCK 188 U.S.A.* on the right side of the tang where the military contract one is not. Both are marked *M9 PHROBIS III U.S.A.* on the left side of the blade tang.

"The major difference is in the wire-cutting feature. The commercial Buck version has a limit stud to help prevent accidents occurring by someone leaving a finger or two between the scabbard and blade when cutting wire. In addition, there is a bright yellow decal on the scabbard warning users to keep fingers behind a specific line when cutting wire. The military contract version has no decal or limit stud. Retail price is a whopping $159.95, but several dealers tell me they are selling quite well," Karwan says.

The enthusiastic response of the M9 MPBS on the civilian market points out one other factor that has increased interest in bayonets. This is the wide sale and interest, during the last ten years or so, in civilian versions of the world's assault rifles. The list is a long one, including various Berettas, the Armalite AR180, the Valmet series, the H&K series, the Galils, the M1A, the AR-15, the SIG series, the Dae Woo series, various AK-47 spinoffs, numerous FAL variations, just to name some of the more prominent guns that have been or are on the market. Practically all mount a bayonet and consequently have created a market and interest in bayonets to fit them.

"This has brought about a new and unique phenomenon. That is the production of commercial bayonets, in many cases of a type not used by any military, for sale to civilians to put on commercial as well as military rifles. A good example is the line of new commercial bayonets made in West Germany and imported by Springfield Armory, Incorporated. It includes commercial variations of the U.S. M4 through M7 series of bayonets, plus a number of exotic variations that fit the AR-15 that are not used by any military I am aware of. Who would have thought there ever would be a civilian market for commercial bayonets to go on commercial civilian rifles?

"Be the bayonet a commercial civilian or a military veteran, the current interest in all types is nothing short of phenomenal. For the average civilian, they constitute the consummate collectible, because they really serve no useful purpose. No civilian needs one. I know plenty of veterans who say no soldier needs one either!

"However, they complement the various rifles they go on quite nicely and offer an interesting cutlery field completely by themselves."

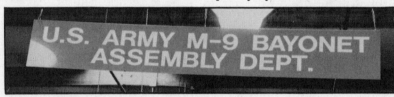

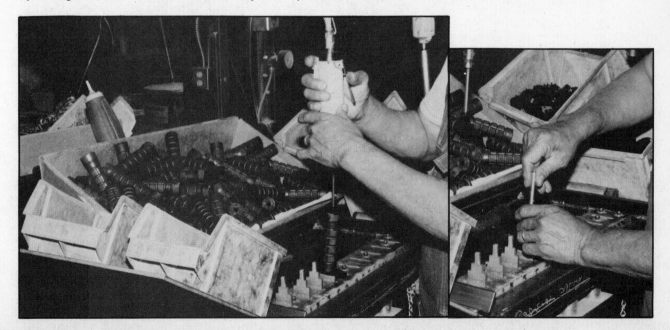

*Assembly of modular parts of M9 bayonet is fast and simple, as it should be. Completed blades are slipped into assembly jig, with parts bins at hand. Below right, a tang extension is screwed into tang, followed by crossguard, handle with latch assembly and cap screw, below left. Work is done in Buck factory, above.*

Case, above, and Kershaw, below, present two versions of typical survival knives. The Case carries a small sharpening stone on the sheath, along with a small thermometer and flashlight. Kershaw's includes the usual hollow-handle gear, a compass and a survival guide card file.

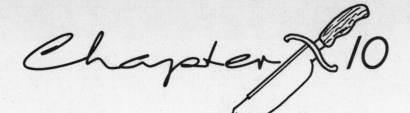

# Chapter 10

# SURVIVAL KNIVES

## *It Takes A Big, Rugged Knife Of Special Design To Qualify For This Category*

A SURVIVAL KNIFE usually is thought of as one with a long blade, heavy enough to chop and cut through wood, rope, sometimes aluminum or nylon webbing, with a hollow, threaded-cap handle. The handle is filled with various emergency items with which one may save a life in a difficult situation or when existing for many days in the wilderness. We may accept that general description of a survival knife, but there may be more to it than that.

We have to define a few terms or set some parameters here, before discussing survival knives. When the situation demands, any knife may become a survival knife. If all you have with you when the emergency arrives is a tiny folding pocketknife and you have to cut through a seat belt or slice some wood chips to start a fire, that becomes a survival knife. The best and biggest survival knife in the world will not help a bit, if it remains at home while the emergency is miles away.

We might also rule out military and hand-to-hand fighting knives for this chapter, as they are covered extensively in Chapter Nine. And while warding off a mugger with a properly wielded survival knife is an act of survival, we'll restrict this discussion to the knives designed to accomplish life and death or comfort tasks, mostly in the field.

The survival knife design usually has some provision for carrying fishing line and hooks, waterproof matches, some sort of signaling device — which may be a whistle or the side of the shiny blade itself — basic medicines such as painkillers and/or antibiotics, a sharpening stone, compass and perhaps a length of heavy cord or light rope. Some survival kits also include a small flashlight for emergency signaling at night or finding one's way down a mountain in a heavy rainstorm. Some survival knives may include additional medical supplies such as a razor blade, snakebite kit and several bandages. Carrying capacity of the hollow handle or other receptacle is the limiting factor to what is carried.

The blade of the knife may be at least four inches long; more likely, five to seven. The blade should be of a thick, heavy steel, measuring up to a quarter of an inch in thickness. Stainless steel is used frequently for the blade, but many survival knives are made from tool steels which are easier to sharpen and have been coated with some sort of finish to resist corrosion. It is a matter of choice whether the blade should be brightly polished so as to easily reflect sunlight to signal rescuers or carry a dull matte finish that will not give off unwanted flashes to frighten away animals or fish. If a dull-finish blade is selected, the wilderness-

Jeff Spivey carried his own design survival knife throughout a horseback trip from Canada to Mexico, down the Rocky Mountains in 1984. He carried the original Saber Tooth model, top, with birdseye maple handle. Newer model features black walnut.

Damascus USA can offer forged-to-shape Damascus blades complete with saw teeth already cut, right.

goer might be wise to carry a small signal mirror.

The blade shape is generally of the drop-point type, rarely of the upswept, skinner design, although there is nothing really wrong with such a design. The steel must be tough and strong, able to withstand what might be considered knife abuse under more civilized conditions.

There are several survival knives available with saw teeth or serrations on the back of the blade. The value of these designs must be questioned. If the blade is intended to saw through a small log or tree trunk, the design of the teeth must be a genuine saw design, not simply grooves cut into the back of the blade. Some of these so-called saw blades do nothing but catch on the material they are trying to cut, thus being worse than nothing. If the knife is heavy enough, one can chop through small logs in the same time it

takes to saw through them, with less frustration and more success.

If the "teeth" on the blade are serrations, such as those found on the blade design of some Spyderco knives, the blade is intended to cut through tough materials such as thick rope, vines, rubber hoses and the like. These things are notoriously difficult to cut with a regular blade and the serrated or scalloped edge makes a difficult job considerably easier. In addition, these edges can be touched up and honed in the field when necessary, while the saw teeth, when they become dull, are almost sure to require professional help once back home.

A handguard is a must. Under the best of conditions, when cutting anything tough, requiring lots of exertion in wet conditions, a knife without a guard can be dangerous.

*Gutmann Cutlery features several survival knives, some with hollow handles and saw teeth blade backs. Leather sheath has provision for sharpening stone.*

*Gutmann's Model 21-049 has a blued 440 stainless steel blade measuring 6¼ inches long with false edge and saw teeth on the back. Hilt has tie-down holes for emergency spear; leather sheath included.*

In an emergency, life-threatening situation, no one needs further stress caused by a slipped hand and a cut finger. The guard can be a simple, straight-across affair or a curved shape to accommodate the thumb on one side and the fingers on the other. Some makers will fashion special tips — intended to be screwdrivers — on the guard metal. Some are drilled through with the idea that a cord may be threaded through for lashing the knife to a pole, thus serving as a harpoon or spear.

The handle may or may not be hollow with a threaded butt cap. If so, a limited number of emergency items may be carried inside as outlined earlier. The threaded cap must have a plastic or rubber grommet to ensure the hollow is watertight. Wet matches, even the so-called Lifeboat waterproof matches, do no good, if they cannot be used to start a fire. Most medicines, too, must be kept totally dry to be effective when taken.

Some knives have a liquid-filled compass built into the cap. Others have the compass positioned on the underside of the cap, more out of harm's way. Some might use the cap to crack rocks, nuts, bones or anything else and such treatment surely would break a good compass. One may argue that no knife should be so treated, but we're thinking in terms of emergency situations; cosmetics of the knife are of minor importance.

Every survival knife handle must be of a material or finish to provide a firm, non-slip grip under the most trying conditions. One must assume the knife will be used in hot, humid weather; cold and wet; in icy conditions; with or without gloves. Some survival designs include finger grooves formed into the handle for control, but this would seem to restrict the use of the knife to but one position in the hand. The value of deep finger grooves is questionable, in our opinion.

A rubber polymer composition — soft to the touch and often with checkering moulded in — is a common material used for handles of some knives these days. This material is impervious to most corrosive or damaging substances

Pete Klicka imports the LifeKnife Commando knife, offering it at a rather lower price. Hollow handle will hold standard survival gear and butt cap has a built-in compass. Handle is made of cast aluminum.

Custom knifemaker Chuck Stapel designed the first Outsider knife; small, lightweight and easily carried. New model has dark matte blade finish.

and offers a firm grip, especially in cold, wet conditions. It is non-reflective, but can be damaged by another knife blade, barbed wire, sharp metal or broken glass edges. Most such materials are affixed to the knife handle by epoxy cement and/or screws or rivets and won't come loose even under considerable abuse.

Other knives — especially those with hollow handles — often feature machine-cut or moulded checkering for a good grip. This system works well under some conditions, but when the weather is cold and wet, even icy, the metal handle will be as cold as the air and can present problems.

Some, especially custom makers, wrap the handle with a length of nylon or cotton cord. The heavy cord provides a

firm gripping surface as well as providing a length of emergency line that can be used to fasten the knife to a pole, to make a snare, lash shelter poles together or used for any number of other tasks. Several makers favor this cord-wrap technique as a convenient way to always carry extra cord along on any trip. The cord usually is green, gray or black; a color which will be unobtrusive in the wilderness while not showing too much dirt after a couple of years of use.

Speaking of color, most survival knives have featured a black or gray handle, but camouflage coloring is coming on strong. Using plastic or multiple-layer linen micarta, almost any camo pattern — green or brown — may be built into

*Some will argue that a rifle bayonet is the ultimate survival knife, in or out of a combat zone. The Phrobis/Buck M9 bayonet does many things, including splitting firewood, if required.*

*Another custom knifemaker, Mike Franklin, designed this lightweight knife, likely to be carried. Handle will not be the most comfortable, but the skeletonized handle, light weight makes it practical.*

the handle. Some companies prefer handles of a plastic-impregnated wood, a technique that is meant to make the wood as impervious to the elements as plastic. Companies have to sell their products to stay in business and the impregnated wood makes for an attractive knife, appealing to the consumer while remaining plenty tough.

Another method of storing items in the hollow handle rather than utilizing a threaded cap, is to hollow out the handle halves, locking them closed with one or two easily removed screws. Some of these handles will leave one screw fixed as the handle slab pivots out of the way on a hinge to open the cavity. One must always use care so as

not to lose the locking screw in the bush. A couple of custom knifemakers use this method of storage.

Not so common as two or three decades ago, but still found on at least three factory-made knife handles, is a series of leather washers held tight by a threaded bolt or fitted butt on the end of the tang. The still-popular Ka-Bar USMC fighting knife is produced with that type of handle, as is Camillus' Pilot's Knife and a newer commemorative knife by SOG. The leather washer handle fell into disfavor years ago when it was discovered that, in parts of the world where heat and humidity swing from one extreme to the other, the leather tends to expand and shrink with alarming

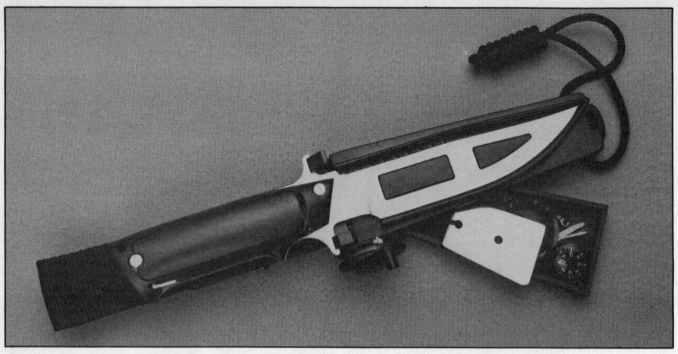

*Teckna's Wilderness survival knife takes a slightly different approach to the problem of carrying gear along with the knife. Equipment, including a tiny fishing reel, is carried in a compartmented sheath.*

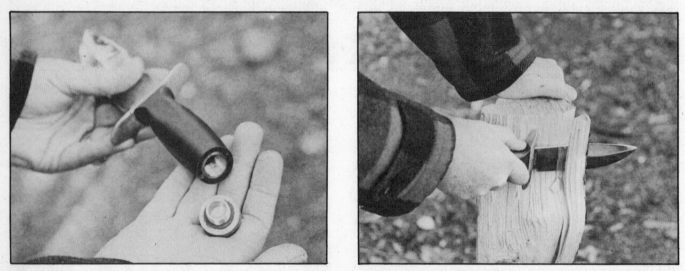

*The Bianchi Nighthawk is a rugged knife made in and imported from Germany. The knurled brass cap is precision-threaded for a secure, watertight fit, left. Nighthawk is heavy and rugged enough to split kindling off firewood, if necessary. Sometimes, survival is simply a matter of having a good campfire.*

rapidity. Eventually, the washers would loosen on the tang and re-tightening them seemed difficult, if not impossible. These days, knives using this handle material have a chemical sealant applied to the leather washers to protect them from moisture-caused variations and they seem to hold tightly for years. Grooved slightly, the new models offer a firm gripping surface and an attractive appearance. There are many such knives still to be found at swap meets, gun and knife shows, as well as new at retail dealers.

Yet another storage method for packing along small emergency items involves the sheath, rather than the knife handle. A number of makers have experimented with an extra pouch sewn onto the outside of the belt sheath to carry a sharpening stone as well as other gear. With this design, the sheath becomes as important as the knife itself, but under most circumstances, neither is carried without the other. Such a small pocket or pouch can carry considerably more gear then the hollow knife handle, too. Additional bandages, antibiotics, snake bite kit, matches and the like may be carried in the extra room.

There is something to be said for the extra sheath pocket and a hollow, waterproof handle combined. The pouch alone has the disadvantage of not being reliably watertight. It is not unlikely that the wearer may be submerged in a stream or river, or be soaked by heavy rains or snow while hunting, fishing or backpacking in the mountains. Bianchi

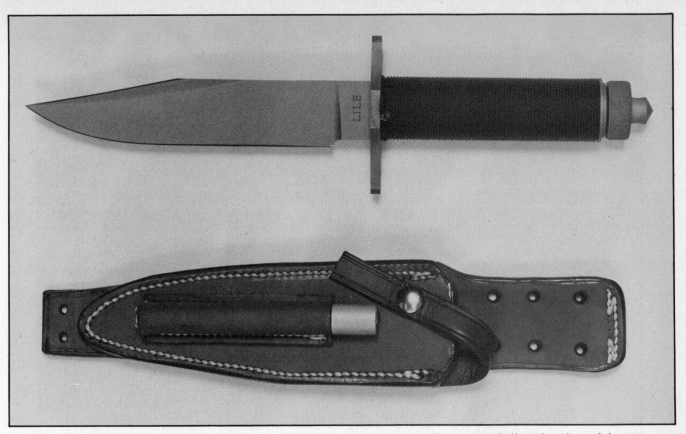

Jimmy Lile, custom knifemaker down Arkansas way, was making handsome survival knives before the "Rambo" movie. This 6½-inch-blade model features a hollow handle wrapped with heavy nylon cord.

The Tru-Bal Battle Blade is a combination throwing and survival knife and axe. The knife is a foot long overall, weighing just under a pound. It will chop or cut through just about anything in the field.

International currently is importing a survival knife from Germany which has such an arrangement.

Several other factory-made custom knives are intended to be or are easily adaptable as survival knives. Depending upon the situation and terrain, a machete, with a blade as long as two feet or more, can be an excellent survival knife. Many of our Latin American and Oriental neighbors survive in jungles thicker than anything North America has to offer with only a machete to keep them company. With it, one is able to provide food, shelter and even primitive clothing by wielding the long blade. Mostly, the machete is used to slash or chop through heavy brush, vines and small trees. But the big blade will easily split kindling, dig holes,

pry loose shellfish and butcher animals. It would be a bit clumsy to try to field dress or skin out a game animal with a machete, but it can be done.

For more then thirty years, Harry McEvoy, from up Michigan way, has been making and selling a line of throwing knives. They are big, balanced primarily for throwing and made of excellent steel. One model in particular, the Bowie-Axe, seems ideal for a survival knife. It comes in a thick leather belt sheath and is strong enough to chop wood as well as do most everything a machete might do. The Bowie-Axe weighs almost a pound, but feels lighter in the hand due to the easy balance.

A new survival knife that was not designed as such is the

*There should be no question about these Bucks' abilities to perform under tough conditions. The same blade with serrated false edge and saw teeth may have either a hollow handle or lighter thermoplastic-covered model. They are the Buckmaster, left, and Buckmaster LT.*

*Another cord-wrapped handle knife is this one from Jack Crain. Saw teeth are cut in the blade back and the ends of the hilt are cut as screwdrivers.*

Buck/Phrobis III Military bayonet. The M9 bayonet was designed by a team from Phrobis and Buck and is being produced by Buck in its El Cajon, California, plant. A civilian version is available, identical to the military except for one detail. The civilian M9 bayonet has a blade stop on the sheath tip to prevent any possible accident when the knife is being used to cut wire.

About two inches down from the tip of the 7½-inch blade is an oblong oval cut out of the blade. The oval cutout fits over a similarly shaped male stud attached to the tip of the sheath — or bayonet scabbard — which acts as a pivot point. Just below the stud at the tip is a half-inch by quarter-

inch cutout in the metal tip designed to catch the barbed wire to be cut.

With the wire in the slot, the back of the bayonet blade is pivoted on the stud and the wire is cut. On the civilian version — and this is the only difference between it and the military bayonet — Buck has included a blade stop to keep the sharp edge from cutting the user's fingers. In addition, there is a printed warning on the outside of the hard plastic sheath, "When using wire cutter, keep fingers this side of dashed line." A good idea!

The blade sheath is a dark-green hard-plastic material to which is attached matching green nylon webbing and a belt

**136**

The Ek Commando knife gained fame in WWII and Ek Knives continues to produce the design. Whether it is a combat or survival knife depends on where you are.

Al Mar makes the rugged lines of his Special Forces One-Zero knife look graceful. Arguably, this may be survival or a combat knife, but it will do either.

attachment designed and built by Bianchi. It is the same attachment device used on Bianchi's military handgun holster. Built into the solid sheath, on the inner side, is a small sharpening stone about an inch wide and 4½ inches long. It is solidly inset in the sheath and protected by webbing. An extra six-inch-long nylon pouch attaches to the sheath with a Velcro strap; ideal for carrying emergency items.

With the 7½-inch blade, the bayonet measures a full twelve inches long. The handle is manufactured of a hard plastic material that is checkered and grooved for a firm grip. The stainless steel blade is a quarter-inch thick with a hollow-ground edge and three inches of real saw teeth on the back. The design of the teeth makes it possible to actually saw through wood, light metal or other substances, as conditions dictate.

The M9 bayonet scabbard is of hard plastic as dictated by military specifications. Most other survival sheaths are of leather or nylon. Typically, the leather will be brown or black; green or black are the most common colors used for nylon sheaths. However, several sheaths are available in camouflage patterns and are especially popular for big survival knives.

Nylon is cheaper to make and lighter in weight than

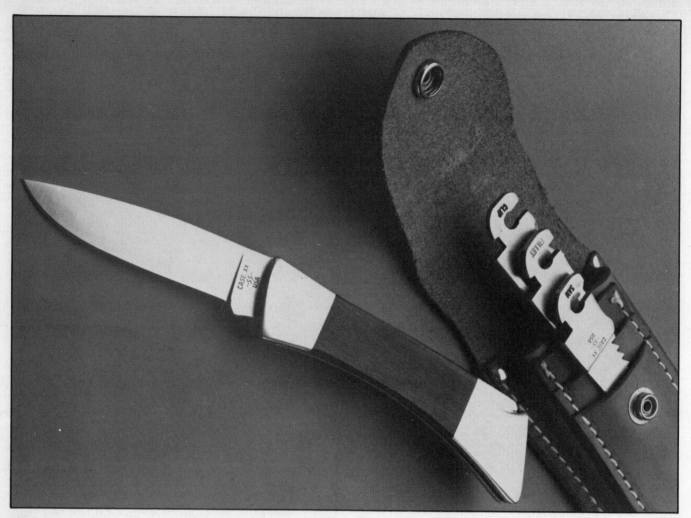

*W.R. Case & Sons calls this one their XX-Changer, a folder with sheath that carries an extra three blades. Different blades are marked clip, saw and fillet. This one should do it all in the wilderness.*

*The Calmont knife blade does not fold, but the blade guard does. It is used to prevent unwanted cuts in intestines while skinning a game animal. With its serrated back, the model qualifies as a survival knife under any definition we choose.*

leather, giving the manufacturer more flexibility in design possibilities. A survival knife may be worn on the hip, leg, strapped to the lower leg or upper arm or, as some prefer, attached to the backpack strap on the upper chest. The latter position offers instant success to the big knife, while not interfering with the pack's hip strap. (Knife sheaths are discussed in greater detail in Chapter Four.)

All this discussion on survival knives has been about large fixed-blade sheath knives. There are those who would consider a rugged folding knife as the ultimate survival knife. Folders have a certain disadvantages, however, when it comes to this kind of work. In an emergency, under adverse weather conditions, opening the blade could be difficult because of nerves, cold, wet fingers or gloves. A fixed blade knife is ready for employment as soon as it is drawn

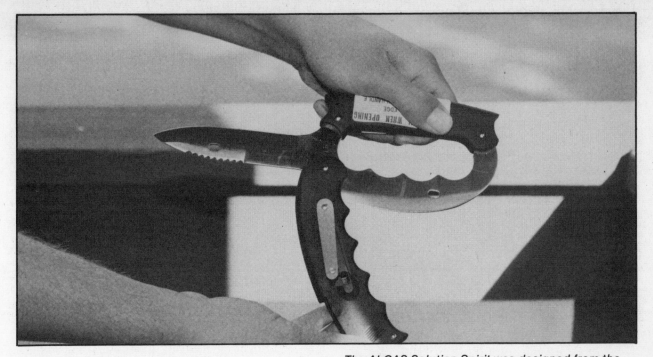

The ALCAS Solution Spirit was designed from the start as a survival knife. The handle folds around right or left, exposing either the knife blade or the axe. It is a bit cumbersome to carry, but it will perform any of several tasks.

from the sheath, while the folder must be drawn and the blade opened before it can be used to cut anything. On the other hand, if the folder — the typical generic "Buck Knife" — is more likely to be carried in the first place, then a folding knife is the better choice. As we have said, no knife is any good, if you don't have it when the emergency arrives.

Several manufacturers and importers market folders large enough to fit into our category. Al Mar, Gerber Kershaw, Case, Camillus, Blackjack, Spyderco and the Buck folder are among the best. A heavy, rugged stainless steel blade is essential for this work, as is a positive, easily operated locking mechanism. No knife should be considered for such use that does not have a positive method of locking the blade open, with no possibility of malfunction during hard use.

Handle materials for folders have the same requirements as for fixed-blade knives. They must be tough, impervious to most elements or corrosive materials and they must provide a non-slip grip. Man-made plastics or rubber polymers are almost universally preferred.

Such large folders usually are carried on the belt in a pouch of leather or nylon. The flap which closes the pouch must not open accidentally, but at the same time, must be easy to open under stress conditions. Most utilize a snap or Velcro closure; some use both.

There are other survival tools available, but they are not knives. An axe, a hammer, pliers and various combination tools have found their way into the marketplace from time to time. Some have found popularity, while others are now available only at swap meets and garages sales. Most such inventions are simply substitutes for a tough, ready-to-use survival knife and should be regarded as such. Nothing can take the place of a good knife when the chips are down. Don't leave home without one.

Coleman/Western's neat package puts a hand axe and a hunting knife in one sheath for easy access.

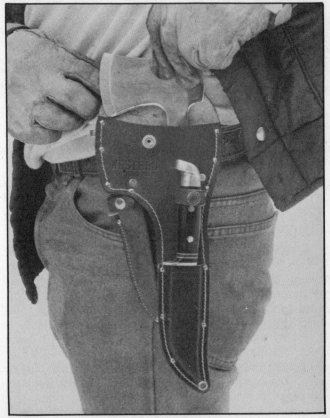

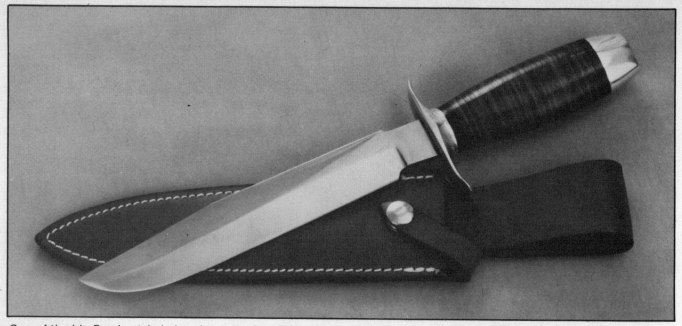

One of the big Bowie-style knives imported by Atlanta Cutlery would serve as a survival design any time.

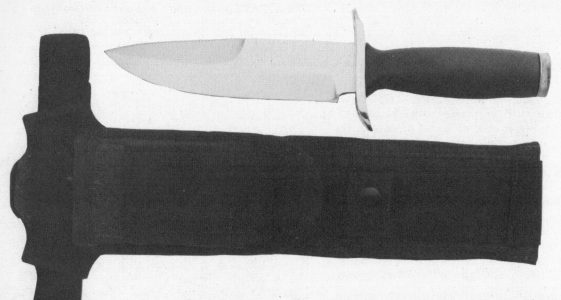

A newer model, the Bianchi Nighthawk II, features a serrated false edge on the blade back and a nylon sheath designed to carry several emergency items. Clever pockets contain such things as a map compass, a container of matches with striker, nylon thread, a plastic box for bandages, scalpel and some medicines. The inside box top doubles as a signal mirror. Affixed to the rear of the sheath is a ceramic sharpening stone. Tie-down strap included.

One of the most unusual survival knives we have seen in recent years is a new model from ALCAS Cutlery in Olean, New York. It is called the "Solution" and was designed by custom knifemaker Dan Harrison. The Solution and its younger brother, the Solution "Spirit," are considerably more than simply a knife.

At first glance, one can see that this is a strange looking tool. The Solution is actually a knife with gut-hook and saw-teeth on the back, which really work, and it is also an axe. The handle pivots on a central hinge pin in either direction, to change from knife to axe and back again. The handle of the Solution is a watertight compartment for

storage of emergency items. The Spirit does not have the storage compartment, however. Instead, there is an additional gear pocket sewn onto the black nylon sheath. Back of the Spirit Knife blade is recessed for cutting cable, rope or hose, rather than being formed with saw-teeth.

Changing from axe to knife mode is simple, but requires the utmost care for safety reasons. Doing it wrong may result in a nasty cut. First step is to unlock the safety latch on the side of the handle by raising the spring clip and moving it into the rest position. Then, what ALCAS calls a Saf-T-Guard at the butt of the handle is unlocked. Left closed, the knife blade will not move into its closed position; while

*Frankly and obviously designed as a survival knife, the Gerber LMF displays widely spaced saw teeth on blade back. Nylon sheath is lightweight, includes heavy cord for thigh tie-down or other emergency use.*

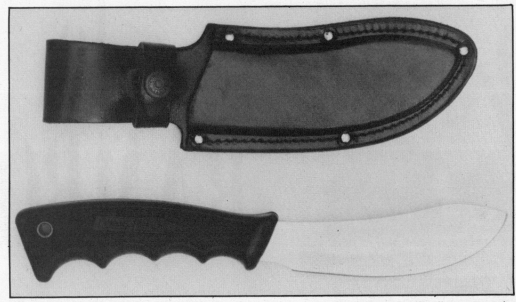

*The Coleman/Western Model R14 skinning knife was not designed specifically as a survival knife, but it is big enough to do the job. Most hunters carry but one knife for all tasks.*

in the axe mode, the guard keeps the blade in the handle during use. Once freed, the handle rotates 180 degrees to lock into the opposite end of the knife/axe, exposing the other blade. In either mode, the handle provides finger grooves for firm control while chopping or cutting.

The original Solution comes with a leather sheath with belt loop and rawhide tie-downs. The Spirit model features a black nylon sheath with belt loop and nylon tie-downs. The knife and axe blades on the Solution are protected by a Parkerized oxide coating, while the Spirit leaves the metal brightly polished. Both have safety straps to securely lock the tools into their respective sheaths.

Another full-time survival tool is the latest from Break-Free, better known for their special high-grade lubricants. Their multi-purpose folding shovel compresses down into a twelve-inch by six-inch carrying package, weighing less than three pounds. The shovel blade is sharpened along one edge to act as a machete for clearing brush and has a saw edge on the other edge for cutting small limbs. The tip of the shovel blade is concave and sharpened to cut easily through roots. The foot lip is designed to double as a hammer.

The handle is made of strong, lightweight aircraft aluminum, internally ribbed for strength. The blade locks into two positions for digging or trenching, or into the compact carry position. Using the folding handle, the whole thing will serve as a small stool, when the need arises. Open, the Break-Free shovel measures a full thirty inches in length. It all carries in a small nylon pouch, black or camouflage, with double belt loops on the back. It's the type of tool that will get you out of any number of tight spots, as well as serve you well when in the wilderness.

# Chapter XII

# from BOWIE to RAMBO... to INFINITY

Roger Williams played Bowie in a 1937 film, "Heroes of the Alamo." Knife in his right hand was insignificant.

Robert Armstrong was Bowie in 1939 film, "Man Of Conquest." Knife was from Republic's prop department.

MacDonald Carey portrayed role in "Comanche Territory," circa 1950.

## The Movie Mob Has Long Had

## A Big Thing For Big Knives

## And It Doesn't Look

## Like It'll Ever End

Ken Tobey was Bowie in Disney's 1955 TV series, "Davy Crockett," with big knife. As time passes, the knife gets bigger!

Scott Forbes portrayed Bowie in a series that ran from 1956 to 1958. He used one of the knives made for "Iron Mistress."

Jeff Morrow fought off Mexican army in "The First Texan" in 1956. Knife used probably came from Stembridge shop.

HOLLYWOOD has a well deserved reputation as the land of the Gimmick. This is true, when it comes to action movies. Every action star seems to want a gimmick that will draw the public's attention...and this syndrome has been going on almost from the time that Thomas Edison introduced his first movie camera.

Going back a long way, the late Tom Mix, the first cowboy star to make it big, had several gimmicks. First was his white hat. No matter how tough the battle, when it was all over, he still wore that hat without a smudge. Of course, the fact that he ordered them from J.B. Stetson by the dozen was one of the secrets of those early days. His other big gimmmick was a horse called Tony, which came to be billed on the screen with his name in the same size type as his owner. He was called The Wonder Horse and was the first of a whole line of movie cowboy mounts with names like Silver, White Flash, Topper, Champion, Trigger, *ad infinitum.*

Another Mix gimmick was the pair of matched pearl-handled six-guns he always wore. Most of those who know anything about guns realize that mother-of-pearl has roughly the same toughness qualities as your family crystal. It is not something you put on a using gun and expect to remain intact, if you're going to be using that revolver with any great frequency. Drop it just once and it's all over.

On a more modern note, there is Clint Eastwood. In his portrayal of *Dirty Harry,* he helped greatly to make the Smith & Wesson Model 29 .44 magnum famous. Ask anyone on the street what Dirty Harry's last name was in the series. Most of them can't tell you it was Callahan, but they surely can tell you he carried that big *pistolo* and identify it. That goes for kids, school teachers, little old ladies and even those of the anti-gun fraternity. The latter may not like it, but they know it.

Knives always have played an important part in action films. In the early days, it was always the henchmen who were excellent knife throwers and were constantly threatening the hero with that excellence. It probably wasn't until the movie moguls settled on Jim Bowie as a potential box office hit that knives began to gain a degree of respectability. That and the Tarzan films. The idea of Tarzan wandering the jungle without a knife is akin to the *USS Constitution* fighting without a sail.

Sterling Hayden used "Iron Mistress" knife in a 1962 film, "The Last Command." That knife did get around!

In the first chapter, we covered much of the factual material — or what is known of it — about the knife favored by Jim Bowie that became the pattern for similar knives around the world. Truth of the matter is that more Bowie-type knives used on the frontier of the last century were made in England than in this country.

The first film to feature Jim Bowie and his knife is lost somewhere in film history, but the film that starred the knife itself, and had actor Alan Ladd along to hang on to it, was called *The Iron Mistress* and was adapted from the historical novel by Paul Wellman.

There have been a number of individuals who claimed to have designed and made the knife carried by Ladd in his role as Bowie, but truth is that the knife was the brainchild of a team at Warner Brothers studios. Philip Jefferies, the production illustrator on the film, did the original sketches of the knife; John Beckman, the *Iron Mistress* art director, designed it and Allen Smith, the set designer, drew the blueprints, which were used to make the knife in the studio prop shop.

In addition, the "star" knife had its stand-ins just as do living actors. There was a near copy made that had a sheet metal blade. Both later were used in Disney's *Davy Crockett* and in the *Jim Bowie* television series. The version with the sheet metal blade also saw service in the hands of Sterling Hayden when he portrayed Bowie in a film called *The Last Command* and still later in John Wayne's epic, *The Alamo*.

Richard Widmark was Jim Bowie in "The Alamo," a John Wayne starrer. Again, the knife used in the "Iron Mistress" film of decades before was featured blade.

There are many tales about origin of the "Iron Mistress" knife; it was created (from left) by Phil Jefferies, production illustrator on the film; John Beckman, the art director; Allen Smith, who served as set designer.

There have been a lot of less ambitious — and less authentic — films in which Jim Bowie and his knife have been featured. An example, is one called *Heroes of the Alamo*, circa 1938. A long-forgotten actor named Roger Williams portrayed Bowie and fought off the Mexican army with a butcher knife that looked as though he'd brought it from his own kitchen.

Then there were the Tarzan knives. The late Johnny Weissmuller was the first to play the jungle man in a sound film, although there had been a host of portrayals during the silent era. During the long-lived series, made by two different production companies, Weismuller carried at least two knives, but both of them were modified Bowie patterns.

This is the point at which we totally disillusion all of those now of middle age — or older — who recall Weissmuller wrestling a crocodile underwater and slaying it with his knife. That knife was a collapsible model. Pressure on the point caused the blade to slide up into the handle. What happened to that particular knife is a question that may never be answered, but chances are it was sold at the Metro-Goldwyn-Mayer auction more than a decade ago. That was when Scarlett O'Hara's dress and Judy Garland's Ruby Shoes from *The Wizard of Oz* went on the block, too.

According to collector Joe Musso, "There were a bunch of Bowie-type knives that were mislabeled as having been used in *Julius Caesar* and *Ben Hur*. It isn't likely that

It may disillusion Tarzan fans, but the knife carried in films starring Johnny Weismuller has a wooden blade. A sponge rubber version and one with retracting blades were made also by property experts for fast-action sequences.

*From left: Knifes used in "Iron Mistress" are stiletto carried by Anthony Caruso; wooden mock-up Alan Ladd was supposed to have whittled as a pattern; the sheet metal version that has been used in action scenes in many of the other Bowie films; steel blade with brass strip. All made in the property shop at Warner Brothers.*

The wooden knife carried by Weismuller as Tarzan now is in the collection of Joe Musso, a film studio artist.

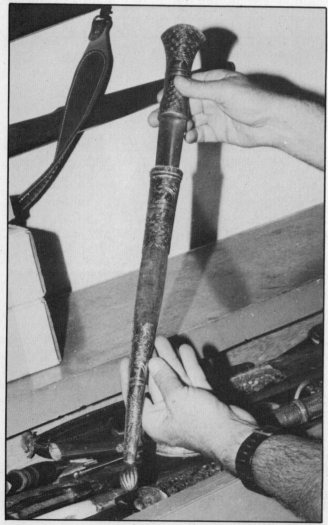

Stembridge Gun Rentals furnishes firearms and cutlery to the film industry. Some are genuine antiques, while others are manufactured to fit a special movie need.

Caesar was stabbed with a Bowie, since it wasn't designed until about seventeen centuries after that, but it is likely that one or more of the Tarzan knives went in the auction under that misnomer."

Weissmuller carried this particular knife through six of the MGM Tarzans, but when he transferred to RKO-Radio Pictures to make the rest of the series, he carried a different knife in several of them. In the final few pictures, he again had the big MGM Bowie-type.

Today, Musso owns two of the Weissmuller Tarzan knives. One is fashioned from wood and is painted to look like the real thing. The other is of sponge rubber and probably was carried as Weissmuller or one of his doubles swung through the jungle on vines. If a vine broke, he might fracture his neck, but he wouldn't stab himself to death! Whether there ever was an actual, steel-bladed knife used in the series is a fact that is lost somewhere in the past.

Incidentally, the knife that Weissmuller carried early in the RKO adventures later was carried by the late Lex Barker, when he portrayed the jungle hero. The two knives in Musso's possession were found in an RKO prop trunk, when the company was sold to Paramount Pictures a number of years ago.

The late Buster Crabbe, who portrayed the apeman in a bad, bad serial early in his career, carried what looked to be a $3 knife then being sold by Remington Arms. Considering the budget of *Tarzan the Fearless,* that is a distinct possibility!

Later Tarzans, in keeping with the times, had become gimmick conscious. Jock Mahoney, for example, had a Swiss bayonet cut down and fashioned into Tarzan's knife when he starred in two of the leather diaper epics. The others who have swung through the trees without puncturing themselves with a blade usually have settled for whatever the studio property department supplied them...as long as it was big!

But not all of the movie knives have come out of the studio prop shops. In the days of Errol Flynn, Tyrone Power and other derring-do types, there were plenty of swashbuckling pirate films and movies about European kings and knights. In these celluloid extravaganzas, hundreds of actors and extras were assigned to carry swords and knives to fulfill even minor roles. Such films are less common these days, but when the need arises, there are several movie equipment rental houses in the Hollywood area ready to fill the requirement.

One such organization is Stembridge Gun Rentals, which is operated by Syd Stembridge in Glendale, California. For many years, the outfit was situated on the Paramount Studios lot. An employee, when he wasn't scalping settlers in Western movies, was the late Rodd Redwing, a full-blooded Indian, who was an expert on both firearms and edged weapons.

It was Redwing who set up the classic stunt in *Shane,* which starred Alan Ladd. In a key scene, Jack Palance, as a hired killer, was to shoot Elisha Cook, Jr., who portrayed a harmless settler. To make the scene more realistic, Redwing attached a wire to Cook's belt at the back. When Palance triggered the blank cartridge, Redwing gave a magnificent tug on the wire. Cook was jerked — supposedly by the force of the bullet — off a raised board sidewalk to die in the mud. The scene made a star of Palance. Cook's recollections have been dutifully censored.

Rodd Redwing also did a personal appearance act in which he drew a six-gun from a holster with one hand and pulled a knife from behind his neck with the other. He would fire at a target with the revolver, then throw the knife. The knife invariably would stick into the bullet hole left by the bullet. In short, he knew his cutlery and coached many an actor in how to use it in knife-fighting scenes.

Stembridge Gun Rentals still specializes in guns for movie use, furnishing anything from flintlocks and single-action revolvers to the most modern machine guns, all modified to fire blanks or special ammunition. But in the drawers throughout the establishment are hundreds of knives and swords that will fit almost any period of history — or any fantasy. When the script calls for a dagger of a specific period, a fencing foil, an executioner's axe or a mugger's switchblade, the film producers know that Syd Stembridge can supply what they want and the item will be

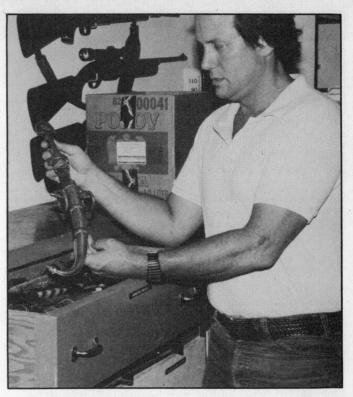

*Syd Stembridge inspects one of the movie props that he furnishes to producers on a rental basis. Almost any type of knife is available or will be made as required.*

*Arkansas custom knifemaker Jimmy Lile designed, made the survival knife used by Sylvester Stallone in the first two Rambo films. Lile-made copies of this blade were made in a limited edition to sell at up to $2250.*

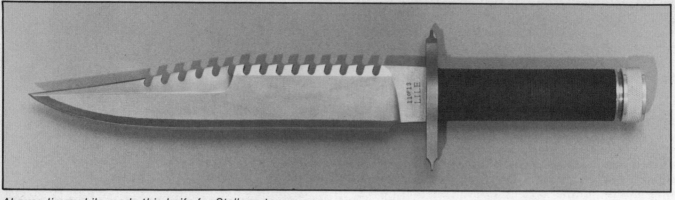

Above: Jimmy Lile made this knife for Stallone to use in "First Blood" Rambo film. (Below) Similar in design, the same maker created this survival type for "Rambo."

authentic in appearance, although it may be a careful reproduction of the original.

In recent years, modern Hollywood mayhem and splatter scripts have proved to be a veritable bonanza for custom knifemakers. Much of this must be credited to Sylvester Stallone and his *Rambo* portrayals.

For the first of the series, which he produced, Stallone decided that he needed a special type of survival knife that could be used for various imaginative chores. The actor was familiar with the reputation of Jimmy Lile, known among his contemporaries as The Arkansas Knifemaker. He contacted Lile at his shop in Russellville, Arkansas, and they discussed Stallone's ideas on what he thought he needed.

"He said he wanted a knife like no one else had for a

movie he was making," Lile recalls now. "I didn't know he was talking about *First Blood,* the first of this Rambo series, but I did get an idea of what he wanted and I went to work.

"Stallone had given me an overview of the story he was going to do and I tried to put myself in a situation where I would be totally dependent on a knife to provide me with the basic needs of survival: food and shelter." The knife was ground from 440C stainless steel.

Lile doesn't talk about how much the actor paid him for the knife used in *First Blood,* but part of the agreement was that the knifemaker could make a hundred exact copies. He did, each of them numbered. They were marketed for

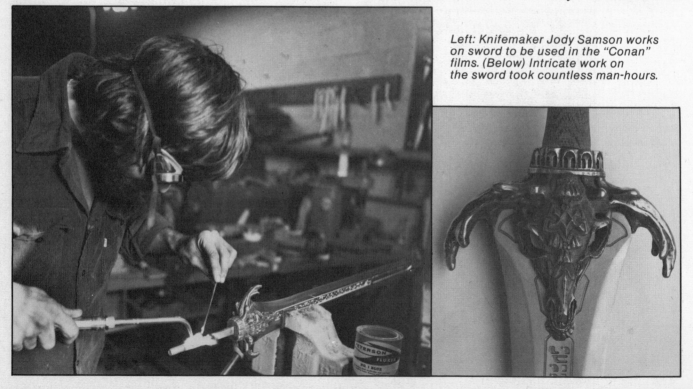

Left: Knifemaker Jody Samson works on sword to be used in the "Conan" films. (Below) Intricate work on the sword took countless man-hours.

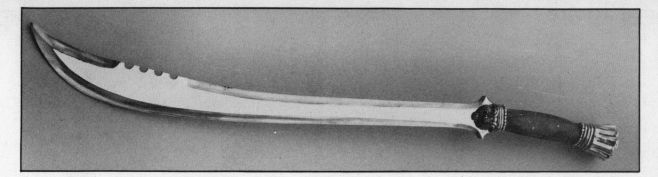

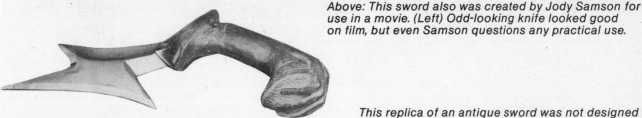

Above: This sword also was created by Jody Samson for use in a movie. (Left) Odd-looking knife looked good on film, but even Samson questions any practical use.

This replica of an antique sword was not designed by Samson, but he was commissioned to accomplish the job.

up to $2250, depending upon the number.

For the sequel, Lile made a different knife for Stallone to use in the film. This was a stiletto, with copies selling for up to $950!

Still another knife for Stallone is being made at this writing to use in another Rambo film that is being shot in Israel. But under terms of their agreement, no details of its design will be released until late this year, when the film is shown in theaters. After all, it isn't good to give away the gimmick too soon!

Sylvester Stallone set the trend and other blood-and-guts performers have followed.

One of the blades, for instance, that received a lot of attention was the one carried by actor Arnold Schwarzenegger in *Conan The Barbarian*. The sword, big enough to match Schwarzenegger's muscular build, was crafted by one of the better custom knifemakers, Jody Samson.

Samson's shop is in Burbank, California, which may account for the Conan sword assignment, as well as the many motion picture jobs he's had since.

"We're right next door to a recording studio," says Samson. "They do a lot of sound recordings for movies and television and we have several of the actors who drop into the shop when they're in the neighborhood. I guess that's how the studio people have come to know my work."

The Conan sword took months of Samson's time, day and night. Producing the movie version was not simply making one sword for the actor to use in the film. The maker had to produce five or six each of two different designs to be submitted to the studio for approval. Original design work was the product of A-Team Productions of Hollywood and Samson also had to produce a couple of aluminum replicas of the final version to be used in the film, which was written and directed by mayhem expert John Milius and produced by Dino DeLaurentis.

The design of the unique butt and hilt was the work of Jody Samson. The artwork was first carved in wax, then a mould was made for bronze casting. "It's hard to estimate the time involved, for I worked quite a long time at the wax artwork before the actual start of the sword blade," Samson recalls.

This array of knives was made by Chuck Stapel for use in the film, "Little Nikita." The partial blade that is affixed to the metal plate was used in scene to show the penetration of knife carried by one of the actors.

The Conan sword was constructed of 440C stainless steel, with a blade length of twenty-nine inches; the width tapers from three inches down to two inches near the tip. The hollow grind down the center was done freehand as were the outside hollows of the blade. The basic form was done on a stone wheel grinder, according to Samson. Later he switched to his trusty Burr King belt grinder for final shaping of the quarter-inch-thick steel blade.

Known for his understatements and modesty, Samson commented that, "The swords were kind of fun, but an awful lot of hard work."

The completion of the Conan sword and the success of the movie have brought Jody Samson a measure of fame and fortune. "People just keep popping in and wanting me to do more work for various films and television shows" he says.

He has built swords or knives for such diverse outlets as the Universal Studio's tourist display of *Conan,* plus stage plays such as *Othello, Salome* and *Macbeth.* He has produced props for *The Sacketts, Kung Fu, The Movie* and *Sidekicks* for television. Other motion pictures that have featured Samson blades are *Under The Rainbow, My Science Project, The Big Brawl, Red Dawn* and *Sharky's Machine.*

Another Southern Californian who has been making excellent custom knives for a dozen or more years is Chuck Stapel of Glendale. A movie called, *No Mercy* starring Richard Gere and Kim Basinger had brief popularity. The Bad Guy in the story used a curved-blade and decorated knife in the film. Stapel made it.

Another film for which Stapel made several knives, some of which have collapsing blades, rubber blades and half-blades — none of which have sharp edges for safety sake — is *Little Nikita.* In this movie, a young man, played by River Phoenix, discovers his mother and father are actually agents of the Soviet Union. Sidney Poitier is the

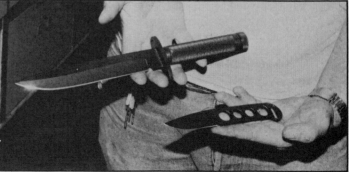

Left: Stapel displays one of the knives he created for a film titled, "No Mercy." More and more filmmakers are seeking unusual knives. (Below) A number of Stapel's early knives are stocked by Stembridge Gun Rentals.

Knifemaker Jack Crain (left) meets with Jim Frost of Frost Cutlery to sign contract for the latter's firm to mass produce Crain models used in "Predator" movie. (Right) Crain made medieval war hammer for "Running Man" film, but script changes deleted its appearance.

Good Guy FBI agent, while Richard Lynch plays the Bad Guy who uses the Stapel knife to no good end.

As mentioned earlier, Arnold Schwarzenegger is one of those who discovered "the gimmick" early in his career. This has been beneficial to several custom knifemakers, including Jack Crain of Weatherford, Texas. The actor chose to use three of Crain's knives from what he calls his Life Support System in a film called *Commando*. These knives were of varying sizes and designs for survival. Some of these knives also made their appearance in television's *Air Wolf* and *The Fall Guy*.

The actor must have been satisfied with the products of Crain's grinding wheels, because the producers of *Predator,* another Schwarzenegger film, came back to him

to design several knives and a big machete for that film. The Crain machete, incidentally, has gone the commercial route, with the Frost Cutlery Company contracting to produce it *en masse*.

In *Predator,* knives are carried by not only the star, but by every actor in the film. All the knives in the film are the work of Jack Crain. In the film story, an alien being gradually kills off all the Good Guys trying to track him down in a South American jungle except Arnold Schwarzenegger.

*All of the knives pictured are part of Crain's Life Support System series, which he has patented as a trademark. All of them have been used in Arnold Schwarzenegger action movies.*

A number of custom knifemakers have been well paid for the knives made for films and also have received publicity that was an aid to their reputations. Both the knife at Arnold Schwarzenegger's hand and the machete in the hand of another actor were made especially for "Predator" by Jack Crain. The resultant publicity has helped business.

Finally, with no other weapons left except his knife, the hero is forced to fight the alien with only a knife and the bow and arrows he is able to fashion with the blade.

Crain is proud of the obvious visibility of his knives in the hands of the actors in this movie. Crain, too, is offering duplicates of the *Predator* knife, fitting the survival definition, but at prices considerably higher than most of us can afford.

Another Sylvester Stallone movie that achieved considerable box office success was one called *Cobra*. Here is

a story of a Los Angeles cop who is alwasy called out to run down the worst and most vicious criminals. Among the Bad Guys, one carries a special knife and uses it to slash up pretty girls. That particular knife — one not forgotten by those who have seen it or the movie — was made by custom knifemaker Herman Schneider.

Schneider, one of the more successful custom makers, to judge by the sale and prices of his artwork knives, has had several of his knives purchased by Stallone, but they never had met. One day, a telephone call from Stallone to

This knife was created for Stallone's film, "Cobra," as a weapon carried by a villain. It is made of 440C stainless steel and was designed, custom made by Herman Schneider.

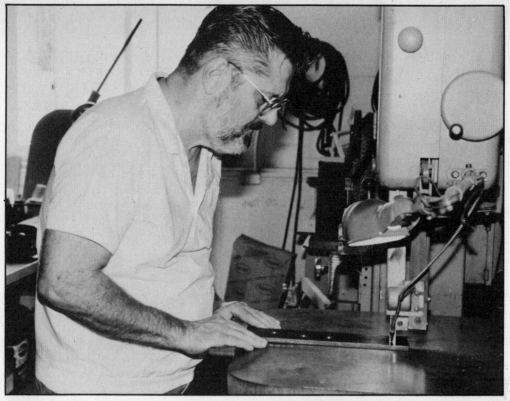

Herman Schneider, renowned for collector-quality custom knives, cuts a piece of ⅝-inch steel to start the "Cobra" knife. He conferred with Sylvester Stallone on style.

Schneider outlined the *Cobra* plot and the actor's need for a special, never-before-seen knife. The bad news was that Stallone needed it within three weeks.

A face-to-face meeting took place in Hollywood, not far from Schneider's Southern California home. Stallone outlined how he envisioned the knife design. He wanted a sort of cross between a hatchet and a big knife with plenty of belly to the blade. It had to look modern, slick and fearsome. Schneider returned home and soon had some sketches for Stallone to examine. The blade has a deep curve, the

*With a long way yet to go, the cut-out blank for the "Cobra" knife hangs in Schneider's shop, while he does other knives of the type for which he is best known.*

handle has two finger holes in it, but the most arresting feature is the ten steel spikes protruding from the knuckle guard portion of the handle.

It is wicked looking! Stallone approved the design concept and Schneider made a plastic model for final examination. The star was not satisfied with the look of the ten spikes and made a suggestion which led to the final design seen in the movie.

The final design is frightening looking, while maintaining a certain grace. Herman Schneider made the knife — in the required three weeks — of 440C stainless steel, a full five-eighths-inch thick. The handle material is 6061-T6 aluminum anodized black. The handle is held on by four spline-drive screws with three hidden alignment pins near the screw holes. The handle may be removed, although only with a special spline-drive screwdriver. The ten handle spikes are of 303 steel. There is a carved devil mask on the side of the deeply hollow-ground blade.

The original, as used in the *Cobra* movie, went into Stallone's private collection after the filming, but Herman Schneider produced five — and only five, he stresses — duplicates which he has sold to collectors. The knives, he says, have sold for several thousand dollars each. He will make no more, but he has completed an agreement with a Japanese manufacturer to produce a limited number of the Cobra knives, but reduced in size by ten percent. This will retain the value of the five Schneider-made Cobra knives.

The number and variety of sharpening tools available today is large and may seem a bit bewildering to the knife owner. Each item, though, has its use and makes the work a breeze.

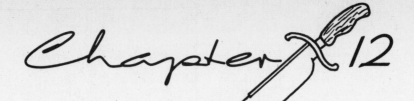

*Chapter 12*

# of
# SHARPENING
# and
# SHARPENERS

*There's Not All That Much Mystery About
Creating A Cutting Edge!*

*The close-up view, above, is the finished edge of a correctly sharpened utility knife. The edge angle is beveled at a desirable twenty-five degrees.*

*Comparing blade widths of common knives, below. On the left is a Buck Hunting utility knife, with a G-96 fish fillet knife on the right. The Buck should have a twenty-five-degree edge taper while the G-96 will cut best using eighteen degrees.*

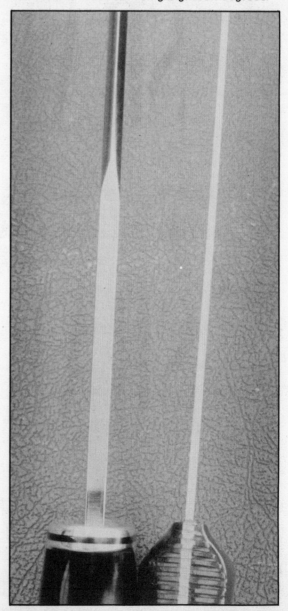

"A DULL KNIFE is worse than useless; it's dangerous. Far more injuries are caused each year by dull knives than sharp, because the dull blade cannot perform as intended. This greatly increases the potential for serious accidents." That is the philosophy of gunsmith Jack Mitchell, who also sharpens things. We asked for his input for this chapter.

There are a great many excellent sharpening accessories available to the knife owner today. Unfortunately, if not used properly, most produce less-than-perfect results. The only way to produce the proper edge for any given knife is to understand how to use the sharpening equipment and obtain the type of edge best suited for the jobs for which the knife will be used.

"A surgeon's scalpel is great for the human body, but try whittling tent pegs with it and see how long it lasts. A knife is a tool and the type of edge must coincide with the tasks it will be called upon to perform," Mitchell decrees.

A blade's edge and, equally important, its durability are dependent upon the type of steel used in its manufacture, the care taken in its heat-treating, the methods used to give it an edge. The first two features are covered elsewhere in this book. This chapter concerns the sharpening aspects.

"To begin with, any blade is simply one large bevel, widest at the top or spine, gradually tapering to the edge. The actual cutting edge is created by a smaller second bevel extending from the edge. Most frustration in knife sharpening is caused by how much relief (thickness) is directly behind the cutting edge. It is this angle or degree of taper that makes for sharpness and an ability to stay sharp.

"This second taper or edge *must* be consistent in angle and straightness from ricasso to point (back to front). The amount of angle *must* be compatible with the type of knife and its intended uses. The only way to efficiently accomplish these tasks is to work with the right sharpening tools in their correct order."

A wide variety of excellent power and hand sharpening tools is available. As we look at each proper technique for using these tools — matched to the particular knife we are sharpening — it will become apparent that putting a proper edge on a knife is neither mysterious nor difficult.

### POWER TOOLS

"Power tools offer one big advantage over hand tools in that they achieve results much faster," Mitchell points out. There are also some disadvantages. Power tools such as buffing or polishing wheels turning at high rates of speed quickly build up heat which can damage or discolor a knife edge.

"Used improperly, they can be dangerous. This is particularly true when working either the point of a knife or back near the quillon. I've seen knives ripped out of workers' hands and whipped to the floor, or worse, into their feet. Also, the wheel can catch the knife and whip it around and up — either to stick into the ceiling or between your ears. I do not recommend anyone sharpening a knife with power equipment unless he is experienced and uses all proper safety precautions."

Possibly the most useful power tool ever to come along for the custom knifemaker is an abrasive belt grinder manufactured by Burr King.

This California-based manufacturer makes a variety of models for different industries, but one — with a number of accessories — is made specifically for the knifemaker. The knifemaker can use a solid backing behind the belt for precise grinding or polishing or hold the work above the backing for contour or loose-belt grinding. The seventy-two-inch-long belts, two inches wide, are available in 40 to 600 grits, allowing the maker to actually contour blanks of steel and mirror-polish the finished work on the same machine.

The Burr King belt grinder is particularly useful tapering the relief on new knives or repairing damaged old knives. It also will quickly complete initial sharpening of any knife through a technique called "forming a burr." This is done using either a 240- or 320-grit abrasive belt with the blade

The Burr King belt grinder is particularly suited to knifemakers and sharpeners. It is fast and efficient. Here, a 220-grit belt is being used to re-shape an improperly tapered pocketknife blade.

*Stitched muslin buffing wheels impregnated with buffing compounds of various grits will make short work of removing the edge burr, but use caution!*

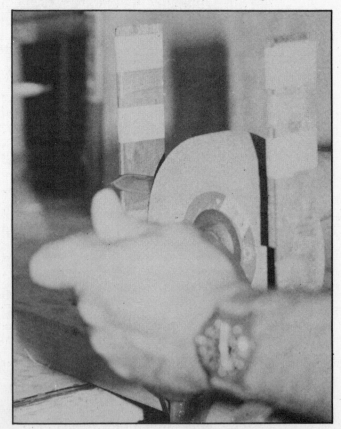

*Phill Hartsfield designed the Little Cranky, a geared, hand-powered sharpener that is simple to use, always results in extremely sharp edge.*

held against the unsupported belt. Utility knives usually are held at about a twenty-degree angle, while thinner blades like the kitchen varieties are angled slightly less; about 18 degrees.

"By carefully running the edge back and forth at the proper angle, a visible burr is formed along the entire edge. The burr indicates equal sharpness wherever visible and is as sharp as it can be with that particular grit belt. The burr is formed because the steel becomes so thin at the leading edge it has no rigidity. By changing belts to progressively finer grits, the edge becomes more polished, leaving only honing or stropping to produce an extremely sharp edge," Jack Mitchell reports.

Safety glasses should be worn when using this or any power tool. Gloves ordinarily would be another safety accessory, but they don't allow the worker to feel that heat buildup of the steel which could be destroying the temper in the metal.

"Sewn or loose muslin wheels impregnated with 600-grit Tripoli or Matchless compound are excellent for final stropping. However, as stated, they can be dangerous and great care should be exercised. Since the wheels are flexible, they actually contact the edge of the blade as it is passed back and forth and almost underneath it, completely removing the burr formed by the abrasive belts or coarse hand-polishing stones." The metal on the leading edge of the blade is displaced (buffed) as much as polished, producing a finely sharpened edge. The blade should be held at about a thirty-five-degree angle for this operation.

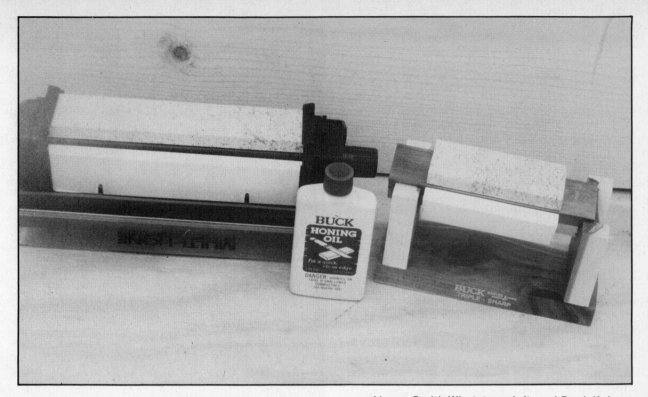

*Above: Smith Whetstone, left, and Buck Knives offer quality stand-mounted natural stones of various hardnesses. In use, the Arkansas stones must have a good honing oil, frequent cleaning.*

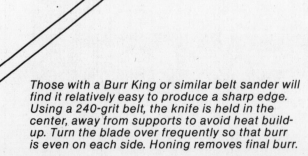

*Those with a Burr King or similar belt sander will find it relatively easy to produce a sharp edge. Using a 240-grit belt, the knife is held in the center, away from supports to avoid heat build-up. Turn the blade over frequently so that burr is even on each side. Honing removes final burr.*

## HAND TOOLS

"Phil Hartsfield's 'Little Cranky' has put more razor-edged knives back into use far faster and more efficiently than any other. This sharpener actually is a transition between power and hand tools," Mitchell states.

Hartsfield suffered a near-fatal accident while using a power tool some years back. Realizing conventional hand tools required more time to produce the same results as power tools, he improvised to come up with the Little Cranky. It is basically a geared crank device using a medium-grit wheel surrounded by a steel alignment frame with wooden shims. The knife is placed on one side of the wheel in one hand while the other turns the crank. When the desired relief or taper is formed on one side of the blade, it is placed on the other side of the wheel and the crank is turned in the opposite direction.

"It is much easier to use than it sounds and provides a perfectly uniform taper at exactly the right angle — about twenty degrees — leaving only the stropping operation to result in an extremely sharp edge," Mitchell has found.

The Little Cranky provides fast, efficient results without the possibility of over-heating the blade, as can occur with conventional power equipment.

Priced at around $45, it is quite inexpensive when compared to power equipment and costs only about twice as much as one good eight-inch natural oilstone!

## NATURAL STONES

The State of Arkansas appears to have a monopoly on natural oilstone; also called whetstone. The only place in the world where quality natural stones are found is within a fifteen-mile radius of Hot Springs. The largest supplier is the Smith Whetstone Company which has been hard at it for one hundred years.

Not all Arkansas oilstones are perfect; dark streaks in otherwise white stones are caused by impurities. Some will also have pits or hairline cracks. It is best to avoid "cheap deal" Arkansas stones and stick with established companies like Smith and A.G. Russell.

Quality Arkansas stones contain high-grade novaculite — a hard, compact, silica crystal. This substance is the key to polishing an edge, as it sharpens.

The two most common Arkansas stones used are the medium, which is mostly white or gray in color, and the Arkansas surgical black. The latter is used for putting the final edge on razors and surgical instruments.

"When it comes to purchasing Arkansas stones, buy the biggest one you can afford. They are easier to use, if secured in a wooden block or between soft jaws in a vise," Mitchell advises.

In using a whetstone to sharpen a knife, first rub a liberal coating of light oil such as Buck's Honing Oil over the stone. The oil permits the knife edge to be drawn easier across the stone and helps float steel particles over the surface and out of the pores of the stone.

When the pores of a whetstone become plugged, the stone should be cleaned, using a rag with a solvent or kerosene. An old knifemaker's trick is to wrap the stone in a kerosene-soaked rag and bake it for a few hours in an oven at 250 degrees.

For best results, natural sharpening stones are first coated with light machine or honing oil. The oil floats away minute metal chips from the blade as it sharpens. Stone must be kept clean.

The Norton Pike Company is an old and large maker of artificial India stones and supplier of an array of natural stones, below. Hundreds of sizes and shapes will fit almost any metal polishing job.

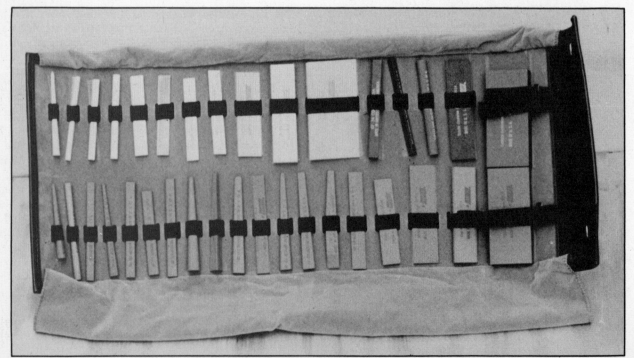

Man-made ceramic stones and rods are manufactured in a variety of shapes and sizes, ideal for putting on the final working edge. The triangular cross-section rods are Spyderco; the stones, Colorado Ceramic Abrasives.

## MAN-MADE STONES

Man-made whetstones — commonly called India stones — are indispensable for initial phases of knife sharpening. The largest manufacturer, Norton Pike Company, produces a vast number of different sizes, shapes and grits. The most versatile for knife sharpening is the two-sided coarse- and fine-face six-inch stone.

India stones are lower in price than natural stones, yet are excellent for putting a good edge on a knife. When used first for initial tapering of the edge, then finished on a fine Arkansas stone, sharpening goes fast and efficiently. The India stones should be used with a good light coat of oil and cleaned in the same manner as the Arkansas naturals.

Another man-made stone, relatively new in this country, is the Japanese waterstone. Although much softer than India stone, it produces an edge comparable to the finest natural oilstones.

A major factor in popularity of Japanese waterstones is the speed with which they produce a razor edge. Due to their consistent size of grit, they produce a fine edge several times faster than India stones. Japanese technology has succeeded in controlling two critical factors that determine the quality of each stone: consistent size of particles used in each stone and even less impurities than in top-grade natural stones.

Before you run down to the store to stock up, be advised that the Japanese stones wear rapidly and do not hold up to abuse as well as American oilstones. Hard use means gouges, cracks and chipping. They must be kept in water, even when stored, and must be re-faced flush against another flat surface to restore their shape. They sell for about the same as a quality oilstone.

Today's high-grade, wear-resistant ceramics are excellent for polishing an edge and obtaining excellent sharpness. They are available in a wide variety of sizes and shapes, as well as two basic grits distinguished by gray and white colors.

## SHARPENING BY HAND

The two most important factors in sharpening any dull knife involve maintaining the same precise angle throughout and knowing which abrasive stone to begin with and when to graduate to the next finer stone.

As mentioned, most utility knives should be sharpened at a twenty-degree angle. Thinner knives like kitchen knives should be sharpened between seventeen and eighteen degrees. Large cutting tools like cleavers or hatchets require a twenty-five-degree angle.

The best way to take the guesswork out of setting the correct angle is to use an angle-holding fixture. Buck's Honemaster clamps onto the spine of the knife by means of a thumbscrew. It holds the blade precisely at any angle selected while sharpening each side.

If a knife is dull or has nicks or chips in the edge, the relief or taper must be re-established. That means removing metal until all nicks have completely disappeared.

"Attempting to do this with a hard stone like the black Arkansas is an exasperating lesson in frustration and futility," Mitchell reports. "Start with the coarse side of an India

*While the bevel angle may be just right, left, a slight burr left on the blade will cause the knife to catch or slip in use. Text contains several useful techniques for eliminating that metal burr.*

*Illustration at right shows the correct stroking method for honing a blade which is bigger than the sharpening stone. The blade moves evenly across the stone as if taking a slice off the top.*

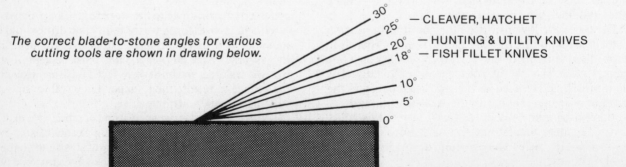

*The correct blade-to-stone angles for various cutting tools are shown in drawing below.*

30° — CLEAVER, HATCHET
25° — HUNTING & UTILITY KNIVES
20° 
18° — FISH FILLET KNIVES
10°
5°
0°

The Lansky sharpening system relies upon a special jig to hold the knife and the ceramic stones always at the same precise angle. The blade will sharpen up quickly and safely, because of the unvarying stroke.

stone liberally coated with a light oil. Removal of metal will be faster and the correct relief will result in a sharper edge after final stropping.

"Begin sharpening with the stone positioned securely in a block or set in a vise. Make cutting strokes from the back of the blade toward the tip as though slicing off a thin layer of stone. With today's Space Age knife steels, especially 440C or 154CM, definite downward pressure must be applied, if you want to finish the job before becoming eligible for Social Security."

A dozen or so swipes on one side followed by a like number on the other of a coarse India stone should be enough before switching to a finer-grit stone, unless the edge has deep nicks. With each stroke, the most troublesome area will be near the point of the blade. The knife must be raised and slightly pivoted to maintain the correct angle in this section of the blade.

"As you progress from the coarse India stone to the medium grade, then to the medium Arkansas, do not be deceived by the feel of the edge," Mitchell cautions. "Each swipe creates a tiny burr, confusing the issue. Just work on the proper angle. By holding the knife up to a light at an angle, this burr should be quite visible. It will also show whether the new taper or relief is consistent from one end of the blade to the other."

Once the relief has been established and the knife has been sharpened on succeedingly finer grit stones, it is time for final honing.

A knife blade which is new, or one which has been improperly sharpened several times may result in an edge which looks like the one on the left, below. Re-sharpening the blade at left will take a great deal of time and patience. Note how the right blade contacts the stone, with its easily sharpened taper.

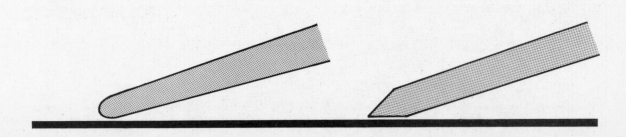

## HONING A KNIFE

Honing or stropping a knife both do the same thing. They remove the microscopic burr left by abrasive stones. One way to remove the burr is to sink the knife into a piece of wood and draw it back out. Another is to slice through a piece of lead. It can also be accomplished with power buffing equipment (600 grit with muslin wheel) as described previously. However, Mitchell insists the easiest and safest method is with a leather strop.

"I'd like to tell you where you can get barbers' leather strops, but I don't think they're available any longer. Barbers stopped using straight razors years ago," Mitchell says. "I bought mine from a retiring barber several years ago and found it was made in Russia. Fortunately, any piece of leather such as an old belt will work if treated with a fine compound like Matchless 600 or green Tripoli."

To strop properly, secure one end of the strop and hold the other end with your hand. Move the blade away from

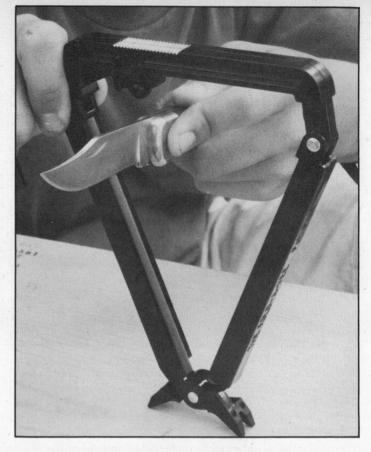

*Another Lansky sharpening device, Hold-A-Vee, right, is simple and compact. Opened up as shown, the knife blade is quickly sharpened by vertically running it down the ceramics.*

*A quick, sharp edge is obtained by holding the knife blade vertical while stroking down along the ceramic rods. The Spyderco sharpening kit includes brass rods to protect the user's hand.*

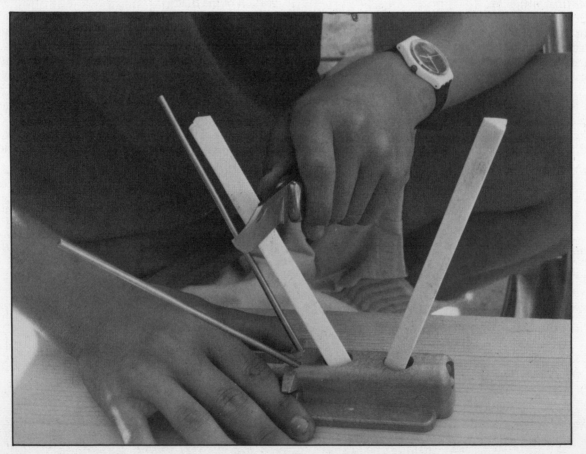

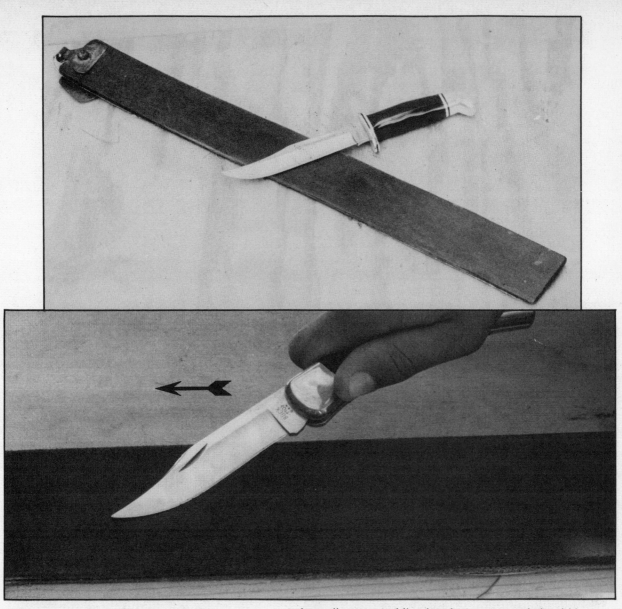

*A small amount of fine lapping compound should be added to the face of the strop before beginning work, above. For this final honing and de-burring operation, the blade is stroked away from the edge.*

*Good leather razor strops are a vanishing breed in this country, because of the changing barbering business, left. Swap meets, garage sales, catalogs are places to search.*

you, the spine or back of the knife leading the way. In other words, this operation is opposite of how you've been running the edge toward the stones. The stropping motion will eliminate the burr, leaving a fine sharp edge.

## ALTERNATIVE METHODS

"With manufacturers jumping into the knife-sharpening accessory business, I was skeptical of anything new at first. However, a sharpening system called the Lansky Knife Sharpener Kit is one of the most ingenious and idiot-proof systems I have found to date. It differs from the hand-sharpening method described previously in that it brings the sharpener to a stationary knife edge rather than the other way around. The Lansky sharpener consists of a clamp that holds the knife securely in place. Several holes are drilled on either end of the clamp. Using guide rods inserted in a hole marked to give any desired angle, a sharpening stone attaches to the guide rod. It is a simple matter to push and pull the rod across the knife's cutting edge at precisely the desired angle. A number of abrasive stones come with the kit, ranging from an extra-coarse diamond hone to a fine diamond hone. Each one is color-coded to avoid confusion. The system is easy to use and produces results rivaling the best conventional sharpening means.

## SERRATIONS OR SCALLOPS

Serrated-edge knives present a peculiar sharpening problem. They cannot be properly sharpened with India or whetstones. Spyderco, Inc., a company manufacturing both knives and sharpening accessories, has developed a system known as the "Tri-Angle." It consists of a base and triangular ceramic sticks, along with brass rods to prevent accidental cutting of the hand holding the base of the kit, should the knife slip during sharpening.

The key to successful knife sharpening using the Spyderco Tri-Angle lies in the fact that the operator need only keep the blade of the knife perpendicular. Since the ceramic sticks are already anchored at twenty degrees in the base,

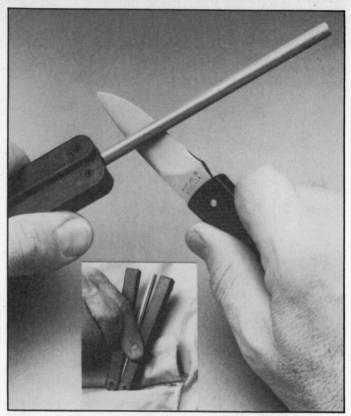

*Folded up and taken to the field, the Diamond Machine Technology field hone is ideal for quick touch-up work. Rod is embedded with fine diamonds.*

*Buck's diamond rods are set in a carefully drilled block to ensure the correct honing angle with every stroke. Rods are stored within cavities in base.*

*Serrated edge knives such as this from Spyderco may be re-sharpened, but only on ceramic or steel rods. This edge will cut quickly through tough nylon belts or ropes, but requires special care to bring back an edge.*

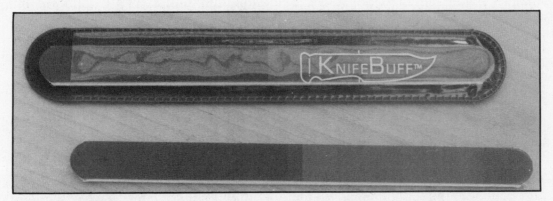

*The Knife Buff flat has two grits at ends of rods. Tight grits put the final buff to blade edge.*

excellent results can be expected. Each kit comes with two sets of ceramic sticks, gray or coarse, and white or fine.

Initial sharpening should be done with the stick edges contacting the knife edge. This is necessary for sharpening serrated-edge blades like those found on electric knives. The sticks may be turned so that the edge contacts the stick flats as well. This works well with thin-bladed knives like fishing fillet models.

### FIELD EXPEDIENTS

"Getting a sharp edge on a knife and keeping it that way during heavy field use are two different things. If a blade edge is gouged or nicked there is little you can do to recontour the taper and get a new fine edge. However, following normal use that only dulls a knife somewhat, a fine edge can be regained with a variety of accessories. A regular sharpening steel works quite well to put an edge back on a knife while caping out an animal. Smith Company makes a retractable sharpening steel that takes up no more room than a ballpoint pen.

"One of the best knife sharpening accessories for quick use in the field is another brain-child of the Lansky Company. Weighing only a few ounces, it is composed of two ceramic sticks that quickly assemble into the same triangular shape as the Spyderco Tri-Angle. With a grip located on the outside of the sharpening area, it prevents accidents.

There is also a gripping base on this device that helps keep the unit stationary during knife sharpening."

For more information write to:

BUCK KNIVES, P.O. Box 1267, El Cajon, CA 92022

BURR KING MANUFACTURING, 1875 Penn Mar Avenue, South El Monte, California 91733

COLORADO CERAMIC ABRASIVES, Box 141, Littleton, Colorado 80160

KNIFEBUFF, 2365 Avon Industrial Dr., Auburn Heights, MI 48057

LANSKY SHARPENERS, P.O. Box 800, Buffalo, New York 14221

"LITTLE CRANKY," Hartsfield Knives, 13095 Brookhurst, Garden Grove, California 92643

NORTON PIKE COMPANY, 1 New Bond Street, Worcester, Massachusetts 01606-2698

SMITH WHETSTONE, INCORPORATED, 1500 Sleepy Valley Road, Hot Springs, Arkansas 71901

SPYDERCO, INCORPORATED, P.O. Box 800, Golden, Colorado 80402

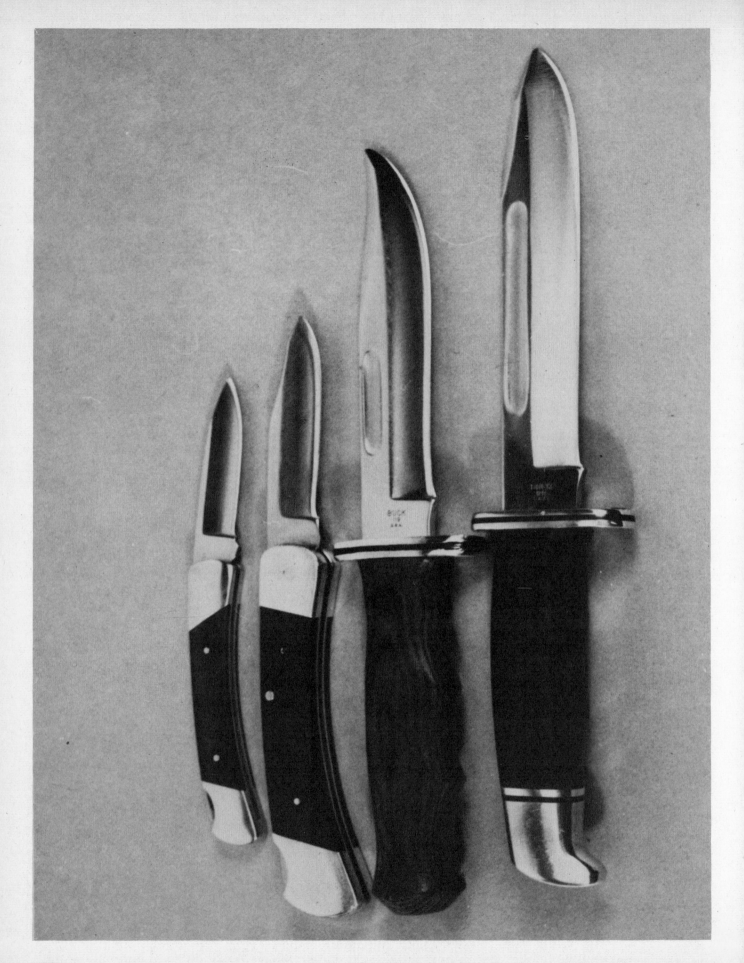

# Chapter 13

# CLEANING and REFURBISHING

### Knife Care Is A Lot Easier Than Repair, But When Necessary, Here Are Some Easy Steps To Take

**B**OB LEARN has been a tinkerer, repairer and gadget maker for more than thirty years. He has also written dozens, if not hundreds, of "How To" articles for the nation's outdoor press on the care and repair of almost any kind of equipment or gear known to mankind. We figured he was a natural to come up with some ideas on how to repair and maintain your favorite blade or handle. You will agree that he has a unique outlook on the task. Here is his report:

We all use and sometimes abuse our knives, says Learn, sometimes beyond repair. Many knife companies offer replacements, unless there are certain signs of mistreatment. We know we should not throw, hammer or use our knives as screwdrivers, but people still do those things rather than obtain the proper tool for the job.

When we do things like this, which basically ruin a knife, we will often try to repair it ourselves rather than send it back to the maker. There are times when you want to keep

Safety is an important consideration when working around any power tools or sharp points. The heavy leather sheath will hold blades when buffing or grinding handles. The stainless steel-reinforced Kevlar glove will withstand most knife accidents.

Use of a woodworking belt sander will save a lot of time and effort when refinishing knives. A new belt should be attached for knife metal work.

a particular knife you damaged, because someone special gave it to you and it has sentimental value. Bob Learn says there are some simple ways to refurbish that knife as well as prescribed methods of cleaning a dirty knife.

The fixed-blade hunter is one of the popular types frequently abused. Friends bring them by Learn's place and ask if he can possibly do anything to restore them. His first and simple answer is to send it back for a replacement, but nobody wants to, for some reason.

There were several examples in the shop that had come into Learn's temporary possession that showed how people can abuse a knife. One was a Buck General, one of that

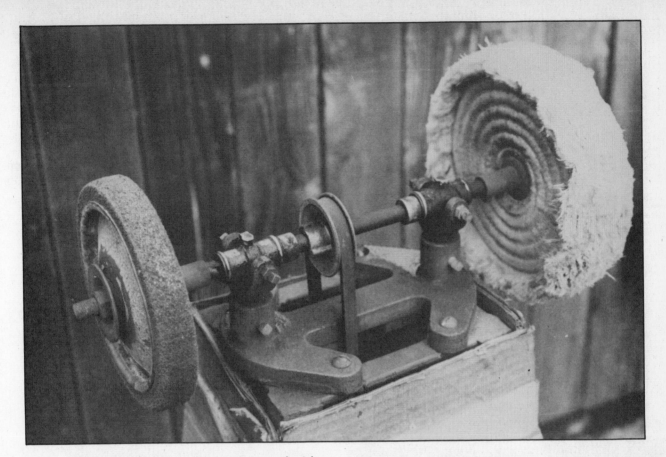

Dangerous as well as time-saving, an electric buffing and grinding wheel is one found in many workshops. Most of the materials shown can be picked up at swap meets or junkyards.

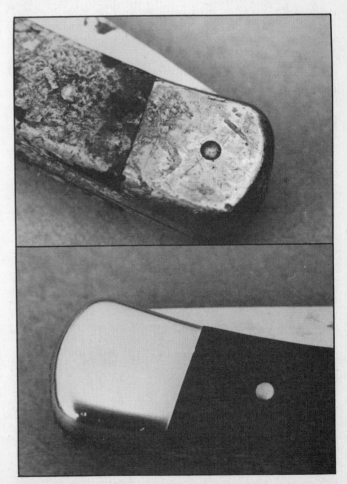

The brass bolster at right may have been used as a hammer by the previous owner. The knife was handled by someone with a sticky paint or epoxy on his hands. A fine-tooth file, sandpaper and steel wool transformed the knife above to the almost-new looking folder shown at lower right.

company's many fixed-blade designs. It looked as if they had hammered on the aluminum butt and in turn had broken off the tip of the blade. Not a total disaster, but it wouldn't do much good in its present condition.

The remedy for this is to take the blade down slow and easy on a sanding belt. Some people try to rework or change a blade style by using a high-speed grinding wheel. About all they usually succeed in doing is to ruin the blade by burning it. This comes from too much pressure on the blade while grinding. The first rule, says Learn, is don't use a grinding wheel.

Safety is the watchword here. The first thing Learn puts

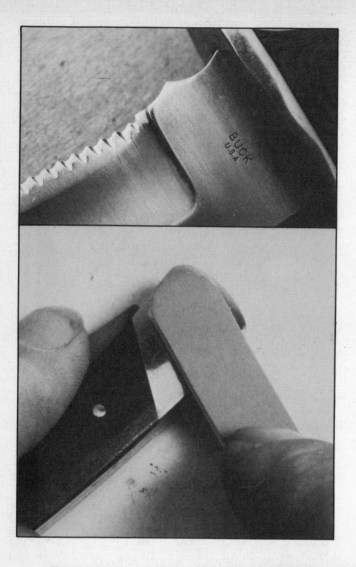

on is his safety glasses. He puts a can of water beside the belt to dip the blade in if it gets too hot to the hand.

The Buck knife had an edge that someone had tried to file; the file marks still showed, along with the broken tip. The edge of the blade was held against a new 120-grit sanding belt and worked slowly. Learn held his right hand on the blade's back to feel the temperature. He made a grind, moving in a smooth motion. A new edge soon appeared with little time and effort.

Changing the tip on a broken-ended knife is simple, claims Learn. Originally the Buck General had a trailing

*Upper left: While there are some knife models made with serrated blade edges, those who serrate their own are sure to void any warranty from the maker. For final polishing, the KnifeBuff, left, will do an excellent job. Each buffing stick has two grit ratings at each end, one side.*

*Non-abrasive Flitz may be used to put a high polish on soft brass, wood or synthetic handles, below.*

tip blade. To cut to the same style would make the knife shorter on the cutting edge. The new blade style became a drop point. Sand slowly and smoothly to round the old tip. The back edge is thick and will cut slowly, but the edge side is thinner and will cut too fast, if you are not careful. A marking pen will outline the blade for the new shape.

When you have the blade style you want, clean up the cutting edge by slowly moving it on the belt to obtain a sharp edge again. Learn prefers to thin out the tip of the blade as well as the upper edge. But not too thin!

After the blade sanding was finished, Learn took out the

*Blackened and burned knife blade tip, upper right, is the result of too much pressure on buffing belt or wheel. The temper is changed and the tip must be cut off and re-ground, or the knife discarded. Blades may be re-ground for use, depending upon the severity of the break, final length of blade.*

*Careful filing and sanding restored the Buck Model 110 blade, below. It was the bottom blade in the photo at right. The Roman nose shape may not be as attractive as original, but it cuts.*

*The copper riveted, heavy leather sheath is a smart safety measure when handling sharp blades. The thick leather should protect hands against blade.*

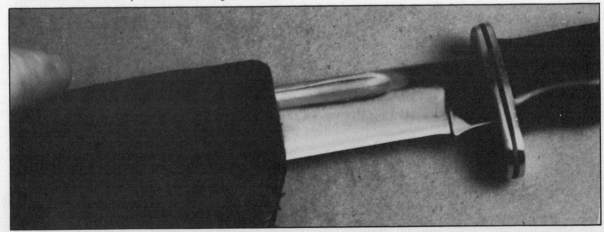

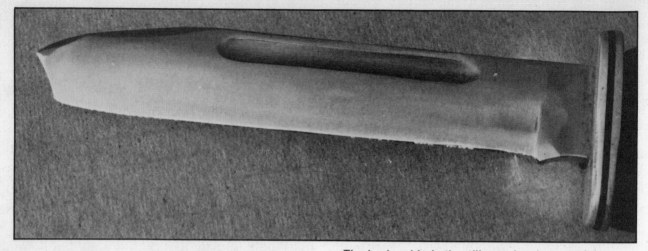

The broken blade tip still remains, but careful file work and 120-grit belt sanding have begun to remove the worst damage. Blade is sharpened last.

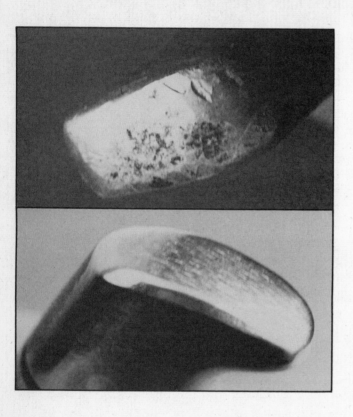

Left: Before and after on the Buck butt cap. Brass is fairly soft and easily worked. Butt may be left as in lower photo for a semi-matte finish, or may be polished to a high gloss.

The craftsman filed and ground the tip of the Buck General down to a drop point pattern, one not found in the Buck line. If cut up from bottom edge, trailing point shape is retained.

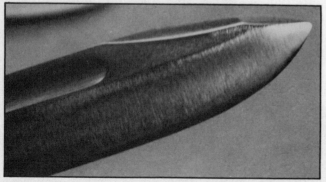

hammer marks on the hilt and smoothed up the Buckarta handle material. It looked as if someone had used a pair of pliers on it.

Another Buck knife had a damaged handle. The blade was good, but a bit scratched. Handles are easier to work on than blades and you have no steel burning problems. Replacing the handle on the Buck Special requires removal of the old handle. The aluminum butt is held on with a rivet, but don't try to drill it out, warns Learn. Use a hacksaw to cut down the middle of the butt cap. When you reach the tang, stop. A large chisel will spread the cut apart nicely and the butt cap will fall off, leaving the open end of the tang.

If you are lucky, you may drive the Buckarta handle material off the tang by placing it in a vise and tapping the tang. If you're not lucky, says Learn, you can grind or hammer it off. Use care, because it is tough stuff and flies all over the shop when shattered.

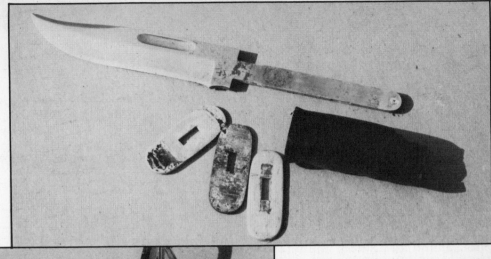

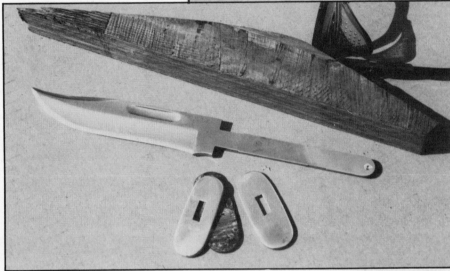

Above and left: The broken handle has been removed and will be discarded. The finger guard spacers — three ovals — will be cleaned up, as at left, and re-used. New handles will be fashioned from piece of laminated wood, left.

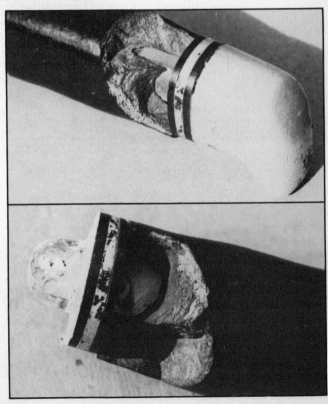

The Buckarta handle as it appeared broken before it was removed, right. The butt is held to the tang with a rivet and epoxy, but was taken off.

Clean up the tang and aluminum guard to remove the old cement. You can clean and reuse the guard, if you don't want to make a brass finger guard to replace it, says Learn.

Learn located a chunk of new laminated hardwood someone was going to use for rifle stocks. This has different colors of laminated hardwood, and when sanded, produces interesting patterns. Rosewood or cocobolo wood will also make nice knife handles.

Tang hole in the wood had to be cut just the right diameter. Too large and the tang will be loose, too tight and the wood may split as it is tapped onto the tang. Cavity is filled with epoxy cement.

Cut a block bigger than the handle that came off the knife, says Learn. Matching rivet holes for butt caps is too difficult, so make a single-unit handle of wood. The block needs to be big enough for your hand and long enough so that the butt cap won't be needed.

Drill a hole straight down the middle of your block of handle wood. Learn made his a full half-inch in diameter as the tang on the Buck Special is wide. It should be tight enough so the tang can be driven into the block, but not so tight that it will split the wood. Fill that hole with a good two-solution epoxy cement, drive the block onto the tang

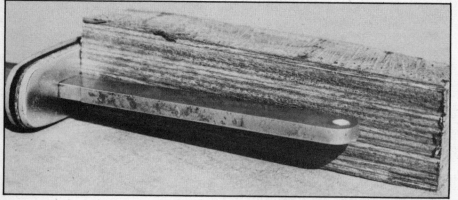

The block of wood chosen for the new handle has an interesting pattern of multi-colored laminates. It will produce an attractive handle when finished. Spacers are in place.

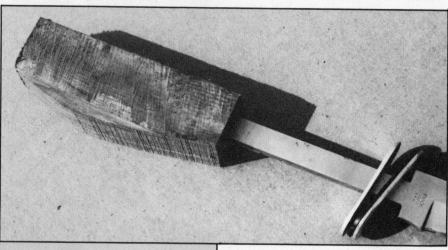

The rough handle block looks uglier than the broken handle in this stage, but making something from nothing is part of the fun of this project.

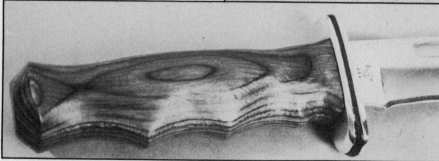

The new laminated handle might match your latest rifle stock. It may be finished with or without grooves, as shown. A light application of wax or oil will seal wood against moisture.

and let it set until the epoxy cures. After the epoxy has hardened according to directions, go back to your sanding belt and form any shape you want.

Full-tang, fixed-blade knives require thinner sections of wood to fit on each side of the tang. Any type of wood and much smaller pieces may be used than for a slip-over tang style. If you like the new synthetics, declares Learn, you can use almost any color you prefer. Micarta is much cheaper than ivory and actually wears better, because it will not shrink or crack with time.

To make a slab handle all you do is make the slabs over-

*Field dressing a game animal is often wet and messy. Dropping the knife in the mud can ruin your day, especially if it is your favorite.*

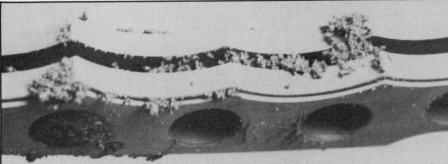

*The knife may be a dirty mess, but if it is a Buck Titanium folder there is little to worry about. The light-weight metal will not corrode; knife is designed to take apart in seconds.*

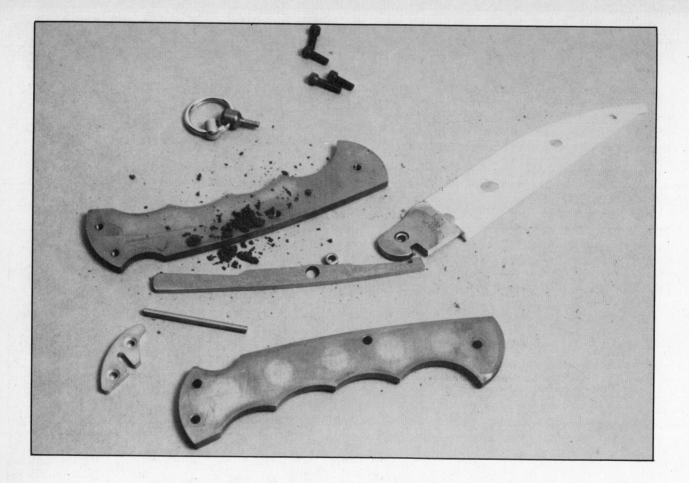

The lanyard ring of the Buck Titanium is also a keeper for a small Allen wrench designed to fit the four bolts holding the knife together. With the bolts out, above, the knife breaks down into its components for cleaning and lubrication. Buck also provides a temporary plastic blade sheath for protection during this work. Once cleaned, below, the knife is ready for careful reassembly.

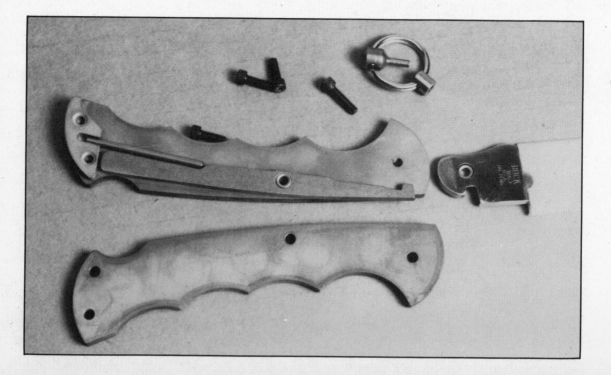

sized, then sand them to the shape you want. You can polish them with a buffer or finish with a coat of epoxy or polyurethane.

Learn had two folding lock blade knives with tips that had been broken off. The blades are hollow-ground and quite thin. This means they will be fast and easy to work, but will also be easier to burn. Learn was able to bring up the bottom cutting edge, move the upper tip down and clean up the cutting edges on both. A folder must have the tip below the knife handle section when closed, or it will catch on pockets or your hand when you reach for it. Keep that in mind when grinding the new blade shape.

One of the folding hunters with the broken tip must have been used by a painter, according to Learn. The handle, brass and all sides were covered with a tough, white/gray guck that he didn't want on his buffing wheels. Learn used a file to get the rough marks, which were too deep for the buffers anyway, then some steel wool on the surfaces.

Cleaning a knife is one thing none of us ever seems to do.

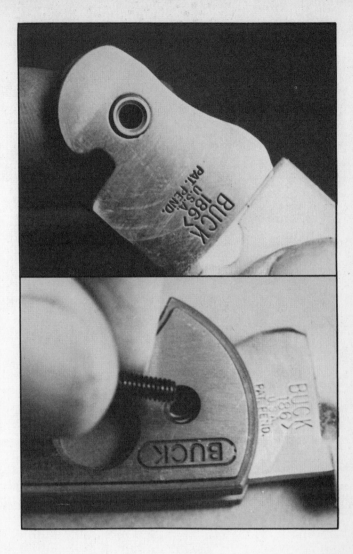

*The tiny ring bearing through the blade tang, upper right, slips right out after the Allen bolts are removed. It should be oiled before the knife is reassembled. Use care to not lose any small parts while cleaning and oiling.*

*The knife is clean, assembled and ready to use.*

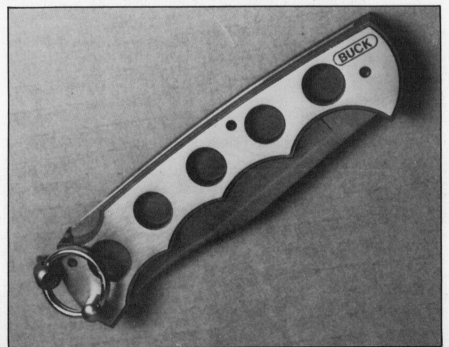

*A little investigation will reveal dozens of cleaning and polishing products on the market. They all work.*

*Among the handy little items contained in the Buck Cleaning and Oiling Kit, is a nifty brush, something like a small neck brush. With it, the handyman can get down inside blade channel.*

We use the knife, return it to the sheath or the pocket, swearing we'll clean it later, but seldom do. Stainless steel is rust resistant, but it will and does rust with improper care. Oil-hardened tool steel blades will rust even faster.

Cleaning a fixed-blade knife is simple, says Learn. Wipe it with a clean cloth or paper towel, then apply a light coat of oil to the blade and grip area. That is about all we have to do for most knives.

Cleaning a folder can be a bit different. One has to clean the inside as well as the outside. Bob Learn claims he has broken off many cotton swabs trying to find one small enough to get into the channel of folders to get them clean.

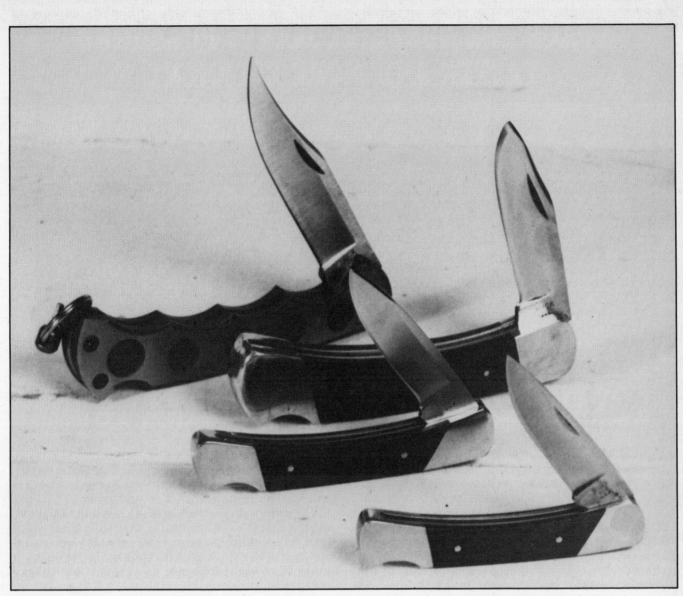

*The two folders in the foreground have been reworked and refurbished to look almost like new. Most knife users will operate on the premise that if it isn't broken, don't fix it. But some maintenance is necessary.*

Buck Knives now sells a folder cleaning kit that has a slick little double-ended brush that gets down into that channel. Along with the brush, they pack a small bottle of Buck knife oil used for the pivot section of the blade. Learn placed a drop into the channel of his pocketknife to oil the pivot on the locking arm. It really did the job and the knife worked much smoother, according to Learn.

Buck has a new titanium knife out and to test it, I took it hunting. The titanium is simple to clean as it is a take-down knife. The blade is a basic 110 Folding Hunter style, but the entire handle comes apart with four bolts. The four bolts are removed with a neat little Allen wrench that is

fixed to the lanyard ring which, in turn, is screwed into one of the long bolts on the knife body. Unscrew the lanyard ring and use the small wrench to remove the four bolts from the knife. Rinse or wipe the mud, dirt and hair from the parts, add a light touch of Buck knife oil from the kit and reassemble for a perfectly clean knife.

Learn warns that any alterations to handles or blades will void your warranty with most knife companies. Take your time and have fun in the repair job.

Clean and oil your knife after you use it. It only takes a minute or two and will pay big dividends in years to come.

# SPACE-AGE ABRASIVE MAKES POLISHING FASTER AND MORE EFFICIENT

*Micro-Mesh is available in several grit ratings, from 100 to an unlikely 24,000. Other industries have used the product for some time, but it just now is moving into cutlery. It polishes any metal.*

JACK MITCHELL, who did the research for us on the chapter about sharpening your blades, has also discovered an unusual product for final-polishing knives — or anything else. The material seems to fit right in with what Bob Learn has been sayng. Here is what Mitchell found:

Mirror-finished blades or gun barrels command premium prices, for good reason. As the metal is polished to each succeeding degree of sheen, any scratches, pits or impurities in the metal are highlighted. In order to produce any metalwork with a mirror-finish involves lots of time, plenty of elbow grease and years of experience. The job is further complicated, says Mitchell, because conventional abrasive paper comes with its own built-in problems and power buffing wheels have a tendency to "run" engraved or stamped lettering, cause round holes to become oval and obscure sharp lines or angles in the work. A company called Micro-Surface Finishing Products has developed a product called Micro-Mesh that greatly eliminates many of these aggravations.

This company has been around for several years, but catered to industries outside the gunsmithing and knife-making trades. Producing unique abrasive cloth with a variety of grits from 100 to 24,000 married to cloth in a uniform manner, they have proven extremely popular with a number of industries.

Commercial airlines use Micro-Mesh to remove scratches from Plexiglas windows. Mitchell recently learned that the violin maker's craft in Europe bestowed an award on Micro-Surface Finishing Products because their product proved to be the best to final-buff oil-finished wood on stringed instruments.

Micro-Mesh MX is a cloth-backed cushioned abrasive designed to produce super finishes on a variety of metals. Even coarse meshes — 180-grit — will polish surfaces to an approximate conventional 400-grit luster.

The cushioned construction of Micro-Mesh MX allows the crystals to flex and depress in order to seek a common level, thus reducing the peaks of the previous pattern *without* gouging deeper channels. This is the secret of why it works faster and better than conventional wet-and-dry abrasive papers.

This product is a new concept in the finishing and polishing of a variety of materials. Unlike other abrasives, it is manufactured with a resilient sub-strata. The crystals are firmly, but not rigidly, bonded to this sub-strata to allow all component parts to be flexible. When applied to a work surface, this flexibility permits the crystals to seek a common level. There is a loss of aggressive stock removal, because of the resiliency, but a sharp increase in polishing potential. A much larger crystal can thus be used to produce a highly polished surface. The benefits of this system are many. Slower work speeds can be used resulting in increased material life, less heat generation, a reduction of "loading" of abrasive, little if any fracturing of crystals, constant pattern production and a definite increase in surface integrity.

Almost all conventional sandpaper is so structured that the sharp points of the abrasive crystals are predominantly oriented toward the work surface and locked in place by the adhesive. This holds true in even the finest of lapping compounds. The sharp points effectively cut, gouge and abrade the work surface, aggressively removing material in relation to the size and type of crystals used. During use,

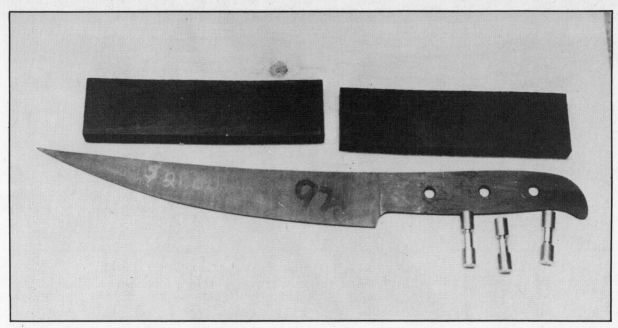

Long before the final polishing on a knife kit such as the one above, files, wheels and belts must be used to remove the rough surface of the steel. But for final finish, various grits of Micro-Mesh may be applied. The polishing crystals are bonded to a flexible surface, permitting them to seek a common working level.

the points fracture off, forming new, smaller points, thus rapidly reducing the work life of the crystals. It follows that by starting with a large crystal, continued use of the piece, with crystals becoming smaller and smaller, will produce a smoother pattern. Unfortunately, this does not happen. The fracturing occurs randomly and there are soon thousands of crystals of varying size. The largest keep the smaller ones from contacting the work surface while the larger gouge deeper channels — deeper scratches — and create uneven patterns.

Because of the extremely high heat generated at crystal points using conventional abrasive paper, these crystals actually fold over, further reducing their effectiveness. This tends to trap abraded particles from the work piece within the abrasive — called "loading" — and as the heat increases, these particles are transferred back to the work piece and literally welded in place, creating a false finish.

Micro-Mesh MX is available in belts, rolls, sheets and discs in grits ranging from 100 to 1200. The MX designates use on metal. Although a bit more expensive than hardware-variety abrasive papers, they will outlast conventional abrasives by almost ten to one.

Mitchell recently worked on a Loveless custom knife with a 600-grit mirror finish that contained some rust and light pitting on the blade. To have attempted removing the beautiful original metal finish by hand would have taken several hours and been almost impossible to achieve perfectly. However, by starting with Micro-Mesh MX 180-grit to remove the rust and get down past the pits to fresh metal took less than an hour by hand. Mitchell noticed the metal continued to take on a higher sheen as well, which would not have happened with conventional paper. Moving through successively finer grits, he was able to polish the entire blade with 800-grit, getting a final finish without any scratches and uniform polish in less than two hours.

The Kershaw Bowie knife has a shiny, reflective finish as it leaves the factory. A mirror polish helps reduce potential rust damage as it does not tend to hold water molecules to the surface. If needed, however, the owner may take advantage of the Micro-Mesh to restore, or even improve, the polish following Mitchell's example.

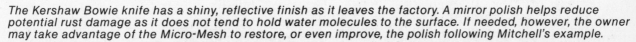
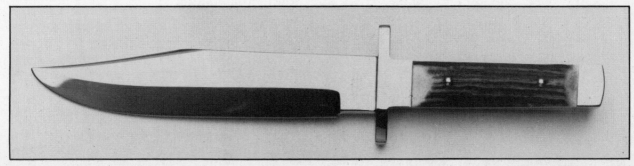

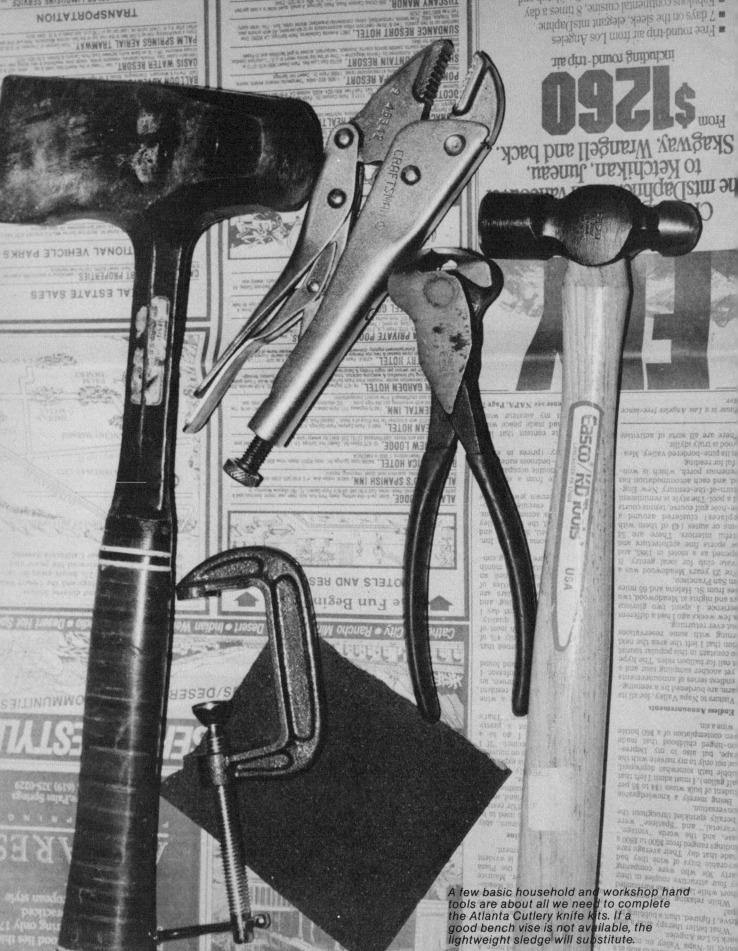

*A few basic household and workshop hand tools are about all we need to complete the Atlanta Cutlery knife kits. If a good bench vise is not available, the lightweight sledge will substitute.*

# Chapter 14

# DO-IT-YOURSELF

## *Make Your Own Knives? It's Easier — And Cheaper — Than You Might Think!*

A KNIFE is a wonderful invention. It may be the most practical tool we will ever see. A knife can do many things in the hands of the skilled. Knives can be a lot of fun. They can be traded, bought and sold, admired and handed down to future generations. They also can be built right at home with a minimum amount of manual skills.

It's true, a knife can be built from simply a slab of steel and a piece of wood in much the manner as the highly skilled custom knifemakers. Most of us do not have that artistic ability, but we can wield a hammer, a file, a pair of pliers and can use glue and sandpaper with some skill. Those prerequisites are about all that is required to build one or two really nice knives from modern do-it-yourself kits. There are several on the market which are assembled easily in a short time to result in attractive knives. Another benefit is a real sense of accomplishment and pride in workmanship after completing a kit knife.

One of the simplest knife kits is for a straight sheath knife. Such a kit may be composed of only five pieces; a finished blade, two handle slabs of wood or a man-made material and two rivets or screws to hold everything together. A variation will add three more pieces; a bolster or guard and two more rivets to hold it on. Usually, the maker must furnish his own two-solution epoxy cement which is used to hold the handle slabs to the tang. This type of adhesive always is used for a knife with a round tang and a single-piece handle. The accepted procedure for larger knives is to use epoxy cement, plus pins, rivets or screws to ensure a firm, tight handle that should not come loose, even after years of use.

Several companies produce complete kits of the type just mentioned, while other suppliers offer a variety of blades and handle materials that the home craftsman may use to assemble his own selection of components.

Most of these blades are finished, except for final sharpening. Care must be exercised during assembly to avoid a nasty cut or stab wound. While working with the blade, it is good practice to wrap the edge and point with heavy paper and tape. This not only protects the hands, but offers some protection to the steel.

Dozens of shapes and blade styles are available. A glance through suppliers' catalogs will reveal drop points, upswept skinning blades, dirks, Arkansas toothpicks, Bowies, straight and hollow-ground blades, full tangs, half-tangs, round tangs, tapered tangs, even Damascus steel forged-to-shape blades. Prices are considerably lower than for a comparably finished factory-made knife. Most blades are of stainless steel, but less expensive tool steel blanks also are available.

Handle slabs may be furnished completely finished or simply as a wood block which is formed and finished after attachment to the tang. Several kinds of handsomely grained wood, Micarta, horn, antler, shell and rubber polymers are the choice of most makers. Indian samber stag horn is a popular material for some hunting knives and is available in North America at reasonable prices. Sambar stag also is used as the handle material for many factory-made production knives. Stag looks good and holds up well, although it is as subject to damage as is any other natural substance. Wood is one of the easiest materials for the beginning knifemaker to work with. It may be filed, sanded, cut, filled

One of the important kit construction aids in Atlanta Cutlery's package is what they term a slackner. The thin metal piece helps establish the correct clearance in the blade pivot mechanism. Once used, it is discarded. Inside the kit envelope, small metal parts are packaged inside plastic pouches to help limit loss in shipment.

and finished rather easily and can be stained to almost any color. It also is the least expensive in the small quantities needed.

Untreated, natural wood tends to be somewhat less than stable under difficult weather conditions. If the knife is to be used in the outdoors, an alternative handle material is something called pakkawood, a material that may be dyed to almost any color. The pakkawood can be buffed to an almost glass-like finish that is virtually impervious to the elements.

All makers and importers of knife kits and component suppliers include instructions for the completion of the knife. The folding knife instructions offered by Atlanta Cutlery are extremely detailed, yet easy to follow. Photographs of each step are included with the written instructions. Building a fixed-blade knife, such as those available from Atlanta Cutlery, Rigid Knives, CAM III and Bob Engnath's House of Muzzleloading, is almost self-explanatory. Illustrated instructions are available with each kit or component.

The simplest knife is the full-tang design. Most of the blades are formed and ground in Japan or Europe, with polished blades and the tang area left rougher for better cement adhesion. The blanks also are pre-drilled for pins or screws in virtually all cases. Knife equipment suppliers or your neighborhood hardware store should have supplies of the necessary two-part epoxy cement. Follow directions on the package. Each brand varies slightly in the amounts of each part to mix for a really strong bond. Mix the epoxy and set the compound aside for the required period of time before using.

Most kits call for at least two C-clamps to hold the handle slabs to the knife tang while the cement sets. A padded-jaw vise may be used or even two sets of vise-grip pliers can be substituted for the C-clamps.

Position and clamp one slab to the tang without cement. Use care to not tighten it down too far, as the wood — if that's what you are using — will crack under too much pressure. All we'll do at this step is drill out the handle slab using the pre-drilled tang as a guide. For this work, a hand drill will work as well as a power drill.

With one side drilled through, re-clamp the second slab carefully, then drill through the second side. The sets of holes should line up perfectly. Remove the clamps and apply epoxy as smoothly as possible to both sides of the tang, leaving no gaps or spaces uncovered. Re-clamp the two handle slabs, using the pins, rivets or screws to align the drilled holes. A certain amount of cement will ooze from the tang area, which may be cleaned off later, as the knife is finished. Some epoxy cement will set within five minutes, while other types require half an hour or more. Most need twenty-four hours to cure completely.

Screw rivets, if used, are available in different lengths to fit the thickness of the knife handle exactly. All one needs to do at this point is to tighten the screws while the epoxy is still soft, then remove the clamps when the cement has cured. If soft metal cutler's pins, included in most knife kits, are used, excess length may be trimmed off after the cement has cured. Instructions usually call for the use of wire cutters or diagonal-cut snips to trim these pins. Cut the pins down as close to the handle material as possible.

With this type of construction, it is not necessary to open the pins as the epoxy and pin combination will hold the assembly together even under stress. When the epoxy is hard, the excess may be removed with a shop file. If necessary, the pins can be filed flush, using care not to take down too much of the handle material around the metal. Avoid scratching or gouging the handle and the metal tang. Use short, brisk strokes, maintaining control of the file. A padded-jaw vise may be used, if one is handy. Otherwise, the knife may be held in the hand while filing. During this phase, the exposed blade should be covered.

If the epoxy was applied smoothly and the clamps evenly tightened, the cement will leave an attractive line between metal and handle material. Epoxies are available which harden up clear or in various shades of gray. The adhesive can leave a nice contrasting line around the visible tang edge, depending upon the color of the handle slabs.

If your knife kit has finished handles, the knife is complete except for sharpening the blade. However, some filing and sanding probably will be necessary at this point. A round or semi-round file works well when shaping the handle, followed by successively finer grits of sandpaper. Use a sandpaper block or flatten the paper on the workbench and slide the knife across it for an even finish. Substances such as sambar stag or Micarta may be treated the same as wood at this step.

This is the most basic of fixed-blade knives, without bolsters, guard or pommel. With a bit more skill and experience, one may want to try completing kits that include those additions to the design, as well several other decorations. But keep your first knife simple and easy to make.

*Each wood handle slab part has a matching brass liner which must be mated before construction begins. Liner has an extra machining hole.*

*The pivot pin is inserted up through the pile side wood handle and liner, then spring is slipped down on top. Spring will pivot smoothly on pin.*

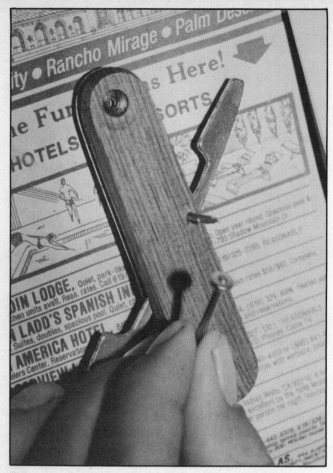

Three pins and three bird's eyes are furnished with the Atlanta folding knife kit. Wooden handle pieces are pre-drilled and countersunk to accept the small washer-like parts. Rounded side fits away from wood.

The rather unusual looking part shown above is the catch disc. The disc rides against the back spring to limit its travel as the blade is opened and closed. Drilled end of disc also holds lanyard ring.

That way, you will have success and know you can make more — and probably better — knives in the future. Adding nickel silver bolsters, fancy spacers or other embellishments adds to your knife's appearance, but they also require care and skill in construction.

Making a folding knife is easier than one might think. Atlanta Cutlery has three folding-knife kits which they have sold in the thousands. There is a single-blade folder, a two-blade version and a locking-blade folder.

No power tools are necessary to complete either of these knives. If you can read and follow instructions, you can build any of these styles. They are inexpensive and can result in some really nice pocket or purse knives for yourself or to give as gifts.

The instructions Atlanta Cutlery includes are as complete as any we've seen and each booklet contains a couple dozen photographs to guide one along. With the kit, all you need is a ball peen hammer, a second-cut flat file, wire cutters, a bench vise with protected jaws or a pair of vise grips and a sheet or two of 400-grit sandpaper. If you do not have access to a bench vise, you will need some sort of steady rest for peening; something impenetrable. Some builders have resorted to using an axe or sledge hammer head on the workbench for this purpose. It's a bit shaky, but will work, if nothing better is at hand.

There are fifteen parts in the Atlantic Cutlery single-blade knife kit, requiring twelve steps to complete. An experienced builder can put one of the knives together in a matter of minutes; we've seen it done. Carefully reading the instructions as we go, the rest of us may require an hour or more.

It's always a good idea to read a set of instructions through before proceeding with construction. It is particularly important with the Atlanta Cutlery kits, because of the little component called a *slackner*. This is a little rectangle of aluminum stapled onto the outside of the plastic bag which holds all the parts. One must be careful not to lose this slackner, as it plays an important role in peening the pin that holds the blade. From there, the instructions include an excellent line drawing of each part and how to assemble it.

To get started, the builder must examine the jacaranda wood handle slabs — Atlanta calls them handle covers — to determine which piece goes down first. They are referred to as the "pile" side and the "mark" side covers. It's called pile side, because it is the side that goes down first and upon which everything else is piled. The mark side ends up on top and it is the side on which trademarks, nameplates and medallions are fastened. Also, the nail nick and any identifying marks on the blades are on this upper side.

To build this knife, one must identify and start with the pile side handle cover. Both pieces of wood and body liners are pre-drilled for the pins that will hold them together; the outer covers are countersunk to accept the so-called bird's eyes which secure the pins. The covers are slightly wider on one end than the other; the blade is fastened to the narrower end. Place both wood covers on the work surface, the wider end to the left. Look at both, and the one with the middle hole drilled nearest you is the pile side cover. Simply match up the metal liners atop each cover to determine the pile side and mark side liners.

The remaining parts, carefully described in Atlanta's instructions, will practically fall into place as construction proceeds. With the flat surface of the pile side cover facing upward, one pin with its bird's eye is inserted up through the wood in the center pin hole. The point of the pin also must face upward. Place the matching pile side liner on the same pin. The fit is intended to be tight and some force may be necessary. To do it right, close the vise jaws almost together, turn the liner and cover down with the pin between the jaws. Now carefully tap the pin down until it is nearly flush with the wood surface. Next, slip the backspring onto the assembly pin, followed by the mark side liner and cover. The backspring pin hole is deliberately off-

center so it can fit only one way. Line up the narrow and wider ends of the liners and covers to face in the same directions.

The nickel silver catch disc is a rather odd little part. Looking a bit like an amoeba, it is the only part like it in the kit. Put a pinned bird's eye through the hole in the wider end of the handle, then start the pin into it. In the middle is the catch disc and an aluminum washer, also one-of-a-kind. The disc and washer are fitted between the liners. The instructions, and experience, tell us the fit of the pin through all the parts is extremely tight and it has to be hammered through. The bench vise, closed to within a quarter-inch, will work well. The fit of the pin through the bird's eye is the tightest.

One side of each bird's eye is flat, the other rounded. When the pin is through the eye, the little, rounded side should face away from the wood; the flat side is in the countersink. Meanwhile, the straight edge of the catch disc meets the bearing surface of the backspring.

Pound another pin through another bird's eye in the same direction as the first one. Squeeze the backspring with your bench vise or vise grips until the opposite end of the backspring clears the pin hole. Slip the knife blade into the handle and align the holes. Hammer the pin with its

After the assembly pins have been clipped off as close a possible, they must be carefully peened flat on each end. A bench vise was not available, so an axe head was substituted. Pins are soft metal and not difficult to work, but care must be exercised to prevent hammering too hard which will cause an internal bend.

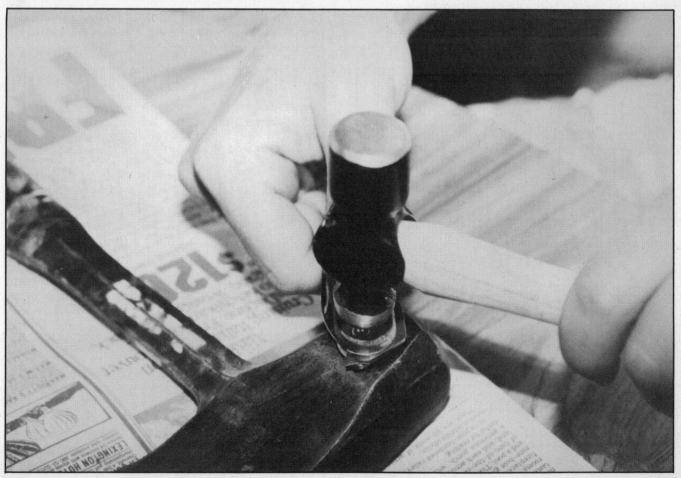

bird's eye down through the covers and the liners, using the same degree of care as before.

Bird's eyes now are applied to the opposite open ends of the two pins protruding from the knife handle. They have to be hammered down, using the technique utilized to drive the pins through the eyes. You will see the reason the pins have not yet been rimmed off until now.

The nickel silver pins are relatively soft and should be trimmed at this point to within one-sixteenth inch of each side, using wire cutters or diagonals. The excess is left on the pins for peening.

Now for the slackner. Use an ordinary pair of scissors and put a small "V" in one side of the slackner so it can be slipped into the knife, between the blade tang and the liner, going around the pin. The thickness of the slackner will be just enough, after peening, to allow the blade to pivot evenly without binding, but without too much freedom. After the pins are peened, the slackner is pulled out and discarded.

The pins are peened — with the slackner still in place — on both sides, using the rounded end of the ball peen hammer. The job should be done on a non-yielding surface, such as the bench vise of the sledge hammer head mentioned earlier. Tap gently and evenly. Hit the pins too hard or miss them, and the wood covers can split, ruining your project.

If you did no more work, you would have a functional, but rough pocketknife. But some filing and sanding still are in order. The excess assembly pins should be filed down flush with the wood covers. Don't work too fast or press too hard, because the wood can be scarred forever. Holding the knife firmly, use the small file to smooth down all the parts, especially the covers, until they all are even and functional looking. Work slowly and carefully; you've spent too much time and effort to spoil it now.

Sanding can be done with a block or with the 400-grit paper flat on the bench, sliding the knife across it. The amount of sanding is up to the individual. Jacaranda wood sands down nicely to result in a reddish finish. You may leave the natural wood or apply a thin coating of wood wax or furniture polish.

You may want to add some custom touches, filing finger grooves or do some engraving or carving on the wood. Finally, there is a little lanyard ring included in the kit that can be attached to the hole in the catch disc which protrudes from the larger end of the handle.

Constructing the two-blade knife kit is accomplished in similar fashion. The small pen blade of the Atlanta Cutlery kit is installed first in the wider end of the knife, as was done with the previous knife. Then the larger master blade is pinned into the knife at the narrower end. Use of the slackner during peening, cutting off the excess pins and finishing the knife all follow the same technique. In this case, you end up with a double-bladed pocketknife.

The third folding-knife kit from Atlanta is a locking-blade knife. It is a bit more complicated to make, since there are seventeen parts in this one. For this knife, the backspring looks different because of the locking mechanism

*When basic assembly of the knife is finished, edges of liner or wood handle slab may be filed smoothly to match. Care is used to avoid scratches or gouges in softer jacaranda wood handle. Edges may be rounded or left with flat angular line for high-tech appearance.*

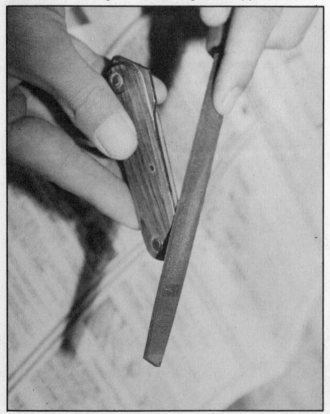

*Easiest method of sanding is to place full sheet of coarse sandpaper on bench top and slide knife across, with the grain. Soft metal pins, bird's eyes and wood will sand smooth in a relatively short time.*

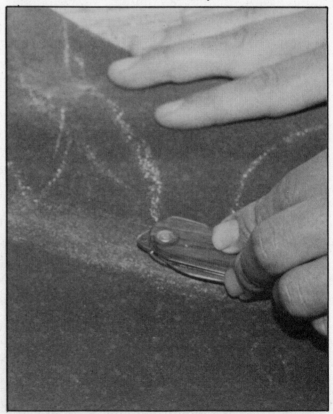

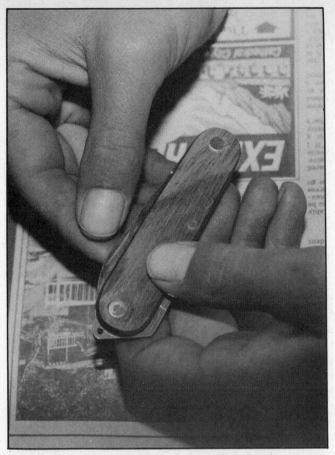

*Finished wood may be waxed, oiled or left in natural state as above. This is the single-blade version of Atlanta's three folder kits. Lanyard ring was left off for lower profile while carrying knife in a pocket.*

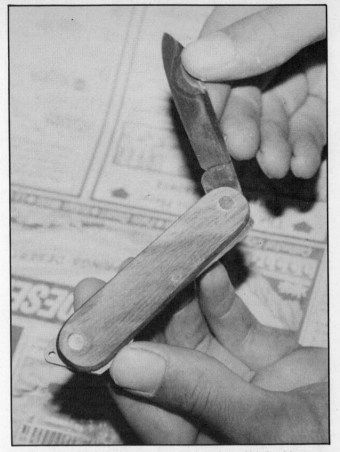

*As the blade is opened, one may see how the locking spring temporarily rides out of the liners before snapping back into place when blade is all the way open. Additional Atlanta Cutlery kits offer a two-blade knife and a locking single, all easy to make.*

and there is an interior spring and an extra washer not included among components for the non-locking knife kits. Two aluminum washers are stacked on the pin at the opposite end of the handle from the blade pivot. They balance the space between the liners so that, when the blade opens and closes, the knife remains even and symmetrical.

Installation of the first center pin on the locking blade knife is done the same as before. When the second pin is installed at the wide end of the handle, two aluminum washers are placed on the pin against the pile side liner. They can be hammered down utilizing the same technique used for the bird's eyes.

The internal spring and backspring are joined together before they are installed in the knife. Correct installation is essential for proper functioning of the knife. You will note that one end of the internal spring has a bend in it about a quarter-inch back. This short end fits into a recess in the backspring so the remaining, longer end of the internal spring bends down toward — not away from — the inner surface of the backspring. If it is put in wrong, the knife won't unlock — ever. The two springs are a tight fit and may have to be hammered together.

The lock release end of the backspring is installed in the knife toward the wider end. The lobe that locks into the blade tang faces the narrow end.

Next, the mark side liner and cover are mounted on the center pin, but are not tightened down. They are pressed down on the pin just far enough to hold them in place. They will be hammered down later. The second pin is inserted through the mark side cover and liner as described previously. The backspring at the lock release end is left hanging out of the handle for the moment.

Installing the blade requires a slightly different technique, because of the backspring and the pressure it is under from the internal locking spring. In order to line up all the pin holes so the blade can be inserted, the protruding backspring must be depressed until almost flush with the covers and liners. The easy way to do this is with a bench vise. The last pin is pounded through a bird's eye and is pushed down as far as possible through the cover and liner, through the pin hole in the blade tang. Then the knife can be taken out of the vise and the pin hammered home as before. With a final bird's eye tapped onto the pin and into the recess in the cover, trimming, peening and finishing the locking blade knife is the same as previously discussed.

Completing any of these knife kits gives a sense of accomplishment, but the lockback model is particularly rewarding because of the extra mechanical requirements. If you have done your work, it will work like a charm, giving you something to show off to friends. Actually, these knives make pretty nice gifts. Friends will appreciate your efforts.

*Chapter 15*

# KNIFE PRODUCERS and IMPORTERS

## Old Or New, Large Or Small, Knifemakers Turn Steel, Brass, Wood And Plastic Into Usable Tools

FACTORY KNIFEMAKING is more than simply inserting several pieces of steel, plastic and other materials in one end of a factory building and shipping finished cutlery out the other; much more.

Knife production requires careful selection of the best materials, whether steel for the blades, nylon fabric for the sheaths, plastic or stag for handles, or strong steel pins and rivets to hold folding knives together for years to come. In addition to just the right materials, a knife factory must have a management staff and production people who can see that the blades going out the door are a credit to the company name; that the product will last the customer — or the customer's children — for many years. Personnel

must have the training and skills required to turn out a mass-produced knife which looks as good as it is. They must be able to design, operate and maintain the machines in the factory which make mass production possible. And the facilities must be housed and powered within a building at a location which can accommodate the work and has smooth shipping facilities.

In the earliest days of the Industrial Revolution, cutlery manufacturers were located at the source of the power required to run the machines; beside swiftly flowing rivers and streams. Water power was harnessed to operate the grinders and other machines used to produce knives. This is the way it began in Europe and the way it continued at

Buck Knives is a large corporation with international connections, but Chuck Buck, right above, third generation of the family, makes it a point to visit with his California factory employees on a daily basis.

Above: The modern Buck facility may seem cluttered, but each mass production machine and station has a purpose. Workers must wear eye-protective glasses.

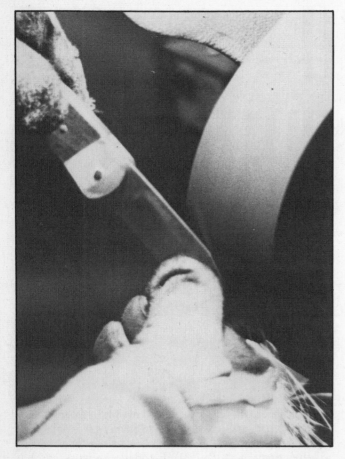

Final blade grinding on factory production knives still is done by hand on belt sander. Note hand protection.

the beginning of the Nineteenth Century in America. The power to run factories is now from electricity and the buildings are located wherever management may choose.

The manual skills need not be, but often are, passed down from one generation to the next. Production workers may be recruited and trained for even the most technical tasks from almost any population. Needed specialists can be hired and brought in from other areas, if the need arises. The basic requirements are the same whether the work force is thirty or three hundred. Production workers must convert raw materials, using their hands, skills and machines, into the finished cutlery products. The products must then reach, be purchased by and satisfy customers. The factory where this takes place may be a corrugated iron lean-to near a rice paddy in the Orient, or it may be a modern steel, brick and glass building in Japan or Southern California, just off the freeway. The production problems are basically the same, although the solutions may differ from one factory to the next.

The primary ingredient of any knife, no matter the size, shape, design or intended use, is steel; high quality steel which can be forged, worked, cut, ground, shaped and polished to perform at all times under the most adverse conditions. There are several standard blade steels produced in several parts of the world — the 440 stainless series is a popular example — commonly used by many manufacturers in the United States, Germany and the Far East. There are no secrets to its manufacture and these steels are used by the tons at factories around the world.

Other knife companies, however, have developed special blade alloys by working with small steel producers. Some have exclusive rights to these special metals and their formulations are closely kept trade secrets. Quality control often extends back to the steel manufacturing plant where chemical and metallurgical tests are constantly under way to satisfy the knife producer. Many makers routinely re-test and analyze their supplies of blade and spring steel

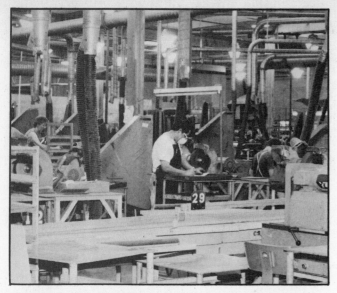

A major concern at the Buck Knives factory is metal and wood dust. Dozens of ventilation ducts are built into the facility to ensure clean air for workers.

Most factory production knife blade grinding is done by semi-automated machines. Machine maintenance is an important function in any production facility.

at the factory before the production process begins.

Typical of the care rendered are the steps taken by Camillus Cutlery of New York. Blade steel used by Camillus is blanked to an accurate shape without disturbing the special strength-structure rolled into the steel at the mill. The next step — one that Camillus considers most important in the production of knives — is heat tempering and hardening steel for blades and springs. Large producers accomplish this within their own factories, while some smaller makers job this special task out to local heat treaters. Either way, heat treating is critical to the lasting quality of the final metal components.

A knife is the product of its components. A quality knife must start with quality components. The quality of the brass for liners of folding knives and the nickel silver used for bolsters and other parts is just as important as the blade steel. Every knifemaker is aware of this and attempts to use the best.

Modern, often specialized, equipment and skilled operators combine to produce the best knife for the money. Older workers take pride in passing their skills along to their younger successors. The use of lasers, computers with electronic controls and gauges may speed production and ensure uniformity, but only experienced hands produce top-quality knives. Production tolerances on folding knife parts must be held to within a few thousandths of an inch. Quality control at this level could be achieved only with the greatest difficulty and cost a couple of decades ago, but modern optical, electronic and mechanical equipment puts this precision at the fingertips of any manufacturer, foreign or domestic.

All the machines must be inspected, calibrated and maintained by skilled technicians who may never actually produce a single knife, but their contributions to factory production are recognized by enlightened management. Inspections, spot checks and constant monitoring of parts and procedures are essential to knife production. Many

A large wholesale order is filled near the end of the production cycle. Final inspection and packaging will follow after the order count has been completed, above.

One of the newer knife factories in the United States is the modern Coleman/Western facility in Colorado. Ownership by Coleman is new, but Western Cutlery was family-connected to Case, before turn of the century.

components of folding knives are not visible to the consumer, but if any of them fail or begin to malfunction in a few years, an unhappy customer will be created. Businesses fail from too many unhappy customers.

No knife manufacturer can survive on tradition alone. New designs, new materials and new products must be designed and introduced to keep the public buying. Some traditional designs have gone on for decades — for more than a century, in some cases — and probably will always be made. The popularity of the Bowie knife is one example. But consumers demand new products in any industry and cutlery is no exception. Recent trends in handle materials

comprise but one example of the research and development work done in the knife industry. Lightweight plastics and rubberized handle materials have proven wildly popular on some folding knives, exceeding the sale of those with traditional jigged bone or stag. Large hunting folders were introduced and have continued as best-sellers during the past quarter century. The big Buck folder was a pioneer. Different metal alloys and ingenious blade locking designs always are under consideration. The use of heavy nylon fabric, in place of leather, for many knife sheaths is another recent development which has added excitement to the knife industry. There will be others.

On the Camillus production line, a jig holds the folding knife parts as they are "stacked" and ready for riveting.

Each blade size and style must be sharpened by hand, according to rigid specifications on abrasive wheels.

*The Camillus Cutlery factory worker at right glazes, scours and hand-buffs a folder to remove rough spots.*

Complete automation seems unlikely for the knife industry. The size of the industry and the limited profits, as compared to, say the automobile industry, seem to rule out factories run by a handful of robot technicians. Skilled hand work still is appreciated to a high degree by knife customers. One need look no farther than the custom, handmade knife movement to realize that fact. There are more than a few production steps which must be done by hand, unlikely to ever be automated. True, there are robots and automatic machines at work in most modern knife production facilities, but the need for hand work is still considerable. One no longer sees row upon row of workers bent over giant, water-powered grinding wheels, common a century ago, but each modern machine has a human in attendance.

The final edge on each factory blade is the result of a special human function. A mechanical device is used, but the honing and polishing is still done by hand. So are the last inspections before wrapping and shipping the knives.

There was a time, perhaps a hundred years ago, when the bulk of knife production was done in Europe and England. Solingen, Germany and Sheffield, England were the centers of knifemaking. Soon, the industry swung across the Atlantic to New England, New York State and Pennsylvania, following the settlement routes and power sources. Many remain there today. Several of the larger American producers have moved to or have built in the western United States, particularly since the end of World War II.

In more recent decades, there has been industry penetration by producers in Japan, Taiwan, the Philippines, Hong Kong and other exotic locations such as Singapore, India and Pakistan. Labor costs enable knife production — some of them high quality — at a fraction of the cost in other countries. As standards of living rise, however, manufacturers in places like Japan are finding themselves undersold by new production facilities located in such countries as Korea. Now, the pendulum seems to be swinging back to again favor the quality and attention to detail found in factories in the United States. Some of that trend, it must be noted, is due to economic and currency factors which have nothing to do with quality of product from any country.

American knife producers still have a couple of advantages going for them. As the world's biggest market for knives is the United States, local makers have a greater

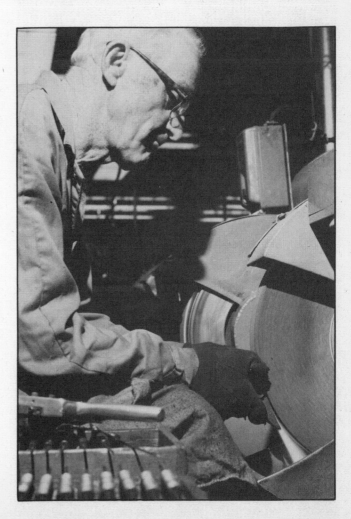

*Old-line knife companies, such as Coleman/Western, are finding their products in demand in North America, as well as overseas. Cheap imports still have a market throughout the world, but there seems to be growing demand for quality production knives.*

Before this group of Camillus folding knives is placed in packages, excess oil is removed, another step that cannot be done by machines. Wrapping is next step.

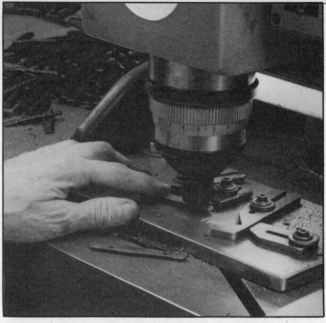

A Camillus production worker unites handles and covers, above, making them ready for riveting. The components are held in assembly jig during machining.

Most of the knifemaking skills were imported from England and Europe during the last century. Today, older workers pass their skills on to the younger generation, maintaining quality of their product.

knowledge of their market than do most foreign producers. American manufacturers are accustomed to committing part of their annual budget to research and development and introducing one or more new models each year is not unusual for some producers.

For the U.S. market, the supply lines are shorter for domestic producers. While some Far Eastern knock-off artists have been known to copy a hot new design with incredible speed, the advantage is usually with the local developer/producer. California manufacturers are still closer to customers in New York than are factories in the Orient. Distribution systems usually are well established, operated by people with long experience in their business. Customers with problems will get a more sympathetic hearing dealing directly with the U.S. manufacturer than with an importer who is faced with a language and cultural barrier. The best importers, however, are equally responsive to customer problems; local manufacturers must stay on their toes.

In the following pages, we shall present a number of commercial knife manufacturers' stories in words and pictures. Arranged alphabetically, these are the leading producers and importers of cutlery in America and throughout the world. Some date themselves back a century or more; others have been in business for only a couple of years. Each has found a niche in which to sell knives. Some sell tens of thousands of knives a year while others number their production in only several hundred. Some are industry leaders and some follow along with the tried and true.

Many of the knives from these same companies have been discussed under previous chapters, but what follows are the stories of the factories which produce or import them. Most businesses are reflections of the personalities who, past or present, started them. The knife business is no exception and we think you will enjoy learning about some of the leaders of the cutlery industry.

# ALCAS BEGAN AS A MARRIAGE BETWEEN ALCOA AND CASE; THEIR OFFSPRING ARE GROWING AND MULTIPLYING

Olean, New York, is the home of Alcas Cutlery. In 1983, the company put a million dollars in upgrades.

ALCAS CUTLERY may be one of the least-known large knifemakers in the country. The firm has been in business for almost four decades and hardly anybody knows about them, except housewives and cooks who use their extensive line of blades put out under the Cutco banner. This is about to change, though, through the introduction of the Alcas Solution and Spirit knives, discussed in more detail in Chapter Ten.

As with most knife factories, much of the manufacturing is hand- and labor-intensive. Alcas boasts that sixteen percent of its employees have been with the company for more than a quarter of a century. The factory provides a stable employment base and the workers seem to provide the company with a reliable, hard-working labor pool.

Dan Harrison, a custom knifemaker from Texas, designed the Solution knife/axe combination tool to satisfy his hunting needs. With the design set, Harrison searched out a manufacturer. He found Alcas willing to take on the project. All construction of the Solution and Spirit is done at the Olean plant, south of Buffalo. The design requires more hand operations than the standard survival knife or folder. Fit and finish are critical and the people at Alcas do a good job.

Alcas Cutlery Corporation began in 1948 as a subsidiary of the Aluminum Company of America (ALCOA). The roots of Alcas go back to a decision by officials of WearEver Aluminum, another ALCOA subsidiary, to market a line of cutlery to supplement their quality cooking utensil line, then sold directly to consumers.

The W.R. Case & Sons Company of Bradford, Pennsylvania, was approached by ALCOA to jointly establish a cutlery manufacturing facility to be built in Olean, New York, just fifteen miles from Case's Bradford facilities. ALCOA chose Case because of its product, technical and manufacturing expertise. The name Alcas derives from the combination of *Alcoa* and *Case*. The joint venture was established to manufacture a household cutlery line to be

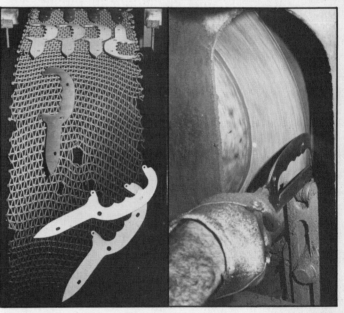

The unusual Solution Spirit knife components move through heat treatment on a conveyor belt, left. Grinding needs special care because of shape on double-header, at right.

sold by WearEver under the Cutco trademark.

Case management provided much of the early technical knowledge and production decisions for manufacturing top quality cutlery right from the beginning. The first knife of the original nine-piece set was produced in March, 1949, and Alcas has been manufacturing the Cutco line at its Olean facilities ever since.

From 1949 until 1972, John O'Kain was president of Alcas, and was concurrently the president of W.R. Case & Sons. Mornings were devoted to Case, afternoons to Alcas, with a fifteen-mile commute over the hills between Bradford, Pennsylvania, and Olean, New York!

The Spirit handle has more moving parts than most knives, needing more assembly steps to finish.

While much of the Alcas Olean plant is thoroughly mechanized with assembly-line machines, plenty of hand work is still required for the Solution Spirit, above.

Alcas' fisherman's Solution knife was introduced in late 1987. A number of blades await grinding.

During this period of its involvement with Case, Alcas broadened its activities. Included was its first manufacture of sporting knives, on a low volume basis for Case, as well as the Alcas-designed professional cutlery line marketed by WearEver to the restaurant, hotel and institutional market. This line is a significant part of Alcas production today.

In 1972, W.R. Case & Sons sold its forty-nine percent share of Alcas to ALCOA, thus making Alcas a wholly-owned subsidiary of ALCOA. This was the start of events which formed the Alcas Cutlery Corporation as it is today. During the period 1972-1982, Alcas expanded its product lines primarily into the private label sporting knife area for which Case had provided a beginning. It also developed and/or manufactured a number of major, well known sporting knife brands. It was in this connection that Alcas became known as "The Knifemaker's Knifemaker." According to an Alcas press release, their specialty throughout the industry was the manufacture of premium quality lock back knives, as well as fixed-blade and folding sporting knives that rivaled hand-crafted pieces in areas of finish, assembly details, grinding, edge honing techniques and other manufacturing details.

In January of 1982, under the leadership of President Erick J. Laine, Alcas took over the Cutco marketing responsibility which had been with WearEver for thirty-three years. This arrangement between the two companies of ALCOA gave Alcas increased control over Cutco's marketing. Cutco products still constituted half of Alcas' production volume.

In September of 1982, Laine and four of his officers purchased Alcas from ALCOA. Alcas became then, and remains, a privately held corporation held entirely by the officers of Alcas. Laine is majority owner. Since the purchase of Alcas, its new owners have taken steps to strengthen its position. In 1983, Alcas invested more than $1,000,000 in updated manufacturing equipment to assure cost competitiveness in an increasingly tough marketplace.

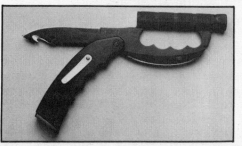

The original Alcas Solution knife with blued blades finds success with rugged construction.

In 1983, Alcas started an aggressive pursuit of the export market, primarily for its Cutco product line, which is now sold worldwide. In Japan, the traditional Japanese respect for quality makes Cutco attractive.

Early in 1985, Alcas acquired its two largest U.S. Cutco distribution companies; one on each coast. These two operations were merged into one wholly-owned marketing company — Vector Marketing Corporation — so Alcas would have stronger control over the marketing of Cutco, which remains its single most important product line.

Today, Alcas continues to pursue growth, profitability and product line expansion. Its main operations are divided between manufacture and marketing of its own Cutco line and the manufacture of premium quality sporting knives for a growing list of Original Equipment Manufacturer and private label customers.

Alcas Cutlery Corporation has a work force of two hundred craftsmen who maintain the highest design and production standards in manufacturing quality cutlery and rugged sporting knives. American-made Alcas products reflect nearly forty years of excellence and technology. Alcas Cutlery supplies the military and the consumer from its 85,000-square-foot manufacturing facility which remains the center for ongoing materials and product research and testing programs.

# AL MAR AND THE WARRIOR'S EDGE ARE SYNONYMOUS, BUT HE MAKES KNIVES FOR ALMOST ANY PURPOSE, TOO.

*Al Mar Knives is largely a family operation with Mar doing the designing, his wife, Ann, handling administration and daughter, Ryann, functioning as the sales manager.*

A SMALL office building stands far back on a lot, away from the main thoroughfares in Lake Oswego, Oregon. Except for the few vehicles in the parking lot, the structure appears to be new and unoccupied at first glance.

Hanging from the eaves in front of one of the offices — in letters no more than four inches high — is a sign announcing:

This is the home office of the family industry that has given knife design a whole new look over the past couple of decades. Ann Mar, the designer's wife, is president of the company, and his daughter, Ryann, is the company's sales manager, after serving her apprenticeship in inspection, shipping and other facets of the enterprise.

But Al Mar Knives didn't just happen. Mar is of Chinese ancestry. Raised in Seattle, he gained his initial exposure to edged weapons while serving in Laos and Thailand with Special Forces' First Group in 1959-60. At that time, his unit was based in Okinawa, but conducted training missions in the Southeast Asian countries.

Over the years, he has been involved with law enforcement and conducts training for an Oregon sheriff's department as well as doing some undercover work for the department. He also has spent time with the Japanese Special Police, an anti-terrorist unit, and with the Hong Kong Customs Police, learning their techniques.

A graduate of the Los Angeles Art Center, Mar originally was involved in package design for a Southern California firm. On one assignment, he was sent to Gerber Legendary Blades in Portland to solve a packaging problem. He liked what he saw there, signed on as a knife designer and stayed with Gerber for nearly a decade before launching his own operation.

Much of the Mar operation in Lake Oswego is devoted to move-'em-in-and-move-'em-out. For the most part, his knives are designed at his own drawing table, then are sent to Japan, where prototypes are made for his approval. Once approved, production is carried out there and the completed knives shipped to Oregon. With some models, handles are installed by Mar's staff of helpers before the knives are shipped on to dealers around the world.

Oddly enough, one of Al Mar's biggest markets is in Japan, where his knives are made. "There are countless collectors there," the designer explains, "and a lot of them collect our knives. It has become a lucrative market for us."

*Unusual design combined with function is one of the hallmarks of Al Mar's efforts.*

Osprey (below) and Hawk (right) are small versions of designs that have found high favor with customers. The handle for the Hawk is now of Micarta, not rosewood.

The knives in Mar's Tanken series illustrate influence of his Chinese heritage. Handles are of Du Pont Zytel, while the blades are fashioned from AM-P stainless.

But there are Al Mar collectors in this country, too; lots of them. "But it isn't until we discontinue a particular model that there suddenly is a rush to gather them in by collectors," Mar explains. "Once there aren't any more being made, suddenly everybody wants one." Prices on some of his early styles are several times the original price.

Al Mar has an interesting philosophy about the blades he produces. "We have one survival knife in the line," he acknowledges. "Personally, I feel the interest in the knife with the hollow handle and enough stuff packed into it to set up a military base camp has waned. However, we can't keep up with the demand for what we call our SAS-10. Everyone thinks the letters stand for something military. Actually, the SAS stands for Survive Anywhere Safely." Oddly enough, all that Mar includes in the handle of the knife is a thermometer and another knife, a small folder.

"I feel that whoever buys the knife is going to make his own decision as to what he wants to carry in it," is Mar's opinion.

While his success has been built on mass production of his own designs, more recently Mar has started to offer a limited number of custom-made models. All of these are his own designs that are turned out by selected custom knifemakers. "This service gives our dealers the opportunity to offer their customers additional high-quality knives of unique design," Al Mar explains.

The Lake Oswego operation also offers special order knives, with engraving and scrimshaw of the customer's choice. This is farmed out to experts in their own right. A

The Fang I and Fang II, the larger knife, both have been good sellers. Blade of Fang I is 3½ inches, the blade on the other, 5⅜, using RS-30 stainless.

lady named Bonnie Schulte in Newport, Oregon, does all of Mar's custom scrimshaw work, including four-color renditions. The engraving is handled by Bob Vlade of Seaside, Oregon.

In some instances, Vlade incorporates other materials into knife handles, since he was a lapidary before he taught himself engraving. He utilizes jade, jasper and turquoise to dress up special-order knives. Two such Al Mar knives, incidentally, were made for President Ronald Reagan and presented to him in a White House ceremony.

Leather sheaths for Al Mar knives are made by Tex Shoemaker, the Southern California holster manufac-

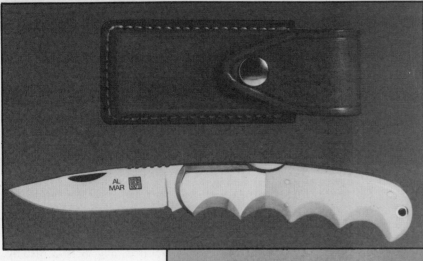

The Buzzard model was one of Mar's early designs. Featuring a four-inch blade, it has an ivory Micarta handle. Blade is of stainless steel; is manufactured in Japan.

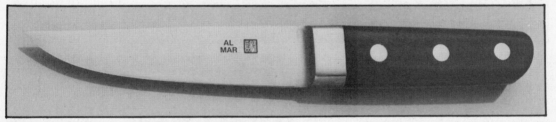

The designer is another who has recognized the popular appeal of lightweight knives and has added a series of lightweight folders with Zytel handles to his line-up.

Mar's utility tanken style has either a conventional point or a chisel point. The handle material used is black pakkawood. It comes with a hand-made sheath.

turer. For those that require nylon sheaths or pouches, another Oregon firm, Eagle Industries, handles production.

If you want a carbon steel knife from Al Mar, you're out of luck. All of his blades these days are strictly from stainless steel. The primary material is RS-30, which is made in Japan and is not exported. The entire production is used by cutlery firms within the country and Al Mar Knives must settle for a specific allotment of this material. Another knife steel is listed as AM-6 and is what Mar refers to as a "proprietary steel" the formula for which is regulated by the Japanese company that manufactures his blades. A more familiar-sounding stainless that also is used in some of the knives is 440-A.

Al Mar admits there has been a degree of confusion with his name. "Since *mar* is Latin for sea, there have been those who thought I was Italian or Spanish, until we met," the knife designer offers with a grin. "But they didn't know that *mar* also is Chinese for horse." On each of the blades coming from his operation, the Chinese figures that mean

"horse" are worked into a standard signature.

In spite of the much publicized tradition of animosity between the Chinese and Japanese down throught the ages, Al Mar has developed a unique relationship with his Japanese manufacturers. He makes several trips a year to Tokyo, taking with him plans and designs for the knives he would like to produce and market. In a marathon session, involving engineers and casting specialists, it is determined which of the designs are economically feasible — and those that are selected are put into production almost immediately.

In more recent months, Al Mar Knives has expanded from its approach, which seemed to go along with the mentor's motto that "every knife is a survival knife." One gets the feeling that, when he makes that statement, he is thinking of urban survival as much as anything else.

But new additions to the Mar line include gift items such as belt buckle knives, money clips that incorporate a hidden blade and key rings that also contain a knife.

With the expanding line, there is little doubt that his Green Beret series remains his own favorite. This line includes a number of heavy-duty folding combat knives, some with wood Micarta handles, others featuring a new rubber handle. Added to the Green Beret series is a fixed-blade knife he calls the Special Forces One-Zero. It is an improved version of the knife issued in Vietnam.

Recent additions also include several variations of the tanken, which was the personal knife of the Japanese samurai warrior. He has designed what he calls a utility tanken in two different styles, one with the tanto-type blade. The utility blade is 5⅜ inches in length, while the tanto is half an inch shorter, due primarily to its more blunt point. These feature black pakkawood handles and are of AM-6 steel tempered to a hardness of 57-59C on the Rockwell scale.

The recent popularity of lightweight handles has not been lost on the Mar organization and another series of tanken knives — the Shugoto I, the Shugoto II, the Scout and the Phantom — vary in blade length and blade shape. But each is of AM-6 stain-resistant steel and has a handle cast from Zytel, which reduces weight.

When one wants to discuss the so-called tanto blade, incidentally, Al Mar is quick to explain, "The term *tanto* is a generic term that has come to describe a wide variety of cutlery having Japanese styling in their design features. The word *tanken,* on the other hand, translates from the Japanese to mean "short sword."

Most of these knives, along with his other combat designs, are marketed under the Warrior's Edge designation.

But, as suggested earlier, you don't have to be warlike to own an Al Mar knife and like it. He has knives in all sizes and shapes, ranging from small, lightweight pocketknives, through the standard stock knife designs favored by ranchers and livestock handlers.

All of this means a lot of long hours at his drawing board, where Al Mar designs what he thinks is going to interest the public next. The result of his predictions — laid out on paper in his designs — is reflected in the fact that a great many of the knives he has introduced have been copied by other makers, several of them much larger in staff, factory space and production than Al Mar Knives.

While all of his knives are manufactured in Japan, Al Mar uses Oregon craftsmen for special presentation knives that feature engraving and custom scrimshaw.

Mar's own experiences with Special Forces were used in designing what he calls the Special Forces One-Zero. Handle is of leather, with a brass guard and butt cap.

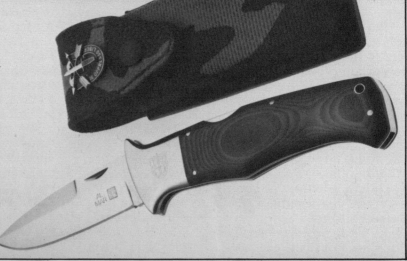

The SERE (Survive, Escape, Resistance, Evasion) model is popular with military buyers. It was inspired by an officer at Fort Bragg for special operations use.

# ATLANTA CUTLERY OFFERS SOME OF THE MOST UNUSUAL BARGAINS TO BE FOUND IN THE WORLD OF KNIVES

The Atlanta Cutlery crew; president Bill Adams is the gray-bearded one standing in the back row, third from right. Below: The old bank building at the corner of Center and Commercial now is the home of Atlanta Cutlery. Visitors are welcome.

BILL ADAMS heads up Atlanta Cutlery in Conyers, Georgia. One look at his many-faceted catalog of knives should convince anyone that Adams not only knows a lot about knives, but that he has a charming sense of humor.

Atlanta Cutlery offers literally hundreds of knives for sale, produced in the United States, Japan, Taiwan, mainland China, Pakistan, India, Germany, Spain, France, England, Finland, Norway and seemingly dozens of other exotic locations. Knife styles include just about anything one might be able to think of, except generally illegal knives, plus some you might never knew existed. Almost every kind of folder, sheath knife, bayonet, machete, fight-

*The largest part of Atlanta Cutlery's business is, by far, mail order, but the company also enjoys a healthy retail business in Conyers, Georgia.*

ing knife, survival knife, throwing knife, axe, pick, entrenching tool or military knife to be found anywhere is for sale under the Atlanta banner. Furthermore, Adams has located and offers many kinds of sharpeners, knife kits and hobby components for the amateur and professional craftsman.

Conyers is about twenty-five miles east of Atlanta and the company operates a retail outlet and a small knife museum at the location. The building, incidentally, is an old yellow brick bank building just a block off the railroad

The retail sales room also displays covers from past sales catalogs, some of which have become collector items in themselves. Allow plenty of time for a visit; knives are many and varied.

tracks, near the center of town. The showroom is open to customers and browsers during normal office hours, according to Adams. There are lots of knives to be seen, so plenty of time should be allotted for the visit.

Knives from Atlanta Cutlery may be large or small, decorative or completely utilitarian. One of the latest models, a side-lock folder made in Italy, utilizes Swedish steel for the blade. Because of the side-lock, the knife can be closed using only one hand; the lock will not let go accidently, even under hard use. The handle is formed from hard, checkered plastic shaped in what is called a shotgun style.

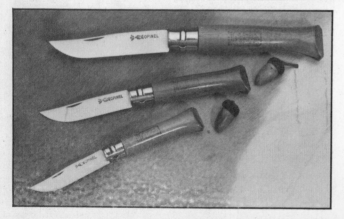

Knives are imported from many countries. The Opinel folder, left, is from France. The blade is locked in place by a twist of the bolster. Price is cheap.

Another nice folder design that reflects the international nature of Atlanta Cutlery is found in a couple of lightweights from Germany. The larger of the two, with a 3½-inch blade, weighs only four ounces. The smaller knife has a 2¾-inch blade and weighs only three ounces. The handle slabs are made of a special olive drab lightweight polypropylene. The single blades are of stainless steel.

From France, another unusual folding knife available from Atlanta is called the Opinel. This twist-lock design is intended for mountaineers who may have to lock and unlock the blade with one hand, presumably hanging on to a steep cliff with the other. The mechanism requires a one-

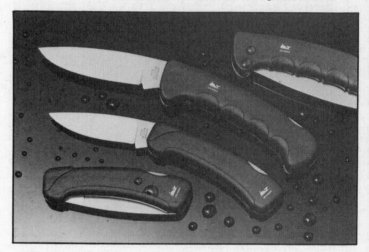

Two folders imported by Atlanta: the lightweight lock-back from Germany, above, and the Royal Eagle from Italy, below. German knife has lock placed near rear while the Italian has a lever on the side.

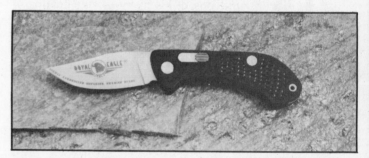

eighth-inch twist in either direction to open or close. The high-carbon steel blade folds into a varnished hardwood handle and the Opinel design is available with blades of 3⅛, 3½ or 4¾ inches in length. They weigh little and are quite reasonably priced.

One of the more unusual designs is the String Bean stiletto, also made in Italy. The String Bean has a blade six inches long, with an overall open length of more than a foot. The blade is of stainless steel, the handle is some sort of imitation shell and the design includes what is called a traditional stiletto crossguard integral with the bolster. The blade has a rear-locking mechanism.

One of the most popular knife designs ever imported by Atlanta cutlery is the Gurkha kukri. The distinctive curved

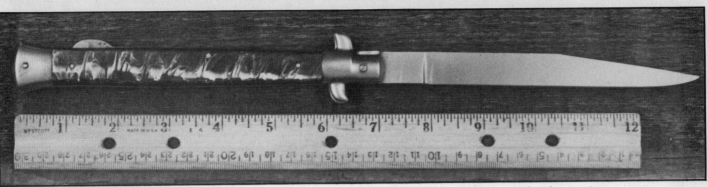

*Made in Italy, the folding String Bean stiletto has a six-inch blade with positive locking mechanism on top.*

blade is still in use by the Gurkha regiments of Nepal and anywhere in the world where they may serve. The kukri has been and continues to be extremely popular with collectors all over the world.

The kukries are offered in three different blade lengths. The original import has a twelve-inch blade and includes two accessory knives and a black leather sheath with wooden liner. The kukri has been in use by the Gurkhas since the middle of the Nineteenth Century, through World War I, WWII and as recently as the Falkland Islands operation. The kukri is sold with a copy of an eight-page government contract, the ordnance drawing and a specifications sheet, all sure to please the collector/buyer.

With the popularity of the original design, Atlanta Cutlery has added two more kukri styles for aficionados of exotic knives. The officer's kukri is somewhat shorter, with a 9½-inch blade and a buffalo horn handle. It comes with two accessory knives and a regulation officer's sheath made of black leather. This knife includes a copy of a letter from a "Colonel of the Regiment," verifying the authenticity of the heritage of this sacred weapon, a five-page government contract plus an ordnance drawing and spec sheet covering the knife.

There also is a huge ceremonial kukri knife, with a blade measuring 22½ inches. These knives are rare and certainly are not carried in uniformed duty by Gurkhas. The ceremonial knife is used once a year at an event called *Dushera*. At this event, the regiment selects its strongest young man,

*Given the popularity of the original kukri, it is no surprise that Atlanta has added the Gurkha officer's model. A regulation sheath, two accessory knives, copies of issue letter, contract and ordnance drawing are included with purchase. The 9½-inch blade is hand-forged of high carbon steel, 3/16-inch thick.*

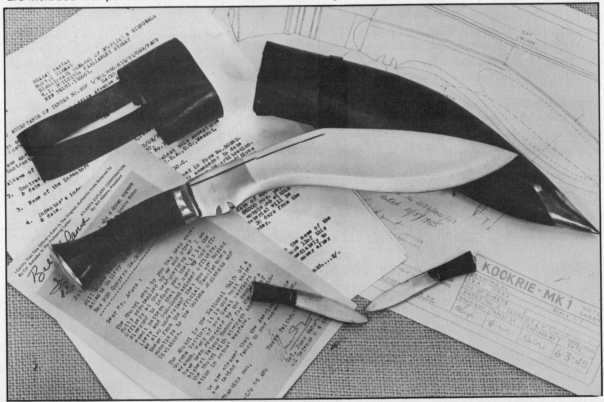

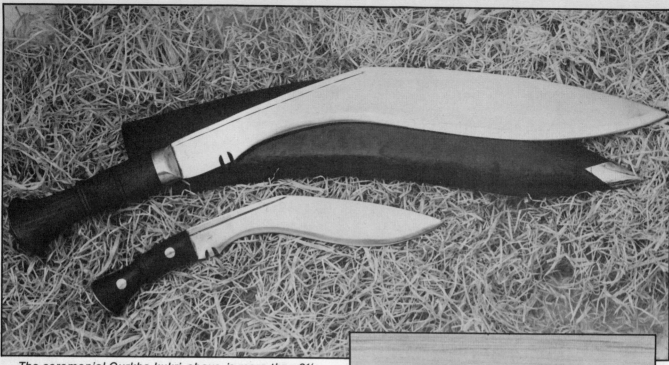

The ceremonial Gurkha kukri, above, is more than 2½ feet long, weighing more than four pounds. For large knife fanciers only! Atlanta Cutlery also specializes in handle materials, such as the buffalo horn at right.

who is required to sever the head of a water buffalo with one stroke. If he does this, he ensures good luck to the entire regiment for the year. Bill Adams says that only one of the ceremonial kukris is issued to each regiment, but his supply is the result of an overrun by the manufacturer. It certainly should be a conversation piece for any collection.

An earlier chapter told how to make your own knives from kits in general and the Atlanta Cutlery folders in particular. The firm has a large supply of knife components, including dozens of blades and various handle materials for the maker to assemble. Two traditional blade styles for skinning knives Atlanta calls Skinner Supreme and Absorka.

Both have upswept blades for smooth skinning action. The Skinner Supreme is a high-carbon steel blade while the Absorka is made from stainless steel. The former measures

Knife blades for the handyman to haft are popular at Atlanta. Skinner patterns, below, are of high carbon steel, upper, and stainless steel. Pommels are pre-threaded for handle and pommel attachment.

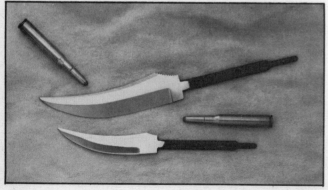

five inches long and the latter is 3⅝ inches. Both blade blanks have a threaded tang end for screw-on pommel attachment. Each blade is reasonably priced and should present no problems when it comes to forming and attaching a handle.

Just right for a skinning blade or any other knife handles are the black buffalo horn blocks that Bill Adams has included in his catalog. The buffalo horn comes from India, another of Adams' globe-trotting finds. The horn takes a real polish, says Adams, and the material is shot through with natural white streaks for added attractiveness.

As Bill Adams and his staff continue to scour the world in search of new and unusual knife designs, each annual catalog tends to reflect their finds. For example, Adams was on a trip to mainland China not too long ago. It was a vacation trip but, ever on the lookout for new things, Adams noticed a group of elite Chinese police specially trained to deal with unruly citizens. Each officer carried an unusual knife on his uniform belt. These turned out to be most unusual designs with blades that retracted into the handle. Adams was able to arrange for importation of several of the knives, which have since proven popular with the collecting crowd.

The Chinese police knife is not pretty to look at and is certainly not made of the highest quality materials, but it is different and that is what appeals to buyers.

# BERETTA U.S.A. HAS ADDED A LINE OF QUALITY KNIVES TO ITS LINE OF FAMOUS FIREARMS

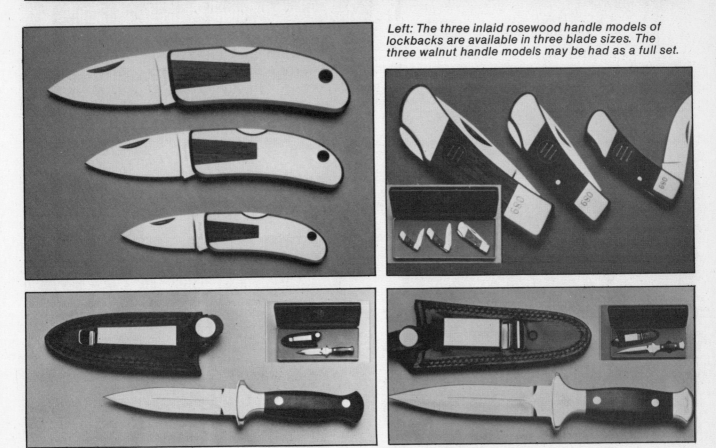

*Left: The three inlaid rosewood handle models of lockbacks are available in three blade sizes. The three walnut handle models may be had as a full set.*

*The Beretta double-edge model is a typical boot or belt knife, with a spring clip belt loop and safety strap. Model has 3⅝-inch blade and ebony handle.*

*Larger double edge knife, above, features a five-inch blade. It has a spring clip sheath and comes with a display case. Three lockback folders, below, have rosewood inlays; replicate Beretta shotgun receiver.*

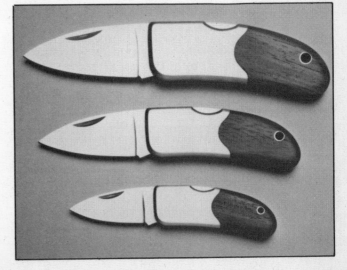

**B**ERETTA, the old-line Italian gunmaker, has invaded the American marketplace in a big way. When the United States government decided to replace the seventy-year-old Colt Government Model 1911A1 pistol as the official sidearm for its soldiers and sailors, it conducted several years of intensive trials, open to all comers. Firearms makers from all over the world competed for the coveted contract, finally awarded to Beretta's 9mm pistol.

A couple of years later, Beretta USA introduced a series of nice-looking knives to be sold through the same outlets as their firearms. The designs are interesting and attractive. Some of the folders with inlaid wood and metal handles are the most unusual, reflecting some genuine attention to quality control. The level of workmanship seems high enough to satisfy most knife users.

There are twenty-one knives in the Beretta knife collection. These are separated into three categories: the Collector's series, the Sportsman's series and the Hunter's series

*Two Beretta skinners, above, each features sturdy clip blade made of 440C stainless steel. Handles are of weather-resistant, kiln-dried rosewood. Both have thumb and forefinger rests for steady control at work.*

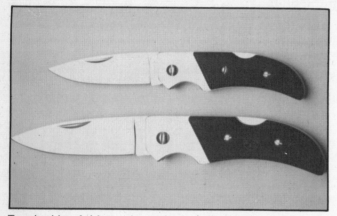

*Two locking folders, above, feature drop point blades of 440C, 2¾ inches or 3-7/16 inches long. Handles are of Micarta with Beretta logo on sides.*

*Additional folding designs have same Micarta handles with Beretta logo, but blade style is a clip point, 2¾ inches or 3⅞ inches long.*

The Collector's series includes walnut-handled lockbacks (K-101 through K-104), stainless steel lockbacks (K-201 through K-204) and classic double-edges (K-301 and K-302).

Beretta's models follow a logical numbering system and inventory of Collector's series knives is as follows: Walnut knives are numbered individually and in sets. Sets are numbered from 006 to 700. Individual knives are available in limited quantities. The large walnut knives are from numbers 006 to 165; medium walnut knives from numbers 006 to 115; and small walnut knives from numbers 006 to 100.

The Sportsman's series includes two styles of premium-quality folding lockback knives (K-601 through K-606) and a gentleman's money clip knife (K-701).

The Hunter's series includes two styles of folding lockback knives (K-401 through K-404) and two fixed-blade skinning knives (K-501 and K-502).

The Beretta knives range in retail price from about $25

up to about $150. Blade lengths are as small as an inch-and-a-half, up to five inches for the double-edge boot knife. Folders all are single-blade knives, except for the little money clip knife which has a pen blade and a nail file. Most of the knives have blades in the two- to three-inch range.

Handle materials are stainless steel, walnut, rosewood and Micarta. Most of the blades are of 440C stainless steel.

We were unable to determine who the Beretta knife designer is, but they may be utilizing the talents of some American custom knifemakers. Late in 1987, Beretta launched a program to involve custom makers in the design and production of the Collector line. One of the first names to be announced in this connection was Gary Barnes of New Windsor, Maryland. Barnes' first efforts were to create new deeply engraved German silver handle scales for the standard drop point lockback model. Bob Loveless also has signed a design contract with the company. Other makers, says Beretta, will be adding their artistic touches to the Collector's series for Beretta USA.

# BLACKJACK KNIVES IS NEW, BUT IS CARVING OUT ITS NICHE IN A HURRY

**M**IKE STEWART, who heads up Blackjack Knives, is serious about his new company. Stewart is a lifelong martial artist and knows what he wants in the way of knives. He is confident he has found and is filling a need in the knife business.

Until 1986, Stewart was a part of Pacific Cutlery, another Southern California knife company. Stewart had been of the opinion for some time that there was a part of the knife market which a company such as he had in mind could supply. Blackjack knives was formed to concentrate on the outdoor/survival knife segment; to supply products for those who appreciate better knives designed for specific purposes. Blackjack began with an imported line of knives from South Africa, all of them handmade by Chris Reeve. Initial custom production from Reeve showed more than a dozen designs, all with a basic fixed-blade configuration which includes a hollow handle with threaded butt cap to carry small emergency survival items.

What makes the Reeve-made Blackjack knives unusual is their construction from a single solid piece of steel. Handle and blade are of the same billet, machined from high

Mike Stewart stands before the modest headquarters of Blackjack Knives in Chatsworth, California. He is holding one of his newest creations, the Mamba.

The series of Chris Reeve knives designed and built in South Africa, imported by Blackjack. The series includes blade lengths of from 8¾ inches to the shortest with a four-inch blade. All have hollow handles closed by a threaded butt cap and seal. The hexagonal shape of the cap facilitates tightening.

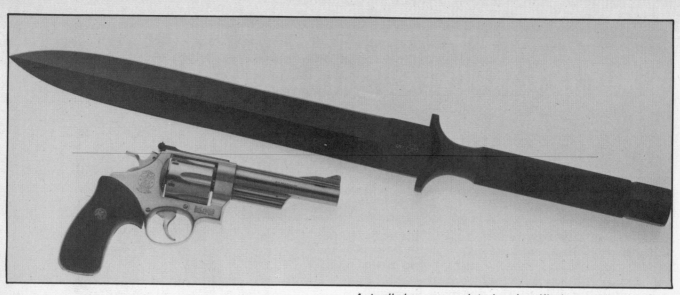

Actually long enough to be classified as a small sword, this Chris Reeve knife was specially made for Blackjack's Mike Stewart, who likes 'em big.

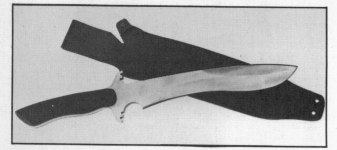

The Blackjack Mamba knife has a distinct blade shape, not unlike a snake; thus, the name. The final handle design will resemble snakeskin when in production. Mike Stewart is the designer.

carbon steel and finished in a black-gray material called Kalgard. The Kalgard finish is a dull matte, precluding most light reflections as well as protecting the metal from most corrosive substances. Each blade, according to Stewart, is hardened to a Rockwell C reading of 56-58 before it is coated with Kalgard. The only separate piece is the air- and water-tight threaded butt cap.

Balance of the knife in the hand is quite good. The thirteen models — as of late 1987 — range in size from the Jereboam with its 8¾-inch blade to a compact version with a four-inch blade that most hunters and backpackers seem to prefer. Blade styles include clip points and spear points, drop points and upswept tanto shapes. The steel is made by Thyssen-Marathon of West Germany.

Reeve produces all the knives by hand, with an annual production of about 250. Blackjack imports them all and has no trouble finding buyers for them, while maintaining a considerable waiting list. In early 1988, Stewart was considering dropping a couple of the designs and adding another blade shape or two more suited to the American market.

The overall impressions of the Reeve knives is one of massiveness. Because of the color, they tend to seem a bit bigger than they really are. One might think they could be unwieldly in use, but to the contrary, the models we tested are well balanced and easy to use. On a spring black bear hunting trip to Alaska, the seven-inch-blade Mark IV model was used to field dress and skin out three animals. It

This publicity photo is intended to illustrate the feature that Blackjack's South Africa imports are built of a single piece of steel. Machining steps take place about as shown. The finish is Kalgard.

The locking folder, Model FM-11, was named the "Best Cutlery Buy Of The Year" for 1987 by The Blade Magazine. The knife, also known as a folding Mamba, features a snakeskin-like handle.

Oregon custom knifemaker Bob Lum is given credit for the design of this Chinese fighting knife which Blackjack is producing. Note slightly curved handle.

Design of this Blackjack dagger is reflected in company's logo: the blade piercing the Jack and Ace of spades — Blackjack! Handle material is soft, rubber-like substance for a firm, non-slip grip.

Reverse side of blade above reveals the triangular cross-section which gives the knife its strength. Dagger is an ideal boot-knife for those, such as some law enforcement or paramedic personnel, who carry one.

was tough work and the Blackjack Mark IV needed only slight sharpening touch-up during the extensive work. One hunter, who is a custom butcher by trade, communicated his surprise that such a big knife handled so well. He was favorably impressed at how well the edge held up throughout the hours of work.

Not all the Blackjack knives are made in South Africa. Some models are being contracted out to be manufactured in Japan, while others are built in California. Some are designed by Mike Stewart, while others are the result of considerable thought by custom knifemaker Bob Lum, who now maintains his shop in Oregon.

Mike Stewart has been mentally harboring a large camping, hunting and trail knife design for several years. Four years in development, the new design is called the Mamba, named after a deadly African snake. The blade is nine inches in length and the knife measures fifteen inches long overall. This knife is machined from a solid quarter-inch-thick steel bar of a specially blended and rolled material. The knife is cut from the blank by laser which is said not to put any stress on the steel and is highly accurate and precise in dimensions. The handle attracts as much attention

as the large sweeping blade itself. The handle is a snake-skin textured rubber polymer material held on by a special cement and three hollow pins which are flared larger toward the ends to lock the material to the full tang.

The dramatic blade shape of the Mamba has been engineered to serve as a continuous working-cutting surface, according to Stewart. The exact curve design has been tested extensively by Stewart and his crew to obtain maximum cutting capability with minimum effort. The sweeping, curving blade shape aids in cutting. In balance, the knife weight is slightly forward, which helps when chopping wood in camp — something the big knife is perfectly capable of doing. The finger-size cut-out choil at the rear of the blade permits easy choke-up gripping for that extra control necessary for finer cutting tasks. The knife has not been designed as a skinner, but could be used for that purpose if required by the situation. The integral lug guards are radiused forward on top and rearward on the bottom to give the proper thumb and first finger support in field use.

For all its size, the Mamba weighs only fifteen ounces. When handled, it feels much lighter because of the balance and design. At first glance, the knife seems far too large for

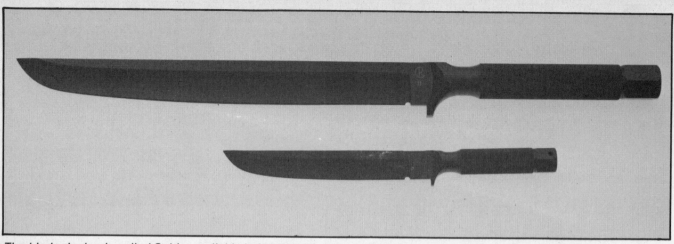

The blade design is called Sable, available in lengths from 8¾ to four inches. Those dimensions coincide with some popular revolver barrel lengths. Even longer blades are available from Chris Reeve through Blackjack.

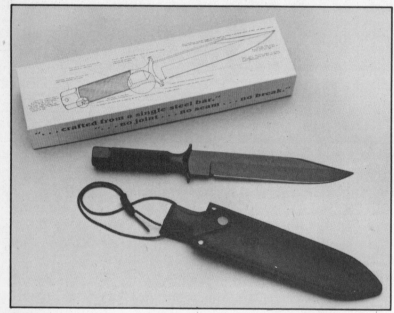

Packaging is often as important to the success of a product as the product itself. Blackjack presents a high-tech look to its boxes, offering important data on the knife inside.

Mike Stewart has been involved in the martial arts since he was 8 years old. His designs reflect his background.

use as a field tool, but after handling it for a few minutes, most skeptics decide the Mamba could do well for most outdoor work. Although Stewart does not advocate such uses, there is no doubt that the big knife would do well in the hands of a trained martial artist and knife-fighter.

We've all heard of spin-offs. Blackjack has spun-off its own design and has come up with a smaller folding knife version of the Mamba, called the model FM-II. The lock-back blade measures 3½ inches. The knife is 7¾ inches long when open, 4¾ inches closed. It weighs only 5¼ ounces. Upon its introduction in 1987, it won an industry award as the "Best Cutlery Buy of the Year."

The smaller blade is of the same basic shape as the Mamba and the handle slabs are of rubber polymer textured in a snakeskin pattern. The lock release is located in the center of the handle spine, a placement, according to Mike Stewart, which is the most convenient and least likely to release accidentally while working. One may see and feel a checkered stud through the blade which helps in

opening and closing the blade. With practice, the blade can be opened quickly with one hand.

Bob Lum is a custom knifemaker; one of the best. He has always been interested in his Oriental heritage and its relationship to knives. Lum was one of the makers responsible for introducing what has become known as the tanto blade style; it's now included in several factory knife and custom catalogs. Lum and Stewart have gotten together and Blackjack Knives is producing Lum's Chinese fighting knife. The design has been researched by Lum as an authentic style which was found in old China.

Mike Stewart continues to seek out unusual and unique knife designs to add to the Blackjack offering. He is confident of the future of the company. The only real problem he faces is that of filling the many orders for his knives. He is moving slowly and carefully, attempting to avoid both over- and under-production. With knife production under way in Chatsworth, California, part of his problem should be solved.

# WITH A HISTORY OF SOME FOUR HUNDRED YEARS, BOKER STAYS ON TOP OF KNIFE TRENDS!

Boker's Damascus steel blades are hand-forged by Manfred Sasche of Dusseldorf. Each blade consists of more than three hundred layers of metal to form its own unique pattern, unlike any others.

"BOKER TREE Brand knives have come a long way," is the opinion of Ernst Felix, president of Boker Germany. The company, which has an off-shoot, Boker USA, headquartered in Golden, Colorado, is some four hundred years old, but has had to undergo continual changes and such shattering experiences as World War II. Today, it continues to survive, turning out and distributing some of the finest cutlery available.

The Boker history is traced back to a huge chestnut tree overshadowing the little factory where the Bokers were manufacturing handtools in the late Seventeenth Century. During a restless political era, Hermann and Robert Boeker decided to start production of sabers in 1829 and the books disclose a weekly production of 2000 pieces in September 1830. These were made by sixty-four forgers, forty-seven grinders and a great number of unskilled workers.

"With an ever-increasing range of tools and cutlery and the growing chances of worldwide distribution, family members realized they had to split up to look after their interests in an efficient way," Ernest Felix reports.

So Hermann Boeker went to New York and established H. Boker & Co. in 1837. Young Robert established the interest in Canada and later, in 1865, founded the Mexican subsidiary that is still a market leader in that country under the name of Casa Boker. Both dropped the *e* from the family name to simplify it.

Heinrich went to Solingen where the German cutlery industry was growing at incredible speed. In 1869, he joined with Hermann Heuser, a well known cutler, to establish Heinrich Boeker & Co.

The family had to identify their products in an easy way for the overseas market, where many consumers had problems with the German name Boeker, apart from the fact that illiteracy was widespread. The logo showing the chestnut tree close to the Remscheid company was ideal, but this trademark belonged to the Remscheid firm along with the second brand, an arrow. One of the few valuable documents that survived total destruction in World War II is an 1874 advertisement of Boeker Remscheid showing both trademarks.

*Folding knives, too, are made with Boker's Damascus steel blades, with unusual design possibilities. The medium pen knife, left, and the locking-blade version have handles of Argentine red bone, Boker medallion.*

"There has always been an extremely friendly relationship among the various Boker companies, so Heinrich took the tree brand with him to Solingen without big argument or check. Since then, no Boker item has left the Solingen plant without being branded with the tree logo.

"The old chestnut tree, over one hundred years old, was hit by lightning back in 1925. A talented whittler carved the majestic appearance of this tree off a piece of the trunk," Felix says. This piece still decorates the office of Boker's president, Ernst Felix, and his partner Ulrich Mennenoeh.

By 1900, the U.S. market accounted for the greater portion of Boker's business. H. Boker & Co. Inc., New York, gave the tree brand products a predominate place. Since the demand grew faster than the capacities, the New York firm started to manufacture pocketknives in Maplewood, New Jersey, and later added pliers to the line. As the tree brand was well established, their German relations gave them the right to use the logo for their products as well.

During that time there have been two different ranges of Boker knives on the market. They had the same style and appearance, same logo, even the same order numbers in

*These two Premium lockblades are offered with a choice of African thuya wood or Argentine red bone handles.*

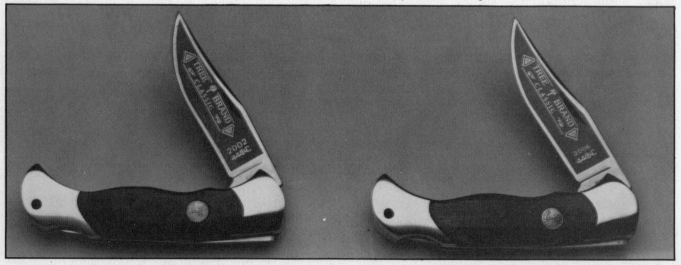

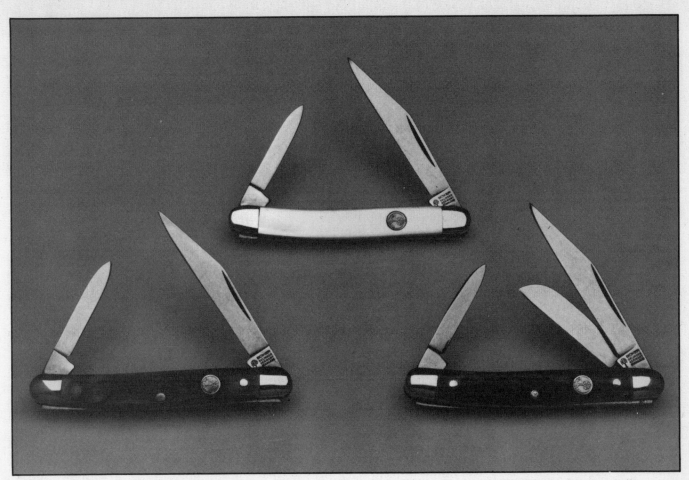

*This trio of folders is offered with handles of stainless steel or mother-of-pearl. The two-blade models have a clip and a pen blade; the three-blade version features a clip, spey and a sheepsfoot blade. All are made in Germany.*

some cases, but one was made in the United States and the other in Solingen. One carried the tang stamp, *Boker USA,* the other, *H. Boker's Improved Cutlery Solingen.*

"During the Second World War, the business was virtually shot to pieces. The Solingen plant was burnt out completely. No equipment, no tooling were left. No catalog material. No samples. The few originals from the past the Boker principals have available today were kept in private homes during the war and donated to the company later.

"They also lost one of their most valuable assets: their tree brand logo and brand names in the American market were confiscated as enemy property. John Boker, Jr., in New York, eventually succeeded in acquiring them in order to secure distribution of his products made in Maplewood," says Chuck Hoffman, now president of Boker USA.

Soon after the war, the Boker factory in Solingen began to emerge from the ruins. Skilled cutlers returning from the war rebuilt one production line after the other, until the pre-war standard was reached again. The American Boker cousins renewed their business contacts with Solingen and submitted orders. It did not take many years to again become the predominate customers.

In the early Sixties, the Boker family sold the business to Wiss & Sons, Newark, New Jersey. Thus, America's largest scissors manufacturer became the new owner of the

Boker business. They continued manufacturing knives in Maplewood and distributing the German products. Less than ten years later, Wiss sold out to the hardware division of Cooper Industries. Boker Germany established a close relationship with this industrial giant. Cooper reestablished the Boker name particularly on their own home grounds: the hardware distribution. Boker was able to modernize their plant and to pursue new product ideas. Recent introductions include Damascus steel with 320 layers, nicely contoured lockbacks with genuine pearl or thuya wood handles and light but solid knives with titanium scales.

Several years ago, Cooper closed the Boker manufacturing facilities in New Jersey. Today, this line is made in Germany as well. As a result of negotiations, Boker Germany has reacquired their U.S. trademark rights and has established Boker USA, Incorporated in Colorado as their own distribution facility for the American market.

At last count, Boker listed nearly eighty different models in their catalog. Among the newer items is a trio of Damascus fixed-blade knives.

In the new Damascus sheath collection, each knife blade of Damascus steel is as unique as a fingerprint, with over three hundred hand-forged layers by Manfred Sasche of Dusseldorf, Germany. Each blade is complemented with an exotic African thuya wood or white micarta han-

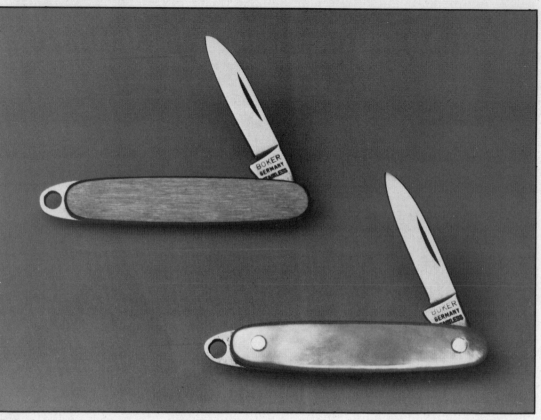

*Boker's little pen knives were introduced in 1987. Blades are only one inch long and customer has a choice of mother-of-pearl or stainless steel handles. Holes make for easy key ring attachment.*

dle. Each comes in a wooden presentation case.

Two others are Boker's 240 Damascus and 1004 Damascus. Both the lockback version (#1004) and the folding, medium pen (#240) have handles of red bone from Argentina. Each comes in a wooden presentation case.

Of the Damascus III, only 999 have been made. With this tree brand limited edition Damascus lockback knife, each is complemented with a handle of red bone from Argentina and each comes in a wooden presentation case.

There also are two new Premium lockblades in the Boker line. Both are folding lockback models, with cor-rosion-resistant 440C stainless steel clip blades. With a choice of an African thuya wood handle (#2002TH) or red bone from Argentina (#2006), each comes with a leather sheath.

Boker also has a pair of new small pen knives that are attachable to a key ring. The stainless steel blades are only one inch long, with a choice of stainless steel or genuine mother-of-pearl handles.

If it's a pocketknife you need, you have many choices from Boker. There are models with steel clip and pen blades (#8288HH, #8288P) or one with clip, sheepfoot and spey blades (#8388HH). Natural handle materials are genuine stag or mother-of-pearl.

*A limited production of 999 knives using the Boker Damascus III hand-forged blades were produced. The handle is made from Argentine red bone and a wood presentation case is included with each lockblade folding knife.*

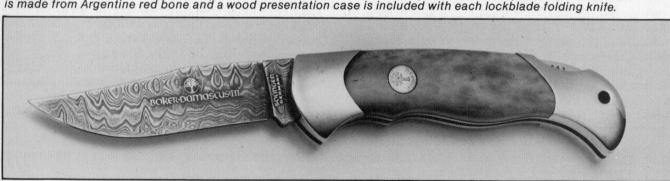

# BROWNING ADDS A SERIES OF PRACTICAL AND ATTRACTIVE KNIVES

*In addition to this line of folding knives, the Browning designers also have introduced a series of limited edition knives, some with blades of Damascus, that have found favor with collectors.*

WHEN FIRST introduced two decades ago, the Browning knife line consisted of only four knives, one of which had a folding blade. The others were typical upswept-blade hunting knives, all made from stainless steel, with Brazilian rosewood handles and brass guards and butt caps. All the sheaths were smooth leather.

The following year, a couple of pocket folders and a fish and bird knife were added to the line, as well as the first Browning sharpening stone. Popularity with dealers and customers was growing rapidly.

The number and design variation was increased year by year. Some of the knives were imported from the Far East, while others were made in a small factory near the Browning corporate headquarters in Utah. Several more folders were introduced, including a Swiss Army knife look-alike. Sharpening stones and honing oil, too, became a part of the knife line. It wasn't long until the Browning knife series included more than two dozen models, plus sharpening stones. All blades were of 440-C stainless steel with handles made of such things as Stamina wood, African ebony, rosewood, Lexan and stag.

Browning introduced several semi-custom-made knives which were produced in limited numbers, selling for somewhat more than the average pocket or hunting knife. These knives featured Wyoming jade handles and had names such as Oregon Trail, South Pass and Great Divide. They were produced in limited numbers at the beginning of the Eighties, each design restricted to 2000. A velvet-lined walnut case was included with each of these jade-handled knives. In a short time, Browning was showing almost fifty knife designs in their catalog. Smaller knives, larger knives, multi-blade folders, fishing knives and additional sharpening stones and honing kits were added. In the mid-Eighties, Damascus blades were in the Browning line.

The latest count of Browning knife styles shows the number reduced to less than twenty models, two limited edition knives and an assortment of sharpening stones, ceramic and steel honing devices. In limited production is a Damascus-bladed Classic Fighter featuring more than two hundred layers of laminated steel. Only a thousand of these have been made, with handles of cocobolo wood.

Browning also is following the recent trend of most factory producers: lightweight models fitted with handles of a rubber-like composite with mild checkering. Some of the lightweights are using Rynite or Zytel for the handle materials. One of the more attractive knives is the Model 810, called a Medium Folding Stalker. It has a combination handle of composite material with wood inlays. It is quite unusual and appealing in appearance. The line rounds out with four pocket folders, five traditional folders with one, two or three blades of up to four inches long and a couple of presentation pocketknives using African ebony or mother of pearl for handle slabs.

# Buck — The First Family Of Modern Knives

The First Family of Knives. From left: Charles T. Buck, president; Alfred C. Buck, chairman of the board; Charles B. Buck, product manager and head of Buck Apparel. The photo at upper left is H.H. Buck, first of knifemaking line, great-grandfather of Charles B. All have been actively engaged in Buck operations.

A BUCK KNIFE. The term is so well known that it has become practically generic, like aspirin and nylon.

The first Buck knives were made back before World War I, when H.H. Buck began forging. Buck knives then were made one at a time, each the work of one man, turned out for friends and neighbors. Each was handcrafted to H.H. Buck's exacting standards.

At the turn of the century, H.H. Buck was a blacksmith in Leavenworth, Kansas, a man who was not satisfied with the way steel blades held an edge. Actually, his first search was for a way to extend the life of worn-out grub-hoes for the farmers in his area.

He began experimenting with cast-off horseshoeing rasps and soon developed some innovative tempering tech-

niques which transformed the high-carbon steel into tough, durable steel that was not brittle. The hoes that Buck made with his new tempering process amazed the farmers: The edges stayed sharp!

Not surprisingly, he soon was being asked to make knives with the same temper. Those first handmade Buck knives held an edge like no other knife his neighbors had ever seen.

Alfred Buck is H.H. Buck's son. During World War II, Al Buck was a sailor stationed for a time in San Diego, California. When the war was over, memories of the business opportunities, the beautiful weather and the fishing possibilities were strong enough in Al Buck's memory that he loaded up his wife and son, Charles T. "Chuck" Buck, and moved them all to Southern California.

All knife-making operations at Buck are conducted under one roof, covering nearly four acres. Heat treating and tempering are critical operations.

Al, Chuck and Chuck Buck, Junior, — actually, not a junior, because the name is Charles B. — all are actively involved in the operation of Buck Knives, Inc., in their new building in El Cajon, a suburb of San Diego. The firm moved, in 1981, to this building specifically designed for the high-volume production of Buck knives. The facility is modern, attractive, efficient and abuzz with the assembly line production of thousands of knives per day. Chuck Buck, president of the company founded by his grandfather, takes keen interest in what is going on out on the production floor. On a recent visit to the plant, we noted how many employees Chuck Buck knows by name.

The self-contained Buck factory is a modern, smooth-running operation. From the arrival and storage of raw steel for the dozens of blade shapes and sizes, through modern machines for cutting, stamping, grinding, shaping, sharpening and fastening, to the inspection, packaging and shipment of products, the flow of work moves along with dispatch. Everything is done under one roof, much of it done by employees with more than two decades with Buck.

Buck has added a custom shop within the factory where some of the more skilled employees produce custom knives which are among some of the best to be found anywhere. Most are produced to the customer's order, but a few standard models are handcrafted by the shop personnel. Navajo Indian artist David Yellowhorse's distinctive work appears on Buck Custom Limited Edition knives.

Another growing area is that of special order or commemorative knives. These are standard Buck knives that are specially engraved or etched in a numbered, limited production run for a specific purpose or organization. Many law enforcement and government agencies have ordered these knives for employee recognition or simply to be issued to all members of the particular group. A large batch of knives was commissioned for the Border Patrol agents in the Southwest. A special machine numbers and engraves such knives.

Buck has pioneered some significant advances in knife design. Perhaps, the most famous was their creation of the Folding Hunter (Model 110) in 1963.

To that time, hunting knives usually had a fixed blade and came in a variety of lengths and shapes. Those knives fit nicely into a sheath that might run halfway down your leg.

Such sheath knives had their place and they still do. For

1988 marks the silver anniversary of the Buck lock-blade folder. Two commemoratives, the Folding Hunter and Ranger models, have specially etched blade to mark the date.

Buck maintains a knife repair facility at the El Cajon site. Knives are received down to the point that there is little steel left, but if it can be repaired, it will be.

many outdoorsmen, there is no substitute. Buck, of course, continues to produce a full range of fixed-blade knives, including a skinner and a caper along with ten others, plus a hunter's axe.

But when they designed that first folding lock-blade, Buck literally revolutionized hunting knives. Now the outdoorsman could have a sturdy, practical field knife that locked open with a full four-inch blade, yet folded down and stored away in its sheath, at an overall length of only 4⅞ inches when closed.

Buck has continued to make evolutionary improvements in both the Folding Hunter and the slightly smaller Ranger (Model 112). In 1984, handle edges and bolsters were slightly rounded for better feel.

Buck also has a new finger-grooved version of the Folding Hunter for those who prefer the added sense of grip, the feeling of control afforded by finger grooves. In addition to the finger-grooved folding hunter, Buck also has added a finger-grooved Ranger.

Newest additions are BuckMaster (Model 184) and BuckMaster LT (Model 185), two rugged multi-purpose field knives created to meet emergency situations. Both have the same 7½-inch blade, 9/32-inch thick and an overall length of 12½ inches. The back of the blade serves as an emergency wood/metal/ice saw; the sharpened clip portion of the blade also is serrated for the tough job of cutting rope, wet or dry.

BuckMaster 184 has a water- and air-tight hollow handle for storage of emergency necessities, with two detachable anchor pins that screw into the guard. A compass, with meridian lines and transparent base for taking map

Employees are required to wear eye and ear protection equipment while working around fast-running machines. All persons entering the factory floor must wear protective eye glasses, even the boss, seen on facing page. Finished projects are placed in trays, above.

Each knife is hand-polished at the end of production and before being packaged for shipment. The last step also provides a final individual inspection of each knife.

bearings, comes in a pouch which attaches to the sheath.

Model 185 is the skeletonized one-piece version, the handle coated in black thermoplastic. Both BuckMaster models have a gray, sand-blasted finish and come in a GripTite sheath with a built-in emergency sharpener.

Three fish fillet knives — the LakeMate (Model 123), StreamMate (Model 125) and OceanMate (Model 127) — have handles made of Kraton. These specially-engineered handles are finger-grooved and shaped to fit the hand comfortably and naturally.

The innovative handles have a tacky or slightly sticky feel to reduce the worry of the knife slipping from your grasp. These handles have a cushiony, resilient quality to them. The mid-flex blade is made of Buck's rust-resistant, high-chrome, high-carbon steel and the full-length tang is permanently embedded in the handle.

From the time Buck's fish fillet knives were introduced, requests came in for the same handle comfort and sure grip in fixed-blade sheath knives. So Buck created two models to meet that demand: the WoodsMate (Model 619), with black Kraton handle in a black nylon sheath with a protective liner; the FieldMate (Model 639), with olive drab Kraton handle in a camouflage nylon sheath.

With increasing demand for lightweight outdoor gear, Buck introduced a series of lock-blade field knives that combine rugged durability with really light weight. The BuckLite (Model 422), the first knife in this series has a steel three-inch blade and the same positive lock-open action and spring as Buck's other folding lock-blades. It weighs only 3¼ ounces in its nylon sheath.

BuckLite's lightweight has a one-piece handle made of Valox, an engineering-quality thermoplastic. BuckLite II has a 2⅝-inch blade; BuckLite III, a 3⅝-inch blade. In addition to the standard tan, brown-trimmed sheath, a camouflage sheath is available as an option. Each of the three models also is available with olive drab handles and camouflage sheaths.

Two new models are designed to meet the uniform requirements of most law enforcement officers. Both have

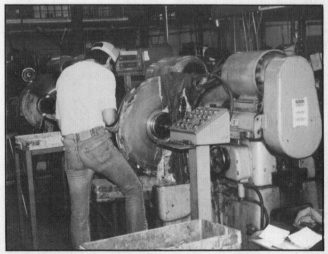

Chuck Buck, left, spends some time each day on the factory floor talking with employees and observing the production flow. Most of the big factory's machines had to be custom made, above.

black handles and come in a black nylon sheath. One has its three-inch blade in Buck's standard brushed-steel finish; the other has a sand-blasted, non-reflective gray finish.

Today, Buck markets a total of more than seventy models, plus a wide range of custom knives. The regular Buck line comprises two full series of pocketknives, fixed-blade sheath knives, heavy-duty folding knives, Slimline lockblades; specialty knives such as the Ultima I, the Gent, the Executive and the colorful Treasury series; the handsome Akonua and Kalinga, which come with a special sheath and presentation case; and the family of three Classic presentation knives.

There's even a Whittler's Kit, complete with knife, honing stone, honing oil, two easy-to-whittle wood blocks and the easy-to-follow twelve-page "Buck Knives Guide to Old-Time Whittling."

Another of Buck's recent reaffirmations of its role as leader in innovative knife design was the introduction of a totally new concept in pocketknives. The Colt (Model 703) is stronger, heftier and has more body. Heavier bolsters are made of stainless steel, as are the knife's liners. Springs are non-rusting. Handle inserts are birchwood, chemically treated to assure long-lasting natural woodgrain beauty. All of the blades — clip, sheepsfoot and spey — are hollow-ground, made of high-carbon, high-chrome steel that tests out at RC 57-59.

The Colt was followed by a similar but larger model, the Bronco (Model 701) then by two small, two-blade executive knives, the Pony (Model 705) and the Yearling (Model 709). Newest in this series is a single-blade version, the Maverick (Model 704).

Buck also offers its 300 Series pocketknives, with eleven models to choose from, including special knives such as the Yachtsman, with a locking marlin spike, and the Bird knife, which has a gutting hook for feathered game.

Buck's reputation is backed by their guarantee: Every Buck Knife is guaranteed for the life of the original purchaser against defects in materials and workmanship.

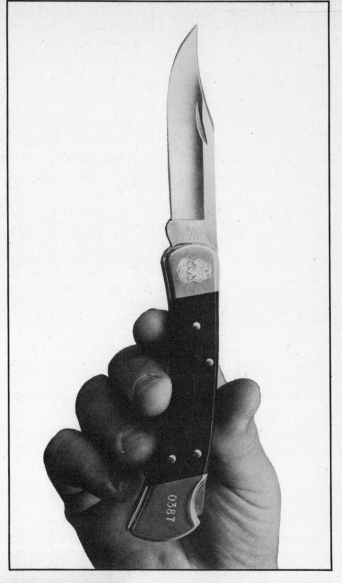

Commemorative and presentation knives, suitably engraved and numbered, have become a major part of Buck Knives' production.

The new U.S. military M9 bayonet is produced at the Buck factory. The civilian version has proven popular with knife buyers, as noted by the maker, Chuck Buck.

# FOR MORE THAN A CENTURY, CAMILLUS CUTLERY HAS TURNED OUT KNIVES IN QUANTITY AND QUALITY

Camillus has been making cutlery for more than a century and, today, has a modern factory with state-of-the-art equipment. But experienced workers oversee production.

This manufacturer's American Wildlife series has become a continuing design concept that has found interest in the ranks of serious collectors of sporting cutlery.

*In recent years, Camillus has come to recognize the fact that smaller knives for daily pocket carrying are an important part of the market.*

*In the design stage, one requirement for the American Wildlife series is that the knife must be practical.*

*The young president of Camillus, Jim Furgal, recognizes the fact that a knife must be useful if it's to sell.*

THE SAME YEAR that the United States celebrated its first hundred-year anniversary as an independent nation, Camillus Cutlery began operations as a producer of quality knives. 1876 was the year the country observed its Centennial with an exhibition in Philadelphia; it also was the year football, telephones and apartment houses were introduced. Land in Texas sold for fifty cents an acre and a train trip from San Francisco to New York City took seven days.

That year, an emigrant from Germany set himself up in the imported hardware and cutlery business in New York City. Business was good until protective tariffs were imposed in the late Nineteenth Century, making imports too costly. A domestic source of good cutlery needed to be found if the business was to continue, so the founder located a supplier at a small knife factory in Camillus, New York, and bought the factory to serve as his source.

Demand for quality knives continued to grow as did the company. After several expansions, today's modern production plant occupies more than 130,000 square feet of covered space. Camillus employs more than two hundred people from the surrounding New York area and turns out more than two million knives annually. All knife production is carried out at the single location, from steel selection and cutting, through stamping, grinding, polishing, tem-

*Catering to collector interests, such multi-knife packages as this have become good sellers in Camillus line.*

pering, assembling, inspection, packaging and shipping.

The Camillus line has a few fixed-blade models, including hunting, skinning, military and fileting knives, but most of its production is devoted to dozens of folding designs. Camillus introduced what it calls its American Wildlife series several years ago and it has proven a winner many times since. These knives all feature the words *American Wildlife* etched on the blades and each handle has an inset medallion of big or small game, birds or fish. All but the fillet knife are folders and all have stainless steel blades and Delrin handles. The knives are practical as well as collectible with their various animal designs on the medallions.

Camillus produces dozens of friction-lock folders with one, two, three or four blades. The larger folders include rear-blade locks, except for the Folding Hunter model, with its side-mounted slide-lock mechanism. Leather belt pouches are included with the largest folders.

In 1987, James Furgal was named president of Camillus Cutlery. A relatively young man, Furgal believes Camillus must become a customer-oriented company with emphasis on quality.

"If the customer is satisfied with a Camillus product," says Furgal, "the benefits will filter down to the company and its owners."

With a philosophy like that, Camillus Cutlery should be around for at least another hundred years.

*The old-line firm has not settled on a few standard items, but has developed new designs, decorations for the market.*

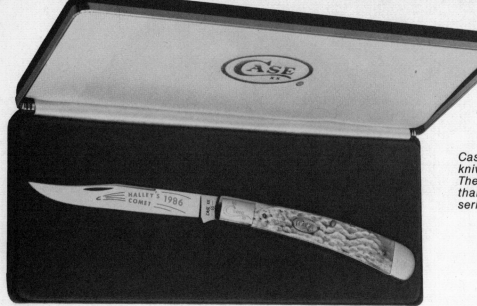

Case has been a leader in making knives that interest collectors. The Case Collectors Club has more than 4000 members who often buy a series of special commemoratives.

Case's Shark Tooth model has been endorsed by Montana Outfitters and Guides Association. It has a laminated black wood handle. (Below) A continual seller is this standard stockman's knife with its jigged bone handle.

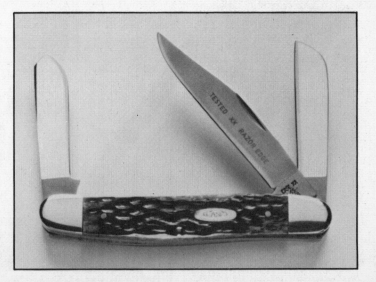

MEMBERS OF THE CASE family have been involved in the cutlery business in the United States for nearly a hundred years. Earlier ancestors were engaged in knifemaking in Sheffield, England. Through the Case family and the Platts family, who founded the firm that became Western Cutlery and now Coleman/Western, the Cases and their descendants are heavily involved in the cutlery history of the country. There is evidence of Debbie Case working for and later marrying H.N. Platts in 1892.

The W.R. Case & Sons Cutlery Co. was incorporated and the first factory was built in Bradford, Pennsylvania, in 1905, still the home of Case Cutlery. For some collectors, a trip to Bradford has been a "trip to heaven."

Case, along with Ka-Bar, is a company that seems to understand knife collectors and their needs, offering considerable support and encouragement. The company's Case Collectors Club publishes a quarterly newsletter which is mailed to club members. It offers information, photographs and collector interviews of old and new Case knives. Many Case dealers display posters and coupons encouraging prospective members to send for one of these quarterly newsletters and to join the club.

The club, established in 1981, has more than 4000 members. Each year, Case crafts a special knife exclusively for its club members. In addition, Case also produces at least four limited edition sets annually for knife collecting enthusiasts.

Throughout the company's rich history, Case has been awarded numerous government contracts. During WWII, the company produced various kinds of military knives; the most famous being the V-42 stiletto fighting knife. In 1965, NASA awarded Case a contract to produce the

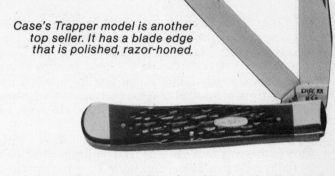

*The Case Folding Hunter is the most popular knife ever manufactured by the company.*

*Case's Trapper model is another top seller. It has a blade edge that is polished, razor-honed.*

famous Astronaut's Knife, which was carried on the Gemini and Apollo manned space flights.

Case demands workmanship and materials that are combined to create knives that make reliable, hard-working field-tested performers. An independent research firm conducted an objective test to determine which knives best suited the needs of professional sportsmen, including the respected Montana Outfitters and Guides Association. Similar lock-blade knives from Case and two leading competitors were tested in the field for an entire hunting season. The Case knife was the overwhelming choice, claims the company. As a result, Case is the official knife of the Montana Outfitters and Guides Association and is the only knife ever endorsed by that organization.

Case uses two types of cutlery steel for its blades: Tru-Sharp, a high-carbon surgical stainless steel, and chrome vanadium steel. Case Tru-Sharp blades hold an edge and resist rust and corrosion. The chrome vanadium blades are known for ease of resharpening.

In addition to using genuine bone and high-impact Delrin for handle materials, Case's more exotic handle materials include genuine stag, mother-of-pearl, natural walnut and other imported exotic hardwoods, ivory and even 28,000-year-old mastodon ivory.

Since 1972, Case has been part of American Brands, Inc., a diversified company serving the cutlery, distilled beverage, food product, office product, hardware, security, golf products, optical goods and services, and personal care markets.

Case manufactures a wide range of cutlery products, including pocketknives, sporting knives, kitchen cutlery, scissors and shears, plus various accessories and sharpening tools.

In answer to a growing consumer demand for quality, competitively priced knives, Case recently introduced the Basics, a line of lower-priced knives designed for rugged everyday use. The Case Basics line includes eight sturdy, lighter-weight knives. In spite of their prices, these knives offer Case quality and attention to detail. All eight Basics feature Tru-Sharp blades. The knives also feature texturized, ergonomically designed handles to fit either the left or the right hand.

*The old-line cutlery manufacturer also manufactures a broad variety of knives favored by housewives.*

COLD STEEL, headquartered in Ventura, California, reflects the philosophy of its president, Lynn Thompson. Examining the knife designs of Cold Steel, it will come as no surprise that Lynn Thompson has been a practitioner of the martial arts for a couple of decades. He works out with knife fighting techniques every day at his company headquarters. It is his avocation as well as his occupation.

Thompson began Cold Steel, Incorporated, in 1980, when two knives that had a reputation for strength and reliability broke in succession while he was practicing martial arts. Thompson won't reveal the maker of these knives, but he was dismayed to learn how brittle and fragile the blade and tips were.

Thompson admits the treatment he gives a knife might be considered abuse by some, but he believes a knife should hold up to the most severe treatment possible. In a real-life situation, that just might be what happens. A failed knife could mean serious injury, or even the loss of a life, in

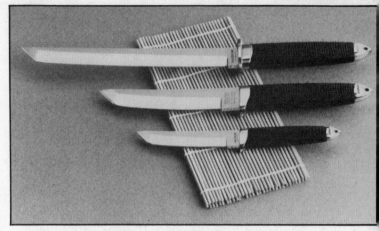

Above, from top: Cold Steel's Magnum Tanto with 8¾-inch blade; Original Tanto with 5¾-inch blade and the Mini Tanto with 4¼-inch blade. All with Kraton handles, they are the first knives to be designed and produced by Lynn Thompson, at left.

already in production, as well as prototypes under consideration, using simulated, but realistic situations. This, he believes, offers plenty of daily contact with the products and immediate identification of any potential problems.

In 1981, Cold Steel introduced its first Tanto design, a blade shape that has won acceptance among knife users around the world. The distinctly angled blade tip now is seen in dozens of knife sizes and shapes from several knife producers. It is disputed by some, but custom knifemaker Bob Lum generally is credited with the modern introduction of the design. Cold Steel's version features a reinforced tip and a rubber-like Kraton handle complete with checkering, which offers firm but soft grip. Cold Steel's Tanto production now has been included in four fixed-blade knives and at least three folders.

Newer folders use laminated San Mai III steel for blades and soft checkered Thermolin on the handles. They are the large, medium and small Shinobu Tantos.

an urban or a wilderness situation.

"Cold Steel was created," says Thompson, "to make only quality production knives that are stronger, tougher and sharper than anything else available."

A knife that will hold up to the roughest testing and tough treatment will not fail in a real emergency situation, Thompson believes. That is why he runs a constant evaluation program for all his production knives.

The daily knife fighting practice Thompson conducts for himself affords him a chance to work with the knives

*Latest model from Cold Steel is made in U.S. with 9½-inch blade of Carbon V steel. Built on the old Bowie pattern, it carries a soft Thermolin handle.*

The Cold Steel Tanto has received rather wide attention and has been featured in books and magazines, televison shows and movies. A popular movie in which one of the characters uses a Cold Steel knife was *Platoon,* but the scene's action was so fast that not many were aware of the knife design.

Until 1983, when Cold Steel moved its knife production to Japan, things were a bit slow for the company. That April, Cold Steel contracted with one of the top knifemakers of Japan, a firm known for its quality workmanship. The knives all are hand-ground and the Tanto points are ground by the owner of the factory himself.

According to Thompson, the owner thus assures himself of his production knives' quality. Thompson will not reveal the name or exact location of the factory, but claims it is as good as it is small.

The blade steel is called San Mai III. The steel for Tantos is actually a three-part lamination of stainless steel spring "skins" wrapped around a hard stainless steel core. The three pieces are hammer-forged together into one piece of blade steel. The laminations are visible upon close inspection of the edge of the large Master Tanto blade. A thin line about three-sixteenths-inch thick runs the length of the blade edge.

Thompson has put considerable effort into promoting his unusual knives. He has demonstrated their strength and sharpness by such stunts as thrusting a Tanto through the door of a car. There was no apparent damage to the blade when it was withdrawn. He is also able to demonstrate the knife's ability to cut through a free-hanging 1¼-inch manila rope with a single stroke. This, says Thompson demonstrates the typical razor edge with which each of his knives leaves the factory.

The Cold Steel line includes the Tanto blade shape in four sizes and three hunting knives — two with upswept and one with a drop-point blade. There are three push knives which have proven popular with some buyers. The blades are as short as an inch-and-a-half and as long as 3¾ inches. Among the latest introduction are three folders featuring the Tanto-style blade made of San Mai III steel. The folding blades range in size from 1¾ to 3½ inches long. Handle slabs for these lock-back folders are an impact-absorbing material called Thermolin, similar in nature to the Kraton used for sheath knives.

The latest models in the line include a series called Trail Mate and a big Bowie Thompson has named Trail Master. The Trail Mates are folders, without the Tanto blade style, but with stainless steel blades and Thermolin soft handle slabs. They are available in three different blade lengths. In 1987, the Trail Mate was named Import Design of the Year by *Blade* magazine.

The Trail Master is a departure from all stainless steel knives common to most factory production. The knife features a 9½-inch blade made of a high-carbon steel alloy called Carbon V. It is specially smelted and hot-rolled into blade stock measuring five-sixteenths-inch for Cold Steel.

Great care, Thompson declares, has been taken in heat-treating and tempering to assure a super-tough stress-free blade. Thompson feels the Trail Master will become one of the company's most popular knives. Another departure from the past is that the Trail Mate is manufactured in the United States, rather than in Japan. Lynn Thompson believes he has the best of both worlds.

*This photographic sequence from Cold Steel shows company president Lynn Thompson slicing through a hanging 1¼-inch manila hemp rope with one of his knives. Thompson claims each of his knives carries a comparable edge.*

# COLEMAN/WESTERN — A NEW COMPANY WITH ROOTS STRETCHING BACK TO THE TURN OF THE CENTURY

*In spite of a company history dating back to the turn of the century, the production facilities for Coleman/Western cutlery are modern in every respect, as are techniques.*

FOR MORE than three-quarters of a century, Western Cutlery turned out quality knives for outdoorsmen before becoming a part of the Coleman Hunting and Shooting Sports Group in 1984. With that absorption, the name was changed to Coleman/Western, but knives still are made in the factory in the Rocky Mountain community of Longmont, Colorado.

The firm originally was established as the Western States Cutlery and Manufacturing Company in Boulder, Colorado, by H.N. Platts, producing a variety of jackknives, sheath styles and even kitchen cutlery and razors, until the opening days of World War II. At that time, the company reorganized its production as part of the war effort and became known for production of the utility sheath knife issued to the Navy's combat construction personnel.

Operations understandably were expanded during the war years and the expansion led to a move to Longmont and the construction of a newer, larger and more modern factory.

From 1911 until 1984, when the company became a part of the Coleman empire, members of the Platts family had been involved on a continuing basis. Harry Platts, great grandson of W.R. Case and Charles Platts, was president of Western Cutlery until 1984. However, the tradition continues with Coleman/Western designers coming up with new, original but nonetheless practical knives for outdoorsmen.

The Colorado outfit continues to produce the line it refers to as the Old Reliables. This includes the model L48, which combines the classic leather washer handle design with a carbon steel saber-ground blade, a solid brass guard and a polished aluminum end knob. Other old-timers of proven popularity are still carried in the line.

But there have been changes and additions, too. In 1985, the line of pocket folders was redesigned. While listed as Old Reliables and familiar in design, new features were added. In all, six knives are included in this line-up.

Coleman/Western also decided it was time to design knives in the field under actual hunting conditions with the help of several leading hunters and guides. The result has been three models known as the Guide Series.

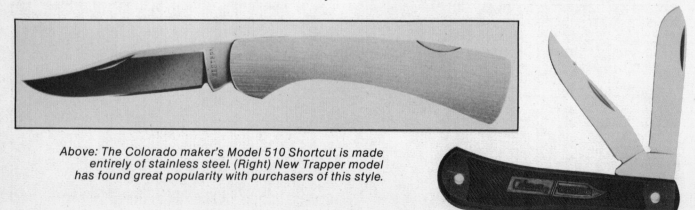

*Above: The Colorado maker's Model 510 Shortcut is made entirely of stainless steel. (Right) New Trapper model has found great popularity with purchasers of this style.*

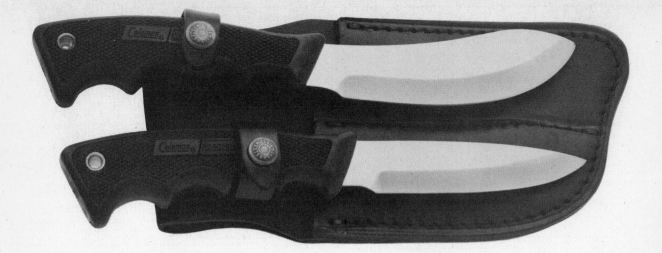

*Coleman/Western's Big Game System offers a deep-bellied skinner and a drop-point style in a double-blade sheath.*

*The Colorado manufacturer is another that has recognized the popularity of lightweight knives and has adopted a line of progressive sizes known as their Mighty Lites.*

The Model C103 Elk Knife was designed by a professional hunting guide, Billy Stockton, to handle the needs of elk and bear hunters, as well as anyone who needs a tough knife for a tough task. It features a thick, heavy-duty 4½-inch blade of 440 stainless steel and a special hip-pocket leather sheath with a medium-grit India stone built in for touch-up sharpening.

The Model C102 Mule Deer Knife was designed by Kirt Darner, a big-game hunter whose Boone & Crockett Club records are recognized in the hunting world.

It was meant to answer the demands of Western mule deer guides who need a knife for a wide variety of purposes, both on the trail and in camp. The features of this double lock-blade include: a clip-point blade with a serrated RoughCut edge for tough cutting tasks and a drop-point, smooth-edge blade for skinning and other precise cutting. The handle is of Fibron wood and the sheath is moulded leather.

For deer hunters and outdoorsmen everywhere, Coleman/Western's Model C101 Whitetail Knife was designed and tested by Leonard Lee Rue III, North America's leading whitetail deer authority, author and photographer. This model features a modified skinning blade of heavy-duty, hollow-ground 440 stainless steel, a Fibron wood handle with a lanyard hole, and a custom leather sheath.

The new 221 Survival System is built around an almost indestructible knife with a 6½-inch epoxy-coated, saber-ground blade of chrome-vanadium steel. Honed to a razor edge, the opposite edge has a saw that will cut through wood or bone.

The end knob can be used as a hammer and the Delrin handle will withstand lots of abuse, engineers claim. The handle is grooved for a better grip and shaped to fit even the largest hand.

The 221 comes with a unique zippered Cordura sheath that has a special hard plastic sleeve for the knife. A front pouch on the sheath contains the rest of the system which

The C102 Mulie model is one of the knives designed for Coleman/Western by a working game guide. One of the blades for this knife is in the RoughCut style now favored.

Coleman/Western's C103 Elk style fixed-blade is another of the knives in the Guide Series designed by a guide.

includes a Silva compass, fishing hooks, line, sinkers, metallic signal mirror, waterproof matchbox and needles and thread.

Overall length of the 221 Survival System is 11¼ inches and it only weighs 15 ounces.

Coleman/Western's RD1214 Big Game System offers hunters two knives — a deep-bellied skinning knife and a drop-point blade — in one sheath.

Both knives feature checkered black Kraton handles with a finger-mould design for comfort and safety. These rubber-like handles offer a sure grip, even when conditions get messy. They are perfect for field dressing, cleaning and skinning, as well as a host of camp chores.

The R12, which weighs five ounces, has a 4¼-inch stainless steel blade in drop-point design. Overall length is 9¼ inches. It is similar to Western's R16 companion knife, which is offered separately, except with a shorter blade. The R14 skinner's blade is 4⅝ inches long. The knife weighs 5½ ounces and has an overall length of 9¾ inches.

Both knives feature full tang construction of 440 stainless steel with a satin finish and handles include a lanyard hole. The double sheath is top-grain black leather with individual compartments for each blade, including separate leather handle straps that fasten securely with heavy-duty snaps.

Some of the most popular knives in the Western line are the Model W75 and W77 boot knives due to their one-piece, full-tang design and patented sheath.

In 1985, Western has added a third boot knife to the line — the Model 777 blackened boot knife.

This knife features the same one-piece blade and guard construction as the others, but the stainless steel tang and blade have been blackened and coated with a blued finish that won't rub or work off. The blade is 4½ inches and overall length is 8¾ inches.

The handle is made of Delrin and checkered for better grip and looks. Also standard is a patented embossed leather sheath that's thin for comfort, but fitted with a super strong spring clip to keep the sheath secured to your boot or belt when drawing the knife.

The W75 has a 3½-inch blade and overall length of seven inches. The W77 is a little longer with a blade length of 4½ inches and overall length of 8¾ inches. Both have hardwood handles impregnated with resin.

Like other major cutlers, Coleman/Western has recognized the trend toward lightweight knives and has added what they call the Mighty Lites. They feature Delrin handles with scallops and a rocker shape to fit the hand. Checkering adds more grip and two of the knives come with black Cordura belt sheaths.

The smallest of the Mighty Lites is the Model 516 which has a clip blade of 440-A stainless steel that's 2⅛ inches

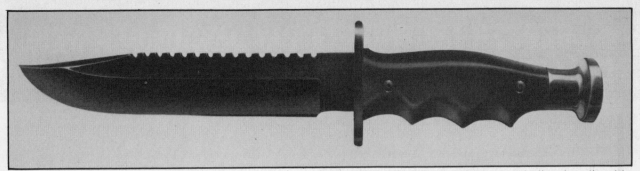

*Model 221 Survival System features a hollow handle with a compass, signal mirror, needles, thread, fishing gear.*

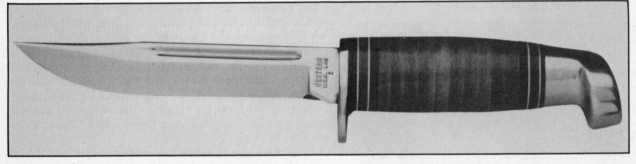

*The L48 sheath knife is one of the Old Reliables that is still carried after many years. It has been updated to a degree, with slight changes in the materials utilized.*

long. The mid-size Mighty Lite is the Model 526 which has a 2¼-inch stainless steel blade suitable for campers, backpackers and other sportsmen conscious about size and weight. This knife comes with a Cordura sheath.

The largest of these lightweights, the Model 546, weighs only 3½ ounces and this includes a three-inch stainless clip blade. This slim knife measures only five inches long closed and comes with a black Cordura sheath.

Western markets a number of fillet knives, but the Model 561 not only is a folding lock-blade, but also is one of the lightweight offerings. It can be tucked conveniently into a tackle box, a daypack or strapped on a belt in its Cordura sheath. Its 5⅜-inch stainless steel blade is strong, but flexible for filleting. The knife's handle is of reinforced Valox checkered for a sure grip. Its sculptured design is meant to give it a nonslip fit. Measuring just under seven inches

when closed and 12⅜ inches when locked open, the Model 561 weighs 4½ ounces.

Coleman/Western also has entered the age of promotion with a vengeance. Every knife now carries a hundred-year warranty and there is a new concept called "hands-on packaging."

"The sure-grip handle is one of the greatest selling points for our new high-tech fillet knives," said Mike Williams, the company's marketing manager, "so we have designed a hangable pack that invites the customer to put his hand around it and feel it for himself."

The fillet knife hangable packaging is part of an overall packaging improvement program, according to Williams. Several of Coleman/Western's most popular models will be available in hangable packaging.

*The Model C101, another in the Guide Series, was tested after designing by Leonard Lee Rue III, one of nation's leading authorities on habits of native American deer.*

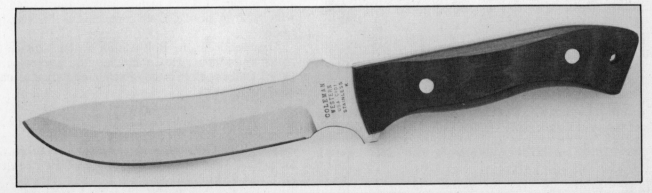

# GERBER LEGENDARY BLADES, UNDER NEW MANAGEMENT, CONTINUES ITS INNOVATIVE WAYS

THERE ARE new faces at Gerber Legendary Blades and some old faces with new responsibilities. The company now is owned by Fiskars Manfacturing Corporation of Wausau, Wisconsin, but the long-time board chairman, Pete Gerber, still lurks in the background, acting as consultant and knife designer.

All facets of knifemaking are accomplished in Gerber's modern plant in Oregon. Many employees have been on the staff for several decades, offering their experience.

"Always before, I was in a panic situation, running the company," Gerber puts it, "making certain we met deliveries. Now I have time to handle the parts that always were dear to my heart, but overrun by other demands."

Fiskars was founded in 1977 and is best known for its quality scissors. The Wisconsin-based corporation is a wholly owned subsidiary of Fiskars OY AB of Finland, which was established in 1649.

Gerber Legendary Blades was established in 1939 by Joseph R. Gerber, Sr., a Portland, Oregon, advertising executive who made knives as gifts for some of his customers. Abercrombie and Fitch asked Gerber to make some for their New York store. This eventually led to a small manufacturing business being established in Portland.

Over the years, Gerber Legendary Blades has grown into a major American cutlery manufacturer. Today, their knives are sold in stores throughout the nation and in more than thirty foreign countries.

Like any manufacturer, Gerber is constantly searching out new knife designs. Some are made, some are discarded. If a knife that was thought to be promising doesn't arouse the interest of the public, it is quietly phased out.

An example of a lasting product is Gerber's Bolt-Action Hunter model, which was introduced in 1984 and still is in the line. The idea for this particular style originated with Steve Timm, an Oregon businessman who also spends a batch of time in the outdoors.

"Steve wanted a folding knife that could do the whole job," James R. Raske, Gerber's president, recalls, "gutting, skinning and all-around camp knife."

The first step was to call in renowned knife designer Blackie Collins. Working with Timm, the shape of the blade was finalized.

The glass-filled reinforced DuPont Zytel handle features the patented Bolt-Action mechanism developed by Collins. The blade features Gerber's exclusive full concave grind for edge holding and ease of resharpening. The blade pivots on nylon bearings for extremely smooth operation.

"In addition to making this knife hell for stout," says Pete Gerber, "I used a high-tech blade finish to go along with the Zytel handle. Each complements the other beautifully."

The sheath for the Bolt-Action hunter is made from ballistic cloth bonded to Cambrelle with a layer of foam between. Ballistic cloth is the same material used in making bullet-proof vests.

Thus, the Bolt-Action Hunter became the third in a series that includes the Bolt-Action Utility and the Bolt-Action Fisherman.

Since then, Gerber has added two more configurations to the Bolt-Action line. Their Bolt-Action Rescue knife is

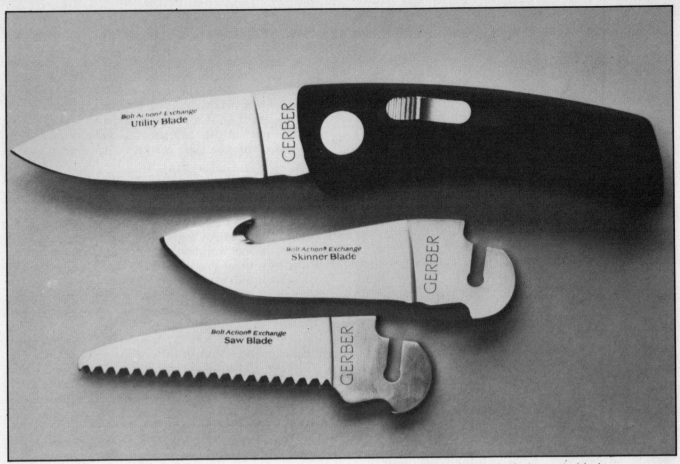

*Gerber's interchangeable blade folder with a Bolt-Action locking system. Blade shapes include a saw blade, a skinning blade with gut hook and a drop point which is termed a utility blade. Knife has a handle of Zytel.*

specifically designed for quickly cutting through seat belt material in emergency situations.

Specially designed blade serrations have proven in testing to be extremely effective for cutting tough nylon webbing and rope. The blade-tip is rounded to protect an entrapped person during extraction.

Again, the one-piece handle is moulded from Zytel. The handle shape and checkering provide a comfortable slip-proof grip. The International orange handle results in this knife being extremely visible to avoid loss.

The Bolt-Action Skinner sports a 3¼-inch blade designed for skinning and field dressing medium to large game. This blade has the belly and the dropped point of the famous old Green River skinners that the old guides and professional hunters preferred over any other type of knife. This blade also features a new, unique gut hook. The gut hook allows

*Another knife model in Bolt-Action series is the Rescue. Serrated edge cuts easily through nylon.*

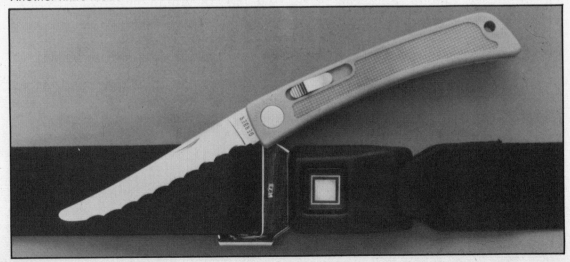

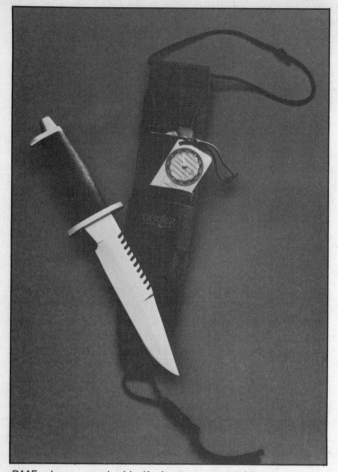

the hunter to quickly split the hide from the carcass.

Over the past decade or so, Gerber has pretty much had a lock on the market for so-called survival knives. In 1984, the Oregon company absorbed Benchmark Knives and, with it, the services of the earlier-mentioned Blackie Collins. Before concentrating almost exclusively on design work, Collins was a widely respected custom knifemaker.

When the TAC series was introduced in 1985, Pete Gerber called this "the next generation of survival knives." The series still is an important part of the Gerber product line.

The TAC is available in five- or six-inch double-edged blade lengths with serrations. A moulded Zytel sheath secures the blade with a unique interlocking mechanism.

The full-tang blade extends through the length of the handle. This provides not only an incredibly strong knife, but also includes a lanyard attachment and allows for pounding with the butt of the handle.

The knife and sheath system attach in numerous ways to a variety of equipment. It can be carried in virtually any position or can be adapted for use with military-type fasteners.

The Gerber basic multi-functional survival system (BMF) is the latest generation of survival/fighting knives.

The BMF is a tough, heavy-duty survival knife designed to withstand heavy use under extreme conditions. It is 13¼ inches long overall with an eight-inch full-tang, high-carbon stainless steel blade. The Rockwell hardness of the BMF blade is RC 54-55. The back of the blade features an effective chisel tooth saw designed for aggressive cutting of wood and other materials. The blade has a non-reflective

BMF, above, survival knife features an eight-inch blade and heavy-duty butt cap built to withstand abuse, nylon sheath for emergency gear.

Below: Gerber's Parabellum is a larger folder with survival possibilities. Bolt-Action blade locking system is tough enough for the most rugged work. Pouch has room for compass.

finish, as do the stainless steel guards and butt cap. The butt cap is designed to endure heavy pounding.

The Gerber BMF handle is of highly compressed, black DuPont Hypalon. This is a closed cell polymer that will not absorb moisture and is impervious to extreme weather conditions. Hypalon's semi-soft composition cushions and protects the hand from abrasion and impact during heavy usage, Gerber designers contend.

Made from black Cordura, the ambidextrous sheath was designed around the BMF. Alpha cellulose fiber material stiffens the sheath and provides protection for both the blade and user. A rubber welt protects the sheath's interior stitching.

For military applications, the sheath has been engineered to be silent, with no hard surfaces or metallic parts that could generate noise. A pocket on the top of the sheath holds a liquid-filled jeweled orienteering compass, which is included. Attached to the back of the sheath is a diamond sharpening hone protected by a nylon cover. An accessory strap on the front of the sheath allows a folding knife, survival kit, or other equipment to be attached. A removable clip assembly allows the BMF to be attached to standard issue military battle dress and harnesses. Black nylon tie-down cords at the top and bottom of the sheath allows the BMF to be tied to the leg or lashed to other equipment. The Gerber BMF weighs in at only fifteen ounces. Overall weight with sheath is 28.5 ounces.

Gerber also has discovered the public's interest in light-weight knives. The first entry in this category was their Ultralight LST. At 0.6 ounce, the Ultralight LST is the "lightest, smoothest and toughest knife of its size on the

Moulded Zytel sheath for TAC survival knife, above, is designed to be carried in any one of several positions. Full steel tang features lanyard hole.

Two-blade versions of Gerber Bolt-Action Hunter, below, with glass-filled Zytel handles. Locking system was developed by designer Blackie Collins.

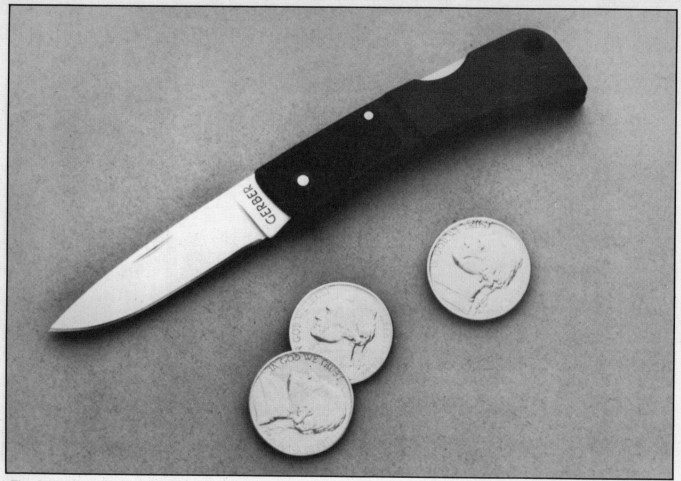

The Gerber Ultralight LST folder has proven popular with the buying public. The drop-point stainless steel blade measures but two inches and is housed in a moulded, Zytel handle. A practical pocketknife!

market." Its two-inch high-carbon, surgical stainless steel drop-point blade pivots on permanently lubricated integral bearings and features Gerber's patented full concave grind for a keener, longer-lasting edge. The Ultralight LST's contoured one-piece handle is moulded from black, blue or red Zytel.

The latest in the Bolt-Action series allows one to change blades. To quickly change blades, pull back on the locking bolt with the thumb release and move the blade to the half-open position. Then, while holding the bolt back, push the blade toward the butt of the handle and remove. The new blade is installed by reversing the procedure while holding back on the thumb release.

The handle is made form DuPont Zytel and its sheath is black ballistic cloth and has a pouch for two extra blades plus the knife.

In 1987, Gerber's Parabellum folding knife captured *Blade* magazine's "American Built Knife-Of-The-Year" honors. The Parabellum knife is part of a revolutionary system that includes its sheath.

The Parabellum is a massive folder that combines strength and light weight due to its high-tech handle design and materials. The blade is ground from high-carbon stainless steel with a finished thickness of .175 inch and a length of

4¼ inches. The Bolt-Action locking mechanism is the strongest locking system available for folding knives. The harder you push against the hardened steel bolt, the tighter it locks.

The handle of the Parabellum is designed with user comfort the major consideration. Its double-guard design offers tremendous safety over conventional designs. The handle is constructed of fiberglass-filled Zytel nylon for strength combined with light weight. The handle material has a special additive that provides permanent lubricaton for the built-in internal bushings that the blade pivots on, resulting in smooth movement of the blade as it opens and closes.

This sheath actually allows you to carry your knife as a fixed-blade knife or as a more compact folded knife. When carried as a fixed-blade knife, the pouch is empty to carry whatever survival items the user desires. With the knife carried as a folding knife, the sheath built behind the pouch accepts a sharpening steel or stone of your choice. On the rear of the sheath is the new Bianchi military web-belt attachment device adopted by U.S. and NATO forces. The unique device allows you to carry your sheath on a conventional belt or military web belt and features instant detachment of the sheath without removal of either style belt.

# KA-BAR: A LEGENDARY NAME NEARS ITS CENTENNIAL

*Probably the best known of the Ka-Bar designs is the Marine Corps combat knife issued during World War II. It still is being produced and is popular with armed services throughout the world.*

THE KA-BAR NAME was adopted by the then-Union Cutlery Company early in its history, when a letter was received from a fur trapper. He wrote that his knife had saved his life when he used it to finish off a bear he had wounded. His gun had jammed after shooting and the bear was about to finish off the trapper. The man scribbled a bit and when he wrote that he had "kill-a-bar," it looked like "KA-BAR." One thing lead to another and

soon the company adopted that trademark and finally, in 1951, Union Cutlery became Ka-Bar.

Today, the fame of the name, Ka-Bar, stems from more recent history: World War II. The Ka-Bar knife was the standard fighting knife issued to the Marines of the Big One. Since then, the term has become almost synonymous with a military fighting knife. It continues as the most popular style that Ka-Bar produces.

*Ka-Bar engineers and designers have recognized popularity of lock-back style knives. This one is called the Ka-Lok.*

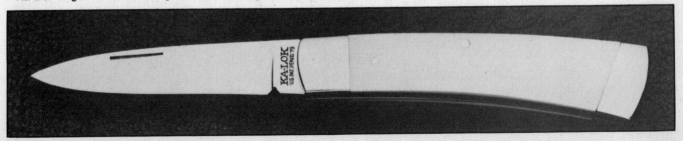

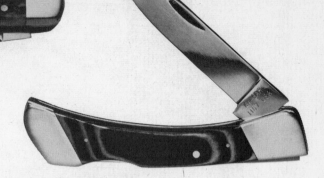

For collectors, Ka-Bar has re-created knives made by early predecessors. The one above, is from the Union Razor Co. The model 1187 lock-back knife with micarta scales, right, has been discontinued and now is being sought by collectors.

In 1941, Ka-Bar was one of the companies that submitted a fighting-utility knife design for consideration by the United States Marine Corps. It was accepted as the standard issue and soon was recognized as a prize possession by every Marine. The Ka-Bar had several mundane uses too — including pounding tent stakes, driving nails, opening ration cans and digging holes — but it was the fighting knife by which all others were measured.

Demand for the knife was such that more than one manufacturer produced the wartime Ka-Bar, much as the .45 pistol was produced by more than Colt Firearms during the war. Some of the original Ka-Bars, made in Olean, New York, had the name struck into the tang; later issues were stamped *Ka-Bar* on the finger guard. Today's production is stamped *KA-BAR* on the ricasso portion of the blade and *USMC* on the opposite side.

When the war was ended, Ka-Bar stopped production on the knife, but a similar style, produced by other cutlery companies, was reactivated by the Marines and saw service in Korea and Vietnam.

Thirty-two years were to pass before Ka-Bar resumed production of its famous knife. In 1978, some of the workers at the Olean, New York, factory, who had worked on the original knife, began production again. All World War II specifications were followed closely. Ka-Bar was able to do this because of the discovery of a set of original blueprints in an old filing cabinet at the factory. The box in which the new Ka-Bar is delivered is printed with a replica of these drawings. The finish and polishing job on the new is said to be better than in those war-rushed days.

The Ka-Bar USMC Fighting Knife is currently the company's best seller, growing in popularity. Knives are being shipped and sold all over the world, including Europe, Asia and the Far East, to collectors and sportsmen. Several direct mail catalogs also feature the Ka-Bar.

Second best selling product for the company is what is known affectionately as the Hobo. Back in the Twenties, Union Cutlery had a patent on a take-apart eating kit which was one of the most popular in the line at the time. Ka-Bar recently reintroduced the same design in stainless steel to almost instant popularity. The Hobo is definitely a specialty or survival knife design, carried in a small nylon belt pouch. It is actually a lock-back folding blade and snap-off fork and spoon when opened.

All the knives in the Ka-Bar line number more than a hundred, including several Swiss Army-like folders, five-inch lock-blades, multi-bladed jackknives, pocketknives, the Ka-Lock hidden lock folder, boot knives, big sheath knives and sharpening stones. But the main production of Ka-Bar is Ka-Bars. Perhaps that is as it should be.

Seeking to expand their market, Ka-Bar has introduced the Hobo, a compact four-inch unit that becomes a complete dining set when assembled, but folds to single unit.

# PETER KERSHAW'S PHILOSOPHY IS SIMPLE: MAKE THE BEST KNIFE YOU CAN, THEN SELL IT TO THOSE WHO WANT THE BEST!

In less than two decades, Kershaw knives had gone from a warehouse in a rented basement to this modern structure. (Right) Pete Kershaw has sold company to Japanese firm, but still has management contract.

A NATIVE Oregonian, whose ancestors date back to the 1840s in the state, Pete Kershaw was a farm boy who knew the value of a good knife. He grew up in a family of orchardists near Medford, but forsook fruit-picking for Lewis and Clark College and a degree in marketing.

He was a marketing rep for Gerber Legendary Cutlery a dozen years ago, when he decided it was to try the knife business on his own.

"What I had in mind," he recalls, "was to make and sell the Nikon of pocketknives." With his wife of more than twenty-five years, Judy, he began with, as he puts it, "Zip. Nothing." But he did have a line of half a dozen excellent pocketknives he'd had manufactured in Japan

Much of his success, he admits, is based upon a long and intense relationship with Japan's Kai Cutlery. They made the knives — and he did the selling. Today, Kershaw Knives is owned by the Japanese firm and Kershaw oversees operations under contract.

"We had done well," Kershaw explains, "but we knew it was time for expansion. Borrowing the capital we needed would have meant mortgaging most of what Judy and I owned." Instead, Kai bought the company and installed Pete Kershaw as president.

"It's been an ideal marriage between an American firm and a Japanese company," Kershaw insists. He runs the company pretty much to suit himself, observers believe, and sends the parent company in Tokyo a financial statement once a month.

In the beginning, there were only the two of them: Pete and Judy. In those early days, the market was limited, because their travel was limited. It was Judy who was in charge of ferrying the inventory back and forth between their home and a rented basement warehouse. Today, Kershaw holds forth in a new, modernistic brick and concrete structure in Wilsonville, some twenty-five miles

south of Portland, Oregon — and knife buyers seem to beat a path to the new doorway.

"I'm no designer," Pete Kershaw is the first to admit, "but I'm not all that bad when it comes to sketching with a felt-tip marker on a cocktail napkin." Some of his initial designs were created in just this way before he took them to a professional designer. The engineering drawings under his arm, he headed for Japan.

Kershaw is quick to admit that everything seemed to fall into place. One of the first Japanese he met was a gentleman named Huo. "He's still our man in Japan," Kershaw says. It was this Japanese gentleman who introduced the Oregonian to a network of Japanese cutlery manufacturers who had been trying for a number of years to break into the international markets.

Kershaw's philosophy was based upon the idea of producing a top quality knife that would sell at an honest price. The Japanese apparently believed in this philosophy, too, for they set aside some other projects and immediately went about turning out Pete Kershaw's first order.

"They told me later they felt they had to work fast, because they were afraid I might starve to death, if they didn't," the blade merchant recalls, with a grin. Thus, the first shipment of Kershaw knives went out in November 1974.

Pete Kershaw is somewhat reluctant to accept the cloak of what might be termed marketing genius. "I really didn't do anything. I got the right people and got them cooking on it. Lucky, I'd say."

But in the beginning, it was an adventure, too. Pete and Judy Kershaw had a Volkswagen van that served literally

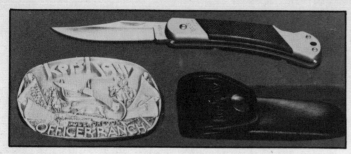

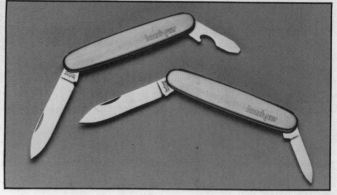

*Kershaw has entered the specialty cutlery market with a series of gift packages such as knife/buckle combo. (Right) The Oregon firm also is marketing a pocket style that comes under the heading of a "gentleman's knife."*

as a mobile warehouse. They used it to transport knives from their home to the basement warehouse that had become an office. He sold knives and she kept the books. Then Kershaw started touring the trade show circuit where sporting goods are displayed and sold. "I knew the knives would sell," he says now, "but I didn't know how fast. The initial problem was to stay ahead of starvation."

At the first trade shows, Kershaw found he had sold orders to Abercrombie and Fitch, a leading sporting goods retailer, but word of mouth was serving him well, too. He sold knives to other exhibitors and to outdoor writers, who would mention them in print. At the end of the first day at the trade show, Kershaw came back to the hotel to find his wife sitting on a bed, surrounded by money. It wasn't long before the Kershaw blades were selling around the world.

They added more salesmen, but it still was a small-scale operation at this point. Kershaw and his wife often worked far into the night, packing boxes, inspecting product and gluing on labels. When they decided they needed display cases, Pete Kershaw built the first of them himself.

"It didn't take long for me to discover I wasn't a cabinet-maker," Kershaw admits. He found a retired carpenter who had become bored with inactivity and put him to work on a part-time basis. It wasn't long before the craftsman was working full-time. When the elderly carpenter died, his grandsons took over the cabinetmaking facet.

Kershaw realized, too, that he had a psychological problem. He needed someone to collect the bills. He was wearing that hat, too, at that point, but came to realize "you can't badger people about their account and sell them something at the same time.

"We couldn't afford another person on the payroll, so I made our dog, Huey, the bill collector. Collection letters went out with his name at the bottom." That, of course, has changed in the interim, but Kershaw maintains his business philosophy has been right.

"The first mistake a lot of people seem to make," he contends, "is that they open a big, fancy place with too many employees. The secret of success, if there really is one, is hard work and wearing a lot of hats." As a result of this type of thinking, more than eleven years passed before Kershaw Cutlery moved into the big, modern facility in Wilsonville from which the business now is operated.

Further evidence that the Kershaw philosophy has been successful lies in the fact that there now are more than a hundred items in the four-color catalog Kershaw Knives furnishes to potential customers. During the Christmas season, the company ships as many as 50,000 knives a day!

There are folding knives, there are fixed-blade knives; there are combat knives and there are kitchen carving utensils, although Kershaw views the last as simply an adjunct

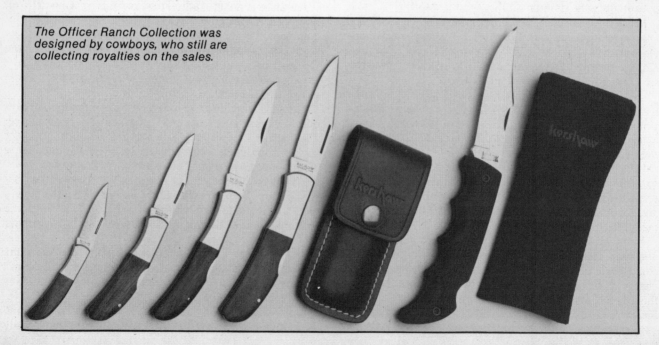

*The Officer Ranch Collection was designed by cowboys, who still are collecting royalties on the sales.*

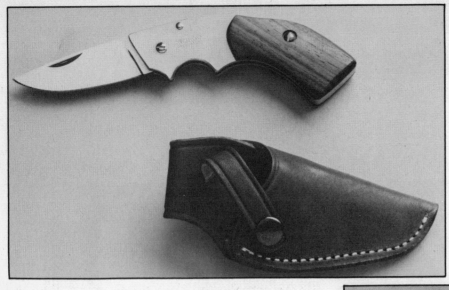

The Kershaw Pistol Knife resembles a small derringer and comes with its own miniature leather holster.

to his line. As a veteran outdoorsman, he feels his market is with his brethren in those pursuits.

In addition to the knives coming from Japan, he currently imports cutlery from Germany. This includes a Damascus steel knife that retails for more than $500. Too, there is a survival knife, although he insists the bloom is off the rose in this particular field. "Today, there are more manufacturers turning out survival knives than there are survivalists," he feels. His survival model, however, has a hollow handle that contains everything he feels one would need to survive in most situations. There's even a quarter in the handle for a phone call!

The Damascus steel blades being forged in Solingen, West Germany, are folded and forged eighty-two times to attain the wavy grain of steel. Each knife is outfitted with a Sambar stag handle and, according to Kershaw, only twenty are being produced a month. That production is sold well in advance, incidentally, mostly to knife collectors.

The manner in which Kershaw does business perhaps is best reflected in his relationship with the Officer family of eastern Oregon. They operate the Officer Ranch and, for some two decades, Kershaw has been hunting, riding and ranch-handing with members of this family. The ranch also has been a tough testing ground for Kershaw knives.

"On a cattle ranch, no tool is required for as many jobs as a knife," Kershaw reports. "If you want to make a good tool, talk to the people who use it."

In an after-work bull session with members of the Officer family and their cowhands, they discussed an ideal knife for ranch work. As the talk became increasingly serious, the cowboys started drawing the outlines of blades they would favor, using a stick to mark the shapes in the dirt.

From this session came one of Kershaw Knives' best-selling series, the Officer Ranch Collection. The Big Joe is a scabbard-carried knife that is named after the oldest member of the Officer family. The Li'l Cody is named for the youngest member; it's what Kershaw refers to as "a goin' to town" knife that can be carried in the pocket for small chores. Others in the line include the Whiskey Gap

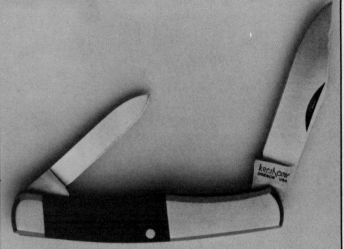

The 45 Ranch model from Kershaw Knives is another of the designs drawn from preferences of working ranch hands. This folder combines needs learned in field.

and Wild Turkey models; these are named for geographic areas on the ranch and feature handles of sandalwood, heavy brass liners and locking clip-style blades. The Black Horse is a rugged knife yet extremely lightweight, with a handle of Space Age plastic impervious to acid, gasoline and changes in extreme temperature. For their efforts, the hands at the Officer Ranch collect royalties on their designs.

During his years of marketing, Kershaw has discovered that customers prefer that their cutting tools have identifying names. Thus, the line-up carries such names as Dude, Good Buddy, Big Foot, Stag and Rustler.

The Amphibian is a knife for skindivers, while the Special Agent and Trooper are compact survival-type knives that some police officers use as back-up instruments.

Kershaw admits that his wife, Judy, objected to some degree when he added such names as Macho, Honcho and Little Stud to the line — until "I reminded her that these knives had helped put the fur coat on her back."

*The 3000 DWO was named for Delley Wade Officer, victim of a hunting accident. (Right) One of Kershaw's newest specialties is a knife resembling a 12-gauge shotshell. (Below) The 1034TF sheath knife has a five-inch drop point blade; grip is made of Task Force rubber polymer.*

In 1984, Kershaw became involved in commemorating the fiftieth anniversary of the Federal Duck Stamp Program by producing a knife marking the occasion. The knives all had a reproduction of that year's duck stamp etched into the handle. Kershaw personally presented a pair of the knives to President Ronald Reagan in a White House ceremony.

Since then, Kershaw has added to his collector series. In addition to the German-made Damascus knife, there is a series of three — matching in design, but varying in size — that features blades of jasper, a semi-precious gemstone found mostly in the Northwest, and a series of stilettos with carved ivory handles. Each of the handles depicts the head of a native American wildlife creature: the grizzly bear,

falcon or eagle. All of the collector knives are marketed in custom-built walnut presentation cases.

There are others, too. There is a line of jewelry knives that includes belt buckles and money clips, with knives skillfully concealed in the design. There are novelty items such as the knives that resemble 12-gauge shotshells and one called the Pistol Knife that looks like a small derringer, the blade folding into what would appear to be the gun barrel. And new items are constantly being considered.

Yet, Kershaw admits that he tends to steer clear of what he calls the "fashion fads that might be popular one year, dead the next. I like longevity. And this industry is just that.

If you have a good product in 1977, it's still a good product in 1987. Making a good knife that the public wants is what it's all about.

*Packaging is now an important facet of the business. This 150 folding field model is packaged with a pouch, as well as a sharpening steel and sheath for the latter.*

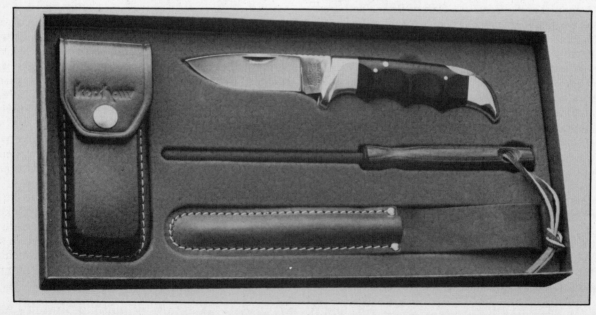

*Original Precise Deerslayer, right, has large stainless steel blade and double-cut saw. Boslters are solid brass and handle is rounded hardwood. Other Field Grade versions, below, all have stainless steel blades and pakkawood handles. They measure from 2⅞ inches to 4¾ inches when closed.*

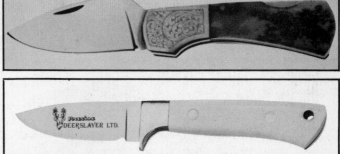

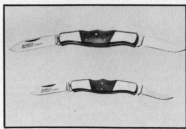

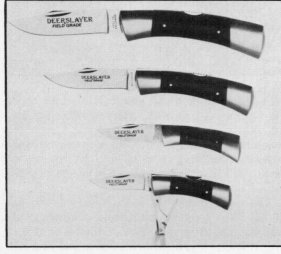

*Golden Classics, top, have bone handles while Deerslayer Lite features full tang and micarta handle, above. Both blades of Tandem 2 & 2 folders, left, have safety locks and polished bone handle slabs.*

PRECISE INTERNATIONAL may not be a household name known to the knife-buying public, as with some other knife companies, but Precise is a producer and importer of a considerable line of knives and associated outdoor gear. As noted in Chapter 6, Precise is the American importer of one of the two official Swiss Army knives. The Precise import is made by the Swiss firm of Wenger. These models comprise a large and important part of Precise International's business.

The company was founded in 1954 by a young man named Rudy Graf. Graf was an Air Force officer who had been stationed in Europe in the latter part of World War II and for a time thereafter. He was enough of a businessman to realize the potential for knife imports through some of the European contacts he had made after the war. His original knives were from Solingen, Germany, still the source of much German-made cutlery.

Sporting cutlery was and is the backbone of Precise's business and, as time went on, the company began to find other sources throughout Japan and the Orient for such things as compasses, outdoor cook stoves, pedometers and other gear. Portable lanterns and outdoor cookwear have been added to the import line in recent years.

In 1969, Precise was acquired by Esquire, Inc., owners of *Esquire Magazine* and about a dozen other properties

at the time. The new owners entered into an agreement with Wenger of Switzerland to become the exclusive U.S. distributor of the original Swiss Army Knife. That agreement is still in effect, two decades later.

During the 1970s, Precise developed the Deerslayer line, which continues as one of the primary products of the company. During that same time, the Wenger Swiss Army Knife sales grew more than a hundred-fold as popularity of the multi-blade folder continued to expand.

Many Vietnam veterans will recall picking up a Swiss Army Knife at the last PX before landing in Southeast Asia, carrying the knife throughout their combat tours. It served many of us well.

Due to several surges in the walking and running fitness booms in the U.S., the demand for the Precise pedometer grew to the extent that the company had to open a second manufacturing facility in the United States to satisfy customers.

In 1983, Esquire sold Precise to the Swiss American Investment Company, (Savest). Savest draws its financial strength from the Swiss aluminum industry. Ownership of Precise is commonly shared with the second largest aluminum company in Switzerland.

Precise management understands the need for cosmetic appeal to attract customers in the competitive knife market. All their knife models have a distinct look. They use a lot of bone handles, highly polished, in the Deerslayer line of hunting knives. The object is to have each knife slightly different from every other knife in the line, because bone is a natural substance and changes from piece to piece. Bone is also quite durable out in the elements.

The Precise motto is, "We make knives for users and price them for buyers." They seem to be living up to the motto.

# GROWTH – COUPLED WITH HEART AND EXPERTISE – IS THE FOUNDATION OF SCHRADE'S SUCCESS

A half-million square feet of manufacturing space is the new home of Imperial Schrade Corporation just north of Ellenville, New York. The new facility was occupied in 1987, employing more than five hundred knife workers.

Many of the Schrade craftsmen are members of third and fourth-generation cutlers, intent upon quality designs.

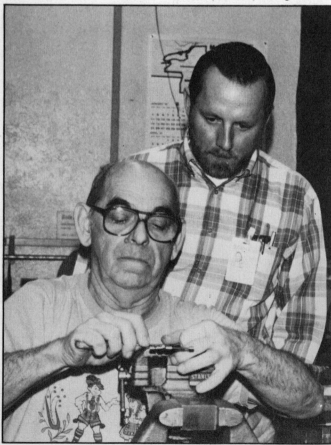

THE YEAR, 1987, marked two milestones in the history of Schrade Cutlery, or what has come to be known as the Imperial Schrade Corporation. The machinery, the five hundred-plus employees and the rest of what comprises lock, stock and barrel moved into a new facility of half a million square feet just north of Ellenville, New York.

The other milestone, a sad one, was the passing of Henry Baer, longtime president, chairman of the board and figurehead for the organization. The line of Uncle Henry knives was built on his image and no doubt will go on with the company as a commemorative institution.

The new plant is located on a ninety-three-acre tract, making it the world's largest cutlery manufacturing facility. It, no doubt, is needed to turn out the sixty or so models of Schrade knives, not to mention the Imperial output, plus various accessories that carry the Schrade trademark.

With the passing of Uncle Henry Baer, his brother Albert M. Baer, has become chairman and chief executive officer, while David A. Swinden is the current president.

For those of us who feel that advancement should come from within a company and that presidents should not be brought in from the soap, washing machine and automotive industries to make knives and guns, the case of Dave Swinden represents something of a Horatio Alger tale.

The new president is a third-generation cutler, who followed in the footsteps of his father and grandfather. Swinden began working for Schrade in the summer of 1948, while still in high school. Upon graduation, he joined the company on a full-time basis, learning the cutlery business from the ground up, working in virtually every department.

The year before his death, Henry Baer took a trip through nostalgia, looking back. "As you advance in years," he said, "nostalgia plays a big part in your thinking and fortunately, at 87, I have been blessed with great memories associated in a most interesting industry: cutlery.

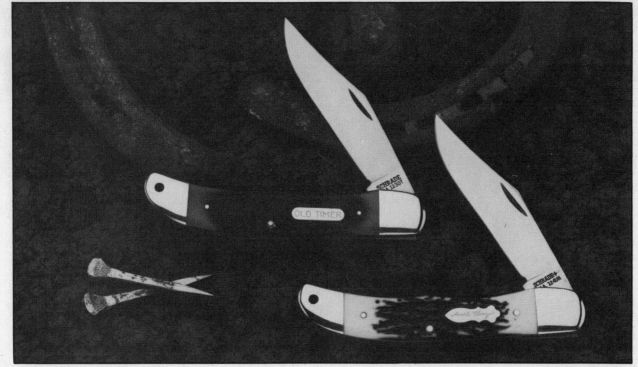

The Old Timer 1230T Pioneer and 124UH Uncle Henry Tradesman folding knives, popular Schrade pocketknives, each feature 3¼-inch clip blades, slim design.

Quality control means frequent spot checks of products against shop specification sheets, below. Schrade brothers began making high quality knives in 1904.

"In the early days, Ellenville and its area were known as the cutlery center of America and, of the many factories that once occupied this area, only Schrade remains. We attribute much of this longevity to upholding a quality that was started in 1904 by the Schrade brothers.

"The industry has seen many changes, but basically, our experience has shown that, with few exceptions, the same patterns and blading that our grandfathers bought continue to be the best sellers. Of course, some Space Age materials have helped maintain the quality and interest of consumers. Our present plan is to continue to keep in step with new developments and to maintain the high quality of product that we believe is today the finest line of pocketknives made in the world."

The philosophy advanced by the late Henry Baer is still in place and is reflected in the continuing policies.

In addition to pocketknives in all shapes and sizes, Schrade produces a line of well respected fixed blades. During the survival knife craze of the early part of this decade, they produced such a knife called the M-7S — only it wasn't exactly a new knife.

Going back to 1943, Imperial — and several other companies — began producing the M-3 trench knife for World War II troops. In time, this same design was altered a bit to become the bayonet for the .30 caliber M-1 carbine. These still are available at this writing.

The Schrade line today actually is several lines. Carrying the Old-Timer designation are seventeen folders and four sheath knives. Under the Uncle Henry banner, the company is marketing fourteen folders, a hunting-type sheath knife called the Golden Spike and several fillet knives for fishermen. Most of the knives in the various lines have handles of heavy-duty plastic called Staglon or of exotic woods. A pair called the Nighthawk and Firebird are small with lightweight handles and one called the Captain, which incorporates clippers and a nail file has scales of what the company calls DuraLens.

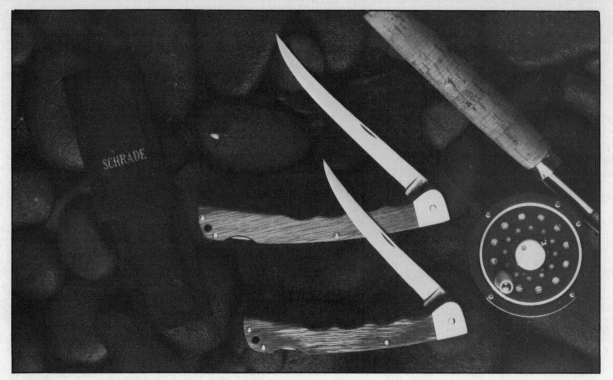

*Two Schrade folding fillet knives feature resin-impregnated American oak handles with finger grooves. Base of the blades is serrated for easier cutting of monofilament or lead core line. A nylon sheath is included with each of the knives. Blade lengths are 4½ inches on lower model, 5½ inches on upper knife.*

The Schrade scrimshaw line has become popular, too. These are models that largely are popular in the line-up, but ivory Micarta handles have been substituted and these have neatly cut scrimshaw patterns that feature a host of animal and outdoor scenes.

Schrade, recognizing the value of the collector, also has begun making a series of limited editions. For example, there was the Silver Anniversary Old-Timer. It was intro-

duced in 1959 by Henry and Albert Baer, who said they wanted to "offer a knife like granddad had, so the name, Old-Timer, was developed. We reached back into the files to find a pattern with the greatest utility. One that was comfortable to hold and that would be practical for whittling and carving, yet husky enough to stand the rough treatment by the home handyman."

To celebrate the 1984 silver anniversary of this model, Schrade turned out 5000 that were suitably marked. They featured sterling silver bolsters and a sterling embossed shield. The handle was of genuine antique bone and each knife carries a serial number. Originally priced at $100, the value is expected to increase dramatically over the years.

In 1987, Schrade introduced a limited series based upon "The Pioneers of America." The first of these was the Cowboy Commemorative. There will be four in all. This particular knife is a pouch-carried lock-back folder that features the company's first full-color scrimshaw work, On one scale is a cowboy with a lariat and a branding iron. On the other side, the scene involves a cowboy roping a long-horn steer. Only 10,000 of these are being made, each carrying its own serial number. Earlier, Schrade produced a series on American Indians which did well in the marketplace and convinced them of the value of such limited runs.

Schrade also has become involved in sponsorship of several outdoor events that they feel will benefit present and future generations of outdoorsmen.

For several years, Schrade has been involved in the

*Two heavy-duty pocketknives reflect both historic and modern designs: Dog Leg jackknife, left, with clip and pen blade in the old peanut pattern and the 30T Bearhead Lockback with locking drop point blade.*

*The Model 1580T Guthook skinner features a blade of high carbon steel custom designed guthook. The design is rare in production knives and is Schrade's only such model. Knife includes a leather belt sheath with safety strap. Knife handle is Schrade's sawcut Staglon material, known for its firm grip.*

Lone Star Bowfishing Championships in Texas. They took the step, as a company spokesman says, "When most outdoor firms didn't even have a working knowledge of bowfishing." Today, this is reported to be the fastest growing participation segment of the archery sport.

In 1986, the company became involved as a co-sponsor of the National Rifle Association's North American Hunter Education Championship, expanding that role in 1987. This particular event is dedicated to improvement of individual hunting skills and safety — not to mention development of a responsible hunter.

The Ellenville company also is deeply involved in the development of the cutlery display at the National Rifle Association Museum in Washington, D.C.

The original Schrade factory was opened in Walden, New York, in 1904. Several years later, a second factory was opened in Middletown, New York, to make only the famed Barlow knife and a larger version called the Daddy Barlow. In 1984, when Schrade celebrated its eightieth year, the Daddy Barlow was recreated as a commemorative piece, with only 8000 of them made.

The four Schrade brothers — George, William, Louis and Joe — all were practical engineers, who worked hard at producing a production system that outdid their competition. They developed their own tooling to produce the knives that led to their ultimate reputation. It was George Schrade who developed and patented the spring-opening pocketknife that has come to be known as the push-button knife.

When Schrade opened its doors for business in 1904, there already were four large knifemaking companies in the town of Walden. The community was considered the cutlery center of the United States at that time. However,

when the Great Depression of the Thirties and World War II had finally come to an end, Schrade was the only one of the companies that had survived.

Schrade moved to Ellenville and a larger factory in 1958. This was some twenty-five miles from the original Walden site and many of the craftsmen continued to commute to their jobs. Such craftsmen as Art Doyle have spent as much as four decades in the Schrade factory. Doyle is a template maker in the company's tool and die department.

Many of the craftsmen in the Schrade factory are third- and even fourth-generation employees of the organization. A great deal of the credit for Schrade's continued success through depression, wars and other trials goes to them. But as one of them stated, "This is a fun business."

His words reflect those of Henry Baer before his death: "I would rather continue in the manufacture of cutlery than work for a living!" It was said in jest, but Uncle Henry probably meant it.

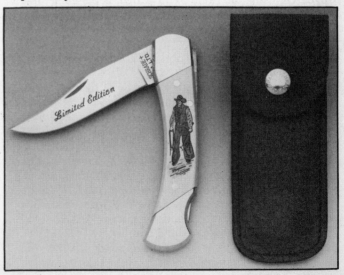

*Only 10,000 of the Cowboy commemorative knives are to be produced, enhancing the collector value of this five-inch lock-back blade, full color scrimshaw.*

# SPYDERCO CONCENTRATES ON A BASIC DESIGN THAT OPENS THE FOLDER WITH ONE HAND AND NEEDS NO SHEATH!

WHEN YOU have a good thing, go with it!

That seems to be the basic philosophy for Steve Gartin and his staff at Spyderco Incorporated, a firm operating out of Golden, Colorado. The firm came up with their first Clipit knife in 1980, a design called the Worker, which Gartin says was "meant to deliver racing performance." It must have worked, because the knife is still in the company line.

Today, or at least at last count, the company is producing seven different versions, but all based upon the same patented concept. In addition to the Worker, with a 2⅝-inch sharpened false-edge blade, there are the Mariner, with a 3½-inch sheepsfoot blade; the Hunter, which features a 2⅝-inch drop-point design; and the Executive, with a 2⅛-inch drop-point blade.

Also included in the lineup are the Standard, with its 2⅝-inch skinning blade and the Police Model, the largest of the group with a 3⅞-inch clip-point blade. The newest addition is the Co-Pilot. Constructed of G2 stainless steel, it is the smallest in the line, the blade measuring only two inches.

"Airline travel severely restricts those who put on their knife when they put on their pants," Gartin explains. "The Co-Pilot is the sensible solution. It includes a money clip and has the same serrated blade that is used on several of the other models."

Introduced in 1987 at the same time as the Co-Pilot was a model called the Harpy, which Gartin says was created for the commercial fisherman "who faces daily cutting chores that would intimidate Rambo." It features what the maker calls a Hawksbill blade with Spyder-Edge serrations directed to the needs of seafaring folks.

Although still on the drawing boards at this writing, Spyderco, using the same basic design, is planning knife styles that they hope will prove popular with paratroopers, skydivers and scuba enthusiasts. "A whole new generation of knives for those who may have to depend upon a knife for life and limb," is the way Steve Williams, the marketing director, describes them.

The clip that is riveted to the handle of the knife does away with the need for a sheath. On the smaller pocket models, it can be used as a money clip or any of the knives can be clipped to the belt or the edge of a pocket. The idea is that this allows easy accessibility.

Each of the Clipit knives has a hole in the blade. The purpose of this is to slip the tip of the thumb into the hole, allowing the knife to be opened with one hand. With the knives having a false edge, a section of it is sharpened. This allows one to cut string, tape, fishing line and other small items without opening the knife completely. The knives also are offered in right- or left-hand configurations, the change being made simply by changing the side onto which the clip is attached.

The Spyderco line, with the hole in the blade for ease of opening, is available in several blade lengths and configurations. (Below) Each knife has the belt clip.

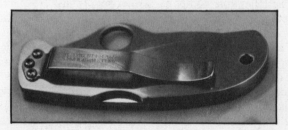

The serrated blades that are standard on some models and optional on others are, frankly, ugly, but they are practical. The maker says one can cut a half-inch rope with a single swing of the blade. We tried it and they don't lie about that! The knives are made of either 440 or G2 stainless steel and are manufactured in Japan at this time.

But Spyderco didn't start with the Clipit knives. The company's origin was in the sharpener business. The firm developed a system called the Tri-Angle ceramic sharpening system back in 1979 and has been marketing it since. The unit features alumina ceramic stones that have a hardness of 9.22 on a scale of 10. These fit into a moulded base that offers the correct angle for sharpening knives, scissors and other cutting tools ranging from dental tools to hatchets. The system is fast and easy, offering an almost fool-proof method to get an outstanding cutting edge on any blade. We tried it and it works better than we had hoped.

# MAKERS & IMPORTERS, CUTLERY & ACCESSORIES

## A

ALCAS CUTLERY CORP., 1116 E. State St., Olean, NY 14760
AL MAR KNIVES, P.O. Box 1626, Lake Oswego, OR 97034
ANDERSON ARCHERY, P.O. Box 130, Grand Ledge, MI 48837
ATLANTA CUTLERY CORP., Box 839, Conyers, GA 30207

## B

BALLARD CUTLERY, P.O. Box 97, Golf, IL 60092
BAUSKA MANUFACTURING CORP., P.O. Box 2270, Kalispell, MT 59903-2270
BEAVER TEETH KNIFE, 1852 Albany Ave., Loveland, CO 80537
BERETTA USA, 17601 Indian Head Hwy, Accokeek, MD 20607
BIANCHI INTERNATIONAL, 100 Calle Corte, Temecula, CA 92390
BINGHAM PROJECTS, Box 3013, Ogden, UT 84409
BLACKJACK KNIVES, 21620 Lassen St., Chatsworth, CA 91311
BOKER, 14818 W. 6th Ave., No. 17A, Golden, CO 80401
BOWEN KNIFE CO., P.O. Drawer 590, Blackshear, GA 31516
BROWNING, Rte 1, Morgan, UT 84050
BUCK KNIVES INC., P.O. Box 1267, El Cajon, CA 92022.

## C

CACOCTIN CUTLERY, P.O. Box 188, Smithsburg, MD 21783
CAM III, 425-A Merchant St., Vacaville, CA 95688
CALMONT CUTLERY, 7 Baynard Cove Rd., Hilton Head, SC 29928
CAMILLUS CUTLERY, P.O. Box 38, Camillus, NY 13131
W.R. CASE & SONS, 20 Russel Blvd., Bradford, PA 16701
CHARTER ARMS CORPS, 430 Sniffens Ln., Stratford, CT 06497
CHICAGO CUTLERY CO., 5420 N. County Rd., #18, Minneapolis, MN 55428
COLD STEEL, INC., 2128 Knoll Dr., Unit D, Ventura, CA 93003
COLE CONSUMER PRODUCTS, 5777 Grand Ave., Cleveland, OH 44105
COLEMAN/WESTERN, 1800 Pike Rd., Longmont, CO 80501
COLONIAL KNIFE CO., P.O. Box 810, Olean, NY 14760
CONSOLIDATED CUTLERY CO., Inc. 696 N.W. Sharp St., Port St. Lucie, FL 33452

## D

DAMASCUS USA, 243 Glendora, Suite B, Long Beach, CA 90803
DAN'S WHETSTONE CO., INC., P.O. Box 619, Royal, AR 71968
DMT, 85 Hayes Memorial Dr., Marlborough, MA 01752-1892

## E

EAGLE BRAND CUTLERY, 6928 Lee Hwy, Chattanooga, TN 37421
EK COMMAND KNIFE CO., Box 6454, Richmond, VA 23230
EYE BRAND, P.O. Box 2122, Austin, TX 78768
E-Z PRODUCTS, P.O. Box 41, Rossville, GA 60963
EZE-LAP DIAMOND SHARPENERS, 15164 Weststate, Westminster, CA 92683

## F

FISKARS MANUFACTURING CORP., 7811 W. Steward Ave., Wausau, WI 54401

R.H. FORSCHNER CO., INC., 14 Progress Dr., Shelton, CT 06484
FROST CUTLERY, P.O. Box 21353, Chattanooga, TN 37421
FULCRAFT KNIVES, P.O. Box 177, Memphis, TN 38101

## G

GASTINNE RENETTE, INC., P.O. Box 3395 College Station, Fredericksburg, VA 22401
GERBER LEGENDARY BLADES, 14200 S.W. 72nd Ave., Portland, OR 97223
GOLDEN EAGLE ARCHERY, 104 S. Mill St., Creswell, OR 97426
GOODWIN ENTERPRISES, P.O. Box 4124, Chattanooga, TN 37405
GUTMANN CUTLERY, 999 S. Columbus Ave., Mt. Vernon, NY 10550

## H

H&D FORGE, Rte. 2, Geisinger Rd., Shiloh, OH 44878
J.A. HENCKELS ZWILLINGSWORK, INC., Box 253, Hawthorne, NY 10532
HOFFMAN DESIGN, 5341-A Derry Ave., Agoura Hills, CA 91301
HOUSE OF MUZZLELOADING, 1019 E. Palmer, Glendale, CA 91205

## I

C.A.S. IBERIA INC., 54 Patricia Ln., South Setauket, NY 11720
IMPERIAL KNIFE CO., 1776 Broadway, New York, NY 10019
INTCO, P.O. Box 2180, Paso Robles, CA 93447

## J

JET-AER CORP., 100 Sixth Ave., Paterson, NJ 07514
JOY ENTERPRISES, P.O. Box 314, Ridgefield, NY 07657

## K

KA-BAR CUTLERY, 5777 Grand Ave., Cleveland, OH 44105
KEN'S FINN KNIVES, P.O. Box 126, Republic, MI 49879
KERSHAW KNIVES, 25300 S. W. Parkway, Wilsonville, OR 97070
KRIS CUTLERY, P.O. Box 133, Pinole, CA 94564
KWIK SHARP CO., 350 N. Wheeler St., Ft. Gibson, OK 74434

## L

LAKER KNIFE WORKS, P.O. Box 216, Taylorville, IL 62568
LANSKY SHARPENERS, P.O. Box 800, Buffalo, NY 14221
LEATHERMAN TOOL GROUP, INC., P.O. Box 20595, Portland, OR 97220
LIBERTY ORGANIZATION, INC., P.O. Box 306, Montrose, CA 91020
LEE BENCH MADE, P.O. Box 1777, Gaffney, SC 29340
LORAY, INC., 16740 Indian Hollow, Grafton, OH 44044

## M

MICRO-SURFACE FINISHING PRODUCTS, Box 818, Wilton, IA 52778
MID-EAST MFG., INC., 2817 Cameron St., Melbourne, FL 32901
MILITARY REPLICA ARMS, P.O. Box 360006, Tampa, FL 33673
MIRANDA IMPORTS & EXPERTS, 1524 E. Santa Clara, San Jose, CA 95116
MORTY THE KNIFE MAN, 60 Otis St., Unit C, West Babylon, NY 11704
MOUNTAIN FORGE CORP., P.O. Box 1345, Cleveland, GA 30528

MUSEUM REPLICAS LIMITED, Box 840 XV, Conyers, GA 30207
MYERCHIN MARINE CLASSICS, P.O. Box 911, Rialto, CA 92376

## N

NEW PATHS, INC., 1272 Washington St, Denver, CO 80203
NORMARK CORP., 1710 E. 78th St., Minneapolis, MN 55423

## O

OLSEN KNIFE CO., Howard City, MI 49329
ONTARIO KNIFE CO., P.O. Box 145, Franklinville, NY 14737

## P

PRECISION SPORTS, P.O. Box 30-06, Ithaca, NY 14850
PRECISE INTERNATIONAL, 3 Chestnut St., Suffern, NY 14850
PROFESSIONAL CUTLERY SERVICES, P.O. Box 2189, Downey, CA 90242

## Q

QUEEN CUTLERY CO., P.O. Box 367, Titusville, PA 16354

## R

RIGID KNIVES, P.O. Box 186, Lake Hamilton, AR 71951
A.G. RUSSELL CO., 1705 Highway 71 N. Springdale, AR 72764

## S

SCHRADE CUTLERY, 26-30 Canal St., Ellenville, NY 12428
SMITH WHETSTONE, 1500 Sleepy Valley Rd., Hot Springs, AR 71901
SOG SPECIALTIES, P.O. Box 1006, Santa Monica, CA 90406-1006
SPORTING IMAGES, P.O. Box 8391, 8659 Olive St. Dr., St. Louis, MO 63132
SPYDERCO, P.O. Box 800, Golden, CO 80402
STAR SALES CO., INC., P.O. Box 1503, Knoxville, TN 37901
SUOMI SHOP, Rte 2, Fergus Falls, MN 56537

## T

TAYLOR CUTLERY CO., P.O. Box 1638, Kingsport, TN 37662
TEKNA DESIGN GROUP, 101 Twin Dolphin Dr., Redwood City, CA 94065
TIMBERWOLF CUTLERY, P.O. Box 757, Clenton, AL 35045
TOLEDO ARMAS S.A., 302 Ponce de Leon Blvd., St. Augustine, FL 32084
TRU-BALANCE KNIFE CO., 2155 Tremont Blvd. N.W., Grand Rapids, MI 49504

## U

UNITED STATES CUTLERY, P.O. Box 418, Wyckoff, NJ 07481-0418
UTICA CUTLERY CO., 820 Notes St., Utica, NY 13503

## V

VALOR CORP., 5555 N.W. 36th Ave., Miami FL 33142
VICTORINOX, P.O. Box 846, Shelton, CT 06484-0913

## W

WENOKA CUTLERY, P.O. Box 8238, West Palm Beach, FL 33407
WESTBURY SALES, 373 Maple Ave., Westbury, NY 11590
WESTERN CUTLERY, 1800 Pike Rd., Longmont, CO 80501
WYOMING KNIFE CORP., 209-2 Commerce Dr., Ft. Collins, CO 80524

# NORTH AMERICAN CUSTOM MAKERS

## A

ED ADDISON, 325 E. Pritchard St., Asheboro, NC 27203
DARRELL ALEXANDER, Box 745, Big Piney, WY 83113
MIKE ALLEN, Rt. 1 Box 1080, Malakoff, TX 75148
STEVE ALLEN, 200 Forbes St., Riverside, RI 02915
TIM (R.V.) ALVERSON, Box 922, Keno, OR 97627
A.W. AMOUREUX, 3210 Woodland Pk. Dr., Anchorage, AK 99517
CHARLES B. ANDERSON, West Shore, Polson, MT 59860
EDWIN ANDERSON, 2050 Hillside Ave., New Hyde Park, NY 11040
VIRGIL W. ANDERSON, 16318 S.E. Taggart, Portland, OR 97236
DON ANDREWS, N. 5155 EZY St., Coeur K'Alene, ID 83814
W.E. ANKROM, 14 Marquette Dr., Cody, WY 82414
WILLIAM J. ANTONIO, JR., P.O. Box 186, Rt. 299, Warwick, MD 21912
RAY APPLETON, Box 321, Byers, CO 80103
DICK ATKINSON, 2524 S. 34th St., Decatur, IL 62521

## B

RAY BAKER, P.O. Box 303, Sapulpa, OK 74067
PHILLIP BALDWIN, P.O. Box 563, Snohomish, WA 98290
JIM BARBEE, Box 1173, Ft. Stockton, TX 79753
ROBERT E. BARBER, 232 Peachwood Lane, Virginia Beach, VA 23452
NORMAN P. BARDSLEY, 197 Cottage St., Pawtucket, RI 02860
JOE W. BAREFOOT, P.O. Box 1248, Easley, SC 29641
TOM AND WILLIAM BARMINSKI, 809 S. Del Norte Ave., Loveland, CO 80537

GARY L. BARNES, 305 Church St., Box 138, New Windsor, MD 21776
A.T. BARR, 54 Fox Circle, Denton, TX 76205
JAMES J. BARRY, P.O. Box 1571, West Palm Beach, FL 33406
JOHN BARTLOW, 111 Orchard Rd., Box 568, Norris, TN 37828
HUGH E. BARTRUG, 505 Rhodes St., Elizabeth, PA 15037
LEE GENE BASKETT, 240 Oakwood Dr., Elizabethtown, KY 42701
PETER BAUCHOP, P.O. Box 68, Hunt Valley, MD 21030
CHARLES BEAR, 4042 Bones Rd., Sebastopol, CA 95472
GORDON H. BEATTY, Rt 1, Box 79, Seneca, SC 29678
DEVON BEAVER, Box 3067 New River Stage I, Phoenix, AZ 85029
P.F. BECK, 1504 Hagood Ave., Barnwell, SC 29812
MICHAEL R. BECKWITH, 48282 Donahue Dr., New Baltimore, MI 48047
RAY BEERS, 9 Manorbrook Rd., Monkton, MD 21111
JACK BELK, 5321 Country Rd. 3, Marble, CA 81623
FRANK BELL, 409 Town & Country Drive, Huntsville, AL 35806
MICHAEL BELL, Rt 1, Box 1217, Coquille, OR 97423
DON BENSON, 2505 Jackson St. #112, Escalon, CA 95320
DAVE BER, P.O. Box 203, Nooksack, WA 98276
LARRY BERZAS, 208 W. 26th St., Cut Off, LA 70345
LEROY BESIC, 40640 Campus Way, Hemet, CA 92344
ROBERT F. BIRCH, P.O. Box 1901, Huntsville, TX 77340
SID BIRT, RR3, Box 269A, Nashville, IN 47448
EARL BLACK, 3466 South 700 East, Salt Lake City, UT 84106

ANDREW E. BLACKTON, 12521 Fifth Isle, Bayonet Point, FL 33667
WILLIAM E. BLAKLEY, II, Rt. 4, Box 103, Fredericksburg, VA 22405
ROY BLAUM, 319 N. Columbia St., Covington, LA 70433
GREGG BLOMBERG, Rt 1, Box 1762, Lopez, WA 98261
L.H. BLOOMFIELD, P.O. Box 3588, Kingman, AZ 86402
CHUCK BLUM, 743 S. Brea Blvd. #10, Brea, CA 92621
BRUCE BOCHMAN, Box 693, El Granada, CA 94018
PHIL BOGUSZEWSKI, 2102 North Anderson, Tacoma, WA 98406
BRUCE BOHRMANN, 29 Portland St., Yarmouth, ME 04096
CHARLES B. BOLTON, P.O. Box 6, Jonesburg, MO 63351
BONE KNIFE CO., INC., 4009 Ave. A, Lubbock, TX 79404
JEREMY BONNER, 85 Phoenix Cove Road, Weaverville, NC 28787
TILTON AND JAMES BOWEN, Rt 1, Box 225A, Baker, WV 26801
FRANCIS BOYD, 2128 Market St., San Francisco, CA 94114
DENNIS BRADLEY, Rt. 3, Box 3815, Blairsville, GA 30512
EDWARD P. BRANDSEY, 406 St. Joseph Circle, Edgerton, WI 53534
LARRY BRANDSTETTER, 827 N. 25th, Paducah, KY 42001
JIM BRAYTON, 713 Park St., Burkburnett, TX 76354
DAN BRDLIK, 166 Campbell St. So., Prescott, WI 54021
WALTER J. BREND, 351 Pine Ave., Walterboro, SC 29488
CLINT BRESHEARS, 2219 Belmont Lane, Redondo Beach, CA 90278
WAYNE BREUER, 400 East Glenwood, Wasilla, AK 99687

JACK BREWER, 2415 Brady Lane, Lafayette, IN 47905
RICHARD A. BRIDWELL, Rt. 2, Milford Ch. Rd., Taylors, SC 29687
E.D. BRIGNARDELLO, Rt. 2, Box 152A, Beecher, IL 60401
DAVID BROADWELL, P.O. Box 4314, Wichita Falls, TX 76308
KENNETH L. BROCK, P.O. Box 375/207 N. Skinner Rd., Allinspark, CO 80510
MICHAEL BROOKS, 1108 W. 6th, Littlefield, TX 79339
STEVE R. BROOKS, Box 105, Big Timber, MT 59011
THOMAS A. BROOME, P.O. Box 4294, Kenai, AK 99611
MAX BROWER, 1721 Marshall St., Boone, IA 50036
DAVID B. BROWN, Box 112, Doniphan, NE 68832
E.H. BROWN, P.O. Box 1906, Eustis, FL 32727
HAROLD E. BROWN, Rt. 7, Box 335, Arcadia, FL 33821
L.E. "RED" BROWN, 3203 Del Amo Blvd., Lakewood, CA 90712
TED BROWN, 8609 Cavel, Downey, CA 90242
RICK BROWNE, 1464 Gertrudita Ct., Upland, CA 91786
C. LYLE BRUNCKHORST, 4106½ Highway 68 GVSR, Kingman, AZ 86401
JACK and MORGAN BRYAN, 724 Highland Ave., Gardendale, AL 35071
BARRY R. BRYNER, 448 N. 1st Ave., Price, UT 84501
BILL BUCHMAN, 63312 South Rd., Bend, OR 97701
BILL BUCHNER, HC60, Box 35 B, Idleyld Park, OR 97447
MARK A. BUCHOLZ, P.O. Box 670984, Chugiak, AK 99567
DONALD M. BUCKBEE, 8704 Forest Ct., Warren, MI 48093
JIMMIE H. BUCKNER, P.O. Box 162, Putney, GA 31782
JOHN BUGDEN, 106 So. 13th St., Murray, KY 42071
SKIP BURNETTE, 14 Wildwood Ct., Spartanburg, SC 29301
DAVE BURNS, 101 S.E. 27 Ave., Boynton Beach, FL 33435
JOHN BUSFIELD, 153 Devonshire Circle, Roanoke Rapids, NC 27870
JERRY BUSSE, 11651 Co. Rd. 12, Wauseon, OH 43567

## C

BILL CALDWELL, Rt. 9, Box 170-S, West Monroe, LA 71291
ERRETT CALLAHAN, 2 Fredonia, Lynchburg, VA 24503
DICK CAMPBELL, 20000 Silver Ranch Rd., Conifer, CA 80433
JOE CANDRELLA, 1219 Barness Dr., Warminster, PA 18974
DANIEL L. CANNADY, Box 301, Allendale, SC 29810
RONALD E. CANTER, 96 Bon Air Cir., Jackson, TN 38305
DON CANTINI, 3933 Claremont Pl., Weirton, WV 26062
BOB CARGRILL, Route 1, Box 501-B, Oldfort, TN 37362
HAROLD J. "KIT" CARSON, 559 Congress Drive, Radcliff, KY 40160
FRED CARTER, 5219 Deer Creek Rd., Wichita Falls, TX 76302
DENNIS E. CASEY, 2758 Devonshire, Redwood City, CA 94063
DOUGLAS CASTEEL, Rt.2, Box 237, Hillsboro, TN 37342
TOM S. CELLUM, 23023 Birnman Wood Blvd., Spring, TX 77373
FRANK and MARY CENTOFANTE, P.O. Box 17587, Tampa, FL 33682-7587
JOHN A. CHAMBERLIN, 11535 Our Rd., Anchorage, AK 99516
ROBERT CHAMPION, 3710 Harmony, Amarillo, TX 79109
GORDON R. CHARD, 104 S. Holiday Lane, Iola, KS 66749
JOHN E. CHASE, 217 Walnut, P.O. Drawer H, Aledo, TX 76008
BILL CHEATHAM, 22 East 61st, Savannah, GA 31405
CLIFF CHELQUIST, P.O. Box 91, Arroyo Grande, CA 93420
D.E. (LUCKY) CLARK, Box 314 Woodlawn, St. RD #1, Mineral Point, PA 15942
J.D. CLAY, R.R. #1, Box 1655, Greenup, KY 41144
WAYNE CLAY, Box 474B, Pelham, TN 37366
TERRY A. COHEN, 114 Barson St., Santa Cruz, CA 95060
KEITH E. COLEMAN, 07 Jardin Rd., Los Lunas, NM 87031
KEN COLEMAN, 45 Grand St., Brooklyn, NY 11211
A.J. COLLINS, 1834 W. Burbank Blvd., CA 91506
LYNN M. COLLINS, 138 Berkley Dr., Elyria, OH 44035
BOB CONLEY, Rt. #14, Box 467, Jonesboro, TN 37659
C.T. CONN, JR., 208 Highland Ave., Attalla, AL 35954
MICHAEL CONNOR, Box 502, Winters, TX 79567
JEFFERY D. CONTI, 3410 6th, Bremerton, WA 98310
ROBERT COOGAN, Rt. 3, Box 347-A1, Smithville, TN 37166
GEORGE S. "STEVE" COPELAND, Star Route Box #36, Alpine, TN 38543
HAROLD CORBY, 1714 Brandonwood Dr., Johnson City, TN 37604
JOSEPH G. CORDOVA, 1450 Lillie Drive, Bosque Farms, NM 87068
JIM CORRADO, 2915 Cavitt Creek Rd., Glide OR 97443
SCOTT COSTA, Rt. 2, Box 503, Spicewood, TX 78669
ELDON COURTNEY, 2718 Bullinger, Wichita, KS 67204
GEORGE COUSINO, 22386 Beechwood Ct., Woodhaven, MI 48183
RAYMOND A. COVER, Rt. 1, Box 194, Mineral Point, MO 63660
COLIN J. COX, 1609 Votaw Rd., Apopka, FL 32703
JAMES H. CRAIG, 334 Novara, Manchester, MO 63021
JACK W. CRAIN, Rt. 2 Box 221 F, Weatherford, TX 76086
LARRY CRAWFORD, 1602 Brooks St., Rosenburg, TX 77471
PAT CRAWFORD, 205 N. Center, West Memphis, AR 72301
HAROLD CRISP, 3885 Bow St. N.E., Cleveland, TN 37312
JACK CROCKFORD, 1859 Harts Mill Rd., Chamblee, GA 30341
ROBERT CROWDER, Box 1374, Thompson Falls, MT 59873
JAMES L. CROWELL, Rt. 74, Box 368, Mtn. View, AR 72560
JOHN CULPEPPER, 2102 Spencer Ave., Monroe, LA 71201
R.J. CUMMING, American Embassy Panama, FPO New York, NY 09526
THOMAS CUTE, RD 4, Rt. 90, Cortland, NY 13045

## D

DAN DAGGET, 1961 Meteor, Flagstaff, AZ 86001
CRIS W. DAHL, Rt. 4, Box 558, Lake Geneva, WI 53147
G.E. DAILEY, 577 Lincoln St., Seekonk, MA 02771
ALEX DANIELS, 1410 Colorado Ave., Lynn Haven, FL 32444
RICK DARBY, 4026 Shelbourne, Youngstown, OH 44511
EDMUND DAVIDSON, Rt. 1 Box 319, Goshen, VA 24439
ROB DAVIDSON, 2419-25th St., Lubbock, TX 79411
DAVIS BROTHERS KNIVES, 1209 Woodlawn Dr., Camden, SC 29020
BARRY L. DAVIS, 1871 Pittsfield Rd., Castleton, NY 12033
DIXIE DAVIS, Rt.3, Clinton, SC 29325
DON DAVIS, 3918 Ash Ave., Loveland, CO 80538
JESSE W. DAVIS, 5810 Hwy. 301, Walls, MS 38680
K.M. "TWIG" DAVIS, P.O. Box 267, Monroe, WA 98272
SYD DAVIS,1220 Courtney Dr., Richmond, TX 77469
TERRY DAVIS, Box 111, Sumpter, OR 97877
W.C. DAVIS, 2010 S. Madison, Raymore, MO 64083
DANE and BARRY DAWSON, Box 10, Marvel, CO 81329
RICHARD DEARHART, Rt.1, Lula, GA 30554
ROBERT A. DEFEO, 12 Morningside Dr., Mays Landing, NJ 08330
WILLIAM G. DEFREEST, P.O. Box 7497, N. Kenai, AK 99635
DAN DENNEHY, 13321 Hwy. 160, Del Norte, CO 81132
DOUGLAS M. DENT, 1208 Chestnut St., So. Charleston, WV 25309
LARRY DETLOFF, 130 Oxford Way, Santa Cruz, CA 95060
PHILLIP DETMER, Rt. 1 Box 149A, Breese, IL 62230
CLARENCE DeYONG, 5211 Maryland Ave., Racine, WI 53406
JACK DIAS, P.O. Box 223, Palermo, CA 95968
JOSEPH M. DIGANGI, Box 225, Santa Cruz, NM 87567
EARL E. DILLON, 8908 Stanwin Ave., Arleta, CA 91331
FRANK J. DILLUVIO, 13611 Joyce, Warren, MI 48093
GREG DION, 3032 S. Jackson St., Oxnard, CA 93033
MALCOLM C. DION, 820 N. Fairview Ave., Goleta, CA 93117
LARRY DiTOMMASO, P.O. Box 12233, Longview, TX 75602
JOHN DOHAGHEY, P.O. Box 402021, Garland, TX 75046
PATRICK DONOVAN, 1770 Hudson Dr., San Jose, CA 95124
MIKE DOOLITTLE, 13 Denise Ct., Novato, CA 94947
DICK DOROUGH, Rt.1, Box 210, Gadsen, AL 35901
DALE DOUGLAS, 361 Mike Cooper Rd., Ponchatoula, LA 70454
T.M. DOWELL, 139 N.W. St. Helen's Pl., Bend, OR 97701
JAMES T. DOWNIE, R.R. #1, Thedford, Ont. N0M 2N0, Canada
LARRY DOWNING, Route 1, Bremen, KY 42325
TOM DOWNING, 129 So. Bank St., Cortland, OH 44410
BERYL DRISKILL, P.O. Box 187, Braggadocio, MO 63826
DENNIS DUBLIN, St.11, Comp. 23, RR2, Enderby, BC V0E 1V0, Canada
BILL DUFF, P.O. Box 694, Virginia City, NV 89440
ARTHUR J. DUFOUR, 8120 Dearmoun Rd., Anchorage, AK 99516
DAVE DUGGER, 2504 West 51, Westwood, KS 66205
RICK DUNKERLEY, General Delivery, Cameron, MT 59720
MELVIN T. DUNN, 5830 N.W. Carlson Rd., Rossville, KS 66533
FRED DUVALL, Rt. 8, Box 677, Benton, AZ 72015
LARRY E. DUVALL, Rt. 3, Gallatin, MO 64640

## E

RUSSELL O. EASLER, JR., P.O. Box 301, Woodruff, SC 29388
AL EATON, P.O. Box 43, Clayton, CA 94517
RICK EATON, 448 Winslow ST., Crockett, CA 94525
THOMAS W. EDWARDS, 3232 N. 79th Ave., Phoenix, AZ 85033
FAIN E. EDWARDS, 209 E. Mountain Ave., Jacksonville, AL 36265
JOEL ELLEFSON, 1233 Storymill Rd., Bozeman, MT 59715
W. B. ELLERBE, P.O. Box 712, Geneva, FL 32732
JIM ENCE, 145 So. 299 East, Richfield, UT 84701
ROBERT ENDERS, 3028 White Rd., Cement City, MI 49233
GEORGE ENGLEBRETSON, 1209 N.W. 49th St., Oklahoma City, OK 73118
BOB ENGNATH, 1217 B. Crescent DR., Glendale, CA 91205
THOMAS M. ENOS, III, 12302 State Rt., 535, Orlando, FL 32819
CURT ERICKSON, 449 Washignton Blvd., Ogden, UT 84404
L.M. ERICKSON, P.O. Box 132, Liberty, UT 84310
WALTER E. ERICKSON, 23883 Ada St., Warren, MI 48091
VINCENT K. EVANS, 556-B Kamani St., Honolulu, HI 96813

## F

MELVIN G. FASSIO, 2012 Rattlesnake Dr., Missoula, MT 59802
HOWARD J. FAUCHEAUX, P.O. Box 206, Loreauville, LA 70552
ALLAN FAULKNER, 6103 Park Ave., Marysville CA 95901
STEPHEN J. FECAS, 117 Allee St., Clemson, SC 29631
DON FERDINAND, P.O. Box 2790, San Rafael, CA 94941
LEE FERGUSON, Rt., 2, Box 109, Hindsville, AZ 72738
WILLIAM V. FIELDER, 2715 Salem Bottom Rd., Westminster, MD 21157
JIMMY L. FIKES, P.O. Box 389, Orange, MA 01364
L.C. FINGER, 1001-113 N. Weatherford, TX 76086
CLYDE E. FISCHER, P.O. Box 310, Nixon, TX 78140
THEO. (TED) FISHER, 8115 Modoc Lane, Montague, CA 96064
JERRY FISK, Rt. 1, Box 41, Lokesburg, AR 71846
JIM FISTER, R.#1, Finchville, KY 40022
DENNIS FITZGERALD, P.O. Box 12847, Fort Wayne, IN 46866-2847
JOE FLOURNOY, Rt. 6, Box 233, El Dorado, AR 71730
ALLEN FORD, 846 Thompson St., Roswell, GA 30075
PETE FORTHOFER, 711 Spokane Ave., Whitefish, MT 59937
AL FOSTER, St. Rt. 1, Box 117, Dogpatch, AR 72648
ROGER FOUST, 1925 Vernon Ave., Modesto, CA 95351
ED A. FOWLER, Willow Bow Ranch, P.O. Box 1519, Riverton, WY 82501
PAUL FOX, 80 Mineral Springs Mountain, Valdese, NC 28690
HEINRICH H. FRANK, Box 984, Whitefish, MT 59937
MIKE FRANKLIN, Rte. 41, Box M, Aberdeen, OH 45101
RON FRAZIER, 2107 Urbine Rd., Powhatan, VA 23139
ART F. FREEMAN, P.O. Box 2545, Citrus Heights, CA 95611
ALBERT J FREILING, 3700 Niner Rd., Finksburg, MD 21048
W. FREDERICK FREY, JR., 305 Walnut St., Milton, PA 17847
DENNIS E. FRIEDLY, 12 Cottontail Ln., Apt. E, Cody, WY 82414
LARRY FUEGEN, RR 1, Box 279, Wiscasset, ME 04578
STANLEY FUJISAKA, 45-004 Holowai St., Kaneohe, HI 96744
JIM FULLER, P.O. Box 51, Burnwell, AL 35038
JOHN W. FULLER, 6156 Ridge Way, Douglasville, GA 30135
W.T. FULLER, JR., 400 S. 8th St., East Gadsden, AL 35903
JOE FOUNDERBURG, 1255 Bay Oaks Dr., Los Osos, CA 93402

## G

FRANK GAMBLE, P.O. Box 2243, Gilroy, CA 95021
CHUCK K. GARLITS, P.O. Box 577, Rosman, NC 28772
WILLIAM O. GARNER, JR., 2803 East DeSoto St., Pensacola, FL 32503
M. D. GARTMAN, Rt.3, Box 13, Gatesville, TX 76528
RON GASTON, 330 Gaston DR., Woodruff, SC 29388
LINDEN L. GAUDETTE, 5 Hitchcock Rd., Wilbraham, MA 01095
CLAY GAULT, Rt. 1, Box 287, Lexington, TX 78947
ROY E. GENGE, P.O. Box 57, Eastlake, CO 80614
TOM GEORGE, P.O. Box 1298, Magalia, CA 95954
RANDALL GILBREATH, P.O. Box 195, Dora, AL 35062
E.E. "DICK" GILLENWATER, 921 Dougherty Rd., Aiken, SC 29801
JON GILMORE, 849 University Place, St. Louis, MO 63132
KEN GLASER, Rt. #1, Box 148, Purdy, MO 65734
RON GLOVER, P.O. Box 44132, Cincinnati, OH 45244
WAYNE GODDARD, 473 Durham Ave., Eugene, OR 97404
PAUL S. GOERTZ, 201 Union Ave., S.E., #207, Renton, WA 98056
JIM GOFOURTH, 3776 Aliso Cyn. Rd., Santa Paula, CA 93060
T.S. GOLDENBERG, P.O. Box 963, Herndon, VA 22070
WARREN L. GOLTZ, 802 E. 4th Ave.,Ada MN 56510
TAI GOO, 506 W. First St., Tempe, AZ 85281
BUTCH GOODWIN, 1345 Foothill Dr., Vista, CA 92084
GORDON (see De Freest)
DANTE GOTTAGE, 21700 Evergreen, St. Clair Shores, MI 48082
JUDY GOTTAGE, 21700 Evergreen, St. Clair Shores, MI 48082
GREGORY J. GOTTSCHALK, 12 First St. (Ft. Pitt), Carnegie, PA 15106
WILLIAM R. GRANQUIST, 5 Paul ST., Bristol, CT 06010
GORDON S. GREBE, 3605 Arctic #1109, Anchorage, AK 99503
L.G. GREEN, 4301 W. 63rd, Prairie Village, KS 66208
ROGER M. GREEN, 3412 Co. Rd. 1022, Joshua, TX 76058
MICHAEL GREGORY, 211 Calhoun Rd., Belton, SC 29627
ROGER GRENIER, 4595 Montee Saint Hubert, P. Que. J3Y 1V3, Canada
HOWARD A. GRIFFIN, JR., 14299 S.W. 31st Ct., Davie FL 33330
RENDON and MARK GRIFFIN, 9706 Cedardale, Houston, TX 77055
BEN GRIGSBY, Rt. 6 Box 510, Batesville, AR 72501
JOHN B. (Butch) GRIGSBY, 5320 Circle Rd., Corryton, TN 37721
W. W. GROSS, 325 Sherbrook Dr., High Point, NC 27260
KENNETH GUTH, 8 S. Michigan, 32nd Floor, Chicago, IL 60603
GEORGE B. GUTHRIE, Rt. 3 Box 432, Bessemer City, NC 28016
BOB GWOZDZ, 71 Starr Ln., Attleboro, MA 02703

## H

PHILLIP L. HAGEN, P.O. Box 58, Pelican Rapids, MN 56572
GEORGE S. HAGGERTY, 414 Hammertown Road, Monroe, CT 06468
ROBERT J. HAJOVSKY, P.O. Box 21, Scotland, TX 76379
JIM HAMMOND, P.O. Box 486, Arab, AL 35016
HANGAS & SONS (See Ruana Knife Works)
ROBERT W. HANSEN, R.R. 2, Box 88, Cambridge, MN 55008
HARBINGER (See Jimmy L. Fikes)
FRANK L. HARGIS, 321 S. Elm St., Flora, IL 62839
WALT HARLESS, P.O. Box 5913, Lake Worth, FL 33466-5913
LARRY W. HARLEY, Route 5, Box 37, Bristol, TN 37620
ROBERT HARN, 228 Pensacola Rd., Venice, FL 33595
MIKE HARRINGTON, 408 S. Cedar, Abilene, KS 67410
RALPH DEWEY HARRIS, P.O. Box 597, Grovetown, GA 30813
WILLIAM W. HARSEY, 82719 N. Howe Ln., Creswell, OR 97426
ARLAN (Lanny) HARTMAN, 340 Ruddiman, N. Muskegon, MI 49445
PHILL HARTSFIELD, 13095 Brookhurst St., Garden Grove, CA 92643
RADE HAWKINS, P.O. Box H, Red Oak, GA 30272

CHAP HAYNES, R.R. #4, Tatamagouche, NS B0K 1V0, Canada
WALTER F. HEDGECOCK, III, Box 175, Glen Daniel, WV 25844
DON HEDRICK, 131 Beechwood Hills, Newport News, VA 23602
LOU HEGEDUS, JR., P.O. Box 441, Cave Spring, GA 30124
J.L. HEGWALD, 1106 Charles, Humbolt, KS 66748
JOEL HEGWOOD, Rt. 4, Box 229, Summerville, GA 30747
RON HEMBROOK, P.O. Box 153, Neosho, WI 53059
LORENZO (Larry) HENDRICKS, 9919 E. Apache Trail, Mesa, AZ 85207
E.J. "JAY" HENDRICKSON, 4204 Ballenger Creek Pike, Frederick, MD 21701
D.E. HENRY, Star Route, Old Gultch Road, Mountain Ranch, CA 95246
WAYNE HENSLEY, P.O. Box 904, Conyers, GA 30207
TIM HERMAN, 7721 Foster, Overland Park, KS 66204
WM. R. "Bill" HERNDON, c/o Jody Samson, 1834 W. Burbank, Burbank, CA 91506
GEORGE HERRON, Rt.1, Box 24, Springfield, SC 29146
DON HETHCOAT, Box 1764, Clovis, NM 88101
THOMAS S. HETMANSKI, 1107 William St., Trenton, NJ 08610
DARYL HIBBEN, 1641 Domain Loop, Rio Rancho, NM 40299
GIL HIBBEN, 410 Production Court, Louisville, KY 40299
VERNON W. HICKS, Rte. 1, Box 387, Bauxite, AR 72011
TOM HIGH, 5474 S. 112.8 Rd., Alamoso, CO 81101
TOM HILKER, 4884 Harmony Lane, Santa Maria, CA 93455
HOWARD E. HILL, Box 3257, Polson, MT 59860
RICK HILL, 576 Clover Dr., Edwardsville, IL 62025
J.B. HODGE, 1100 Woodmont Ave. S.E., Huntsville, AL 35801
JOHN HODGE, III, 422 L. 15th St., Palatka, FL 32077
RICHARD J. HODGSON, 9081 Tahoe Lane, Boulder, CO 80301
STEVE HOEL, P.O. Box 283, Pine, AZ 85544
KEVIN L. HOFFMAN, 6392 Holly Ct., Lisle, IL 60532
D'ALTON HOLDER, 3200 N. Carlton, Farmington, NM 87401
DALE J. HOLLAND, 204 N.E. 82nd St., Kansas City, MO 64118
PAUL HOLLOWAY, 714 Burksdale Rd., Norfolk, VA 23518
JESS HORN, 2850 Goodwater Ave., Redding, CA 96002
GLEN HORNBY, P.O. Box 444, Glendale, CA 91209
DURVYN M. HOWARD, Rt. 5, Box 77, Gadsden, AL 35903
JOHN C. HOWSER, Rt. 9, Box 579, Bell Ln., Fankfort, KY 40601
JIM HRISOULAS, 15258 Lakeside, Slymar, CA 91342
ARTHUR J. HUBBARD, 574 Culters Farm Road, Monroe, CT 06468
C. ROBBIN HUDSON, Rt. 1, Box 128B, Rock Hall, MD 21661
CHUBBY HUESKE, 4808 Tamarisk Dr., Bellaire, TX 77401
STEVE HUEY, 27645 Snyder Rd. #38, Junction City, OR 97448
DARYLE HUGHES, 10979 Leonard, Nunica, MI 49448
ED HUGHES, 280½ Holly Lane, Grand Junction, CO 81503
LAWRENCE HUGHES, 207 W. Crestway, Plainview, TX 79072
MICHAEL J. HULL, 2118 Obarr Pl., Apt. C, Santa Ana, CA 92701
ROY HUMENICK, P.O. Box 494, Cupertino, CA 95015
ROBERT E. HUNNICUTT, 2636 Magnolia Way, Forest Grove, OR 97116
JEFF HURST, Rt. 1, Box 22-A, Rutledge, TN 37861

## I

BILLY MACE IMEL, 1616 Bundy Ave., New Castle, IN 47362

## J

JIM JACKS, P.O. Box 2782, Covina, CA 91722
GERRY JEAN, 25B Cliffside Drive, Manchester, CT 06040
CARL A. JENSEN, JR., R.R. #2, Box 74B, Blair, NE 68008
STEVE JERNIGAN, 298 Tunnel Rd., Milton, FL 32571
SID JIRIK, 11301 Patro St., Anchorage, AK 99516
BRAD JOHNSON, 3477 Running Deer Dr., El Paso, TX 79936
C. E. "GENE" JOHNSON, 5648 Redwood Ave., Portage, IN 46368
GORDEN W. JOHNSON, 5426 Sweetbriar, Houston, TX 77017
HAROLD "HARRY" C. JOHNSON, 1014 Lafayette Rd., Chickamauga, GA 30707
RONALD B. JOHNSON, Box 11, Clearwater, MN 55320
RUFFIN JOHNSON, 215 LaFonda Dr., Houston, TX 77060
STEVE R. JOHNSON, P.O. Box 5, 554 S. 500 E., Manti, UT 84642
W. C. "BILL" JOHNSON, 2242 N.W. 5th St., Okeechobee, FL 34972
CHARLES JOKERST, 9312 Spaulding, Omaha, NE 68134
BOB JONES, 6219 Azrec N.E., Albuquerque, NM 87110
ENOCH JONES, 6219 Novar Dr., Chantilly, VA 22021

## K

JOSEPH F. KEESLAR, R #1, Box 252, Almo, KY 42020
WILLIAM L. KEETON, 4234 Lynnbrook Dr., Louisville, KY 40220
GARY KELLY, 17485 S.W. Pheasant Lane, Aloha, OR 97006
LANCE KELLY, 1824 Royal Palm Dr., Edgewater, FL 32032
KEMAL (DON FOGG AND MURAD SAYEN), P.O. Box 127, Bryant Pond, ME 04219
BILL KENNEDY, JR., P.O. Box 850431, Yukon, OK 73085
J.C. KENNELLEY, Box 145, Leon, KS 67074
RALPH A. KESSLER, P.O. Box 202, Gary Goff Rd., Elgin, SC 29045
JOT SINGH KHALSA, 368 Village St., Millis, MA 02054
SHIVA KI, 5222 Ritterman Ave., Baton Rouge, LA 70805
BILL KING, 14830 Shaw Road, Tampa, FL 33625
JOE KIOUS, Rt. 2, Box 232, Alamo, TX 78516
GEORGE KIRTLEY, Salina Star Route, Boulder, CO 80302
JERRY KITSMILLER, 62435 Gerry Rd., Montrose, CO 81401
ROBERT KOLITZ, W9342 Canary Rd., Beaver Dam, WI 53916
GEORGE KOUTSOPOULOS, 41491 Biggs Rd., La Grange, OH 44050
MICHAEL T. KOVAL 822 Busch Ct., Columbus, OH 43229
STEVE KRAFT, 315 S.E. 6th, Abilene, KS 67410
TERRY L. KRANNING, 1900 West Quinn, #153, Pocatello, ID 83204
DONALD L. KREIBICH, 6082 Boyd Ct., San Jose, CA 95123
JAMES J. KREIMER, Rt. 2, Box 280, Milan, IN 47031
RAYMOND L. KREMZNER, 6620 Bonnie Ridge Dr., Baltimore, MD 21209-1940
PHILIP W. KRETSINGER, JR., Rt #1, Box 158, Boonsboro, MD 21713
AL KROUSE, 1903 Treble Dr. #4A, Humble, TX 77338
MARTIN KRUSE, P.O. Box 487, Reseda, CA 91335
JIM KUYKENDALL, P.O. Box 539, Tulare, CA 93275

## L

JIM LADD, 1120 Helen, Deer Park, TX 77536
RON LAKE, 123 East Park, Taylorville, IL 62568
FRANK G. LAMPSON, 2052 I Rd., Fruita, CO 81521
ED LANE, 440 N. Topping, Kansas, MO 64123
JERRY I. LANE, 1529 Stafford, Carbondale, IL 62901
GENE H. LANGLEY, Rt. 1, Box 204, Florence, SC 29501
MICK LANGLEY, Box 1447, Weyburn, Sask. S4H 3J9, Canada
SCOTT LANKTON, 8065 Jackson Rd., Ann Arbor, MI 48103
KEN LARGIN, 110 W. Pearl, Batesville, IN 47006
DON LAUGHLIN, 190 Laughlin Dr., Vidor, TX 77662
STEPHEN M. LAWSON, 2638 Baker Rd., Placerville, CA 95667
L.J. LAY, 602 Mimosa Dr., Burkburnett, TX 76354
MIKE J. LEACH, 5377 W. Grand Blanc Rd., Swartz Creek, MI 48473
PAUL M. LeBATARD, 14700 Old River Road, Vancleave, MS 39564
HEINS LEBER, Box 446, Hudson Hope, BC V0C 1V0, Canada
BRACY R. LEDFORD, 1917 Northgate St., Indianapolis, IN 46208
TOMMY LEE, Rt. 2, Box 392, Gaffney, SC 29340
BOB LEVINE, 3201 Iowa Drive, Anchorage, AK 99517
NORMAN LEVINE, Spring Valley Lake #7707, Victorville, CA 92392
TOM R. LEWIS, 1613 Standpipe Rd., Carlsbad, NM 88220
JIMMY (James B.) LILE, Rt. 6, Box 27, Russellville, AR 72801
CHRIS LINDSAY, 16237 Dyke Rd., La Pine, OR 97739
GARY M. LITTLE, HC84 Box 10301, Broadbent, OR 97414-9801
STERLING LOCKETT, 527 E. Amherst, Dr., Burbank, CA 91504
WOLFGANG LOERCHNER, P.O. Box 255, Bayfield, Ont. N0M 1G0, Canada
BOB LOFLIN, 404 Burns Lane, Seymor, TN 37865
LONESOME PINE (See Larry W. Harley)
DAVE LONGWORTH, 151 McMurchy, Bethel, OH 45106
A.C. LOVE, P.O. Box 334, Hearne, TX 77859
R.W. LOVELESS, P.O. Box 7836, Arlington Sta., Riverside, CA 92503
SCHUYLER LOVESTRAND, 325 Rolfe Dr., Apopka, FL 32703
MIKE LOVETT, 3219E Rancier, Killeen, TX 76541
BILL LUCKETT, 10 Armantes Lane, Weatherford, TX 76086
ROBERT W. LUM, 901 Travis Ave., Eugene, OR 97404
ROBERT LUTES, 24878 U.S. 6 (R.R. 1), Nappanee, IN 46550
ERNEST L. LYLE, III, 4501 Meadowbrook Ave., Orlando, FL 32808

## M

MIKE MACRI, Box 222, Churchill, MB R0B 0E0, Canada
J. M. "MICKEY" MADDOX, 63 Spring Circle, Ringgold, GA 30736
JACK MADSEN, 3311 Northwest Dr., Wichita Falls, TX 76305
PETER A. MAESTRI, Rt. 1, Box 111, Spring Green, WI 53588
JEFFREY G. MALITZKE, 4804 Lovers Lane, Wichita Falls, TX 76310
KENNETH MANEEKER, R.R. 2, Galiano Island, B.C. V0N 1P0, Canada
DAN MARAGNI, R.D. 1, Box 106, Georgetown, NY 13072
TOM MARINGER, 2306 S. Powell St., Springdale, AR 72764
CHRIS MARKS, Rt. 2 Box 879-R, Breaux Bridge, LA 70517
GLENN MARSHALL, P.O. Box 1099 (305 Hoffman St.), Mason, TX 76856
PETER MARZITELLI, 14143 110A Ave., Surrey, BC V3R 2B2, Canada
BILL MASON, 1114 St. Louis, #33, Excelsior Springs, MO 64024
LYNN MAXFIELD, 382 Colonial Ave., Layton, UT 84041
JAMES E. MAY, Rt. 2, Box 191, Auxvasse, MO 65231
LARRY JOE MAYNARD, Box 85, Helen, WV 25853
TOM MAYO, JR., 67-177 Kanoulu St., HI 96791
OSCAR L. MAYVILLE, 5660 Cooper Rd., Indianapolis, IN 46208
HARVEY McBURNETTE, P.O. Box 227, Eagle Nest, NM 87718
JOHN McCLAREY, 1710 Keysville Rd. So., Keymar, MD 21757
HARRY McCARTY, 1121 Brough Ave., Hamilton, OH 45015
ZOLLAN McCARTY 101½ Ave., E, Thomaston, GA 30286
CHARLES R. McCONNELL, 158 Genteel Ridge, Wellsburg, WV 26070
LOYD A. McCONNELL, JR., P.O. Box 7162, Odessa, TX 79760
V.J. McCRACKIN and SON, 3720 Hess Rd., House Springs, MO 63051
LARRY E. McCULLOUGH, Route 4, Box 556, Mocksville, NC 27028
DAVE McDEARMONT, 1618 Parkside Trail, Lewisville, TX 75067
KEN McFALL, P.O. Box 458, Lakeside, AZ 85929
JOHN McGILL. P.O. Box 302, Blairsville, GA 30512
JIM McGOVERN, 31 Scenic Dr.,Oak Ridge, NJ 07438
TOMMY McKISSACK II, P.O. Box 991, Sonora, TX 76950
THOMAS McLANE, 7 Tucson Terrace, Tucson, AZ 83745
JAMES McLEOD, 941 Thermalito Ave., Oroville, CA 95965
SEAN McWILLIAMS, 4334 C.R. 509, Bayfield, CO 81122
DARYL MEIER, R.R. 4, Carbondale, IL 62901
HARRY E. MENDENHALL, 1848 Everglades Dr., Milpitas, CA 95035
TED MERCHANT, 7Old Garrett Ct., White Hall, MD 21161
ROBERT L. MERZ III, 20219 Prince Creed Dr.,Katy, TX 77450
CHRIS MILLER, JR., 3959 U.S. 27 South, Sebring, FL 33870
MANFORD J. MILLER, 5105 S. LeMaster Rd., Evergreen, CO 80439
JAMES P. MILLER, 9024 Goeller Rd., R.R. 2, Fairbank, IA 50629
RONALD T. MILLER, 12922 127th Ave. N., Largo, FL 33544
TED MILLER, P.O. Box 6328, Santa Fe, NM 87502
TERRY MILLER, 450 S. 1st, Seward, NE 68434
ANDY MILLS, 316 W. Morse, Fredericksburg, TX 78624
LOUIS G. MILLS, (YASUTOMO), 3600 Rentz Rd., Ann Arbor, MI 48103
JIM MINNICK, 144 N.7th St., Middletown, IN 47356
JAMES A. MITCHELL, 1355 Autumnridge Dr., Columbus, GA 31904
MAX AND DEAN MITCHELL, 997 V.F.W. Road, Leesville, LA 71446
HAROLD MOELLER, RR 3,Thorton, Ontario L0L 2N0, Canada
DELMER R. MONTEGNA, P.O. Box 6261, Sheridan, WY 82801
CLAUDE MONTJOY, R.R. 2, Box 470C, Clinton, SC 29325
JAMES B. MOORE, 1707 N. Gillis, Ft. Stockton, TX 79735
TOM W. MOORE, JR., Rt. 7, Reece Church Rd., Columbia, TN 38401
WM. F. MORAN, JR., P.O. Box 68, Braddock Heights, MD 21714
EMIL MORGAN, 2690 Calle Limonero, Thousand Oaks, CA 91360
JEFF MORGAN, 9200 Arnaz Way, Santee, CA 92071
JUSTIN MORGAN, 2690 Calle Limonero, Thousand Oaks, CA 91360
TOM MORGAN, 14689 Ellett Rd., Beloit, OH 44609
TOM MORLAN, 30635 S. Palm, Hemet, CA 92343
C.H. MORRIS, 828 Meadow Dr., Atmore, AL 36502
GARY E. MOSSER, 15605 20th Ave. S. E., Renton, WA 98056
RUSS MOYER, 1622 Rich St., Havre, MT 59501
STEVE MULLIN, 500 W. Center Vasiley Rd., Sandpoint, ID 83864
PAUL MUNRO, RFD 1, Box 32, Franklin, ME 04634
DAVE MURPHY, P.O. Box 256, Gresham, OR 97030
MEL MYERS, 611 Elmwood Drive, Spencer, IA 51301
PAUL MYERS, 128 12th St., Wood River, IL 62095

## N

WOODY NAIFEH, Rt. 13, Box 380, Tulsa, OK 74107
JERRY C. NEAL, P.O. Box 12458, Winston-Salem, NC 27117
BUD NEALY, 822 Thomas St.,Stroudsburg, PA 18360
KEITH A. NELSON, 18D Chughole Ln., Los Lunas, NM 87031
ROGER S. NELSON, Box 294, Central Village, CT 06332
CORBIN NEWCOMB, 628 Woodland Ave., Moberly, MO 65270
R. KENT NICHOLSON, 615 Hollen Rd., Baltimore, MD 21212
FRANK NIRO, Box 552, Mackenzie, BC V0J 2C0, Canada
MELVIN S. NISHIUCHI, 45-006 Waikalua Rd., Kaneohe, HI 96744
R.D. and GEORGE NOLEN, Box 2895, Estes Park, CO 80517
DON NORTON, 3206 Aspen Dr., Farmington, NM 87401
FRANK NORTON, 3964 Redwood Ct., Pleasanton, CA 94566

## O

CHARLES F. OCHAS, 124 Emerald Lane, Largo, FL 34641
KUZAN ODA, P.O. Box 2213, Hailey, ID 83333
ROBERT G. OGG, Rt. 1, Box 345, Paris, AZ 72855
GORDON O'LEARY, 2566 Hearthside Dr., Ypsilanti, MI 48198
MILFORD OLIVER, 3832 W. Desert Park Lane, Phoenix, AZ 85021
WAYNE C. OLSON, 11655 W. 35th Ave., Wheat Ridge, CO 80033
WARREN OSBORNE, 111 Oak Lawn, Waxahachie, TX 75165
ANTHONY L. OUTLAW, 1131 E. 24th Plaza, Panama City, FL 32405
T.R. OVEREYNDER, 1800 S. Davis Dr., Arlington, TX 76013
DANNY OWENS, P.O. Box 284, Blacksburg, SC 29702
JOHN OWENS, 8755 S. W. 96th, Miami, FL 33176
LOWELL R. OYSTER, RFD #1, Box 432, Kenduskeag, ME 04450

## P

LARRY PAGE, 1494 Rolling Rock Rd., Aiken, SC 29801
PHILLIP R. PANKIEWICZ, RFD #1, Waterman Rd., Lebanon, CT 06249
ROBERT "BOB" PAPP, P.O. Box 246, Elyria, OH 44036
MELVIN M. PARDUE, Rt. 1, Box 130, Repton, AL 36475
DUAYNE PARRISH, P.O. Box 181, Palestine, TX 75801
ROBERT PARRISH, 1922 Spartanburg Hwy., Hendersonville, NC 28739
LLOYD D. PATE, 219 Cottontail Ln., Georgetown, TX 78626
CHUCK PATRICK, Rt #1, Brasstown, NC 28902
HILL EVERETT PEARCE, III, Box 72, Gurley, AL 35748
W. D. PEASE, Rt. 2 Box 13, Ewing, KY 41039
LLOYD PENDLETON, 2116 Broadmore Ave., San Pablo, CA 94806

ALFRED H. PENDRAY, Rt. 2, Box 1950, Williston, FL 32696

STEPHAN PEPIOT, General Delivery, Lancaster Park, Edmonton AB T0A 2H0, Canada

DAN L. PETERSON, 327 N. Rim, Billings, MT 59102

ELDON G. PETERSON, 260 Haugen Hts. Rd., Whitefish, MT 59937

JACK PETERSON, 532 Duke St., Nanaimo, BC V9R 1K1, Canada

JOHN PHILLIPS, 4021B Primavera, Santa Barbara, CA 93110

RANDY PHILLIPS, P.O. Box 1303, Temple City, CA 91780

HAROLD L. PIERCE, 7150 Bronner Circle #10, Louisville, KY 40218

DAVID PITT, P.O. Box 7653, Klamath Falls, OR 97602

LEON PITTMAN, Rt. 2, Box 2097, Pendergrass, GA 30567

JAMES POAG, RR 1, Box 213, New Harmony, IN 47631

LARRY POGREBA, Box 861, Lyons, CO 80540

CLIFTON POLK, 3526 Eller St., Ft. Smith, AR 72904

JAMES L. POPLIN, Rt. 2, Box 191A, Washington, GA 30673

JAMES E. PORTER, P.O. Box 2583, Bloomington, IN 47402

ALVIN POSTON, 1813 Old Colony Rd., Columbia, SC 29209

ROBERT PREUSS, P.O. Box 65, Cedar, MN 55011

JERRY L. PRICE, P.O. Box 782, Springdale, AR 72764

JOEL HIRAM PRICE, Rt. 1, Box 3067, Palatka, FL 32077

STEVE PRICE, 899 Ida Lane, Kamloops, BC V2B 6V2, Canada

RON PRITCHARD, 613 Crawford Ave., Dixon, IL 61021

JOSEPH D. PROVENZANO, 3024 Ivy Place, Chalmette, LA 70043

JIM PUGH, P.O. Box 711, Azle, TX 76020

MARTIN PULLEN, 813 Broken Bow WHH, Granbury, TX 76048

MORRIS C. PULLIAM, Rt. 7, Box 272, Shelbyville, KY 40065

AARON PURSLEY, Box 1037, Big Sandy, MT 59520

### Q

BARR QUARTON, P.O. Box 2211, Hailey, ID 83333

WARNER QUENTON, P.O. Box 607, Peterstown, WV 24963

GEORGE QUINN, P.O. Box 692, Julian, CA 92036

### R

JERRY F. RADOS, R.R. 1. Box 151, Grant Park, IL 60940

RICHARD RAINVILLE, 126 Cockle Hill Rd., Salem, CT 06415

MARSHALL F. RAMEY, P.O. Box 2589, West Helena, AR 72390

W.D. and GARY T. RANDALL, Box 1988, Orlando, FL 32802

STEVEN J. RAPP, 3437 Crestfield Dr., Salt Lake City, UT 84119

RICHARD RAPPAZZO, 217 Troy-Schenectady Rd., Latham, NY 12110

A.D. RARDON, Rt. 1, Box 79, Polo, MO 64671

MICHAEL RAY, 533 W. 36th North, Wichita, KS 67204

CHARLES V. RECE, Rt. 2, Box 477, Albemarle, NC 28001

DAVID REE, 816 Main St., Van Buren, AR 72956

CRIS REEVES, 6433 Frederick Rd., Baltimore, MD 21228

WINFRED M. REEVES, P.O. Box 315, West Union, SC 29696

BILL REH, 4610 South Ave. W., Missoula, MT 59801

JOHN C. REYNOLDS, Box 119, Mica Court, Gillette, WY 82716

DAVID RHEA, Rt. 1, Box 272, Lynnville, TN 38472

DOUGLAS RIAL, Rt. 2, Box 117A, Greenfield, TN 38230

ADRIENNE RICE, Rt. 1, Box 1744, Lopez Island, WA 98261

DAVE RICKE, 1209 Adams, West Bend, WI 53095

WILLIE RIGNEY, R.R. 3, Box 404, Shelbyville, IN 46176

DEAN ROATH, 3050 Winnipeg Dr., Baton Rouge, LA 70819

HOWARD P. ROBBINS, 875 Rams Horn Rd.-Moraine Rt., Estes Park, CO 80517

RON ROBERTSON, 6708 Lunar Dr., Anchorage, AK 99504

MICHAEL R. ROCHFORD, Trollhaugen Ski Area, P.O. Box 607, Dresser, WI 54009

FRED D. ROE, JR., 4009 Granada Dr., Huntsville, AL 35802

ROBERT P. ROGERS, JR., 3979 South Main St., Acworth, GA 30101

FRED ROHN, W7615 Clemetson Rd., Coeur d'Alene, ID 83814

STEVE ROLLERT, P.O. Box 65, Keenesburg, CO 80643

MARK H. ROPER, JR., 206 Plymoth Rd., Martinez, GA 30907

ALEX ROSE, 3624 Spring Valley Dr., New Port Richey, FL 33552

RUANA KNIFE WORKS, Box 520, Bonner, MT 59823

JAMES A RUBLEY, R.R. 3, Box 682, Angola, IN 46703

A.G. RUSSELL, 1705 Hwy. 471 N., Springdale, AR 72764

CHARLES C. RUST, P.O. Box 374, Palermo, CA 95968

### S

SUZANNE ST. AMOUR, Oldstore House R.R. 1, Hillsburgh, Ont. N0B 1Z00 Canada

JOHN D. SALLEY, 3965 Frederick-Ginghamsburg Rd., Tipp City, OH 45371

BOB SALPAS, P.O. Box 117 Homewood, CA 95718

LYNN SAMPSON, Rt. 2, Box 283, Jonesboro, TN 37659

JOSEPH D. SAMS, 10640 Prince George Lane, El Paso, TX 79924

JODY SAMSON, 1834 W. Burbank Blvd., Burbank, CA 91506

MICHAEL M. SANDERS, P.O. Box 1106, Ponchatoula, LA 70454

SCOTT SAWBY, 500 W. Center Valley Rd., Sand Point, ID 83864

MURAD SAYEN (See Kemal)

WILL SCARROW, P.O. Box 147, San Gabriel, CA 91775

JACK SCHEDENHELL, P.O. Box 307, Superior, MT 59872

MAGGIE SCHEID, P.O. Box 8059, W. Webster, NY 14580

GEORGE B. SCHEPERS, Box 83, Chapman, NE 68827

JAMES A. SCHMIDT, R.D. 3, Eastern Ave., Ballston Lake, NY 12019

HERMAN J. SCHNEIDER, 24296 Via Aquara, Laguna Niguel, CA 92677

MATTHEW A. SCHOENFELD, RR #1, Galiano Island, B.C. V0N 1P0, Canada

JOHN J. SCHWARZ, 41 Fifteenth St., Wellsburg, WV 26070

STEPHEN SCHWARZER, 2119 Westover Dr., Palatka, FL 32077

WINSTON SCOTT, Rt. 2, Box 62, Huddleston, VA 24104

JIM SERVEN, 6153 Third St., Mayville, MI 48744

ROBERT G. SHARP, 17540 St. Francis Blvd., Anoka, MN 55303

PHILIP S. SHARPE, 483 Landmark Way S.W., Austell, GA 30001

ROBERT A SHEARER, 2121 Avenue T, Huntsville, TX 77304

SCOTT SHOEMAKER, 316 S. Main St., Miamisburg, OH 45342

RICK SHUFORD, 431 Hillcrest Dr., Statesville, NC 28677

CORBET R. SIGMAN, Rte. 1, Box 212-A, Liberty, WV 25124

ROB SIMONICH, P.O. Box 278, Clancey, MT 59634

BILL SIMONS, P.O. Box 311, Highland City, FL 33846

BOB SIMS, P.O. Box 772, Meridian, TX 76665

CLESTON S. SINYARD, Rt. 2, Box 634, Elberta, AL 36530

JIM SISKA, 6 Highland Ave., Westfield, MA 01085

SAMUEL SKIRCHAK, JR., RD #1, Lisbon Rd., Midland, PA PA 15059

FRED SLEE, 9 John St.,Morganville, NJ 07751

JOHN SLOAN, P.O. Box 486, Foxboro, MA 02035

SHANE SLOAN, Rt. 1, Box 17, Newcastle, TX 76372

ED SMALL, Rt. 1, Box 178-A, Keyser, WV 26726

JIM SMALL, P.O. Box 67, Madison, GA 30650

DAVID LYNN SMITH, P.O. Box 36. Duchesne, UT 84021

GREGORY H. SMITH, 8607 Coddington Ct., Louisville, KY 40299

HARRY R. SMITH, 2105 So. 27th Ave., Missoula, MT 59801

JAMES B. "RED" SMITH, JR., Rt. 2, Box 199, Morven, GA 31638

NEWMAN L. SMITH, Rt. 1, Box 119A, Glades Rd., Gatlin-burg, TN 37738

RALPH L. SMITH, P.O. Box 395, Greer, SC 29652

W.F. "RED" SMITH, P.O. Box 6, Gatlinburg, TN 37738

W.J. SONNEVILLE, 1050 Chalet Dr. W., Mobile, AL 36608

G. DOUGLAS SONTHEIMER, 1705 Chester Mill Road, Silver Spring, MD 20906

JIM SORNBERGER, 5675 Meridian Ave., San Jose, CA 95118

BERNARD SPARKS, Box 73, Dingle, ID 83233

JOHN E. SPENCER, Box 582-B-Star Rt., Harper, TX 78631

RICHARD SPINALE, 3415 Oakdale, Ave., Lorain, OH 44055

JEFFERSON SPIVEY, P.O. Box 60584, Oklahoma City, OK 73146

RICHARD STAFFORD, 104 Marcia Ct., Warner Robins, GA 31088

HARRY L. STALTER, R.R. 1, Box 60, Trivoli, IL 61560

CHUCK STAPEL, Box 1617, Glendale, CA 91209

RANDY STEFANI, 2393 Mayfield Ave., Montrose, CA 91020

KEITH STEGALL, 3206 Woodland Pk.Dr., Anchorage, AK 99517

AL STEINBERG, 2499 Trenton Dr., San Bruno, CA 94066

KELLY LEE STEPHENS, 4235 78th Ln. N., St Petersburg, FL 33709

CHARLES STEWART, P.O. Box 514, 2996 Walmsley Cir-cle, Lake Orion, MI 48035

KAY STITES, 4931 Rands Rd., Bloomfield Hills, MI 48013

W.B. "BILL" STODDART, 917 Smiley, Forest Park, OH 45240

G.W. STONE and JIM ERICKSON, 610 No. Glenville Dr., Richardson, TX 75081

JOHNNY STOUT, 1514 Devin, Braunfels, TX 78130

SCOTT STRONG, 2138 Oxmoor Dr., Beaver Creek, OH 45431

GEORGE STUMPFF, JR., P.O. Box 2, Glorieta, NM 87535

HARLAN SUEDMEIER, RFD2, Nebraska City, NE 68410

ROD SWAIN, 1020 Avon Place, South Pasadena, CA 91030

CHUCK SYSLO, 3418 South 116 Ave., Omaha, NE 68144

### T

ANTONIO J. TAGLIENTI, P.O. Box 221, Darlington, PA 16115

MICHAEL TAMBOLI, 12447 N. 49 Ave., Glendale, AZ 85304

C. GRAY TAYLOR, 137 Lana View Dr., Kingsport, TN 37664

DAVID TAYLOR, 137 Lana View Dr., Kingsport, TN 37664

MICKEY TEDDER, Rt. 2, Box 22, Conover, NC 28613

LOU TEICHMOELLER, P.O.B. 282, Dolores, CO 81323

STEPHEN TERRILL, 908 S. Magnolia, Lindsay, CA 93247

ROBERT TERZUOLA, Route 6, Box 83A, Santa Fe, NM 87501

BRUCE LEE THOMPSON, 4101 W. Union Hills Dr., Glen-dale, AZ 85308

LEON THOMPSON, 1735 Leon Drive, Forest Grove, OR 97116

DANNY THORNTON, P.O. Box 334, Fort Mill, SC 29715

MICHAEL W. THOUROT, T814RR1, RD 11, Napoleon, OH 43545

ED THUESEN, 10649 Haddington, Suite 190, Houston, TX 77043

KEVIN THUESEN, 10629 Haddington, Suite 190, Hous-ton, TX 77043

THUNDERBOLT ARTISANS (See Thomas N. Hilker)

TIMBERLINE KNIVES, P.O. Box 36, Mancos, CO 81328

CAROLYN D. TINKER, P.O. Box 51213, Whittier, CA 90607

DANIEL TOKAR, Box 1776, Shepherdstown, WV 25443

P.J. TOMES, P.O. Box 37268, Jacksonville, FL 32236

DAN TOMPKINS, 310 N. Second St., Peotone, IL 60468

DWIGHT L. TOWELL, Rt. 1, Box 66, Midvale, ID 83645

R.W. TRABBIC, 4550 N. Haven, Toledo, OH 43612

TERRY A. TREUTEL, P.O. Box 187, Hamilton, MT 59840

THOMAS A. TRUJILLO, 2905 Arctic Blvd., Anchorage, AK 99503

JON J. TSOULAS, 1 Home St., Peabody, MA 01960

RALPH A. TURNBULL, 5722 Newburg Rd., Rockford, IL 61108

### V

WAYNE VALACHOVIC, RFD #1 Box 215B, Hillsboro, NH 03244

A. DANIEL VALOIS, 4299 Hawthorne Rd., Orefield, PA 18069

MICHAEL VEIT, Rt. 1, 3070 E. Fifth Rd., LaSalle, IL 61301

H.J. VIELE, 88 Lexington Ave., Westwood, NJ 07675

DAVID P. VOTAW, Box 327, Pioneer, OH 43554

FRANK VOUGHT, JR., 115 Monticello Dr., Hammond, LA 70401

ROBERT VUNK, 4408 Buckeye Ct., Orlando, FL 32804

### W

JAMES W. WADE, Rt. 1, Box 56, Wade, NC 28395

JOHN K. WAGAMAN, 903 Arsenal Ave., Fayetteville, NC 28305

HERMAN F. WAHLERS, Star Route 1, Austerlitz, NY 12017

MARK DAVID WAHLSTER, 6108 Radiant Dr. N.E., Salem, OR 97303

MARK WALDROP, P.O. Box 129, Lady Lake, FL 32659

GEORGE A. WALKER, Star Route, Alpine, WY 83128

JOHN W. WALKER, Rt. 2, Box 376, Bon Aqua, TN 37025

MICHAEL L. WALKER, Box 2343, Taos, NM 87571

A.F. WALTERS, 609 E. 20th St., Tifton, GA 31794

BRIAN K. WALTERS, P.O. Box 2124, Des Moines, IA 50310

KEN WARD, 3401 Becerra Wy., Sacramento, CA 95821

W.C. WARD, Rte. 6, Lynn Rd., Box 184-B, Clinton, TN 37716

DAVE WARDMAN, 9910 U.S.-23, Ossineke, MI 49766

BUSTER WARENSKI, P.O. Box 214, Richfield, UT 84701

AL WARREN, 63664 High Standard, Bend, OR 97701

DALE WARTHER, 164 West ST., Box 265, Bolivar, OH 44612

STANLEY WARZOCHA, 32540 Wareham Dr., Warren, MI 48092

DANIEL and BILL WATSON, 350 Jennifer Ln., Driftwood, TX 78619

FREDDIE WATT, III, P.O. Box 1372, Big Spring, TX 79721

FRED E. WEBER, 517 Tappan St., Forked River, NJ 08731

DEL WEDGE, JR., Box 10, Stewartsville, MO 64490

RUDY WEHNER, 2713 Riverbend Dr., Violet, LA 70092

J. REESE WEILAND, JR., 14919 Nebraska Ave., Tampa, FL 33612

DONALD E. WEILER, P.O. Box 1576, Yuma, AZ 85364

GEROME W. WEINAND, Box 385,Lolo, MT 59847

CHARLES L. WEISS, 18847 N. 13th Ave., Phoenix, AZ 85027

WILLIAM H. WELCH, 5226 Buell Drive, Fort Wayne, IN 46807

GEORGE W. WERTH, 9010 Cary Rd., Cary, IL 60013

CODY WESCOTT, 5610 Hanger Lake Ln., Las Cruces, NM 88001

JIM WESCOTT, 4225 Elks Dr., Las Cruces, NM 88005

MIKE WESOLOWSKI, 902-A Lohrman Lane, Petaluma, CA 94952

GENE E. WHITE, 5415 Taney Ave., Alexandria, VA 22304

ROBERT J. "BOB" WHITE, RR1, Gilson, IL 61436

ROBERT J. "BUTCH" WHITE, JR., RR1, Gilson, IL 61436

JAMES D. WHITEHEAD, P.O. Box 540, Durham, CA 95938

JIM WHITMAN, SR3 Box 5387, Chuglak, AK 99567

EARL T. WHITMIRE, 725 Colonial Dr., Rock Hill, SC 29730

KEN J. WHITWORTH, 41667 Tetley Ave., Sterling Heights, MI 48078

HORACE WIGGINS, 203 Herndon, Box 152, Mansfield, LA 71502

JAMES C. WIGGINS 1540 W. Pleasant Rd., Hammond, LA 70403

GERI L. WILLEY, Rt. 1, Box 235-B, Greenwood, DE 19950

W.G. WILLEY, Rt. 1, Box 235-B, Greenwood, DE 19950

SHERMAN A. WILLIAMS, 1709 Wallace St., Simi Valley, CA 93065

JAMES G. WILSON, Moraine Rt. UC 2004, Estes Park, CO 80517

R.W. WILSON, P.O. Box 2012, Weirton, WV 26062

MICHAEL WINE, 66 Westview Ln., Cocoa Beach, FL 32931

TRAVIS A. WINN, 558 E. 3065 So., Salt Lake City, UT 84106

EARL WITSAMAN, 1975 Echo Rd., Stow, OH 44224

BARRY W. WOOD, 38 S. Venice Blvd., Venice, CA 90291

LARRY B. WOOD, 6945 Fishburg Rd., Huber Heights, OH 45424

WEBSTER WOOD, 4726 Rosedale, Clarkston, MI 48016

WILLIAM W. WOOD. P.O. Box 877, Vera, TX 76383

HAROLD E. WOODWARD, Rt 3, Box 64A, Woodbury, TN 37190

AL WOODWORTH, 4420 State Route 316 W., Ashville, OH 43103

JOE WOREL, 3040 N. LaPorte, Melrose Park, IL 60164

HAROLD C. WRIGHT, 1710 Bellwood Drive, Centerville, TN 37033

KEVIN WRIGHT, 671 Leland Valley Rd. W, Quilcene, WA 98376

TIMOTHY WRIGHT, 4100 W. Grand Ave., Chicago, IL 60651

### Y

DAVID C. YORK, P.O. Box 1342, Crested Butte, CO 81224

BUD YOUNG, Box 336, Port Hardy, BC V0N 2P0, Canada

CLIFF YOUNG, R.R.#1, Cotnams Island, Pembroke, Ont. K8A 6WZ, Canada

ERROLL YOUNG, 4826 Storey Land, Alton, IL 62002

YAMIL R. YUNES, P.O. Box 573, Roma, TX 78584

MIKE YURCO, 260 E. Laclede Ave., Youngstown, OH 44507

### Z

DON ZACCAGNINO, P.O. Box 583, Pahokee, FL 33476

DENNIS J. ZELLER, 1791 South West Lilyben Ave., Gresham, OR 97030

TIM ZOWADA, 23583 Church Rd., Battle Creek, MI 49017

MICHAEL ZSCHERNY, 2512 "N" Ave. NW, Cedar Rapids, IA 52405